From the Other Side of the Fence

From the Other Side of the Fence

An Autobiography

by

John Webb

Matador
12 Manor Walk, Coventry Road
Market Harborough
Leics LE16 9BP, UK
Tel: (+44) 1858 468828 / 469898
Email: books@troubador.co.uk
Web: www.troubador.co.uk/matador

ISBN 1 899293 53 1

Cover: The Old Stocks, Berkswell Village

Typesetting: Troubador Publishing Ltd, Market Harborough, UK
Printed and bound by Henry Ling Ltd, Dorchester, Dorset

Matador is an imprint of Troubador Publishing Ltd

For, and dedicated to,

"The big three" in my life

My father and best mate. The breadwinner.
I loved to be with him.
My mother and best friend. Always there.
Never Financially wealthy,
but with a rich supply of love and care for us all.
Olive my wife of almost fifty years. There is no one better.
Wife, mother, carer and best pal.

CONTENTS

FOREWORD

Dr Carl Chinn MBE

We are the Warwickshire lads
We are the Warwickshire lads
We know our manners
We spend our tanners
We are respected wherever we go
Marching down the Danbury Road
Doors and winders open wide
We can dance, we can sing
We can do all kind of tricks
We are the Warwickshire lads

John Webb is a Warwickshire lad. He may not sing and he may not do all kind of tricks but what John has done is to open the doors and windows wide into the life not only of his own family but also into that of the agricultural people of Warwickshire. For that achievement he should be respected wherever he goes.

Too often our view of the way of life of agricultural England is seen through the rosy hues of painters and writers who have portrayed a rural idyll, an Arcadia in which fields are forever green and skies always blue and where the agricultural worker leads a blissful existence. John Webb is not one of those romantics. He could not be for he does not look at rural life from the outside, he feels it from within.

With the intuition and understanding of someone who belongs and who is not an outsider, John Webb makes plain the hard times of the 1930s. He tells us of his granny's home, one of four dwellings leading off three passages. Water came from a pump or was drawn a walk away from a well. Paraffin lamps or candles or both were the order of the day and 'it goes without saying there was no bathroom and the bucket lavatories were way down the garden'. But just as he is no romantic, neither is John a person who exaggerates the hardships, for as he says such conditions as were quite common. What is more, 'the Workhouse would have been worse. My grandmother was very thankful to live out her lifetime there.'

Importantly John points out that 'in common with most people we were happy and contented with "our lot".'

The joy of reading this insightful account of one man's life in Berkswell, Warwickshire is that in a matter-of-fact way John draws us into a world that has gone. Indeed, the power of his writing is that he does not need to embellish his account as through his own words he makes us see and feel the people and places with which he is so familiar.

He tells us how for lunch his father 'took a biggish piece of bread and a lump of cheese, no butter, in later years it always amused me to see all these blokes in the shant holding the bread and cheese in one hand and carving of the lump with their pocket knives, which all outdoor workers carried.' The food was 'washed down with tea from a large bottle with a cork in. No fancy thermos flasks. The bottle was kept warm in a couple of old socks, washed of course now and again. Lunch was carried to work in a fish basket or frail. Made of a sort of wicker about two foot six inches long and eighteen inches deep and about nine inches wide, with a lid over the top. The idea of the basket was to return home with it full of firewood and the bottle was in the poacher's pocket, not that my father did any poaching. I don't think so anyhow.'

With descriptions such as this, John makes us aware of the reality of agricultural life – a life that has all but been swept away – and he evokes a village that was mostly self-sufficient. Before the Second World War, 'there was absolutely no need to go out shopping. Harry Taylor was the village butcher, who killed and cut up all the carcasses at his shop in the village; Norman Taylor was the grocer who called for the grocery order and delivered bread on Saturday dinner time and on Tuesday, with the groceries arriving on Thursday; milk was free from Wheatley's Home Farm; the "oilman" (hardware) man –Mr Pass- called once a fortnight with paraffin candles and so on from him; and Mr Wilcox called with cooked meats 'and we had very nice brown potted meat paste, very nice on toast which was made over the fire – the best way, even now'.

There is so much to grab hold of in this book, from descriptions of farming and business to Sunday school and holidays and the pictures and army service. And, significantly John takes us with him on his journey through Berkswell man and boy, bringing us to the present and letting us hear through his words the world that has gone and the world that is now. Sadly rural England is fading. But because of John Webb, the stories and lives of the agricultural folk of Warwickshire with whom he is bonded will not be forgotten.

INTRODUCTION

The parish of Berkswell is situated in The heart of England, six miles west of Coventry. The village is two miles south of Meriden – the centre of England. Thankfully, the area has not changed greatly during my lifetime of over 70 years. The village is in a conservation area and the surrounding farmland is under the protection of the greenbelt. About 12 new houses have been built in the vicinity of the village since 1939, plus a small council development behind the Bear Inn – which I think melds in very well.

Some of the houses are now privately owned. There have also been replacements and conversions. Naturally, the way of life has changed over the years – the community is no longer as "close knit" as it once was. However, Berkswell is still very much alive. The church of St. John Baptist is thriving, and the CofE school in the village is a flourishing, happy and proficient place. There are no fewer than ten other local organisations in and around the parish, catering for all sorts of interests for all age groups. The Berkswell Museum is well worth a visit, and contains exhibits relating to the parish. (For more information on the museum, contact the local libraries.)

Apart from two years National Service and living in a lovely caravan for three and a half years – when Olive and I were married in 1953 – I have lived in the parish of Berkswell all my life. I lived with my two sisters and parents for 24 years, and in Windmill Lane for 45 years – and have no wish to move anywhere.

In many ways I think my life has been like a jigsaw, but not a puzzle. The pieces have all fallen into place very nicely – with a few more bits still to go in, I hope. I consider I have had a wonderful, happy and contented life – so far. I have never, ever been bored or searching for something to do.

Please read on – and I hope all enjoy reading Johns Jottings *From The other side of the fence.*

ACKNOWLEDGEMENTS

This book would not have been possible without the invaluable help and understanding from my daughter Jenny and son in law Steve. Also our valued friends listed in no particular order,as friends should be: Jill James – Dee and Mike Tracy – Michael Adams – Mary Cotterell – Tracy Williams – Shirley Stirling – The Balsall Common Lions Club.

Special mention must be made to Dee Tracy my mentor and chief adviser, with Mike in full support.

Last but by no means least my wife Olive for "putting up with it all" never a complaint, never a moan.Thanks.

My sincere and heartfelt thanks to you all.

John Webb
September 2002

BERKSWELL

I live in a place that is dear to my heart,
The Parish of Berkswell of which I'm a part.
Hedgerow and woodland, meadow and field,
Produce crops of all sorts, with a very good yield.

The church in the village, a gem to behold,
Preserved, revered and happy, it has to be told.
Our ancient old well, from which the place gets it's name,
And the stocks on the green, with their tales of infame.

A village school, old cottages, post office and shop.
No Sainsburys, MacDonalds, Video or Co-Op.
The Bear Inn on the crossroads no longer a "pub",
But a good place to call for a pint and good grub,

A stroll to the lake and over the park.
Walk a full circle and be back before dark.
Events in the Reading Room and I've had my share,
Whist, dancing and gatherings with lots of fine fare.

The village museum in old dwellings located.
Just memories now, residents long since vacated.
The Pound, thatched cottages, farmhouses and Hall,
I love it in winter, spring, summer and fall.

p.s.

About a country bloke it's oft been said,
They're strong in the arm and weak in the 'yed.
If a fool in the country you are trying to find,
Best bring one with you, we do not mind.

John Webb   September 2002

CHAPTER 1

Before My Time

An early Christmas present arrived at Top Lodge, Kenilworth Road, Berkswell, on the 22nd December 1892, NO, it was not me, but my father Albert.

I suspect it would be one of the very few Christmas presents as my father was the fourth of eight children.

I am sure he was welcome and loved by the rest of the family of which I know very little, my father seldom talked of his family for probably a very good reason which will be revealed later on.

The eldest child was Ada followed by Harry, Fred then my father Albert. Four more children arrived at regular intervals and they were Ernest, Elsie, Nance and "Young Frank". They also had an Uncle Frank.

Top Lodge was a very tiny single story dwelling guarding the North entrance to Berkswell Hall the drive going on through the woods and out into Top Park. Down the hill to the lake where there were two gates to open and close on entering the Park and round to Berkswell Hall.

I expect my Grandmother had to nip out and open and close the Lodge gate, also drop a curtsy to any residents of the Hall that may be travelling, probably to Hampton-in-Arden.

In those days all the London trains would stop at Hampton-in-Arden. When the railway line was built, Hampton station was allowed to be built on condition that all trains to and from London stopped there as Sir Robert Peel MP – founder of the police force or "Peelers" or "Bobbies" could use the train en route to the Houses of Parliament at Westminster. Top Lodge still stands, now sold off by Berkswell Estate and enlarged and moderniscd.

My mother was born at Stockton on May 3rd 1900. She had an older brother Harry and a younger sister Ruth – my favourite aunt. Don't tell the others.

My mother's father died when she was very young and my grandmother moved to a bungalow on the Evesham Road in Stratford-upon-Avon. The bungalow is still standing opposite the Salmon Tail Pub.

Also in about 1900, The Webbs were a bit "thick on the ground" at Top Lodge and moved to another estate house in Meriden Road known now as "Eardley", and then as "Webbs", another cottage nearby is known as "Wilmot". And it was in the early 1800s that John Eardley Eardley Wilmot became Squire at Berkswell Hall, later on he was sent to Van Dieman's Land (now Tasmania) as Lieutenant Governor. Full story in Berkswell Miscellany Vol IV.

My grandfather worked at Home Farm, known then as Chapel Hill. He was a wagoner and an authority on horses as I understand it, also full of fun and a practical joker. He could be found ringing the Church bells on a Sunday. Apparently my grandfather was in the ringing chamber one Sunday when The Rector walked in. It was the fashion then for men to wear very colourful waistcoats – or wes-cot as my father called them – The Rector said "my word Webb that is a fine waistcoat you are wearing" and the reply was "Yes Parson, the missus has put a new front on and a new back as well, but the arm holes are as good as new". According to the late Arthur James my granny was a jolly little soul and always helping others as well as coping with a husband and family of eight – and then Bill came along, not another son, more of him later.

On leaving school my father went to work for Mr. College of Four Oaks Farm, a five minute walk up the road. Later on, working in Coventry as a carter moving coal from the Coventry station to who knows where. I do not think that lasted long as the horses were ill-treated and over-loaded on the orders of the employers, my father loved horses of all sorts and sizes and eventually got a job as groom in the stable yard at Berkswell Hall, where, they had superb animals for hunting and drawing the various carriages, governess carts, traps and so on.

I think it was a fairly easy life compared say with the workers on the farm. But the hours were long being at the beck and call of the Wheatley Family. The "old squire" was a stickler for time – it had to be dead on. The grooms knew how long it took to get to the front door from the stable yard. My father, on his very first time to drive the squire, took no chances arriving at the front two minutes early. The door was flung open by the irate Squire, demanding to know why he arrived at the wrong time. He ordered my father to go away and return at the instructed time.

By and large things were fairly relaxed as long as all the work – and there was a lot of it – was undertaken to the satisfaction of Mr. Fairfax – the head groom, known behind his back as "Fairy Foot".

I remember him as an elderly gentleman in retirement. Another occasion saw my father driving one of the two Miss Wheatleys – who also lived at the Hall – to some function, I think Leamington way. Naturally the

My mother and father on their wedding day, January 1927

groom had to wait hours, sometimes for the function to end. This night it was quite late when they set off in an open governess cart. Dark, wet and altogether uncomfortable, father was driving at a reasonable pace when his passenger demanded the reins and they were soon making progress at a "fair old lick" clipping the grass verges – there were no kerbs beyond the top of Hearsall Lane in those days.

Faster and faster and then the inevitable happened, a high grass verge not negotiated and the whole caboodle, horse and cart and passengers ended up upside down in a ditch full of water. It would have taken some time to sort that little lot out. My father was instructed not to breathe a word about the incident as Mr. Fairfax and the Squire would not have been very pleased. There was a lot of carriage and harness cleaning to be done that night.

Mr. Fairfax retired to Wilmot Cottage, actually named later on by the Wilkinson family, if my memory serves me right, however.....

Mr. Fairfax always seemed to wear tweed clothes, they did wear very well.

The house came "end on" to the road with a small bedroom window in the gable end. My father often suggested to me – perhaps sister Stella as well – that a few prickly chestnut shells thrown through the open window might be a good idea. I never knew if my father had any sort of grudge against Fairy Foot or not. However, all sort went through the window in due season. Beechnuts, Conkers, Chestnuts – you name it, one always obeyed one's father, did one not. The window was always closed when it was snowing.

We never did things like that when the Wilkinsons were there, no way.

My mother first came to Berkswell in about 1920 as nanny and of general assistant to the Hobson family who lived at Hill Close which is on the top of the hill above the station in Dockers Lane, now known as Station Road. What a pity they changed the name, the Dockers lived there for

Grandma, Elizabeth Hough, with sister Stella, 1937

many years. I remember the family as fishmongers in Coventry, the business certainly still going a few years ago.

The Hobsons were the owners of Charles Ager the shoe people. My mother looked after the three children – Ivan, Ken and Edna.

Ivan and Ken later on took over the business and both had a shop, one in Coventry and the other in Leamington. The businesses are still going today, still in the ownership of the descendants of the Agers. Edna Hobson married and became Mrs Sidney Penn lived in Meeting House Lane until she died in 1999.

My mother seldom spoke about her work there but she was well liked by the family and lots of their visitors, many people tell me, "ah I remember your mother at Hill Close". It was then that my father called at intervals to collect the waste vegetables, etc. peelings and the like, there was a hungry pig in the sty and this was the cheap way of keeping the animal fed.

Can one imagine a scruffy, probably unshaven individual calling for the scraps and a smart young lady in a black dress and white collar and cuffs, etc. answering the door. In addition my father liked a glass or three of ale and a few fags – there was very little else anyhow in the way of entertainment. Mother said that when she first saw him she would not have had him if he were the last man on earth.

What changed their ideas I do not know but in January 1927 they were married by a curate by the name of Rev. Standing – who was, many years later, the vicar of Meriden – at Holy Trinity Church, Stratford-upon-Avon. And that is where the trouble started at Meriden Road. More later on.

Mother's brother Harry, who served in the army in the First World War, could not settle on demobilisation and got very fed up with taking orders. So in 1922 he emigrated to Western Australia. He worked in the timber trade felling and cutting up timber for two years before finally acquiring a block of land which I think he was given.

This was at Nannup some forty miles west of Bussleton and about one hundred and sixty miles South East of Perth, Western Australia.

This land was bush, a mixture of mature timber, smaller trees, bushes and undergrowth. Almost jungle in fact. This all had to be cleared and cultivated to grow mainly grass for the planned dairy herd.

On arrival he lived in a "Humpy" which basically was a tarpaulin sheet stretched over a ridge pole like a tent, the ends at ground level were either dug into the ground or tied to a log and kept down by the weight of the timber. This sufficed until he built a wooden hut.

Prior to departing England he was courting and became engaged to Miss Marion White of King William Street, Stratford-upon-Avon. Working in a large drapers shop (Smiths), in the town.

Aunt Marie, as she was known to us, went out to Australia some three or four years after Uncle Harry. All travel was by ship of course, taking four or five weeks from England to Freemantle, the main port in W.A. Perth is about twelve miles up the river Swan from Freemantle.

Harry met Marie off the boat, they were married and after a short honeymoon in the hills east of Perth, it was back to the hard life of the bush.

As I understand events, both my grandparents Webb of "Webbs" had died. Ada and Nance were "in service" out of the family home. I don't know about Harry.

However, Else, unmarried, acted as Mum to the rest of them. But, my father, on his marriage, being the only one employed by the estate and entitled to the tied cottage, asked the others to leave, oh yes, including young Bill. I could not understand it – my father "one of eight" but Bill made nine. However keep reading.

They left alright but not before pulling all the paper off the walls, taking things as theirs saying "Mother always promised me to have this, that or the other.

Not a very happy start to married life. Mid January, no doubt cold. But father had a job and mother looked after him, one thing they would never be cold as there was always plenty of firewood to be had – all legal and free of charge.

A pair of innocents, Stella and I, 1933

It must have been about this time that father moved to work in the estate yard, probably in the saw shed. He worked there for the rest of his life being well over seventy when he finally retired.

My father worked from 8.00 a.m. until 12.30 p.m. An hour for dinner, not lunch as these days. Lunch was bread and cheese at 10.00 a.m. till, depending on who was about i.e. the foreman. Work started after dinner at 1.30 p.m. till 5.30 p.m. in the summer and 5.00 p.m. in the winter.

After tea, would be gardening in the evenings when the weather permitted and in the winter, cold feet would be pushed up to a blazing fire in the front room. A paraffin lamp of about sixty candle power provided light, and hung from a fitting in the centre of the room.

As I imagine candle power was the only other source of lights or maybe a "flash light" as it was known, which was most likely a battery lamp used on the front of a bicycle, rear lights were not obligatory till about 1939.

My parents, in common with the majority, had no mod cons including electricity and all that goes with that. Only saucepans, kettle and the copper in the wash house for hot water. The copper was on once a week for the washing.

No radio – TV was not heard of.

An earth closet "down the back" which joined on to next door and had to be emptied once a year.

My father would arrive the back way with a horse and cart on a Saturday lunch time. Mother, Stella and I would most likely visit grandma in her village alms house whilst Jim Squires and dad would undertake this surely unpleasant task.

No water on tap, it had to be pumped and carried from the pump, which stood in Squire's garden, next door. It was always carried the back way known as the "Bunny Run".

I would imagine mother and father soon settled down to something like "normal". Father would be home to dinner at twenty to one (ish) if he was not working on one of the tenants farms or cottages.

Alice and Jim Squires lived next door, Jim known as "Shep" – because he was the shepherd at Chapel Hill. They came from Shropshire, Alice from off Clee Hill and Shep from Clun. By the time I was "sitting up and taking notice" son Jim was married and managed a grocers shop near Nuneaton. Bill was married to Edith in the early thirties and after spells living in Tile Hill and Shirley Lane, off Back Lane, came home to live at "Charnwood", Four Oakes. George and Marjorie (Madje)were twins. George joined the R.A.F. before the war and later married Helen from Portsmouth. Madge, as she was known, was a very pretty girl – I knew that at the age of five years.

Madje caught TB of which there was a lot about at the time, about 1935 I would think. Sadly she died, the first death I had experienced and one of the few times I saw my mother cry.

CHAPTER 2

Arriving on the Scene

Now back to the Webbs and scenes of great activity on March 12th 1929, a whipper snapper to be called John Henry Webb was introduced into the world. I do not recall anything about being very young at the time. Before the days of the National Health Service which commenced in 1948. Berkswell had it's own midwife and district nurse. Which I think cost participating households 2d (less than 1p) per week to obtain these services. Nurse Sandy brought me into the world – so you know who to blame, although my parents had something to do with it.

In the meantime grandma Hough (she pronounced it Huff) had moved to Berkswell Village and occupied an Alms house on the village green.

By today's standards they were awful. Four dwellings to each of the three passages. One walked into the living room off the passage. My first memories are of no water laid on, a pump in the garden or, a longer walk to the well. No electricity, paraffin lamps or candles or both were the order of the day. A black leaded range with oven

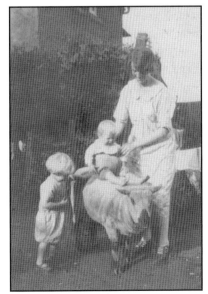

Mother with John (standing) and Stella
on 'Nibby' the lamb

– coal fired was the source of heating and cooking. The pantry and the coal house were under the stairs and on the day the coal man called there was dust everywhere however careful the coal man was. The stairs were spiral only four steps that did not go to a point. It goes without saying there was no bathroom and the bucket lavatories were way down the garden. Every "dwelling" had it's own garden plot, not always managed by the tenant. Having said all that, conditions as describable were quite common. The Workhouse would have been worse. My grandmother was very thankful to live out her lifetime there.

My sister Stella was born on September 30th 1930 and in common with others my memories are blurred until I was coming up to four years.

Most Saturday afternoons Stella, mother and I would visit grandma, known as "Gan Gan". She was a big lady, dressed in dark clothes most of the outer garments to ankle length – the others must have gone a long way as I was puzzled as to what some things were "blowing away" on our washing line at home.

In my grannies eyes I could do no wrong – most of the time – Stella and I usually received a small gift, a big jaffa orange when in season, a tiny bar of chocolate, a half penny or penny caused great jubilation but we were encouraged to save, even then – and we did. Not being allowed to spend at the shop in the village, and one did not ask why?

My granny was a lovely lady and loved us all, she was very fond of my father and he treasured a pocket knife and also his leather belt which were gifts from grandma. Occasionally when the weather was nice, grandma would come to stay with us. She was transported to and fro in a bath chair. A wicker chair on two wheels with a well for the feet. There was a small wheel at the front with a handle for steering. The wheel being on a pivot, I used to pull the handle and mother and Stella push the handle behind the seat. It was hard work – but we thrived on that. There were two bath chairs kept at the rectory for use of anyone in need. We kids often thought our-

selves in need because we sometimes bor-rowed" the bath chair and took it up "Colleges Hill" and took turns to ride down. All went well until father found out, once again we had a good ticking off and that was enough.

Stella had lovely blonde curly hair, all natu-ral, framing a pretty face, like a china doll. I do not know where the idea came from but

Walking 'Dobbin' in the Slang, a long narrow field at the back of our house, 1934

Stella decided to have her hair cut – and – I was to be the hairdresser. She collected the scissors and we departed to the privy "down the back". Quite a few dastardly undertakings occurred in the vicinity of the privy.

I got to work and all must have gone quiet, if kids go quiet they are often up to something. Eventually mother came to investigate, and that was another time I saw her in tears, she was very proud of us two, and I think decked us out very well on a small allowance.

Stella was whisked off to some hairdresser to be sorted out, probably costing more than could be afforded. I don't think we "copped out" to any great extent both being equally to blame. A lock of hair was found when father moved from Meriden Road to one of the estate bungalows near the village green, number one next to the public footpath. Pre school days were happy days, or do we only remember the good times, I remember many hot sunny days.

At the back of our house one could walk straight on to a long narrow field known as the Slange. There were "draw rails" that could be put in position if animals were in the field, but in any case all our drinking water had to be carried from the communal pump in the Squire's garden next door, and father always went round the back way.

Water was caught off the roofs in three big wooden barrels. This was used for washing the clothes, and mother always liked the soft water for washing hair. It goes without saying there was no gas or electricity. The house consisted of a square kitchen with a black leaded range, a hob on either side of the fire and a good sized oven, and many good things came out of there.

My father was first up and first job was to light the fire – winter and summer of course. Working in the saw shed there was always plenty of firewood. He boiled the kettle on blazing sticks, made the tea, then made the fire up with coal. There was always a nice warm fire to come down to, even if the bedroom was like an ice-box. And the tea, made from water boiled on sticks was superb, a lovely different taste. Did some smoke get into the kettle? I don't know but I recall the taste of the tea very well.

The front room was about the same size, no more than twelve foot square. Again there was the open fire grate very sensibly designed to cope with large logs, etc. We almost roasted by that fire from time to time. There were

Mother in 'The Bunny Run' with Stella, the back way to next door, 1932

Playing in the roadway. No traffic worries then (note the knock knees)! 1933

no mod cons at all. Washing up was done on the scrubbed kitchen table, the table-cloth being "oil cloth".

We had no radio or gramophone, i.e. record player.

Washing the clothes was an all day job, always on a Monday regardless of the weather. Father would light the copper fire in the wash-house which was just outside the back door, everything went on that fire, old shoes, boots and slippers all backed up with slack coal. Mother had a dolly tub and wooden "dolly" to pound the clothes with, and a huge old mangle that stayed outside. There was clothes and clobber everywhere, but by mid afternoon the place returned to normal. But there were then baskets of dry washing everywhere to be ironed, so back to the kitchen table, probably in our case the next day because the table was needed for our tea. A few washing aids – there was Rinso and Lux washing powder. "Reckitts blue" whitened the whites and "Robins" starch would stiffen collars, etc. on ironing day. We almost always had our hot meal about twelve forty. Dad "knocked off" work at twelve thirty. It was known to us all as dinner at dinner time. I think they probably had lunch at The Hall, but our lunch time, or rather Dad's was at ten o'clock in the morning in The Shant in the estate yard or probably sitting on a log in the woods.

For lunch he took a biggish piece of bread and a lump of cheese, no butter, in later years it always amused me to see all these blokes in the shant holding the bread and cheese in one hand and carving of the lump with their pocket knives, which all outdoor workers carried. This was washed down with tea from a large bottle with a cork in. No fancy thermos flasks. The bottle was kept warm in a couple of old socks, washed of course now and again. Lunch was carried to work in a fish basket or frail. Made of a sort of wicker about two foot six inches long and eighteen inches deep and about nine inches wide, with a lid over the top. The idea of the basket was to return home with it full of firewood and the bottle was in the poacher's pocket, not that my father did any poaching. I don't think so anyhow. My early memories before starting school were that we did many simple things. Mother used to take Stella and I for little picnics up the Slang or over the next field called the Gypsy field, onto the next one known as The Blackbridge. Primroses grew on the banks of the dry pit over there.

At the age of four I was a thin, skinny kid, probably because I was never still. Father called me Tinribs.

Before the days of the National Health Service – which commenced in 1948 – Berkswell had it's own district nurse and midwife, Nurse Sandy brought me into the world – so you know who to blame.

We were taken on regular visits to the welfare in the Reading Room to let the nurse keep an eagle eye on us, it must have been there that it was discovered I had flat feet and knocked knees. The first action was big jars of cod liver oil and malt, which dad called "jam and herrings". It was very nice and we had a big spoonful every day. My running action was a bit different from the others. I must have been four when I was put in irons. A hole was bored in both sides of the heal of my boot, I don't think I had shoes then, in fact my first footwear was given to me by Mr Hobson of Charles Agers in Coventry, mother's former employers – I digress, again.

Metal rods were fixed, one to each side of my boot, kept in place by two lots of heavy leather strapping. From then on my legs were straight and I could not bend my knees. The flat feet were cured by mounds of soft material placed inside my shoe where the arch of the foot should be.

Coming up to my fifth birthday I was admitted to the Mansfield Orthopaedic Hospital in Northampton for a ten week stay. I learned much later that the local doctor tried to get me into Paybody Home at Allesley but without success. I cannot remember about getting there at all, my memories are of a little lad miles from home, missing his folks, he was a horrible little patient wetting the bed and so on, being a bit of a nuisance to the nurses, they didn't seem to have time for me. I had sores and was in the habit of scratching so much so that in the end I had to wear gloves that were tied on. I bet they blessed me. However in the fullness of time, I was getting over the op. Dr. Wilson Stuart was the surgeon and he removed a small piece of the bone from behind each knee cap.

I had my fifth birthday there, but no visitors, Every other person in Berkswell sent cards, they were postcards then with frilly edges and lovely

The firewood, or timber-fellas, in our backyard.

pictures of horses, country scenes, flowers and so on. Easter Sunday I was well on the mend using a chair to push up and down, what was a very nice ward. And, I had visitors, mum and dad arrived loaded down with Easter eggs that covered the bed. Officially I was not allowed to eat too many, but father made sure I did. They were my first and only visitors, but not many other patients had visitors either. Ted Kerby, who farmed at Holloway Farm, Four Oaks, Cornets End, was the chauffeur in his battered old car with celluloid windows at the side. I don't know what it was but probably a bull nosed Morris.

I was allowed, and encouraged, to explore the garden on nice days, and there seemed to be a lot of them. The ward opened onto a wide terrace and the beds were often pushed out there on major cleaning days. From there on there was this superb garden, the likes I had never seen before. Flower beds, rockeries, shrubs, etc. It was Spring and I can still visualise that garden. The next time I saw mother and father was when I was able to run up to them – still in irons – to inform them that I was going home today. Ted Kerby, once again, provided the transport, my first ride in a motor car. Vivid memories of coming home, a boiling hot day, stopping to buy ice cream, another first. I did not want the trip to end as long as we were getting further and further away from that hospital. However, I have always been so grateful for what they did for me.

Then started the physio, my mother had to take me to the clinic in Dover Street, off Holyhead Road, Coventry, close to the city centre. The only convenient way was to walk to Meriden, with me in the pushchair, aged five. We parked the pushchair at a house by the bus stop and got on the Midland Red bus which was more expensive that the one that passed the door, but they were so infrequent.

Anyhow, at the clinic Miss Wholly usually put me through my paces, and once again the tantrums were in evidence. It was a bit painful now and again but my mother bribed me. If I was good we went to a little café in Spon Street and I had an iced cake with a cherry on top. Then we had to get the bus back to Meriden and I had to be pushed up the two big hills back home.

Eventually it all came to an end and my treatment was completed, I am really sorry for being such a pain to all concerned but will be eternally grateful to all who had to put up with me, and especially my mother's devotion to me.

Time was pushing on and I was at least six months late starting school. My father taught me all the letters and numbers from the newspapers. We always had the Daily Mirror and followed the adventures of Pip (Big dog), Squeak (Penguin) and Wilfred (Rabbit), also Belinda Blue Eyes, Capt. Reilly Foul and I think favourite of most men that would admit it – Jane. Also letters were answered by "The Old Codgers".

Father had little peace after tea until we had done "L and things".

Under starter's orders, Llandudno, 1936

(Identifying letters and numbers from the newspaper).

The bus service, such as it was, was provided by the Midland Red omnibus co. and came to Berkswell via Broad Lane and down the Coventry Road to the Bear Inn crossroads. It then turned right and went as far as Four Oaks. As now. There were only two oaks there in those days. Manned by a driver and conductor the bus would stop at our house. Mother having brewed a can of tea which they would drink at Four Oaks terminal and return the empty can on their return journey.

I never ever remember travelling on the Midland Red, The Bunty Bus Co. later took over the service to Berkswell, on a different route ...... more later.

Very few cars in those days, one regular vehicle was the "Mailman" who collected the letters from the pillar boxes and Post Office. His last run from Four Oaks to Berkswell and on to Coventry passed our house around seven o'clock in the evening and in the summer, Stella and I looked out for the mailman we gave him a wave which he returned and then it was home indoors, get the days dirt off and "up the wooden hill".

CHAPTER 3

School Days in Berkswell

Aged 5 my cousin Gordon, who was twelve months older than I, took me to school on my first morning. There was another problem looming up, it was discovered that I could not see the blackboard properly. So back to the clinic in Coventry for the eye test which involved "drops" in the eyes which I did not go on, anyhow I was soon fixed up with glasses, which I failed to get on with. However, the battle was won and I have worn spectacles ever since.

The school hours were from nine fifteen to twelve fifteen and one forty five to three thirty and Stella and I used to walk and took sandwiches for dinner time. I hated that part of it, taking a few minutes to eat our dinner then what? For the next one and a quarter hours the teachers disappeared, no sign of anyone for well over an hour. We had nothing to play with, no balls, skipping or whatever was not for the nippers. In the end we decided to walk home for dinner. It suited our mum because she always cooked at mid day. About that time we were joined for dinner by "Uncle Bert" Vaughan – my mother's cousin and he was a chauffeur at Berkswell Hall. He lived in The Bothy above the stables and came to us five days a week, for his dinner, paddled his own canoe at the weekends. He married later and lived for quite a few years in the Beehive Cottage in the village.

Stella and I started Sunday School at the same time as I went to Day School. The first Sunday was a foul autumn day, raining and windy with October leaves all over the place. Mr and Mrs Clifford from Four Oaks called for us and we walked there and back under their umbrella. We did not possess one. Sunday School was very nice, we sang all the children's hymns – All Things Bright and Beautiful and "Pennies Dropping" for the collection.

School photo

Pennies dropping, Pennies dropping,
Listen to them fall,
They belong to Jesus,
Jesus needs them all.

Sunday School was held in the village school. There was a small table set up as an alter and if it was anyone's birthday in the week, they were invited to light a candle on the alter. Miss Midgley reigned supreme there. She was head teacher of a junior school in Bedworth and she was an elegant and very smart person, remembered in particular a pale blue suit and one in a lovely pink, another smasher.

The Sunday School met from three o'clock until four o'clock and we attended a service of Matins on the second Sunday in the month, at eleven o'clock in the morning. A high light of the year was the Christmas Party held on the second Sunday, in January at three o'clock in the Reading Room. We all turned up In best bib and tucker in plenty of time. The sandwiches and cakes were laid out on the three lots of tables. Infants, juniors and senior girls and senior boys. We sat ourselves down and when grace had been said by dear old Mr Whittaker, Rector at that time, it was a free for all, but I can honestly say everyone was very well behaved, having been threatened and lectured somewhat before leaving home. There was tea served from large brown tea pots in the old Reading Room dark yellow cups, no one would dare pinch them, they were known to all. We had crackers and balloons certainly before the war, later I cannot recall.

The entertainment was often a magician, we had one or two local ones. Probably a sing song, the scouts made a "camp fire" on the stage one year. And then almost finally Mrs Whitacre, the Rector's wife, would haul herself onto the stage together with the senior teaching staff and she – Mrs W. – would present the prizes. We brought the house down with "Away in a Manager" and made our way home. Stella and I were unlucky the first year only starting in October, but I went on to receive at least six prizes and six medals for never absent never late. Stella made seven first prizes and seven medals. The next day, after the party, saw us back at Sunday School, the best attended days of the year. Mr (Rev) and Mrs Whittacre and Colonel and Mrs Wheatley were always guests always sitting in the old smokers bow chairs at the front. My medals are now in the Berkswell Museum, the only ones I will ever receive!

Up until the war the day school also had a party again in the Reading Room, run on similar lines, but in my day – no prizes. I think Colonel and Mrs Wheatley paid for that. Again this party was held in the New Year but before we went back to school after the Christmas holiday.

Going to school was never a problem for me at Berkswell. Miss Deeming taught us for perhaps a year then numbers attending the school must have fallen because we were all taught in two classrooms for quite a while. In the meantime, Mr Frewin had been replaced by Miss Gwen Tattersall, who arrived in 1936, and the school became a junior and infant school for pupils up to the age of eleven years. The majority going to Balsall Street Central School where Mr "Pop" Seeley was headmaster. Eventually I was under the expert eye of Polly Smith who. Although she had a deep loud voice, was very kind, considerate and above all fair, that is how I saw her anyhow, others may choose to disagree.

The internal school bears little resemblance today as to what it was when I started, although the outer structure has not been altered at the front that is. When it was first built the headmaster lived in the centre section, this is better understood when the building is viewed from the road – Church Lane. There were two entrance porches, long since closed, there was no access through the railings as at present. Once into the porch one door led into the playground and another into a classroom.

The head-teacher had quite a large room at the Church end and Mrs Smith had the central section. The end room nearest the cottages – Eastside was quite large and could be divided by a huge screen which folded back when not in use. I cannot recall any lighting before electricity came to Berkswell village in 1938/1939.

The two large rooms were heated by coke stoves, about three foot tall and fifteen inches in diameter with an iron guard all the way round. Needless to say the teacher sat next to the stove and must have been nice and warm even on the coldest of days – and there did seem to be quite a few in the wintertime. We had a bit of fun with the stove when the teachers back was turned, not very hygienic, but we spat on the top plate and it went round and round in little balls – simple fun.

Polly Smith had the best deal in the winter, her room was smaller and she had the original fireplace of the headmaster's quarters. She had a coal fire and made the best of it, sitting there with her legs apart at something like ten to two. Cannot recall Miss Deeming doing that – or Miss Tattersall. Although I write it myself, I was very good in most subjects especially when I made Miss Tattersall's class. In particular she made history, geography and nature study so interesting for me anyhow.

I did not enjoy P.E. – or P.T. as we knew it – poetry was one thing I could not get on with, perhaps was not interested and could not remember the words, although I do remember one, or part of one. My learned friends of today cannot believe we were taught such stuff, but I can assure one and all that we were

> I wish I liked rice pudding,
> I wish I were a twin,
> I wish some day a real live fairy would just come walking in.
> I wish when I'm at table my feet would touch the floor,
> I wish our pipes would burst next winter,
> Just like they did next door.

Honest truth – and I hadn't got a clue what a burst pipe was. The only pipes I knew about were drain pipes and those that were for smoking. Is it surprising that even today, I do not appreciate poetry?

There were no mod cons at all at the school, I cannot recall water on the tap, it must have come from the well until the water was laid on. When?

The lavatories were up at the end of the playground by the spinney wall, boys backing onto the girls with a staff one at the end which was always locked. No more to be said on that subject, they were awful and seldom used by me. But we had been known to play "furthest up the wall" Horrors! There was an open ended shelter in both playgrounds with a bench along the whole length. Very few possessed a bicycle but those that did left their cycles under the shelter.

Despite not having any luxury, by today's standards, mine was a happy childhood. Everybody, more or less, was in "the same boat". Not many conveniences and not a lot of money.

As I said before, Dad worked on the Berkswell Estate. In the saw shed for sawing timber for estate repairs on the tenant farms, workers cottages and so on. Our house was a tied cottage, we being responsible for the inside decoration and the estate exterior repairs – which was not very often. I think Father did not, or would not, ask. As long as he had plenty to eat, a fairly comfortable chair to sit in and a good fire in the grate to put his feet by, he was happy.

He was always quite a heavy smoker, always Wills Woodbines, known as coffin nails. A pint or two of mild ale at the Bear Inn now and again or when funds permitted made up the pleasures of his life when we were youngsters.

Dad did make parsnip wine though up until the war that is, when sugar and other ingredients became unavailable. He grew a whole lot of parsnips, I am not sure when the wine was made, autumn, winter or spring. It was made in the copper in the wash house and ended up – before it was drunk that was – in a ten gallon crock firkin which was like a barrel. It had a wooden tap at the end and stood just inside the pantry. The wine was made I think for the following summer for when father came in out of the garden dog tired. Owing to my tender age, I never got a sniff of it or, never actually saw any being consumed. Mother had very little, I know, because later on she would only have a small dash of sherry or port, and even that made her "glow". Happy days.

Before the war in the thirties, there was absolutely no need to go out shopping. Harry Taylor was the village butcher, he killed and cut up all the carcasses at his shop in the village. The shop was behind the last house in Spencers Lane beyond the Bear Inn, opposite "The Priory". He was always smoking and most folks had a little fag ash to flavour the meat. Son, Peter, drove an Austin seven and delivered once or twice a week, certainly on a Saturday afternoon.

Norman Taylor (no relation) of Ye Olde Berkswell Stores, Station Road, Balsall (next to Sunnyside Lane and the butchers shop) was the grocer and baker. He called for the grocery order and delivered bread on Saturday dinner time at our home. Bread was also delivered on Tuesday and with the groceries on Thursday. We also had some groceries from the Balsall Co-op, which was where the Italian Restaurant now stands, same building, much altered.

Milk came free in those days from Wheatley's Home Farm. The "oilman" (hardware) man –Mr Pass- called once a fortnight and we had our paraffin candles and so on from him. Don't know why we never had Chatterway's who called next door. Mr Wilcox called with cooked meats and we had very nice brown potted meat paste, very nice on toast which was made over the fire – the best way, even now.

My father was not very good at shoe repairs so they went to Salmons at Balsall, one of the old shops in the row. One was lucky to get them back without a search of the shop, a nice family but not organised at all.

Henry Court could be relied on as a mans outfitter but he did not call on us, although I did have a suit off him many years later. At one time we had three green grocers calling, Mr Sunley was one and he had a tuck box and sometimes we had a halfpenny to spend on a sherbet dab or half a yard

'Dusty', Stella and I with 'Shep'
and his faithful dogs

of liquorice. Mr Williams was another, who sometimes had his daughter Rene, with him. Then there was Ernie Hodgskins from Meriden, a real extrovert who tried to keep one hand on the scales when weighing the fruit or whatever, my mother kept an eye on him alright, always going out to his van rather that letting him do the running about. Mother also got the better of Ernie, twice at least. Once was when he had a small bicycle to sell and one was required for sister Margaret. They haggled away not getting down to a final figure, then Ernie suggested the difference they were haggling about should be "double or quits" – paying double or nothing on the toss of a coin. Mother was no gambler, but she took him on and won.

The second instance was when my folks were interested in acquiring a very large galvanised iron water tank as, by now, the old wooden water butts were past their "sell by date" or non existent. And I think I said before, the females liked to wash their hair in soft water. Anyhow it was a repeat performance of the previous haggle, Ma coming out the winner once again. That was enough for Ernie, he declared there would be no further contests.

Another caller once a month was the man selling tea from Flowery Peeco Tips Tea. His calls stopped when petrol was rationed or unobtainable during the war.

I recall one hot summers evening, my father was digging away in the garden when an Indian gentleman came through the gate with the hope of selling something from his large suitcase. He spoke to father saying "Busy man make fortune". This rather upset father who had to work very hard just to break even making a living. The reply was quite controlled with us kids in earshot, but he did raise his spade above his head and chased the chap out of the garden gate, we never saw him again. That would not be "on" today, no way.

Newspapers were delivered up until the wartime when petrol was limited, afterwards however the papers were delivered to a central point and collected from there, ours were delivered to The Lodge in Meriden Road. Payment was made by putting cash in an envelope which came with the papers once a week.

We also had a postman but in those days very few letters, it was "red letter day" when we had a delivery. All payments were made by cash. I am almost certain my parents never had a bank account. The Post Office savings were the only accounts they had. We youngsters, Stella and I both saved through the National Savings scheme. My account was started for me by my Aunt Ruth, Mother's sister. She bought me three third issue certificates at sixteen shillings each, eighty pence in today's' money. I did cash them in many years later and they produced many times their original value. I must have been a bit favoured by Auntie Ruth, but when she married there were other demands on her money.

Aunt Ruth worked at "Greenfields" in Holly Lane, Balsall before she married Bob Hammond.

We often had gypsies calling selling pegs and attempting to tell fortunes, Mother did not like that at all. None of us ever went very far, my parents both possessed a 'bike'. Father used his for getting to work if he was working away from the estate yard. When working at the estate yard in the saw shed, he would walk to work as it was not easy to carry the basket of wood home on a bike. And it was useful to get to and from The Bear in the village, three quarters of a mile away.

Mother had a "sit up and beg job". I think she only ever had the one bike. When she worked at Hill Close, she often cycled to Stratford to visit her mother on her half day off, then of course back again in the evening, a fifty mile round trip. I have no idea when my Grandmother came to live in Berkswell Alms Houses, she lived in the front flat by Lavender Hall Lane, known as Old Lane in those days, looking up towards the crossroads, probably the one with the best outlook. At the time there were four big elm trees surrounding the stocks on the village green, and two or three other trees as well, which made the Almshouses on the front quite dark.

My first venture on a bicycle was at Barnett Cottage, Four Oaks, where Bob Thomson lived with his mother and father – Tom and Nellie – I was told once that my dad had a soft spot for Nellie who worked at the Hall, or did she fancy him – we will never know.

There was a large lawn at Barnett Cottage with a huge laurel hedge along one side, a thorn hedge along the roadside and various other shrubs including holly's alongside the other edges of the lawn.

Although Bob was younger than me – he still is – he possessed a bike and one day I had a go, pushing off from a very handy bench seat. I found it more or less easy, but came off a few times, no damage to the bike because it fell on the lawn. Eventually Bob was called in for his tea and left me to it. Normally this was the signal to go home, we kids were always instructed to go home when playmates were called in to tea – or whatever. On this occasion "I forgot to remember" the rules and carried on with my self taught riding lesson – becoming braver and braver, going faster and faster round and round the lawn. As I said before, I came off quite a few times, into the laurel, the hawthorn hedge and the holly bushes. Fortunately there was no damage to Bob's bike. I had a few bumps and scratches and went home to announce that I could ride a bicycle. From then on, aged eight to nine, pestered the other cycle owners for "a go" as we came home from school. In addition to Bob, his cousin Jim had a bike also my cousin Gordon who was twelve months older than me and lived almost opposite Bob. We remained very good pals and it is sad to record that Bob died, as did his wife Margaret, within seven weeks of each other early in 2001.

It was sometime after that Bill Squires said he knew of a cycle for sale where he worked as a gardener in Earlsdon, Coventry. He said it was a Rudge and worth every penny of the one pound and ten shillings (one pound fifty) they were asking for it. Mother said I could have it, if I paid for it myself, also I would be responsible for keeping it in good repair. Despite the fact that it made a large dent in my savings, I decided to have it. Bill brought it home for me, riding his own bike one handed and propelling the other one with his other arm outstretched. It was a beauty, well made, very heavy and brake blocks four inches long. I did look after my bike very well and only needed to spend five shillings (twenty five pence) on a new front tyre which father gave me a hand to fit. Well to be honest, he did the job, but I knew then how to repair a puncture and replace the wheel correctly. Some few years later I sold my Rudge bicycle for £1.10.0. (£1.50)

Occasionally we would go on the bus to Coventry, when we needed new clothes, shoes, etc. The Midland Red has been replaced by The Bunty Bus. The route came along Broad Lane, down Eastern Green Lane, which was narrow and quite steep then over a small "skew" bridge over the brook at the bottom and up a steeper hill on the other side, turning left, which was steep and narrow to gain access to Upper Eastern Green Lane. Along this road to Hockley Lane, turning left again down to Broad Lane, turning right and right again to Four Oaks and on to Berkswell village. In those days all the lanes were in fact much narrower, fortunately not much in the way of traffic. The road in Back Lane down past Rock Farm was often bad, a lot of water on the road and in the winter, ice. We could often guarantee that if the bus was late it was in the ditch on the "Rock" hill. It was piped and filled in and a bank made eventually. The bus had various names, one being "The Family Coach". If one sat towards the front, all the news and gossip could be heard, hence, "Didn't you know ? I heard it on the bus".

The bus returned to Coventry via Carol Green, Tanners Lane, Benton Green Lane. Turning right at the end of the lane and once again round Eastern Green. A half-hour run on a good day for six pence and three pence for children. (two and a half pence and you can work the other one out). The service was eventually taken over by the Coventry Corporation buses, we always had single deckers. There were official bus stops but really they were "fare stages", probably a penny fare between each stage i.e. from Four Oaks to Berkswell Village. There were about four a day passing our door at about nine o'clock, one thirty five, five forty and eight o'clock in the evening. Any more than that it was yer bike or shanks's pony.

Farm tractors were very few and far between before the war, none of the Berkswell Estate tenant farmers had one. The first one to arrive at Chapel Hill (Home Farm these days) was an "International", I do not think it was new. However it seemed to go on for ever and ever. Then a brand new Fordson arrived, all orange and posh. Three forward gears and one reverse, everything was towed, no hydraulics then. To change gear the thing came to a stop, the clutch pedal was also the brake, it was around for a very long time. And I would walk over quite a few fields to cadge a ride, sitting on a very wide and stable mudguard. Bill Wilkinson was often sympathetic especially if young George, his nephew, had not got there first. He let us have a go at steering sometimes, but, "don't tell anybody". That was awful, I could not brag about it.

One thing that always sent us rushing to the gate was Rupert Arnold's threshing tackle in transit. It could be heard more than half a mile away. Chuff, Chuff, Chuffing along. The steam driven traction engine looked huge – it was big anyhow – towing the threshing drum and behind that the machine that made the boultings of straw that came out of the back end of the drum when thrashing.

A boulting was about four feet six inches by five foot long, about fifteen inches in diameter of straight straw that passed from the drum to the "tying" machine. Being straight the straw could be used for thatching ricks of hay and corn. Balers had still to be "invented" for use on the farm anyhow. Threshing was a dirty dusty job and I only helped out on two occasions.

Another occasion for me as a kid was the annual cyclists memorial service held at the memorial on the village green at Meriden. In all the years I have never attended this service. Before the war many thousands of cyclists attended this service held in May –I think on the third Sunday in the month. Before the war the service was held in the morning, some of the cyclists travelling through the night to pay respects to those cyclists who died in the First World War. The Second World War was still to come.

Stella and I used to sit on the bench on the side of the road and try and count them as they passed our house on their way home via Berkswell Village. There were thousands and thousands of them, giving us a wave as they pedalled on their way at what seemed to me to be a rather rapid rate. Most of them travelled in their clubs, some of the groups over one hundred strong, with their club pennants flying over the handle bars of their cycles. The weather always seemed to be good on that day. I will make that service one day as it is still held but nowhere near the attendance of pre war, but still quite an event in latter years – The 1990s.

The memory of the Silver Jubilee of King George V and Queen Mary is a bit of a blur. It was celebrated in 1935. Berkswell celebrations took place in the Park by The Hall. I remember a tea for us youngsters all set out under the covered area in the stable yard where the carriages were washed and cleaned in bygone days. By now the Wheatley family possessed a Rolls Royce and Mrs Wheatley drove a huge Armstrong limousine (with never a side ways glance as she passed us kids playing in the road). I digress. After the tea, there was the usual races for all ages, youngsters and grown-ups. Followed by a big bon-fire and fireworks.

Wednesday May 12th 1937 saw the coronation of King George VI and Queen Elizabeth. We had no television, or even a radio then so all the pageantry in London we saw the next day in the newspapers – all in black and white of course – but there were supplements. Again Berkswell celebrated in the park at Berkswell and again I remember a splendid tea in the stable yard, followed by the races for all ages, sack races, obstacle, three legged, egg and spoon and so on. There were side shows including the "walking millionaire". One brave soul with a top hat is walking up and down inside a booth with only head and shoulders visible. One paid for so many tennis balls and tried, by throwing the balls, to knock his hat off. Carters from the shop in the village had a tuck stall, but no ice cream. We very seldom had it, though it was hardly missed. In the evening there was a huge bonfire in the park on the other side of the lake (in Top Park). The reflection and the bonfire was a magnificent sight. My father and other employees of the estate spent many days building this fire and material came from near and far, we walked down one day to have a look.

They started off by building four tunnels with old scaffold poles in the form of a cross so that there would be a draft whatever the way the wind decided to blow. On top of the tunnels a "platform" was made and then the fire material was stacked on top of this. The farm elevator was used to propel material higher than could be pitched or thrown. The elevator was a machine used to elevate hay and corn to the top of a rick at harvest time. A conveyor belt at about 45° going round and round with spikes built into the three foot wide belt to stop the hay or sheaves from slipping down, driven by a stationery petrol engine with a belt from the engine to the elevator. To make sure all went well, they cleaned out the old creosote pit and put gallons of that on and probably one or two old tractor tyres, however all went well, my father was "in attendance" on the night and also went to tidy up next morning and said the fire had generated so much heat that there was no hot ash in the morning.

Not a bit of gleed to light his fag, as he put it. Naturally at both "dos" there was a beer tent but as I was only six years old for the Jubilee and eight at the Coronation, we were not allowed near the place. Kids and booze were kept well apart for us anyhow, never even a lemonade, but we were happy.

Later on Stella and I were taken to the Rex Cinema in Corporation Street, Coventry to see the original extended news reel of the Coronation.

Also there was a trip to London by train to see the Coronation decorations, organised by Miss Tattersall at the school. My folks paid three pence (one and a half pence) per week for quite a long period before the outing to enable me to go. Jim Thompson and I were two of the youngest in the party. I had quite a surprise to see Bill Squires on the train as I made my way to the lavatory, he was on his way to Chelsea Flower Show. I remember clearly all the bunting across the streets and seeing Buckingham Palace. Eventually we were "turned loose" in Woolworths for a while but as we had been told there would be no opportunity to spend money, I only had six pence (two and a half pence) in my pocket, my only purchase was a small trowel which I treasured for many a day – cost three pence.

It must have been after the Coronation that it was decided to form a Wolf Cub pack in the village, according to my research a club pack was formed earlier but it must have folded.

One day we were informed in day school about this idea and all those of eight years and over that were interested were asked to meet at the scout house by the well on a certain Saturday afternoon. There was a good response and very soon there were three "sixes" (groups). I was in the "reds" six and am pretty sure Jim Thompson was as well. Mr Kenneth Hope (Robin Hope's father) was, I am sure, the prime mover behind the scenes. We met at the old scout house for two super hours on a Saturday afternoon. Mr Hope was very well supported by senior scouts. In those days there were not as many distractions as today for young men and others. We started off with a roll call and paid our subscriptions (Subs) of three pence (slightly more than one new pence or 1p) Then there was instruction of some sort, first we had to learn the cub law. Something like – We'll dib dib dib – do our best and dob dob dob. Do our duty, learning knots and lashings, simple first aid and so on to gain a tenderfoot badge.

There was, and still is I suppose, a quite serious enrolling ceremony when all the promises were made. There would always be a good games session, outside if fine, inside during wet weather. We played quite a few games in the spinneys around the village. They were all part of the estate then, we had to restrict our activities a little when game birds were nesting.

The thicket of rhododendrons in Meriden Road was a favourite place to track and ambush. The cubs and scouts had a "roving" concession over estate land in the vicinity of the village and then it was quite safe for children to be out and about even in the dark winter evenings when one game was "Joey, Joey show your light" – when a "Joey" would flash his torch and the others had to catch him. Treasure hunts were very popular. Often the treasure was a small tin of sweets, provided by the seniors. Norman "Granny" Wheeler, Ivan Woodcock and others, Frank Hunter, the scoutmaster was very often in attendance, all of course in their navy blue uniforms, (not the usual khaki) for Berkswell. The jerseys were a bit warm in the summer but we were glad of them in the winter. Mr Hope always attended but never had a uniform. I think he looked after the admin. side, and almost always finished the gathering by reading a story! "Jungle Book" was one, and we all kept quiet. The old scout house was situated along the driveway from Lavender Hall Lane to the well, where the three ugly old garages now stand.

The scout house was an estate cottage until, as I understand, it was condemned for human habitation. Colonel Wheatley of Berkswell Hall then allowed the scouts to use it for a peppercorn rent – I think it was one shilling (five pence) per annum.

There was a passage entrance into the one room which had a nice big fireplace on one wall. Benches on the other three sides. Stairs went up from one corner to two small rooms upstairs, one was the scouters room the other a store room. Upstairs was strictly out of bounds to the cubs. An outer storeroom completed the property as there was no garden.

One of the big events of the year was Parish Sunday, which was St. John Baptist Sunday. Before the war a church service was held at the memorial by the Churchyard entrance. The parading organisations met by Hainsworth's garage (now Carstins) by the railway station. Led by a band, probably The Bedworth Silver Band or one from Bulkington, followed by the British Legion (Not Royal British Legion) for many years to come Girl Guides, Scouts and Cubs. The parade went up Station Road to the island, right along the Kenilworth Road and right again down what is now known as Lavender Hall Lane – Old Lane before the war. Into Berkswell village for the service at 3 pm. I cannot recall very much about the service – only to say it was well attended. After the service the parade formed up once again and marched off to either Berkswell Grange, the home of the Huggins Family or, on alternate years to Berkswell Hall. Only the people in the parade were entertained to tea, so there was always a good turn out, and we all had to be in full uniform and smart, also on our best behaviour. When it was the turn of the Wheatleys to entertain, the parade took the route through what is now the village car park and across the park, long before the "new" rectory was built. There was a big gate on the roadside known as the black gate, which was only opened now and again. On the occasion of Parish Sunday, and when the hunt met on the village green, my father and other estate workers had to cut down the nettles and brambles to make a way through. Again the tea at the hall was under the covered area in the stable yard with the same benches and trestle tables as for silver jubilees and coronations, etc. The house and gardens at The Grange at Carol Green was very nice indeed. Major Huggins and Mrs Huggins had four boys, Michael, John, Patrick and Jeremy. Jeremy was to be known later as Jeremy Brett, the actor. There were all sorts of things for us cubs to explore, a tree house for one. They also had a small pony and a donkey. We were allowed to explore at will. Naturally we had to walk everywhere and we cubs did end up very tired at the end of the day, but the tea was worth it all. Both Colonel Wheatley and Major Huggins – as he was then – were great benefactors to the scout troop, as was Sir Charles Hyde BT, of The Moat.

In the summer time my father would occasionally help out Mr Cudmore, the head keeper on Berkswell Estate. In 1936-1937 the plantation of trees was planted along the side of the footpath between Berkswell and Bradnocks Marsh. There were quite a few hikers and ramblers about then and very few cafès, so they often lit a fire and "brewed" up their tea. Father's job was to forbid fires as the new plantations could have all gone up in smoke had anyone been careless. Patrolling along the path for about four hours on a Sunday afternoon, I often went with him, if there was no Sunday School.

My father always got on well with Mr Cudmore – others certainly did not – without pandering to him that is. Quite often there would be a rabbit in with the firewood when dad got home. "A present from Archie", he would say to Ma.

One summer Sunday morning in 1934, Stella and I were woken quite early to be told we were going out for the day, to the seaside, Rhyll in fact. We walked from Meriden Road to Berkswell Station to catch what was known as a half day excursion. I do not recall much about it, but do remember the sea – looked rather large. Next year we all – Ma, Pa, Stella and I went on a similar excursion to Blackpool, this time I do remember making sand castles and riding on a donkey.

This was followed up another year with a whole week in Llandudno – but father stayed at home. We stayed in a small house about "two blocks" from the Promenade and I think we were all in one room. We had our breakfast in the normal way then went out to the shops and bought whatever we wanted for dinner (lunch now). Then the lady cooked our purchases for whatever time we liked. I think we had our tea out. It was a lovely holiday, I was only eight, or nine at the most. There was a show at The Happy Valley – nice walks, playing on the sands, walking on the pier and one or two donkey rides, oh and Punch and Judy, all things quite new to us. I often went off on my own exploring the locality, an eight year old would not be safe doing things like that today, perfectly OK then, one could ask directions or anything else in complete safety. Generally lots of things are for the better, but I do think we have lived through the best times ever.

Another highlight or treat for us all before the war, was a Sunday trip to Auntie Ruth (Mother's sister) and Uncle Bob who lived in Barford. Strange as it may seem it has been impossible to get to Barford on public transport on Sundays from Berkswell for many years. Before the war everyone worked on a Saturday morning, therefore that only left Sunday when people had one whole day off work per week. Also the majority of workers only had one weeks holiday per annum. It was in 1953 when I enjoyed two weeks annual holiday for the first time – again I digress – must take something for it.

We had a choice of transport to Barford (1) To walk to Berkswell station catching a train via the "branch line" via Kenilworth to Milverton near Leamington where the train went on to. We caught a bus from Milverton to Barford via Warwick. The other option was a bus from the door to Coventry then a Midland Red via Leamington to Barford. Therefore on my father's pay, we did not go very often – or very far. On our first visit, (mother, father, Stella and I). Auntie Ruth and Uncle Bob had not been married all that long and they lived in a little thatched "beehive" cottage, similar to the one in Berkswell village and Aunt Ruth had it all so nice. I can remember all the wood highly polished including bob's upright piano. Outside the garden was immaculate, Bob had quite a few jobs over the years and quite a few were gardening.

There was a tiny pond in the garden and up at the top end a shed cum workshop where Bob made a wooden teapot stand for my mother to bring home. After lunch we all walked up Barford Hill past a big house with a bird aviary by the roadside (Smith Rylands), but in the garden. We walked on down the hill to the large pond or lake at the bottom where there was a waterfall or perhaps a weir, sitting on a wall for a rest before walking back. The sun always seemed to shine at Barford, we would not have made the trip on a wet day anyhow, would we ?

On our second visit, Cousin David had arrived, a chubby "little" lad, made a great fuss of by all and sundry apparently and thought the world of my mum. Eventually the Hammonds were provided with a new council house at the top of Mill Lane behind the Red Lion Pub, which is now known as The Joseph Arch who founded the Warwickshire Agricultural Labourers Union in 1872. He died in Barford aged 92.

My uncle Bob was an accomplished musician from a musical family, born at The Woolpack Inn in Warwick. Later moving to what was The Red Lion in Barford. He and his brothers and sister formed their own dance band. Bob played piano, Phil the drums, Nance played violin and someone else played the banjo.

Bob also played the Church organ at various venues – Sherbourne, Wasperton, Charlecote, Hampton Lucy, Walton to name those I know, not all at the same time of course. He was never "resident" organist at Barford but did play there now and again, I understand for Weddings and funerals. He certainly played at Barford when cousin Kathleen got married, my mother was a guest and said she had never heard the likes before, apparently he must have pulled all the stops out – or pushed them in. However Barford has always, and still is something special, for me. The village has altered very little in appearance although the little "beehive" cottage was demolished soon after Bob and Ruth moved out, a great shame as it was a lovely little cottage. Sometime after we had been to Llandudno Aunt Ruth and Bob came to stay for a day or two. I upset Aunt Ruth by asking how much she was going to pay my mother. I knew we had had to pay in Llandudno you see, Ruth was most offended – naturally, when mother explained and told her "she might have kids of her own one day" all was forgiven.

Stella and I never had any pocket money and in a way I am thankful for that. We had our little treats now and then. Mr Sunley was one of the greengrocers that used to call and he had a tuck box full of sherbet dabs, gob stoppers, yards of liquorice in various forms, acid drops and so on. Now and again we were allowed to spend a half penny (twenty four half pennies equal five new pence). In the summer the ice cream man – Elderodo – would come round on his three wheeler tricycle, two wheels in front with the ice cream container box between them and ringing his bell. Sometimes we had a one penny ice lollipop, which really was frozen cordial – I think – not a lot of flavour but a treat for us nevertheless. We had a proper ice cream sometimes if grandma was staying with us, and that cost two pennies as did a quarter of liquorice allsorts – Bassett's – or a two ounce bar of Cadburys milk chocolate, which we kids could never afford.

Stella and I ran errands now and again, often for "Nan Nan" Squires next door, we would fetch six pennyworth (two and a half new pence) or a shilling (five pence) worth of fowl corn from Mrs James's shop at Four Oaks. The shop, which was a wooden lean-to attached to their semi-detached home, stood about a hundred yards from Four Oaks crossroads along Back Lane, where the bungalows are now. She sold all the groceries that one would need and my father bought most his "Woodbines" from there, I think our mother refused to buy his fags.

Anyhow on these errands, Stella and I would be given one whole penny to spend and making up our minds what to have – again from a tuck box – was the most difficult part. This was alright till one day something happened and we spilt some corn and thereafter we had our reward after the safe delivery of whatever. Then we received our penny and tore back to the shop to spend it. That was not the only disaster I had, my folks also kept poultry, usually about a dozen laying hens and perhaps a cockerel or two for Christmas. In those days before and during the war, poultry was a luxury. Occasionally when the old hens went off laying, they would end up in the pot – one at a time that is – no fridges or freezers remember. They would be boiled for so long then most likely finished off in the oven at the side of the fire.

Anyway, back to the disaster and when we had spare eggs they were sold. The cash did help to pay for the corn which my father bought by the hundred weight (cwt = 112 = lbs) from a local farmer. Probably Mr John Davies from Park Farm where father would help with haymaking and the corn harvest, after work in the evenings and on a Saturday afternoon. Corn! Eggs!

Oh yes, one of mother's customers was Mrs Fletcher, wife of the butler at Berkswell Hall, guess who delivered them, also guess who was picking up conkers and put his foot in the basket of eggs. Yes "Tin ribs", "Sunny Jim" or me. I did not know whether to deliver the few that remained intact, return home, or what; and I cannot recall what I did do. But I did cop out. But my mother never did dwell on anything for long. I lived to tell the tale. In fact I never ever remember my parents having an argument or "falling out".

I started gardening when I was six, father let me have a patch next to our rhubarb bed on one side and two loganberry vines on one end. He rough dug one area of about twenty feet by ten feet and left me to it. Mother provided the seeds, also some out of fathers packets. One used to get huge amounts of seeds for a few pence. We always had seeds from a firm called Fidlers who were taken over many years ago by another seed firm. I did wax and wain a bit with my garden but it was always a joy to produce something for "the pot" or perhaps a nice crisp lettuce. There was an element of competition between father and myself, probably honours were about even although my patch was probably in the best part of the garden.

There was always friendly rivalry between us and Barford. We never won anything, because Barford is always two to three weeks in front of Berkswell being further south and probably being at the end of the Evesham Vale helped somewhat. Also the watershed of England of which I had no knowledge at the time – might have had a bearing on the climate. We now live in Windmill Lane, in the parish of Berkswell and it is possible to trace the rivers, brooks and streams right back to the ditches that drain the fields. There is a field to the east of Windmill Lane – and there must be many throughout the area where the water at one side drains into a ditch which runs into Finham Brook and on into the Avon and eventually into the Bristol Channel. The ditch on the other side of the field feeds a brook that runs into the river Blythe then into the North Sea via the Trent. Another bit of useful/useless information.

As I said before my father would help John Davies of Park Farm, Cornets End with the hay making, and harvest in his spare time. Any overtime cash was his, I understand. Father went shopping to buy his top clothes about once a year. Going to Coventry on the bus on a Saturday afternoon, I think he went to Lynes store which for some many years now is to be found in Well Street, He would return home probably walking from Meriden or Broad Lane terminus, not hanging around for the Berkswell bus which arrived about a quarter to six in the evening. A large brown parcel tied up neatly with string would no doubt contain new corduroy breeches, he wore leather leggings over his legs – a pair of hob nail boots, he never wore a pair of shoes in his life, a pair of shirts and so on. Father never wore wellies or gloves till he joined the Observer Corps in 1938 before the outbreak of the Second World War. Outdoor workers had to be tough in those days, it was thought sissy to wear gloves in the winter, now they are worn by everybody, including me, and cissy footballers.

Before the war I used to write to my cousin Betty in Australia and could not understand that B. Hough, "Hillcrest", Nannup, W.A. would find her. She wrote interesting letters about walks in "the bush" and swimming in the Blackwood River. The letters contained pressed flowers which scented the envelope. Betty was always interested in nature and things that grew – plant life – and still is. It was the war that put a stop to our correspondence, it was not worth it as letters took ages and often went missing. Letters took just over four weeks from door to door, in those days, they take four days now. I never thought I would see "Hillcrest", but I did. Although their dwelling had gone, one could get an impression of what life was like there at the time. Cousin Alan filled in the detail for us in 1990. But I am rushing on too fast – more later. I am far too young at the moment.

In early August 1939, mother, Stella and I went to Stratford-upon-Avon to stay in Great William Street with Mrs White. She was the mother of Aunt Marrie in Australia. The weather was very nice and I found my way around Stratford very well, even taking myself to the cinema in Greenhill Street one evening (age ten). I had to sleep at the Bailey's house next door, I always went in and unknown to the others was fed hot chocolate and biscuits (another first – hot chocolate). The Bailey's got me chatting and apparently I kept them amused telling them all our family secrets.

About two years previous to our trip to Stratford, the Kerby family had moved from Holloway Farm Cornets End Lane in Berkswell to Church Farm at Binton (Ted Kerby was the person who transported me home from hospital in 1934). One day whilst we were at Stratford, we paid a visit by prior appointment to the Kerbys at Binton, travelling by bus. Met by Mr and Mrs Kerby at their huge farmhouse we went into the orchard and gathered early plums and apples, then had dinner (lunch now). I had never seen a piece of beef like it in my life before. Ted Kerby carved and we enjoyed a meal fit for a king. They had three sons, Edward, John and David – who was a little older then me – then Mary and Janet. I cannot recall how many sat down to dinner but seem to recall quite a number at least nine or so. After dinner I went off with the men folk, it was a hot day and every able bodied person was helping with the harvest. They were "carrying corn" i.e. In those days all the corn was cut with a binder, this machine cut and tied the corn into sheaves. The machine started on the outside of the field and finished up in the centre. As now, there were often a lot of rabbits about and as the area of uncut corn got smaller, so the bunnies congregated in the centre. This was the time for the farmer and possibly anyone proficient with a gun – twelve bore or similar – to stand say on each corner of the uncut corn and shoot the rabbits as they came out.

When the binder had finished it's work, the sheaves had to be picked up one under each arm and stood up in stooks, sometimes there were six sheaves to a stook, sometimes eight. The stooks stood for over two weeks as a rule before being carried on the horse drawn wagon to the rickyard at the farm. It was always said that the stooked – some called it shooking – sheaves should hear the church bells three times before being carried. On a big farm it took about seven men to really make a mark. One man taking full loads to the farm and returning with an empty wagon. Another man would unload and pitch the sheaves onto the rick (this was easy before the rick got too tall). Two men on the rick, one to pass the sheaves to the rick builder. There was a correct way to pitch and pass the sheaves, always pitching with the ears of corn to the centre of the wagon and passing the butts of the sheaves to the outside of the rick so that the loader and rick builder would not have to manually turn the sheaves around. Woe betide any rookie making a mistake, he would probably receive three or four sheaves thrown back from a great height.

Again I side track, I did enjoy the afternoon especially when a load of hot strong sweet tea arrived in the field for all to share. All too soon it was time to return to the farm and sit down to a splendid farmhouse tea. Mrs Kerby was a first class cook as were most farmer's wives, and still are. Eventually we said our thankyous and goodbyes and set off to walk down to the Stratford Evesham Road to catch the bus back to Stratford, loaded up with apples, plums, two or three rabbits for the pot and goodness knows what else. We arrived at the main road alright and as we waited for our bus a whole convoy of military vehicles went past the other way. Hundreds – literally – of them. I had never seen the like of some of the vehicles. It was getting quite dusk when a man from the house on the corner – it is still there today – not sure about the bloke – walked down his garden path to the roadside gate, he started off with tales of doom. "There will be a war missis before the weekend, those lorries are taking troops to the docks, and so on. Oh and by the way your last bus has gone"! There was Ma stuck on the side of the road with two youngish kids plus rabbits, apples and plums, etc.

After a bit of a think it was decided we leave our gifts inside this man's gate and walk back up the hill to the Kerby's at the farm. Mother felt awful, having been treated so well during the day and now having to ask Ted to run us into Stratford. Any how we had no choice. Naturally it was no great hardship to Ted, he did not do a great deal of work and so we were soon chugging our way to Mrs White's little cottage in Stratford. As a matter of fact, Ted was more than pleased and when he left us he was going for a game of bowls in Stratford and this trip gave him a wonderful excuse to go. But briefly back to the days at Holloway Farm, Ted Kerby loved recreation, he played darts and also went to whist drives near and far. Being a typical farmer he was very fond of shooting. He was never far from his gun, always handy in the cowshed at milking time. At one time he loved a bit of poaching as well.

Not quite sure when the following episode took place, but the tale was told to me by my father and others during a break when we helping "Uncle" John Davies with the harvest.

At the time, Colonel Wheatley of Berkswell Hall held the shooting rights for game over Holloway Farm owned by Ted Kerby. Apparently Ted could not resist a little bit of poaching, naturally he went onto estate property for this part of his business.

He would light the lanterns in the cowshed to give the impression he was milking, mainly perhaps because the under keeper lived further down Cornets End Lane close to the sand hole as it was known to us (sand quarry). Then off he would go, crossing the road with his gun under his arm towards the woods known as "The Bogs" or others close by. Only a matter of crossing two or three fields. Bang, bang and back again. He might even be lucky and "drop" on a bird or two before getting as far as the woods, who knows. However good things do not go on forever. First of all the keepers were suspicious, then they were ninety-nine percent sure who the villain was, but how to catch him? I understand an effort was made quite a few times unsuccessfully – don't forget he was armed. Eventually he was caught one Sunday evening by quite a posse of blokes and in due course attended court and paid the penalty – whatever that was. But, that is not the end of the story. At this stage Ted did not renew the shooting rights to Berkswell Estate, instead he would encourage young pheasants to come to his farm by providing feed in the way of corn for them They soon "cottoned on " flying from estate land on one side of Cornets End Lane to Ted's fields on the other side. And then in the shooting season all Ted had to do was pot them off with his trusty twelve bore as they flew over the hedge onto his land. Apparently Ted recouped his fine many time over. But the story does have a happy ending and this is no fairy story – both sides "made it up" again but I do not know how long it took. Mr Cudmore, the head keeper, often paid the Kerby's a visit in his old Ford *.

The estate had Holloway Farm shooting rights restored. Ted and the keepers became good pals once again. Whilst I am "on about" pheasants and shooting, etc. reminds me of the time when I assisted by becoming a beater on some shoot days.

At the time I went beating the shoot was on a Saturday. War work did not permit many people, "guns" or beaters to be available during the week. Most men worked on a Saturday morning anyhow, so it was usually men off the estate and farm, also the gardeners and estate workers. Also one or two lads like me. I was no more than ten years old when I went on my first days beating, being quite used to walking miles, but perhaps not used to hacking and clambering through some of the growth of blackberries, nut bushes and so on that grew in the woods. The beaters usually met at the estate yard at nine thirty or ten o'clock. My father would have been out since first light "stopping". Probably four men would have this job. They would walk around the perimeter of the shoot and drive any birds into the centre i.e. the woods. And "stop" them flying away to freedom – poor devils.

The first drive would be from Chapel Hill (Home Farm now) down the

Fordrough (Farm drive) to Meriden Road, beat out the spinney on Old Lane (Lavender Hall Lane now) and Park Lane as we went. Beating meant walking in a line all through the wood or spinney, all armed with a stick – for beating. Rattling sticks in bushes or trees, anything to drive the birds into the sights of the guns waiting at the end of the wood. Some of the "guns" could not hit a pig in an entry, therefore quite a few birds survived till the next shoot or, if they were lucky, the one after that. At the end of each drive, Harry Ayers would be waiting with the game cart, a special horse drawn cart, all painted up spick and span. The horse would be all dolled up with plumes and brasses like a May Day donkey, or was that Harry? In his tweed clothes, polished boots and top hat, not a green wellie to be seen anywhere.

Archie Cudmore, head keeper, and the "guns" would carefully try and account for all the birds that were shot. They would be paired up in braces – a cock and a hen – and hung on special racks on the game cart.

On my first season of beating we ended up near the keepers cottage and whilst the guns retired to The Hall for luncheon, we had our dinner in a brick built shant (a place with a fireplace where workers could have their breaks and in the winter a respite from the weather). There was a roaring fire in the shant at the keepers with trestle tables and benches set out for the beaters. It was always roast beef, a huge joint with lots of fat on, all crackling and bubbling away. I was not a very big kid, thin and skinny but my father had told me what to say and when asked by Bert Vaughan, the under chauffeur and mother's cousin "How much would you like John" says he "enough for a navvy" was my reply. It "brought the house down". The beer flowed freely and I filled up on lemonade, a rare treat for me. Coke was something one stoked the boiler with at that time.

It was not long before things changed, as the war progressed, rationing made catering impossible, in the end it became a DIY job. But there was still a roaring fire.

CHAPTER 4

Berkswell in 1939

Just a little now about how life in general was for the Webb family and life in general just before the second World War in 1939.

In common with most people we were happy and contented with "our lot". We were well fed on plain wholesome food, either corn flakes, porridge for breakfast and a fried breakfast at the weekend. The variety of cereals was somewhat limited but Kelloggs corn flakes, Wheetabix and Shredded Wheat were available. Keeping poultry we always had eggs.

Our main meal was dinner at about 12.30, meat and boiled mashed potatoes and usually two other vegetables. A good pudding to follow, steamed pud, jam roly-poly, spotted dick and milk puddings. At that time we had unlimited free milk from Home Farm. Tea with all meals, we never had coffee.

Tea at around 6 pm consisted of bread butter and home made jam; in the summer months salads featured, but tomatoes and cucumbers were had in small helpings. There was always a big cake around, usually a fruit cake. On Sundays we always had a roast joint of meat – chicken was a rare treat, now and again an old hen – past her "sell by date" – boiled and finished off in the oven. At tea time we had a blancmange or a jelly and sometimes fruit and cream in the summer, a third of a pint of fresh cream collected in a jug was 3d ($1^{1/2}$p).

We had no electricity, radio, etc. No water on the tap, therefore no hot water system or flush toilet. A tin (galvanised) bath in front of the fire, washing up in a bowl on the kitchen table. The ironing was done with a flat iron. My parents each had a bicycle, I learned to ride and paid £1.50 for a very good second hand bike when I was aged nine. The £1.50 came out of my savings. My sister, Stella and I never had pocket money from our parents, it did teach us to be thrifty.

My father was paid once a fortnight and I do not think there was much spare money at the end of two weeks.

We had a large garden with the fowl pen at the bottom end. My father did not really enjoy gardening, I think he must have been tired after his days work on the Berkswell Estate, but it was essential to produce vegetables for our use. All plain stuff, potatoes, peas, beans and lots of brassicas. I had part of the garden from the age of 6 and very soon the few flowers we had were looked after by me. My mother never assisted in the garden, her time was taken up picking and processing soft fruit also shallots, etc., my mothers piccallily was superb, as was everything else that was set before us.

My sister and I had super parents, we never went hungry, we were well clothed and always had a good fire which kept us warm. The bedrooms were cold, as youngsters we got ready for bed downstairs and "shot" into our beds, which were warmed by a hot water bottle. It was quite common in the winter to find any water in the bedroom frozen into ice in the morning.

That was the norm, everybody else was the same, nowadays we have all gone soft – but – I do not wish to go back to those days.

The same can be said for the schools, very primitive. No school dinners, again no electricity (till 1940), no mains water or gas, very few telephones, none at the school. No facilities for sport or P.E. and ad hoc games of rounders or "painting" (called art) on a Friday afternoon had to do. Again I think it was perhaps the same elsewhere. The teachers, in my opinion, were very good, we all departed Berkswell School able to read and write to a good standard.

Just about all of the property in Berkswell village belonged to the Wheatleys of Berkswell Hall, including The Bear Inn and The Garden Café (now The Malthouse) and The Garden House. The Priory belonged to the Hope family, The Well House next to the Church was the Rectory. The Almshouses (12 in those days) shop and the two cottages between the shop and school were, and still are, administered by, and part of, Berkswell Charities, and overseen by seven Trustees and the Clerk.

We had two millionaires in the parish, Colonel C.J.H. Wheatley of Berkswell Hall, and Sir Charles Hyde BT, whose residence was The Moat. A fine house and gardens, a farm and small estate.

There were at least 14 tenant farms, forming Berkswell Estate, as well as numerous smallholdings and dwellings such as the blacksmiths forge in Spencers Lane with Taylors the butchers next door.

Farming was very labour intensive in 1939. The Wheatley family employed well over 40 people at the Hall on the farm and estate workers. At least 12 on the farm. I think it was about this time that the first tractor arrived. At a rough guess I would think that the farm was about 50% arable and 50% pasture, a considerable acreage would be used for making hay, none of the Home Park and Top Park beyond the lake was ploughed before the war.

Different crops were grown at that time. Oats, field beans – similar to broad beans – mangolds, swedes and kale to name a few. I have it on good authority that there is no longer a big demand for oats and the value of the crop makes it uneconomical to grow. Beans were grown to provide protein in animal feed, probably mainly for horses, farmers now purchase diesel oil for tractors instead of horse feed. Mangolds and swedes were very labour intensive to produce and as far as cattle are concerned, silage has replaced those crops, the same can be said for kale. Hay had to be mown and turned a few times – depending on the weather – or, the hay had to be made i.e. haymaking, and "carried" to the rick or farmyard, if the hay was a bit green and damp when carried it could combust and fire. Great long iron rods (pokers) were pushed into the centre of the rick and often when removed would be very hot indeed. Silage, I understand, began to be made in the early 1950s. I used to really enjoy haymaking and harvesting cereals, evenings after my normal work also on Saturday afternoon. I do not think I could get as much pleasure making silage or working in a grain drier. Do farmers dry their grain anymore? No combine harvesters then, or until 1948 when Rupert Arnold of Back Lane acquired the first one in the area that I know of. Before the arrival of the combine Rupert Arnold, who was a farm contractor toured the farms with his "threshing tackle". A huge four wheel steam driven traction engine, belching out smoke, steam and a certain amount of noise. The engine towed the threshing drum and a machine for tying the threshed straw into boultings.

The farm worker, or woman, has always been a skilled person, but with probably less demands years ago. If a man and his team of horses ploughed one acre in a day or cut and laid 22 yds of a hedge that was accepted. There are no "farm labourers" nowadays, all workers on farms are highly skilled, not only required to know farming skills, they need to be mechanics, scientists and very responsible. There is a lot of expensive equipment and valuable stock to be looked after.

There were very few vehicles on the road, some farmers had a car, often used to take piglets and calves to market, via the back seat. Public transport in Berkswell consisted of 4 or 5 buses to Coventry six days per week, less on Sunday. Frequent buses via Meriden to Coventry or Birmingham and trains from Berkswell Station, about 2 per day ran to and from Kenilworth and Leamington. Most people – by no means not all – had a bicycle of some sort, maybe no brakes and so on.

My mother seldom needed to go shopping, we had milk from the farm, the butcher, baker, grocer, greengrocer, hardware man, the lady selling cooked meats, the Floury Pecoe Tips man with his tea, not forgetting the insurance man, all called at the house. Henry Court could always be relied on to supply anything the male required in the way of clothing. With a few exceptions most housewives were always at home, housework and providing meals was a full time job with steady overtime. Some folk went out some pretended to be out, sometimes depending if the tradesman hoped to collect his dues.

I do not recall anything about travel by air, there were a number of aerodromes locally. Castle Bromwich, Whitley (Coventry), and Elmdon, much later to become Birmingham Airport. With the advent of war, early in 1939, Elmdon aerodrome was used to train pilots for the R.A.F., it started off with just a few but soon the sky was "full" of Tiger Moths buzzing around, the Tiger Moth was a two seater open cockpit bi-plane, easy to fly and very safe, we were informed, I believe some are still flying today.

As a ten year old I was not aware of the horrors of war, it must have been a worrying time for our parents. The great war, World War One ending just twenty years previously. The A.R.P. was formed (Air Raid Precautions), later divided up a bit into air raid wardens, ambulance drivers and the Observer Corps. My mother took a course on home nursing and another on first aid. My father joined the Observer Corps in 1938 and was still doing his duties till the end of the war in Europe.

I was ten and a half at the outbreak of war in September 1939. No memories of any of the politics that lead up to the war itself. We still had no radio, or wireless, as it was known then and it was another fifteen months before the electricity was laid on to us.

CHAPTER 5

The Days and Nights of the Second World War

Sunday the 3rd of September was a lovely sunny warm morning, father had gone off to the A.R.P. (Air Raid Precautions). He volunteered for the Observer Corps in 1938. I presume they had lectures and instructions on various topics, they also had aircraft recognition, both allied and enemy aircraft. There were cards with a head on view, side on view and plan view of the individual aircraft. Blenheim bombers, Junkers 87 (Stukas) and so on. I found this interesting and we tested each other.

The sun is still out on this sunny morning and mother, Stella and I walked round the "bunny" run to Squire's to listen to Mr Chamberlain on the wireless, with the inevitable news that we were at war. This was another occasion when I saw my mother crying tears, she just burst into tears and ran for home. Our mother was just eighteen years old when the First World War ended. From then on I took a great interest in the war – for a ten year old – and never once thought that we would lose. When eventually I went back round home the only thing that bothered me was would father have to join up. I did not know that at the time father was forty seven years old and mother assured me he would not have to join the forces. As an aside my father and three of his brothers served in the First World War and all arrived home afterwards safe and sound. Their names – together with many others – are on the honours board in Berkswell Reading Room. What a pity those that served their country since, were not honoured in the same way. Only the names of the fallen 1939 – 1945 can be seen in the memorial by the church gate. For a start off things were more or less as normal, they were for us kids anyhow. Christmas with the parties took place as usual, cannot recall rationing coming in, it did not concern me, did it? My three square meals a day appeared as usual. By this time the Observer Corps were up and running. There was an observation post at the rear of what is known as Cornbury House in Back Lane. There were two men on duty at all times in four hour shifts. Six till ten, ten till two, two till six, day and night.

Mr Cudmore (the keeper) was head observer and paid visits to the post on a regular basis often at odd times to make sure all was well. They were armed with rifles, so he would be challenged during the hours of darkness. There were observation posts at strategic locations throughout the country. Their job was to locate and plot aircraft, friend and foe alike. The observers had an instrument of some sort, father said it was secret – probably to shut me up – to assist their plotting. They then reported to a central location – Coventry in their case, where a grid system operated and aircraft could be followed. They started off with a shelter in the form of a dug-out also a hut with bunks and a stove and facilities for making hot drinks. I know not from where materials came from but soon they built a raised platform surrounded by a wooden "wall" to keep the wind off, I think it was all quite cosy before too long. Father carried on working on the estate and doing duties during the period from six o'clock in the evening till six o'clock in the morning. During 1940 there was an epidemic of flu and quite a number of the observers were unable to carry out their duties, during that year my father was on duty for 1299 hours during the year and although the snowfall of that winter was one of the greatest on record, the

Members of The Observer Corps (later Royal)
Left to right: Mr Gay, Herbert Vaughan under chauffeur B.H.; Jack Mills, Groom B.H.; Wilf Tingey, under keeper B.H.; Len Harford, head gardener M.; Harry Ford, head gardener B.H.; Albert Webb, sawyer B.H.; Arthur Cheshire, pigman B.H.; Bert Wagstaff, chauffeur B.H.; Archie Cudmore, head keeper, B.H; also head observer

"post" remained fully manned. Throughout that year, father put in more duties than anyone else and was presented with a tankard from his colleagues which reads "Albert Webb. F2 Champion 1940. 1299 Watchful hours". 1299 divided by four (hours) does not go, does it – it was a leap year, and who was watching the stars at the time?

In the early days they were all local men, from all walks of life. Chauffeurs, gardeners, farmers and farm workers. The duties were chosen by the observers at the Bear and Ragged Staff in Berkswell at six thirty in the evening on a Friday. This was a good excuse for staying on for an extra pint or two. And why not, I am sure it was hard earned money which was five shillings per shift (twenty five new pence).

One of the first major upsets of the war of course was the evacuation of the B.E.F. (British Expeditionary Force) and other allied forces from the beaches of Dunkirk in June 1940. We all followed the happenings very closely as best we could, almost entirely from the Daily Mirror which was always our daily newspaper. Usually there was a little map to indicate the various advances and retreats of both friends and foe. I'm afraid we made very few advances in 1940.

The cubs went on as usual – or more or less – after the war started, some of the seniors were soon called up for the various forces, and later on it was difficult to be tested for proficiency badges as examiners were few and far between. Also Berkswell was, or seemed to be, a very long way from Coventry then. On top of that there was a black out – no lights to be visible – half an hour before lighting up time on the roads – if that makes sense.

Berkswell scout group always seemed to plough its own furrow. Being virtually unable to join in area sports or the like we really had no choice, but really we were very fortunate. Colonel Wheatley allowing the troop access to more or less anywhere, certainly within a half mile radius of the scout house by the well. Some of the early scouts built a canoe and we were allowed to take this on the lake, it was a two seater, often leaked, but was enjoyed by all. The cubs were only passengers. I do not recall any life jackets but maybe wrong. "Bunny" Poole was a big strong lad and loved the old canoe and seemed to be tireless at giving us cubs a sail. The troop were also permitted, by prior arrangement, to swim in Sir Charles Hyde's pool at "The Moat". It was always cold but the setting was superb, beautifully kept grounds and gardens all round the lovely house, although they were "out of bounds" to us.

Unfortunately I did not learn to swim, being a bit scared to venture from the side, also I could not trust some of the bigger ones who were fond of ducking the likes of me.

We did witness a near drowning one day. A fearless young lad got into his costume for the first time and took a flying leap into the deep end, he had been on the bottom some seconds before being fished out by seniors who knew how to administer first aid. The lad was back in the water again soon after. I wished I had his venturous spirit, many times.

I was not to realise till some many years after, that I suffered with an inferiority complex. I never thought I was as good as the next kid, owing to my problem with my legs and then having to wear spectacles at the age of five – the only one at school to wear glasses. I was "four eyes" and so on, which at the time did not seem to bother me, but deep down, it probably did.

Back to the scouts and The Moat and Sir Charles – as he was known. He often had a walk around his garden and paid us a visit whilst we were swimming or sun bathing. One of his pleasures was to line up the troop along the side of the pool and poke each one in turn, so that we/they all fell in. Sir Charles was a great benefactor to the troop as he was to Berkswell and many other organisations, quite a few in Birmingham.

He provided our troop – the 53rd Coventry – with our own camp ground which was situated at the rear of Lower Farm in Spencers Lane, just one field further back from the farm. We also gained access via the gate at the bottom of the hill in Spencers Lane, close by the pair of semi-detached houses.

The camp ground was about three quarters of an acre in area and roughly oblong in shape, all fenced in. Water was laid on to a tap. The area was dominated by a huge oak tree which provided shade in the summer.

There was a large shed known as "the hut" for the storage of camping gear, also I recall sheltering there many times when the weather was bad. Unlike Berkswell Estate, we were not allowed to use any surrounding ground as it was all down to farming, often with livestock.

Cubs did not camp very often and when I was old enough for scouts, rationing made things difficult. One occasion I remember camping and went home with stomach ache, etc. – Harry Taylor's sausages were blamed for that.

There were three patrols of scouts, The Otters, Owls and Foxes. I was in the Fox Patrol. Each patrol had their own kitchen area, a place for a fire for cooking and so on. These areas had to be kept very tidy as inspections were carried out.

Sadly, Sir Charles died in 1943 and probably – partly through not being used – new ownership and so on, all facilities at The Moat were lost for good. However, an Almshouse in the village was made available, how or why I do not know, but it must have been a bit noisy on Friday evenings for the elderly neighbours.

To assist in the war effort, the scouts had an ongoing campaign to collect waste paper, Farmer Walter Thompson turned out with his horse and cart and a whole gang of us went as far as Tile Hill and came back with a whole load of paper. This paper, as I understood, was sold to someone and as an incentive to the troop the agreement was for any proceeds to be shared. Fifty percent to the troop and the other 50% to the collector. I set to work with gusto as a means of earning a copper or two, collecting, weighing and delivering waste paper to the scout house on a Friday evening –

troop night. I did collect a lot of paper but never saw a single penny and never knew why. Stella and I were used to being treated fairly and honestly and this "paper business" was quite upsetting to me at the age of twelve to thirteen.

Therefore, what with that experience and the troop not functioning very well, I gradually lost interest. The latter really was the fault of no one, just the upheaval of the war. People having to work longer hours, having other duties like fire watching, Air Raid Wardens, Home Guard and lots more. It is pleasing though that the troop kept going in a fashion throughout, thanks to Bunny Poole, Bill Green and John Bradbury in the main with help from lots of others.

It was about this time that I started doing all sorts of odd jobs – sometimes for odd bods. As the war progressed – or otherwise sometimes – I never thought we would lose, not even in the days and months of crisis during 1941, 1942 and 1943. Thanks, of course, to that old "War Horse", Mr Churchill.

I must have been eleven when I took on a small paper round at Four Oaks (Berkswell). This was after I started at Balsall Street Central School at the end of August 1940, more of which later.

I used to come home to dinner from school and collect my papers, which were very thin owing to the war, from The Lodge in Meriden Road. The newsagent, a Mr Spencer, ran the business from a tiny shop near the station, he also sold tobacco and sweets and stationary. Again owing to the war, restrictions on his petrol allowance only allowed him to come that far. My clients to be at Four Oaks got together and enquired of me if I would be prepared to deliver them. This I took on, delivering the papers during our dinner time break which was from twelve o'clock till one forty five. Saturday and Sunday was soon after breakfast. I was paid by my clients to the tune of three pence (just over 1p) per week. Mrs Perkins gave me an extra one penny as they lived at the bottom of the hill in Berkswell Road, on the way to Meriden.

I had about ten customers with a few more on Sundays, so you see I was "knocking up" two and six (twelve and a half new pence) per week. I only had one problem collecting the cash, this concerned a lady – well she was a female – in Back Lane, very slow to pay me. I was about eight weeks short, so one day when my mother was out at dinnertime, which was a rare event – I put a note inside the paper, short and to the point. Unfortunately there were guests at the house and guess who picked up the newspaper and my note. She came blazing down to our house, slapped the money into my sticky paw and raved on a bit and told me not to deliver any more newspapers to her.

That suited me as I also did a bit of gardening there and the jobs I had were sometimes beyond the capabilities of me at twelve years of age. Some two months later this lady called again all gushy and smiles asking me to deliver the papers again. I politely declined with thanks. One of my favourite spare time jobs was at The Moat, home of Sir Charles Hyde BT. Owner of The Birmingham Weekly Post, The Mail and in those days, The Birmingham Post.

Len Hurford, the head gardener was a pal of my father. Len was also a member of the Observer Corps. One day he enquired as to whether I would like to do a few hours gardening after school. I agreed and duly presented myself one afternoon at about quarter past four. The gardeners were in the potting shed for their afternoon cup of tea and I was invited to sit on an old garden bench and was presented with a big mug of hot tea and sitting on the end of this seat were two others. I had just got settled down when the other two got up and I went down. This trick was played on all new visitors to the potting shed at tea breaks. Originally the seat had six legs, two at each end and two in the centre, however the legs at one end had got broken or rotted away and normally no one sat there, but quite a few got caught out. Two hours was my stint, finishing at six thirty, and then home for tea. The gardens were very nice but were showing the need for far more attention than the present gardeners could provide. Before the war there were six full time gardeners. Work there was most enjoyable most of the time and many lessons were learnt there, two worth relating.

One evening just before knocking off time I was working on a flower bed under a window and could not resist the temptation to look in, just as Mr Hurford came round the corner. "Windows are for looking out of" says he "Not for looking into". He had come back to close down the greenhouse lights and stoke up for the night. Another thing that came to a stop soon after. Coke and coal were on ration.

Another time I was just finishing off work in the kitchen garden and walking down an avenue of cordon apple trees. It was early autumn and I was tempted to pinch one apple off a tree and another from the floor. One never selects small apples when large ones are available and naturally I chose two big ones and stuffed them as best I could into the pockets of my trousers. I was still in short trousers, most lads did not have "longs" till they were over thirteen years old. They did stick out rather and unfortunately – for me – I met Sir Charles at the garden gate and after the pleasantries, he tapped each of my pockets with his stick and enquires as to what was contained within. There was no option but to come clean, if I had heard of such a thing as a rupture there was an excuse but I hadn't. Sir Charles took the apples that were sheepishly produced and after the mildest of lectures we went our separate ways. Next afternoon after we had our cuppa, the other men went off leaving Mr Hurford and me in the potting shed. He had two large apples in his hand and gave them to me and told me if I wanted any more I was to ask him or Sir Charles. That memory has flooded back to me many times since.

I was a bit older when I went to Mr Norman (Gubby) Taylors at Ye Olde Berkswell Stores, Station Road, which was on the top of the hill close to Sunnyside Lane – no houses there then. Mr Taylor was our grocer and baker. During the war one had to register with one grocer for our basic food rations, we also had a points system for other groceries and had to hope that when a delivery of something scarce or special was made, the grocer was fair in his distribution. We always found Mr Taylor most fair, he came on Saturday dinner time for the order, also delivering bread, then the order came with the next delivery of bread the following week.

Anyhow, I went to Taylors after my paper round and worked six hours and came away with three shillings (fifteen new pence). There was no man in the shop at all apart from Mr Taylor and the baker, so I had to fill shelves with the heavies, flour, plain and self raising, sugar, soap powders and so on, also I had to unpack the huge cheeses from the wooden crates. He did have an old delivery bike with a basket on the front and I often had a few deliveries to undertake on the Saturday afternoons. I enjoyed my time there and Mr Taylor quite thought and hoped I would work there when I left school, but my mind was made up long before then that I wanted to be a gardener.

Back to school for a while now and by this time I was in Miss Tatersall's class and by this time the school was junior and infants, pupils went to Balsall Street Central at the age of eleven. Miss Tattersall taught all subjects to classes of pupils from age eight till eleven. I like to think we were well taught, there was no one unable to read, write and gain a reasonable knowledge of most subjects. Then as always there were some more able than others. The '3 R's' were well to the fore and Miss Tattersall made history and geography "come alive" for me anyhow. We had games on a Friday afternoon, rounders in the park where the Rectory garden is now situated. In fact that whole triangle was all part of the park until the Rectory was built in the 1950s. I was no good at sport or PT as it was then. Fortunately there was not a lot of it.

Then, as now, we learnt country dancing and maypole dancing. Performing at the annual church fete in June, which was held at the Rectory, which was next to the church. It is known as the Well House these days. The Reverend Arthur Laurence Whitaker was Rector then and lived there with his wife and son Peter who was an officer in the merchant navy. Sadly his ship was sunk in the Indian Ocean in 1942 and he did not survive. Mr & Mrs Whitaker, I am sure, never got over the shock of losing their son – an only child.

The Whitakers were very keen gardeners and the garden was huge, taking in the area where three houses now stand in Lavender Hall Lane, now backing on to The Well House. Bercul House, by the well, was the old coach house. Years ago the "living" at Berkswell was very good – from the Rector's point of view. At one time there was staff in the house and at least two gardeners. The last full time gardener was Percy Bull, I remember him very well. Mr Whitaker, as he was often known, was very popular and was respected by all. In the "pecking order" of the parish he came next to Colonel Wheatley. At all the village concerts, etc. Colonel and Mrs Wheatley sat on the front row with Mr and Mrs Whitaker also in the front row but on the other side of the central isle. They were the only people who sat in arm chairs – smokers bows. Mr Whitaker was always a guest gun at the estate shoots, no idea what sort of shot he was.

During the war in the event of an air raid, all the school children had to run along the Churchyard drive, through a door in the wall by the yew trees – bricked up since the house has been privately owned – on through the back way down into the cellar. Good shot or not he always had his pheasants, I can recall going past them hung up on the way to the cellar – and seeing lots of maggots squirming about on the floor. We never did have to run to the shelter during my days at Berkswell School, in the event of an air raid – thank goodness.

They were happy days by and large but I always had a problem with maths – sums to us. So much so that in the end I copied Jim Thompson's work which did me no good at all. No one could understand why I was a failure at exams. However I was just about equal in all other subjects but it was only Jim that won a scholarship and he went off to Leamington College.

We had our school milk in the early days. A third of a pint in bottles with cardboard tops with a centre disc which we pushed in with a thumb, sometimes a dirty one. We drank our milk through a straw, later on the morning drink was horlicks and to me it was awful, so I went without. In the winter Miss Tattersall's room was heated by a coke stove about three feet tall and fed through the top which got very hot, we used to spit on this and it used to go round and round the top getting smaller and smaller.

Came August 1940 and time to move to Balsall school. All those pupils that lived three miles or more from the school were provided with a brand new Hercules bicycle (value five pounds) or one pound per annum to maintain ones own bike. Guess which I chose, anyhow my faithful Rudge which I had looked after well was getting a bit small, also I had a job to keep up with some of the others. Therefore on the first day I cadged a lift to school with Nurse Whetter whose daughter Sydney was also starting that day – picturing myself riding my new 'bike' home at the end of the day.

What a difference to cosy little Berkswell school. Talk about a rude awakening. First of all the boys from the other neighbouring schools, i.e. Eastern Green (in Warwickshire then), Burton Green, Barston, Beausale, Honily and so on were put in one class together with evacuees from Frederick Bird school in Coventry. The girls were integrated into the main school classes, of which I think there were eight. Mr Dobson taught us lads aged from eleven to fourteen in three classes which I always thought was unfair on him, also on us lads. However, there was a war on and he was a very good teacher who had come to Balsall from Frederick Bird together with Mrs Farndon.

However Mr Dobson was soon called up and for the next four terms or so, we all had Mrs Farndon – and she was stuck with us. I understand she had never qualified as a teacher, but she did her very noble best. We were quite divorced from the rest of the school as regards being taught. Mrs Farndon took us for all subjects apart from sports on a Friday afternoon.

The first day was very long indeed, I also hated the long dinner break and, to cap it all, no new bike to go home on, yes once again there was a war on. Nothing else to do but walk it and it was a long way, what happened to the other starters I do not know, only that Sydney was picked up at the girls gate further along the road. The survival rate was pretty good and I went on the Rudge the next day and in fact, it was two weeks before our bikes arrived, so all's well that ends well.

I had not been at Balsall School long when one Monday morning in early October Mr Seeley (Pop) the headmaster came into the classroom seeking volunteers to help a farmer plant cabbages. Two hours after school at six pence (two and a half new pence) per hour. I put my hand up and was selected not thinking about being home late, there was pocket money at stake.

The farmer was Mr Napier and he farmed at Barston Lane, by the crossroads between Balsall and Barston. All went well until I got home, by this time my mother was frantic and dad was none too happy either. Where was her little lad? What was he up to? When I had explained and Ma had come down to earth all was well, the job lasted about a week and one evening about five o'clock we heard the roar of an aircraft coming towards us, flying low and lo and behold it was a German Dornier. The identification marks on the wings and fuselage could be seen quite clearly, also the silhouette of the pilots head and shoulders. We stood and watched in amazement as he was only flying at about two hundred and fifty feet above the ground. We later heard that the paint shop at the Standard Motor Company at Canley had been bombed, no doubt we saw the culprit. I also learned later on that this aircraft made it back home by "hedge hopping" all the way to the coast. Information via the Observer Corps.

It was during October 1940 that bombing occurred in Coventry, one night a whole lot of bombs were dropped in Radford near to Wallace Road. We understand they were trying to bomb the Daimler works. In amongst the bombs there was an aerial torpedo, which caused a lot of casualties and damage, also an unexploded bomb. This action and others like it started the flood of people seeking overnight shelter in the countryside. We had a call next day from a Mr Mallard who was an insurance agent for the Royal London. Could we, or rather my mother, accommodate him and his wife please? Mother said she could and so began a friendship.

Part of Mr Mallard's round was in the Berkswell area and therefore he came most nights on his cycle. Mrs Mallard came on the bus, and they settled in very quickly. They were so grateful to have a roof over their heads at night, and they felt safe. They lived in Stevenson Road and all the neighbours were evacuated until the unexploded bomb was dug out, made safe and disposed of. I understand Mrs Mallard's main job for a while was making tea for the disposal squad, but they had to fetch it.

The Mallards soon became Uncle Bert and Auntie Connie. He was once a footman for Lord Methuan in Wiltshire and Lord Methuan unveiled the Berkswell War Memorial in 1921. Uncle Bert, a real old soldier of the first world war – as was my father – was wounded in all four limbs, he was also gassed, but survived and lived to "soldier on". Auntie was a Lancashire lass and suffered with angina. Altogether a lovely couple and I think they probably liked the company of Stella and I because they never had children of their own.

In a way, for me, they were exciting times, thankfully as a kid I did not comprehend the full horrors of war, the killing and maiming, etc. of thousands of men, women and children and make no mistake the people of London, Coventry and many other cities and towns were as good as in the front line.

The evacuation at Dunkirk was nothing short of a miracle, and then we all waited to be invaded. To me, as a youngster, it was more like a game, again I could not comprehend the realities of it all.

For some reason we were in Warwick a short while after Dunkirk and the town was full of soldiers, I assume evacuated from France or Belgium. Some of them were in shabby uniforms and quite rough appearance, they were probably from the battlefield and stationed in Budbrooke Barracks, three miles from Warwick, and not been re-kitted out after their evacuation. And we all wondered how long it would be before Adolph tried to invade us. Thankfully it was not to be.

It was just prior to this that the Webbs acquired our first radio set – or as we knew it a "wireless". We did have a little crystal set given to us by the Squires next door. If I remember correctly, this little device needed an earth-wire and a simple aerial. We listened in through a set of earphones and found the broadcasting station by gently searching over the crystal with a very thin wire attached to a sort of lever held firm in a pivot arrangement.

The electricity had come to Berkswell village and the Ford's were having an all electric job, and Ken Ford told me they wished to part with their battery set for five pounds. That was a hundred hours of duty as an observer that my father would have to do to be able to purchase this set. I did pester him and together with some persuasion from our mother, he relented, all be it a bit grudgingly. It ran on a big heavy dry battery with what was known as a grid bias combined, also there were two wet batteries or accumulators, like small car batteries. One was used at a time, whilst the other had to go to a garage to be re-charged, cost six pence (two and a half new pence). Part of the deal was that it was my job to transport the accumulators to and from the garage. I always took it to the garage opposite "The

Shay House", on the Kenilworth Road. Owned in those days by the Coopers, on my way home from school in the afternoon.

All went well until the dry battery packed up, some time after the Mallards came. Owing to the war we could not get another. By this time we really did enjoy the wireless and probably above all could keep track of what was going on regarding the war. Also there were some superb programmes on then. Lots of variety shows featuring all the top artists of the day. Father enjoyed most of it as well.

Our set was a Marconi and it was Mr Mallard that eventually got us fixed up by means of a device called an eliminator. The only problem was we could never get a lot of volume out of it so we had to sit quiet to hear it. We did get our – or rather father's – moneys worth out of it and after quite a few years mother replaced it with a small round radio set – a Bush. All electric job and I did not have to cart those blinking accumulators to and from the garage any more. Great joy, and we could turn up the volume to our hearts delight.

The next major happening was the blitz on Coventry on the night of November 14th 1940.

My father always seemed to be on duty at "The Post" when "Gerry" was performing and this evening was no exception, he was on six till ten. The bombing started quite early and went on for about twelve hours. The Mallards were with us as usual and "things" got very bad what with the noise of the bombers and their bombs going off. Also our anti aircraft guns opening up. This included "Big Bertha" which I understand was mounted on a special railway wagon and was in the Tile Hill area. It went off with one almighty bang, and if the shell had ever made contact or exploded near a plane that would have been the end of that I am quite sure. There was a rumour at the time – one of many – that Big Bertha was there to give confidence to people and to ensure one and all that the Ministry of Defence were doing their best.

However the evening wore on and I noticed mother was doing her best not to be frightened, a term used then was that one "had the jitters". Stella and I did not go up to bed at our usual time, and on seeing our mother, I declared to all that Ma's got the jitters, that seemed to cure the problem and I think we all had a bit of supper.

Mother made a rarebit with cheese and onion on toast for supper sometimes which I thought was superb, especially as I would not eat cheese uncooked. There was only one or two things that I "turned my nose up to" and cheese was one of them, parsnips was another. There was no way that Stella and I could imagine what was going on in and around Coventry, and of course one had to be there to fully comprehend the horror of it all.

What Auntie Connie and Uncle Bert were thinking, I will never know, wondering if there would be anything left of their house, or in fact of the city itself in the morning.

Father was late coming home. He and all the observers were punctual getting to their duties on time and father was usually home ten minutes after his "turn" ended. It was probably getting on for half past ten when we all went out into the road to see if he was coming, including our mongrel dog Bonzo – good name for a dog.

The sky over Coventry was all red and orange for about ninety degrees of the horizon, a bright moonlit night, one could have read a newspaper, it was so bright. It was not long before two pinpricks of light came down the hill from Four Oaks and round the corner. "Goodnight Len" (Hurford) "Goodnight Albert" then "what the devil are you lot out here for, shrapnel and all sorts flying about, get inside". We all trooped in, the dog first and ma put the milk on to warm and we all had cocoa. Then father declared he was off to bed as there was work to do tomorrow. There was various questions regarding our safety what with what was going on five miles away.

We were informed that Coventry was ablaze from end to end and "Gerry" could not miss with his bombs. So we all went to bed but I bet it was only Stella and I that slept through it all, father claimed he did.

We did not go to school the next day, but did have to go to Balsall and Taylors for bread because the baker did not turn up.

We did not know then what was going on in Coventry but quite soon there were people around asking for overnight accommodation, the first arrived at our door were the Bollands from Broad Lane, just a few houses from Hearsall Common. Mrs Bolland was a widow, she had with her her son Lewis and daughter Dorothy and their huge Alsation dog Bill. We were already full up upstairs as the Mallards were in the front room which mother and father usually had. Stella and I were in "my room, she on the floor on a mattress. Mother and father had Stella's small room. However mother felt very sorry for them and said she would put up a three quarter bed for the two ladies and we had an easy chair that folded flat if Lewis would like that. They were glad of any refuge and accepted. We had a big screen – or was it a clothes horse with a blanket draped over it? I forget. Stella and I were in our beds by then anyhow.

Quite a few people were sent on their way afterwards, a mother and her grown-up daughter turned up, and I think it was almost dark. In the end mother said they could have my bed and I joined Stella on another mattress on the floor in the same room. They were overjoyed.

That made eleven people and two dogs in a small semi-detached house.

The mother and daughter were supposed to look for somewhere else, but everywhere was full, even the school, Reading Room, the "big room" at the Bear Inn, even the scout house.

The Mallards and Bollands were very nice people. The late Mr Bolland was a builder and both Lewis and Dorothy had been well educated, in fact Lewis was a teacher and was studying for his M.A., which he passed at his first attempt. The other pair were not quite as refined shall we say, but the daughter whose name I forget, was very nice looking, and I was told later, took quite a fancy to Lewis and apparently took the dogs for a walk most evenings when there were no air raids and the weather permitted, I suppose. They told me Mrs Bolland was very worried as naturally she wanted the best for her son. And naturally Mrs Bolland would not say anything because they were so grateful for a roof over their head at night.

All went well for a while, the Bollands came out in their car until they could no longer get petrol, then they had to use the bus. We were a bit "thick on the ground" but it was nice for Stella and I as we clicked for a few extra sweets from time to time.

After a while events did get a little strained but it all came to a head after mother found empty gin bottles in the bed from time to time, that was it and they had to go – mother and daughter that is.

We had some bombs drop in Berkswell. The first I recall was between Four Oaks and Meriden Road. Bob Thompson took me to see the "bomb holes" made as the thing exploded. A whole string of bombs were dropped one night mainly across The Moat estate at the top of the hill behind the Bear Inn. There were also a lot of incendiary bombs (fire bombs) dropped in the village, soon put out, I understand by Air Raid Wardens. Apparently one dropped right through the overhanging thatch of Beehive Cottage, thankfully causing no damage. Mother's cousin Bert Vaughan, his wife Evelyn and daughter Brenda lived there at the time.

The only time I was really frightened was one night. I was in bed in the back room and was woken up by a sound like an express train coming up the garden. Louder and louder this noise went on – all of a sudden there was an almighty yellowy blue flash followed by a huge explosion. The whole place shook for a moment and then the crashing of glass, I quite thought the whole window had been blown out. As far as I can recall no one came into my room, perhaps dad was "on the post" and the others had got "the jitters" I will never know.

The incident seemed to go on for a long time but probably was only a couple of minutes, however the upshot of it all was an aerial torpedo which landed in the Rushy Meadow near to Mercote Hall, a good mile away as an aerial torpedo flies. (Apparently they had a propeller built into the fin at the end of the bomb.) One pane of glass was cracked in my bedroom window before this incident and half of it fell to the brick yard below. It was years before the window was repaired, typical of Berkswell Estate, but there was a war on.

We all remained friends with the Mallards till they died and the Bollands for many years. Lewis was called up eventually. Dorothy was a tracer for Armstrong Whitworth.

Christmas 1940 was the next important thing, in my life anyhow. Oh, by the way the Mallards and Bollands properties did not suffer any damage to speak of during the bombing. The Mallards were invited to stay with us over Christmas and they accepted with glee, also the Bollands still came every evening.

At that time there were only two days holiday, Christmas Day and Boxing Day, also there were no office parties or much of the commercial "trappings" that go on now. Dad worked, as everyone else did, till five o'clock in the evening as normal and no decorations were put up till after Stella and I went to bed.

Progress was being made in the locality, however. Berkswell village had had the joys of electricity for some time. Now it was the turn of the Four Oaks area. It was being laid on mainly for the benefit of farmers and any small industries that would benefit. My folks declined the idea at first, but again I think mother was the influence that persuaded father to relent. They, my folks, must have been a bit better off what with the extra money my father earned as an observer, also the few shillings our evacuees – as we called them in general terms – paid for their stay.

The cost was one pound per light and we had one in each of the living rooms down stairs and one in each of the bedrooms, i.e. five fittings cost five pounds, paid in cash. My mother always thought our job was a "foreigner" but the electricity board passed the work as OK and it was switched on at four o'clock in the afternoon on Christmas Eve. We thought it was miraculous and it was for us after using paraffin lamps up until then. The old lamp in the front room had a tiny leak in the paraffin tank which was brass, or that colour anyhow, in fact it was porous and probably every third day a bead of paraffin would collect on one of the "feet" of the tank. The lamp was above the table as it hung rather low. Auntie Connie was quite house proud and would "fly off " for a duster if she thought a drop of paraffin would be likely to drip off. It did pong a bit anyhow, but probably the Webbs did not notice things like that.

So, Christmas Eve was a bit special and the "vaccies" turned up as usual. An evening or two before Christmas, ma and pa were out of the room and we were all talking about the forthcoming festivities and Father Christmas in particular, when one of the Bollands said something about not believing in that Father Christmas rubbish, when up piped Auntie Connie saying "Shush", they still believe in Father Christmas and so on. Well I was eleven and Stella nine, and we had been informed of the true facts by our school friends, also our grandmother, two or three years previous.

We both pretended to be deaf and did not hear the previous conversation. One must keep a good thing going, we thought. It is almost certain that our folks knew that we knew and that they rather enjoyed it all as well, parents do, do they not?

We hung one of father's socks at the bottom of the bed. None of this pillow-case lark. We had an orange in the toe, perhaps a colouring book and crayons, a new penny, an apple and one or two other little novelties. We also had one nice gift from our folks, maybe a jigsaw puzzle, a book, and one year I remember a model timber carriage with two horses. I did treasure that for a long time. Where did it all go, I wonder?

Our Christmas tree, I found out some years after was four or five branches of berried holly tied together and hung on the wall in one corner, all decorated up it looked super, and that together with the paper streamers really made our front room look nice.

However, back to Christmas 1940, Stella and I decorated Auntie Connie and Uncle Bert's bedroom with paper chains, streamers and holly in the pictures, they could not get over it.

Rationing had not begun to bite too much by this time and most housewives had a few goodies in their store cupboards. Our guests arrived well loaded and my mother played her part, so much so that it was far and away the best Christmas we had ever had at Meriden Road. Having said that, my mother could always be relied upon to produce "the goods" at Christmas, we never went short at any other time, especially birthdays.

We always had a cockerel for Christmas, usually one of our own. Most people in the country and also the urban population kept a few fowl. We had two quite large fowl pens at the bottom of our large garden, each with it's own fowl shed. The number varies but probably the average was a couple of dozen hens of various ages, and a cockerel or two. As I said before, mother sold a few eggs to regular customers and in the summer when the new pullets came into lay, usually at about six months old, all the surplus eggs would be "put down". A compound called Waterglass was mixed with water and stood in a two gallon bucket and the eggs were put into the solution. They were then used mainly during the following winter and in our household mainly for cooking purposes, i.e. cakes, etc. We usually had enough fresh eggs for the frying pan.

During the war we gave up our ration of eggs in exchange for an allowance of meal which mixed with boiled up scraps from the kitchen made a nice warm mash which the fowl enjoyed.

Mother usually bought day old sexed chicks from Pickerings in Frog Lane, Balsall Common. I used to go along with her one evening on our bikes. They were specialists in the Rhode Island Red breed. Good layers and when they were past producing eggs, one was left with a good size bird for the table. Known as old boilers, because they were boiled in the pot and could be finished off in the oven to brown them up a bit. The day old chicks were quite expensive to buy, but our folks thought it was worth while as we did know what had been purchased. The alternative was to put say a dozen eggs under a broody hen, wait three weeks for them to hatch, feed them for quite a while and probably discover the majority were young cockerels.

We got these precious little bundles of yellow fluff and kept them in a large cardboard box in front of the fire in the hearth in the kitchen for a day or two, making sure the box was cat proof as we always had at least two cats. They were fed for a while on hard boiled egg, chopped up and very fine breadcrumbs mixed up. Mother was most successful rearing these chicks, losing the odd one in a season.

Very little was bought in tins then, or glass jars for that matter. We never had coffee, wine or spirits, baked beans or tinned fruit. Most of our needs were home produced, potatoes, vegetables, etc. from the garden. We had a superb Bramley apple tree which grew in the fowl run, and naturally did well every year without fail. It was a red Bramley and was a lovely sight just before the apples were picked in October. They kept very well in the wash house and we always had apples till the following May. The tree still survives today. Mother did quite a lot of bottling as fruit came into season, all delivered to the door by the green grocer, no pick your own then, also jam making, getting the sugar during the war was a problem though. Sometimes there were extra rations, probably in exchange for ration book "points" used for groceries.

It must have been about this time that the Wheatleys decided to keep pigs in the Slang, the long narrow field at the back of our house. Chain link fencing was put up all round the field and it was divided off into areas of about an acre in each area. There was a substantial hut, which I think was intended for farrowing purposes.

In the next field was built four more sheds and runs, they were for the boars. The Wheatleys specialised in the Tamworth breed of pigs, they are a sandy colour and the boars were big with huge tusks. They were quite friendly until provoked. The runs were made of corrugated iron sheets and some kids were known to run along the side with a stick touching the tin. They tell me it made a sound like a small machine gun going off – no they did not go a lot on that – so I'm told. The Wheatley family still rear "Tamworths" in Wiltshire. Superb bacon breed.

When the Bollands came in the day time as they sometimes did, Stella and I would take Bill the big alsation and our Bonzo for a walk over the fields. It was a problem having to climb over the wire fence which we did if no pigs were in residence. The alternative was to go up the jitty or "bunny run" alongside the Squire's garden to the access for farm vehicles, etc., which enabled the farm workers and their machinery to gain access to fields beyond the pigs in the Slang.

One day for a bit of a lark, we shut old Bill in one of these huts, no problem to Bill, he jumped out through the glass window, which was quite small, and closed at the time. Father found out of course and was not amused, saying things like "you kids will get me the sack" and so on. One's job was pretty safe at Berkswell Estate and farm but my father was always conscious of the fact that we lived in a tied cottage, and no job – no home.

Sometime prior to this Ronnie Squires came to live next door with his grandparents, he was a bit of a ruffian when he arrived and that is why Nan Squires took him under her wing, he was not being brought up very well in his foster home. In a way Stella and I took him on under our wing, he was five or six years younger but well able to look after himself – well more or less. Nan Nan named by her other grandson Reg, son of Edith and Bill Squires who could not say "Granny" or "Grandma". Soon got Ron to use the lav outside down the back, all was well till he was ready to leave when he would bawl our "Gramma – I've finished", he did get a bit impatient. When he got older, Nan Nan would probably pop out to take her husband Jim some tea when he was lambing. One day Ron decided to go out before she had returned, put the key in the usual place and a big notice on the back door which read "key in lav". Bill Edith and young Reg would walk from Four Oaks to see his folks most evenings and at weekends. One evening father had been to the pump for water and came back and told me that Edith had gone into the lav, which backed on to the bunny run and – "why didn't I get a brick and rub it over the wall", apparently it creates quite a horrible noise to those inside. It appeared that Edith took a little while to recover. My father was good at putting us up to a few harmless tricks.

Another evening for some reason I had gone down to play in the village, there was quite a gang of lads there at the time. Great excitement on my return to discover Ron and others had been playing with matches just across the field by the boar pens and accidentally set fire to the huge rick of unthreshed corn. Poor old granddad Squires (the farm shepherd) was beside himself, quite thought he would get his "marching orders". Anyhow all was well, but I never heard what was said by those in charge. If in fact anything was said at all.

The Home Farm or Chapel Hill as my father knew it was not very well run at that particular time, I do not know all the details so least said the better.

At times there were quite a few youngsters in our locality. Ron, I have mentioned. Georgie or "Judd" Wilkinson, who also lived with his grandparents just up the road. There was Bob Thompson from Four Oaks – poor old Bob, he was that one that always ripped his trousers, fell in the pit, cut himself on old bottles and fell through thin ice on frozen ponds. His mother was always nice, never blamed any of us for Bob's misfortunes.

We played anywhere more or less, over the fields, at the back of our house. Father kept two eyes on us most of the time. Our favourite playground was in a huge pit hole just up the slang. Most of the time it was dry in the bottom – but in the winter it would fill up with water and was quite dangerous, fortunately we did not play outside in the winter months anyhow. This pit was the tip for all the waste for The Hall and other places besides, no refuse collection then. Lots of householders would bury their refuse in the gardens. There were all sorts of goodies that appeared from time to time, old prams which we soon had the wheels off for a trolley or truck. Smashing bottles was great fun, lining then up on an old tank and letting fly with anything we could lay our hands on, this was fine until one day we played a new game by throwing a bottle up in the air and aiming another at it on the way down, highly dangerous but we did not see any danger till Ken Ford threw up a bottle and aimed another at it. What he did not know was that the second bottle was cracked and as he picked it up the bottle fell in half onto his hand and forearm. There was blood all over the place and we all ran for home. Fortunately mother was in and she patched him up after a good wash first. Just before the war my mother had completed a course on first aid and another on home nursing so was able to render first aid. Fortunately there was no serious damage done and that particular sport was abandoned.

We made huts in the pit, "secret" paths in the bushes and so on, many happy hours spent there.

If we were not at Sunday School, we would often go with Shep Squires round the sheep, they had to be counted and fed, and naturally there was a lot more work at lambing time in the spring. Quite often there would be a few lambs in the Squire's kitchen laying on old clothing in front of the fire, they were bottle fed until they could fend for themselves. The shepherd kept one one year when we were quite small, there was a biggish yard next door and the lamb was kept there. Nibby grew up to be a big tup and I think he began to get aggressive, so he had to go. Father had to "run the gauntlet" going to the water pump in the yard.

When there were crops in the fields we played in the road outside the house, if there was enough, it was rounders or French cricket, games went in seasons or fashions then – probably still do, I know not. The girls would skip and would join in. There was no-one around as in the school playground to call us lads "cissy". Whip and Top, marbles and lots of simple games would keep us occupied for hours or until we fell out, then the one with the ball would clear off and that was that. There was very little traffic on the road, and what there was went at a more sedate pace. Now it is quite dangerous just to cross the road at that spot, vehicles whiz along as if there is no tomorrow.

Another pastime was catapults and bows and arrows. "Cattys" were made from a forked stick cut from the tall hedge opposite our house, also the bow was made from a length of hazel wood with strong string attached to both ends of the wood and bending into the shape of a long bow. Arrows we made from anything that was long and straight. The dead stalks of golden rod were very good, especially if they had a small metal nut at the sharp end. I could stand under the electricity wires and hit them quite easily. That was something I could do on my own after someone had pushed off with the ball. Great fun.

The elastic for my "catty" came from an inner tube, cut about half an inch wide and each end lashed on to the forked stitch. Some of the lads had "cattys" with quarter inch square elastic, if we owned one of them we had "arrived". I was not supposed to have a catapult and thought that dad was a spoilsport, till one day George Wilkinson and I had a battle, all for fun, no animosity. We were next door in the Squire's back yard, he was in the dog kennel and me in the coal house – with pockets full of pebbles. And then we were pot shooting at one another, eventually we both hit one another – and it did not half hurt – and decided to call it a day.

I did a swop with George one day and acquired a water pistol, but there was not much to squirt it at – till dad came home. I let him have it just once before he went indoors and took it all in good part – more or less anyhow. However, I could not work out why I never saw my water pistol after that day.

Young George was a bit of a pest as a kid, well my dad thought and said so many times. He would try and cadge anything from anybody. "Mr Webb can I have this, that or the other", an old bike wheel, bits of wood – anything. But most of the time, he and I got on very well.

One year he had a pet magpie called Jack. Magpies at the time were not all that common, as the keepers on the estate would keep their numbers down by shooting them because they raided the young game birds – pheasants and partridges. Anyhow, this magpie – Jack – who was allowed his, or was it a she, freedom. It visited a lot of the local gardens and was very fond of pinching and flying off with anything that took it's fancy, often coloured and shiny objects. But worst of all it would pull the pegs off the washing hanging on the clothes line; it was no joke having to swill it out and re dry washing owing to the antics of George's "thieving magpie".

It is a bit of a gruesome tale but dad was digging away in the garden and Jack appeared, "come on Jack", said dad, and sure enough he hopped up quite close – too close in fact because dad hit him with his spade and that was the end of poor old Jack. Mrs Wilkinson (George's granny) was not at all pleased. But it made little difference to young George as he was soon round and on the scrounge again.

All sorts of other things were tried, fires in our huts in the old pit-hole, trouble was the smoke gave us away. Smoking cigarettes was tried, even an old pipe George found. We tried dried beech leaves in that but could not understand "the pleasures of smoking".

Going out for entertainment was the next worry for my parents, I suppose. After I started school at Balsall School, I discovered a lot of young folk were going to "the pictures".

Stella and my first visit to the cinema was to "The Palace" – as it was then known – at Balsall. It stood were Cameo Court now stands. Mother took us to see Shirley Temple. We also went to "The Rex" in Coventry, a brand new posh cinema in Corporation Street in Coventry. That was to see the film of the coronation of King George VI and Queen Elizabeth in 1937. My word, that was the cat's whiskers, quite the poshest place I had been to. Sadly the Rex did not last, at the time of the blitz it was showing "Gone with the wind", and it did, "Gerry" either blew it to bits or it burnt out with incendiary bombs.

I was probably twelve when I was allowed out once a week, mother had to know where I was going and with whom. Also, I paid. That was no problem as I was earning some pocket money by then. I also had to pay for any repairs to my school bike, which unlike the one I bought previously, got rather knocked about and seldom cleaned – after the first week or two of ownership.

Usually it was Balsall cinema, by now "The Cameo". The films were usually getting on a bit by the time they were shown at Balsall, but we had not seen them so it mattered little. We went on our bikes and paid two pence (less than one new pence) to park them in a covered and enclosed lean to shed at the side of the cinema. No one came in a car that I can recall, no petrol for one thing. There was no ice cream or sweets at the interval but we could buy a bag of chips from Reg French's chip shop, which was where the dry cleaners now stands. It really was little more than the front room of a semi-detached house. The French's sold wet fish, some greengroceries and groceries in the day time, fish and chips in the evening. As rationing tightened it's grip, so the chip shop was forced to cease trading later on.

There used to be R.A.F. personnel from Honiley and American GI's probably from Packington. They always had some sort of transport. We tried to cadge chewing gum from them, I was only successful once. He came from Chattanooga, of Choo Choo fame. A while before I got to hear of Glenn Miller and his famous orchestra – my all time favourite music.

We did like our old picture house, I was there one night during an air raid. The audience were informed if the air raid warning was sounded, but seldom anyone took any notice. However this particular evening bombs were dropped at nearby High Cross – which no-one heard, must have been a western on that night. We did hear the lumps of shrapnel falling on the roof but I for one did not know what it was until later on. All was quiet as we made our way home.

Another night we were riding home on our bikes in quite a posse and Ken Ford had no rear light (compulsory now). So we put him in the middle of the group because we had to pass the police house which was opposite where Rose Court now stands on the Kenilworth Road. Sure enough, PC Thornborough was standing on the side of the road outside the "cop shop" but he could not see the offender until we had passed. He then enquired – as we rode on – "where's your light", to which Ken rather naughtily replied "up my a——e". As quick as a flash – get it? – back came the reply, "well sit on your mudguard". This naturally caused great merriment all the way to Berkswell. But, on the next outing to the pictures Ken had his rear light back on because Ken knew that "Thorny" knew who was riding without a rear light in the first place.

On another occasion some time later, I was not so lucky. Again, coming out of the cinema, by now the "Cameo". It was raining "cats and dogs". John Kirby and I retrieved our bikes and half ran and half rode round the traffic island – the wrong way, and a fed up and soggy copper was waiting for us by what is now the restaurant on the Kenilworth road. It was the Co-Op shop then. Out he stepped and stopped us and without any more ado we were "booked". We had no option but to tell our folks, John's mother went into hysterics, "you will have a police record" and so on. We did not attend court, sent a letter of apology instead and in due course received a fine of five shillings each (25p), which rightly and properly came out of our pockets.

I must introduce John Kirby. The family, John's father, Stan, mother Beatrice (Beatty) and younger sister Enid were bombed out of their home in Coventry. They came to live first of all in one of the alms houses in the village, one room upstairs plus a small "boxroom" and one living room downstairs. They later moved to Banbury Cottage round the corner opposite the school. Mr and Mrs Kirby becoming school caretakers.

John continued his education in Coventry at John Gulson school I think, cycling all or part of the way. I did not know him very well until one night I was at the "Pictures". The "little picture" supporting programme had started when John came in and sat in the vacant seat next to me. Some time later he began to be uncomfortable and said he had a pain in his stomach which got much worse. The end result being him being sent to hospital with what turned out to be appendicitis. How he was taken, I do not remember but I took his bike home, riding mine and guiding his with my left hand. From then on we became firm friends which lasted until he died. He was just one day older than me, but tragically died aged about fifty three. More about JSK later.

Time moves on and leaving school looms up. But before that my "schooling" did take a turn for the better about twelve months before I left. By this time most of the evacuees from Coventry had either gone back home or left school altogether and so Mrs Farndon's class of boys was absorbed into the main school.

There were only six classes in the whole school. There were two, Miss Tidsalls and Miss Berry, teaching infants and juniors Miss Butler (Eyeky – Ivy Kathleen) with eleven years olds. Mr Bob MacLaren (Mac) teaching twelve years and Miss Effie Wake taking the top class.

I was put in the lower stream for a start. Miss Wake was one of the "old school". Tall and thin as two lath boards nailed together. Boney hands and her hair done up in a bun at the back. She was sharp featured as well. No-one fooled Miss Wake. She never missed a trick, or anything else anyone got up to in class. Generally acknowledged as being the best teacher, certainly the best that I came across. She demanded one's best work always attention in class and respect. One never spoke to Miss Wake with hands in pockets. She was known to reprimand pupils and even past pupils on meeting in the shopping area of Balsall. Even now people speak and remember Miss Wake with the greatest of respect, me included. She would thump her boney fist on her desk and say " Wake's my name and Wake's my nature". And so it was.

By today's standards there was next to no facilities at the school, basically the three R's and more three R's. It probably did us no harm.

The woodwork and metal work master was called up for the forces just as I arrived at Balsall School. The senior school all crammed into what was known as "the art room" for assembly and there was also some religious instruction also prayers and hymns. We then trooped off to our various classrooms for arithmatic until playtime. Afterwards we always had some form of English perhaps a composition, spelling or dictation. History, Geography and Nature Study was in the afternoon, with games on a Friday. And again owing to wartime restrictions, games equipment was a poor old lot, no sports wear and few football boots were evident. However we all got through.

Discipline was quite strict, we knew where we stood with Mr Seeley, and although the classes were large – Miss Wake had about forty. There were three streams certainly for maths. No one left school unable to read and write up to a good standard. "Did you ever have the cane?" they cry, yes once only. I was only caught once you see, and then it was only partly deserved – in my estimation.

I think I have said before I was often on the last minute, and delivering newspapers around Four Oaks took up time, especially if there was a comic or interesting news to read. This particular day, Georgie Wilkinson and I were just a couple of minutes late and dumped our bikes at the end of our classroom and ran round and joined on the tail end of our class going into the classroom. Unfortunately for us "Pop" Seeley spotted us and gave us a sort of beckoning sign with his fore finger. Results – up the stairs and a few of the best, he thought we were being devious. Probably were, a bit.

Mr W.F.E. Seeley was the headmaster known to his friends as Frank, and to his pupils as Pop, behind his back of course. Pop Seeley was immaculate in all he did, his dress was smart, the creases in his trousers were ultra sharp, his shoes always shone and his moustache always seemed to bristle. He demanded punctuality, which was sometimes a problem to me, I was always "on the last minute". He did not take a class on a regular basis, but supervised the gardening, there were garden plots all neatly laid out, but I was never fortunate enough to have one. I was a bit slow in coming forward in those days and to be honest always thought I was not quite as good as the others.

Again at Balsall sport was just about non existent, basically no one to supervise. Cricket and football was played in season on Friday afternoon, but I hadn't a clue anyhow, and no one to teach or coach.

Mr Seely was a man of many interests, gardening was one of his favourites, he used to write the gardening column in the old Coventry Standard newspaper which came out on Fridays. Philately was another passion, I understood he had a huge collection of stamps. The late King George VI was a great philatelist and apparently Pop went to London occasionally to view the collection. I do not know if he ever met the king. However he did organise and run a stamp club at school. The only after school activity I knew of.

I did join it and it was most interesting, we all gathered around his big desk in his study and most likely he would talk for a few minutes on one particular country then he would produce stamps for us to buy, all neatly fixed into small booklets. I think perhaps it was a little earner for him. My stamps are still in the wardrobe. I wonder if they are worth any more after those fifty years or so.

He took a keen interest in the weather and had a "mini" weather station at the school, recording maximum and minimum temperatures and rainfall. Pop was a founder member of the Balsall Horticultural Society, a member of the Cricket Club, also The Berkswell Association for the Prosecution of Felons. He took a great interest in fungi (what is the name for that?). Travelling around the place on his big "sit up and beg" bicycle. It was a sad day many years later when Mr Seeley was killed by a lorry wheel that came off a lorry being driven in Station Road not far from where he lived.

On our way to school we nearly always met Captain (and Alderman) Gee. He was the postmaster and owned the post office and quite a lot of property in the area. He was a tall upright man, always wore a trilby hat and often a long mackintosh coat, every inch an ex army man. We used to greet him "Good morning Mr Gee". He would wave his rolled umbrella and shout back "Captain Gee". This went on most mornings and he did get a bit irate by Friday.

Balsall was very different then from now, about fifteen shops in Station Road area. The National Provincial Bank (now Nat West) stood on the corner. Chatterways was there, they also had two vans on the road covering the area and selling hardware and paraffin, etc. Next came the barbers shop kept by Frank Enstone. He never missed anything that passed by, there was a small crack in the blind just enough for him to see through. He was a real character and knew all that was going on. He also sold cigarettes and tobacco and catered for the "gentlemen" of the village regarding other requirements that may be needed. The third shop was kept by Mrs Knight and she sold groceries, and where the Midland Bank is now, Mrs Turney sold mainly groceries from what was really the front room of the house.

On towards the station was Mr and Mrs Taylors. Ye Olde Berkswell Stores with the butchers next door. Both properties are now apartments and a private residence.

Opposite where the Royal British Legion club is now, Mr Spencer ran a newsagent business. Again a tiny shop up on top of a flight of steps to the front room of the house. It was "his papers" that I delivered round Four Oaks, his petrol allowance only got him to Berkswell. Opposite Green Lane was Elsons. Bakers and grocers, they had horse drawn bread vans, the driver wearing breeches, boots and leggings – a real smart outfit.

The next shop was the shoe shop kept by the Salmons. The shop was on the island side of the entry to the car park. Then it was the entry to the bedstead factory owned by Owen Thornell. A good percentage of the Balsall school leavers started work there. All the machinery was driven by a steam engine, which chuffed away all day long and could be heard over quite a wide area.

Mr Salmons was the snob and did quite a good repair job on boots and shoes, the only problem being the place always seemed to be upside down and they had a job to find our shoes on calling for them after repair. They always found them – eventually.

On one again came the post office run by Mr David Gee, the old chap we sometimes upset on our way to school. Next to the post office was a dark and dingy looking shop kept by the two Miss Warners, again selling grocery. Across the entry was Hull the butcher and then another newsagent, stationer, sweets and tobacco. All sold during the war when the items were available. Sweets eventually were rationed, I think two ounces per person, per week. Joe and Gladys Smith were the newsagents who were not good business people. I would imagine they were "twisted" out of many pounds worth of newspapers. They did not have any system like today – it was mostly "in the head".

The last shop was French's fish shop, also some grocery and green grocery. They also sold fish and chips until fat became unobtainable. This shop again was converted from the front room of a semi-detached house. The adjoining semi was a private residence until Mr C. Brown opened up a cycle shop some years after. Our own "Charlie Brown".

On the corner stood "The Palace", "Cameo", "Flea Pit", call it what you will, but over the years the local people were able to enjoy an evening out there. Fair enough, it sometimes broke down, which sometimes added to the fun depending on who one was sitting next to. It all went dark when we had a break down and there was more than one embarrassing moment when the film started up again. There were three programmes every week. i.e. Mondays, Tuesdays and Wednesdays and then changing for Thursday, Friday and Saturday. Sunday was another programme, one house at six thirty in the evening.

Across the road was Regent House, the same type of merchandise as today, haberdashery, etc. On the corner was R.G. Hollick the chemist. He was a bit strange, one would walk into the shop which had big black cabinets all round and there were three big coloured glass containers in the window. Mr Hollick would just seem to appear from round the cabinets. Peeping round, I'm sure he didn't care if he served one or not. Mrs Hollick was a small lady always dressed in black, it was sometimes quite a job to see her. They also sold seeds for the garden. In those days on the rare occasion that medicine was required, it was made up by the doctor himself and collected from the surgery.

Mr Hollick had a car, an oldish Austin 7 I understand. He had trouble starting his car but rather than getting it repaired, he built a platform with a ramp, and on returning home, drove his car onto the platform. All he had to do when he wanted the car again was to jump in, roll it down the ramp into gear and away.

He was the scout master, so I'm told and had the scouts performing all sorts of things, like stretching a rope across the road and so on.

We cross the road again to end up opposite the Nat West bank and Mrs Jeffs had a dress shop in the corner and the other shop was a confectioners. The Co-op store was where the Italian restaurant is now. And that was it. Kimberleys had a garage business were the Shell station is now. There were three coal merchants in the immediate area. Dennis Gibbs operated from Hurst Villa on the Kenilworth Road (opposite Elmwood Close). Reg Sage came from Truggist Lane and Tom West lived near to Skew bridge on the Kenilworth Road. My father's brother Ernest later bought that business and together with his wife Nance, worked very hard and I hope and like to think they prospered.

I am not sure when it was, but the Mallards were at our house and Auntie Connie said something about my mother putting on weight, to which she replied that there was a good reason for it. I think that was when the Mallards also Stella and I were told we were going to have a new brother or sister. Such things were seldom spoke about then, certainly not when we youngsters were about. I think my mother had a bit of a rough pregnancy and it must have been decided by the doctor at the last minute that mother would go to Loveday Street in Birmingham for the birth. I was to go on my bike to stay with Aunt Ruth and Uncle Bob at Barford. David and Kathleen were a few years younger and cousin Robin had arrived in the previous autumn, 1942.

I arrived home for dinner in February 5th 1943 to scenes of some anxiety. Mother was in labour and ready to go into hospital but the driver of the village ambulance would not leave work to drive it. Berkswell had it's own ambulance during the war with this man, Mr T who lived in the village designated as official driver. When he would not turn out to drive to Birmingham because he would lose time at work, my father was livid and never forgave Mr T. Father would have paid whatever he asked, so really there was no problem. However, Bert Wagstaff who was the chauffeur at Berkswell Hall undertook the job. Naturally there was some considerable delay and I think my little sister Margaret was born just outside the hospital.

When mother had departed in the ambulance, all I thought of was getting to Barford. My satchel was packed and off I went on my bike, something I had done a few times before. Stella must have stayed at home being looked after by Nan Nan Squires.

I had the time of my life at Barford. The Hammonds lived in Mill Lane in one of twelve council houses. There were lots of youngsters there and we were soon into allsorts of mischief, fairly harmless stuff really. I was there at least three weeks and went to school there. Cannot recall much of that but I did spend some time bundling up and tying parcels of waste paper for the war effort. It was all good stuff really and I was quite sad to return back to Balsall school and get my head down for the last weeks before leaving for good.

One day some of us Webbs and Hammonds met up and father and Uncle Bob were talking about becoming fathers again after quite a gap in both families. We youngsters were kept in the dark – I heard Uncle Bob say "I blame the bombing Albert". They both had a good laugh but it was a long time before the "penny dropped" and I got the message.

On returning home I was quite disappointed as Robin was sitting up and taking notice but now sister Margaret was very much a baby, however she did very soon begin to take notice of things around her and although I was fourteen, she kept me amused for many an hour after tea in the evenings.

Time marches on and at the age of fourteen years and one month, I leave Balsall Street Central School for the last time just before Easter in 1943. Although I had known since the age of five that I wanted to be a gardener, little or no attempt had been made to get a job.

In 1943 it was possible to decide on a profession and go out and get a job more or less whatever one wanted. I certainly did not want farm work, not that I was afraid of work, but it was more or less a seven day week occupation. Even if one was not stockman one had to fill in on some weekends when the cowman or shepherd had his weekend off. I vowed never to learn how to milk a cow, a promise to myself I kept!

CHAPTER **6**

Starting Work "With a War On"

I have no idea how it came about but I found out that they were looking for a lad at "Stratheden Nurseries on the Kenilworth Road at Bradnocks Marsh. It is now "Manor Nurseries".

Can one imagine it? My mother came with me, on our bikes of course. We met Mrs. Morris who was the boss, a very nice motherly lady. We walked round the nursery where there was a lot of glass, 500 running feet of greenhouses in fact. It was April and Spring was in full swing, and really I could not wait to start. Yes, I was taken on, replacing a lad that had been called up for the R.A.F.

My pay was £1.00 per week for a forty-four hour week. They were very cushy hours as all other jobs started at 8 o'clock or before. After two weeks, when my card came through, Mrs. Morris was not very pleased to learn that the minimum wage was £1.2.0. per week (£1.10p), so I very soon had my first rise.

I did not make a good start because, after a day and a half, I went down with a chill and had to have the rest of that week off. It was embarrassing as I had never been poorly before, well hardly anyhow. I think I had a chill probably from running in and out of greenhouses, which I was not used to. I was tall and very thin at the time, probably because I was never still, always on the go, whatever I was doing.

It was embarrassing again when I went back on the following Monday morning. At tea break Mrs. Morris said that she thought perhaps I was not a very strong young man, to which I replied "I used to be". The others fell about laughing. My pride was severely dented and I was determined to prove that I was capable of anything they could throw at me.

Mrs. Morris, as I said, was the boss, her husband was the general facto-tum. Son Gordon was about twenty-one and never got called up. Mrs.

Ayers also worked there, spending some of the time in the house and the rest on the nursery.

On the whole we were a happy little band. Mrs. Morris was very kind and thoughtful. The "old man" was a bit "crusty" – resented not being in charge, I think. He had his own routine, more or less, and seemed to prefer to work on his own on whatever job he undertook. That was after he had fed the fowl and taken in the sticks and coal and all sorts of other odd jobs that usually took him till tea break at 10.30. We all trooped into the living room for our cuppa. There was a fender round the fire with two wood boxes, one at either end, and I sat on one of those. They all sat at the table and tucked into bread and jam and cake.

Gordon was a bit of a dreamer – and I do not mean to be disrespectful. They had a tiny 6 cwt Morris van and Gordon was the driver, taking the produce and plants, etc. to the shops they supplied; also to the wholesale market at Stratford Upon Avon. Although Gordon was over twenty years old, he could not, or would not go on his own, so mother went as well. It was a bit of a change for her anyhow, she did work hard. The only other machinery was a stationary Lister engine with a pump attached. This was used to pump water from a well to the greenhouses via a hose pipe for watering purposes.

There was also a small Rotatilla, a super little rotavator for tilling the ground prior to planting. It was a great help.

I think I soon made amends for my chill, or whatever it was, absolutely in my element doing whatever jobs came along. As there was a War going on they had to grow eighty per cent vegetables or foodstuff in general – 20% flowers.

All sorts of veg was produced in season. One year a big area of onions was grown to be dispatched to the R.A.F. and Bomber Command in particular.

We grew vegetables, plants, loads of them, and there was a big demand for them, especially as there was a "Dig for Victory" campaign. Every one was encouraged to do their bit. Lawns were dug up and garden wilderness tamed for the War effort.

We grew tomato plants for Warwickshire Women's Institutes. Each branch sent their orders to the H.Q. We had the total number and they all turned up at the end of May with boxes to take them home in. The plants were mostly grown in whalehide pots, which were made out of thinnish card coated with a tar-like substance (non caustic). They were waterproof and just held together till the plants were big enough to plant out, pot and all. A lot of the greenhouses were planted up with tomatoes and people would come from miles around when word got around that they were available. People went away quite cheerful with half a pound per customer, until they were more plentiful.

The Morris's had a married daughter and they were farming; also a son,

Hugh, who was in the army and somewhere out East. For a long time they did not know where he was, dead or alive, then one day a very formal and brief telegram arrived to say he was alive and well, but a prisoner of War in the hands of the Japanese. Before his time in the army he was very fond of the latest swing music of the likes of Joe Loss and Glenn Miller, and I was instructed by Gordon never to whistle, or even hum, "In the Mood". He loved dance music and ballroom dancing.

Work was always full of interest for me, new and different jobs as one season rolled into another. No plastic to be had or seen anywhere, paper bags, plants wrapped up in newspaper – bring your own if possible. All seed trays were wooden. We "knocked them up" with wood all sawn to size. This was a job for the winter. All flower pots were clay. 3" pots were 60s, 5" were 48s and so on. All made from a "cast" of clay, i.e. one cast would make 60 3", or 48 5" and so on.

Peat was just becoming available, to us anyhow. Sorbex peat was the brand we had. Most nurserymen had their own "pet" recipes for compost, all secret and closely guarded. A bit of this and some of that. Old mortar rubble was much sought after, which really was only lime after all.

It was probably the War that helped to get rid of their old-fashioned ideas and lots of others too. Nevertheless, I take my hat off to those old gardeners who tried, and succeeded, to grow all sorts of plants, most of them foreign to us on these islands, but a lot of them working on large estates had time, and plenty of money could be spent on heating green-houses and conservatories before the war.

Agricultural and Horticultural growers had a lot of help and advice given free during the War, known as the "War agg". Never did know their proper handle. Sometimes this advice and help was scorned upon, especially when – "some little whipper snapper tries to tell us how to go on" – was a phrase often heard.

However, we at Stratheden Nurseries pressed on, mostly successful, but, as with all things that are grown, there are bound to be failures and disappointment. I still get some of each today, with all the modern com-posts and devices, etc. etc.

At Christmas time I was introduced to making holly wreaths. "We" were allowed to do this as it was a time of the year when little could be done in the way of food production.

The first year the wire frames and stub wire were still available, but thereafter we made the "frames" from willow sticks bent into a circle. The grass/moss mixture was bound on with string. The stub wire for wiring the holly had to be cut into lengths off a reel. The job is – and was – always time consuming and labour intensive and this made it more so. However, when needs must as they say, we all got stuck in and made the best of it.

A lot of our raw materials came from "Weavings Wood" as it was known to me; it was at Honiley. Turning for Honiley Church by the Honiley Boot

Hotel, a small country pub then, the wood was on the right. There was moss in there and quite a lot of suitable holly. The best holly for wreath making is the non prickly variety, not only easier to work with, but it also stayed green and fresh much longer than the prickly forms. There were no artificial berries then, so the berried holly was cut quite early, before the pigeons had them. They can and will strip a tree of all its berries in a single day at the onset of frost and hard weather in November.

It was work I really did enjoy. We cleared out a small greenhouse, one which was economical to keep warm and was safe from the elements for a few weeks.

Mrs. Morris was quite a good florist. Flower arranging as we know it now was still a long way off. Also, floral tributes were either a wreath, cross or a spray. A bride's bouquet was a large arrangement, usually of carnations with asparagus fern (Sprengeri or plomosa) hanging almost to the ground and filling in between the flowers. Mrs. Morris catered for all those requirements. She would go to market in Birmingham for the flowers. Gordon would take her to Hampton Station or the Corps bus at Sheldon. She would say "I'm going on the corps bus". I had no idea what she was on about. It was the Corporation Bus.

It was probably my second wreath making-year on the nursery when Mrs. Morris was that busy with floral work and going to market, etc. that the assembly or actual making up of holly wreaths was behind schedule somewhat. She was very worried as an order had to go to a shop next day. I had seen her make many a one so whilst she was out, I decided to have a go myself and was quite pleased with my efforts. I had a few completed when she came back. My work was given the approving nod and she was very pleased. The order went out on time and we shared that job thereafter. That experience stood me in good stead for many years later on.

It was the year after I started – 1944 – that Mrs. Morris was "at the end of her tether" – worn out, tired, and worried to death about son, Hugh, who was never mentioned except by Gordon, known to some as "Dugger". Apparently, as a kid he was mad on cars. He pretended to be a car and went along muttering "dugger, dugger, dugger", imitating an engine.

However, the Morris's decided to go away for a week's holiday. How it was arranged I don't know, but I think they went to Bournemouth. It was difficult to holiday during the War. Travelling was frowned on, with posters about saying "Is your journey really necessary?". One would need to take ration books and so on.

At the tender age of fifteen I was left to look after the place. I was in charge of myself, with instructions regarding the nursery, feeding the fowl, and not to serve anyone that came to buy. All went very well, but I could not resist taking money from calling customers. I was used to serving people when Mrs. Morris and Gordon were out and Mrs. Ayers not there. She only worked mornings. The "old man" never served at the door. He always kept a low profile. There was quite a nice sum in the till when they returned. I had started off with no float but managed O.K.

My Christmas present was an outing to Birmingham to see a pantomime. It would be a job to imagine nowadays a mother taking her twenty-one year old son and a young lad like me to anywhere in fact, but a pantomime, well I ask you. Anyhow, I presented myself in "best bib and tucker" at the nursery, then on to Hampton Station in the van, me sitting on a produce box in the back. We saw a matinee performance at either the Theatre Royal or The Alexandra Theatre. We came out and then went to Pattisons for high tea. This was a posh place in town, on a par with a Lyons Corner House; thick carpets on the floor and I think a trio or quartet playing away on a raised dais. I did feel a bit uncomfortable, but Mrs. Morris soon put me at ease. Never having been in such surroundings before, I did not quite know how to handle it, but that first time it was a bit daunting. Then it was back on the train and home, and I must say it was very nice and enjoyable. Four years we had the same outing. I was seventeen on the last trip – and in the army four months later.

It really was home from home there and I more or less did as I liked, knowing what needed doing and so on; I could start the Lister engine for watering, most of the time anyhow; it was "getting on a bit" and just a bit temperamental.

Eventually I was allowed to use the Rotatilla, which gave me great satisfaction to see a piece of ground all nicely cultivated. "The old man", although a bit grumpy at times, was a perfectionist in his work, hoeing, digging or in fact everything. I learned a great deal from him. When he was in a good mood, which was quite often really, he had a good sense of humour. I am thankful to say he had the job of emptying the lavatory bucket in the outside loo. He referred to it as "a bucket of grunts". Sorry about that, but it's true.

Not all that long after leaving school, having given up the Scouts some time before, I decided to join The Air Training Corps – 1459 Heart of England Squadron – (A.T.C. for short). No real thoughts about going into the R.A.F. or anything else at the tender age of fourteen and a half. A lot of the lads at school had joined and probably the air force blue uniform might just have had something to do with it. The "parades" took place at Balsall Street School, two evenings per week and Sunday mornings. We were taught "square bashing" – marching drill, forming ranks of three, etc. Class work included maths, aircraft recognition, allied and enemy aircraft, navigation, etc.

I must say I felt rather proud in my uniform; just about half the population seemed to be in some sort of uniform or other at the time.

We had a break for refreshments and as soon as one of the helpers, Mrs. Simpson, discovered I worked at the nurseries, was asking "Could I possibly get some tomatoes for the sandwiches?" Mrs. Morris obliged and it was a regular order when tomatoes were available.

August came and the prospect of the annual camp; there was only one week's annual holiday at the time. The week's camp was at R.A.F. Cosford, near Wolverhampton, all free and all found, except for spending money for the N.A.A.F.I. (Navy, Army and Air Force Institute). Usually, where there were serving personnel there would be the N.A.A.F.I.

Having joined the A.T.C. – 1459 Squadron – Heart of England – (there were numerous other Flights making up the squadron apart from ours known as Berkswell, there were Flights at Keresley, Coleshill, Shustoke, and Arley), I was persuaded to sign up for the camp, to which I agreed. We set off after dinner on the Saturday afternoon, I had to work in the morning. We had an old coach to take us to Cosford, which was an R.A.F. training establishment with aerodrome attached. We were given the rest of the day to settle in and had a free pass to the camp cinema in the evening, a way of keeping us out of mischief probably, although it had been laid on the line to us all about behaviour, discipline, and so on at some length, also what was expected of us. In plain English, we were not there for any sort of holiday.

Sunday morning was Church Parade followed by N.A.A.F.I. break and a lecture of some sort. Sunday afternoon the week's programme was mapped out.

There was the square bashing, of course. We had to march to our meals. We had all sorts of instruction, including the workings of an aero engine and other engineering technicalities, most of which went right over my head. At times like that I thought of Bill Squires who said "Always try to look intelligent and it might work". Well, they never set us any exams so there was no problem.

P.T. was on the agenda, also an assault course, with all sorts of nasty obstacles to negotiate; one thing that I did hate, even when I got into the army.

There was a route march one day, also arms drill with 303 rifles, which were a bit heavy for me. We also had a trip to the butts and all fired off ten rounds. Although there was a bit of a kick on firing, I quite enjoyed that. I did quite well, considering my eyesight was not so good.

The highlight of the week beyond any doubt was the flight we had, I think in an Avro Anson, which was great and lasted about half an hour. My parents had to give written consent to this which I do not think my mother was very keen on, but with all the other parents in agreement "poor old ma" had little choice really. It was 1943 and there were still air raids taking place but by now they were few and probably far between, certainly here in the midlands anyhow. Although "D" Day – the landings in France – were still nine months away, we were taken up by a young pilot officer who gave instructions as to what he was doing, etc. and naturally I answered with a "yes" or "no" and tried to look intelligent. He got rather irate with me and

I suddenly realised I should call him "Sir". After that, all was well. I had only recently joined, of course, but he didn't know that.

It must have been into the early hours before we got to sleep on the first night. After lights out, some of the guys started telling stories and jokes. It started off with ghost stories and went downhill from thereon.

However, I had a good week and I like to think it did me a lot of good. It taught me to stand on my own two feet a bit more and be more self assertive.

I went to camp three times in all. I could not go in 1944 but 1945 saw us at the Bomber Command Station at Swinderby in Lincolnshire. We were there in August at the end of the War and the whole place erupted. Union Jacks were all over the place and all our tuition came to an end for two days. There was a big dance on the Station but we youngsters never got a look in with the W.A.A.F.s (Women's Auxiliary Air Force). I think I had one dance. However, there was a bar, and some of the older lads got our beer in. I was sixteen and just getting used to the stuff. Some of us lads used to hang around The Bear at Berkswell from time to time, and had done so for some time.

The end of the War in Europe I remember well. The Bear Inn then was a real country pub, really only used by the locals. There were a lot of people there on V.E. NIGHT – May 8th 1945, me included. Father was with his cronies in the little tap room; we were in "the passage". "Poor old ma" was at home with sister Margaret, aged two and a half. Well, somebody had to stay home, and my mother never went into a pub in her life – as far as I am aware.

We had a good night and "time" was called, when a whole gang of us was invited to a party up Back Lane, so we bought some bottles of beer and set off, calling in home to let mother know where I was. This "do" went on till about three in the morning, and ended with an invite to another party the next evening. Most of us turned up but it never got off the ground as had the previous evening, but the food was good and plenty of it. How the ladies provided it I will never know.

The Observer Corps carried on until the end of the War in Europe, goodness knows why really, because "Old Jerry" was obliterated from our shores long since, apart from the odd reccy – although there were the V1 (doodlebugs) and V11 rockets launched against the South of England. My father was on duty when the War ended.

Berkswell Flight A.T.C. had its own drum and bugle band and, eventually they gave me a side drum to play with. Again, it was a good thing to be part of. I like to think I managed quite well, taking part eventually in Church Parades, and some years later, back at Cosford, we – the band – led the Church Parade for the whole camp. I could not get a note out of a bugle though, one cannot be good at everything.

I attended Sunday school until the age of fifteen, when after attending

1459 Squadron A.T.C. in camp at Swinderby, Lincs, 1945

Confirmation classes given by the Rev. (Mr.) Whitacre the class of boys and girls were confirmed at Meriden, St. Lawrence's. My mother was very concerned and keen to see Stella and I confirmed. By this time Mr. Whitacre was getting to be quite doddery and elderly. They had lost their only son, Peter, who was an officer on a merchant ship, which had been torpedoed in the Indian Ocean. The Whitacres never got over this tragedy, which at the time sent the whole village into mourning. I only just remember him, my grandmother said what a really nice chap he was.

It must have been in 1943 that the Wise family came to live at Four Oaks Farm, just up the road from our house. The Colleges had died or left the farm – I know not which – of about fifty acres. Mr. Harold Hewitt bought the place. He was a builder from Coventry with an invalid wife who sadly did not live long after coming to Berkswell. They had one son named Bob. It was generally thought that Mr. Hewitt knew very little really about farming, and he was referred to by some people as a "book farmer".

I was only a kid when he arrived, but over the years I liked the bloke and we got on very well.

The farm was probably too much for one to manage and Bob was only six or seven years old when the Wises arrived. Jack Wise was the cowman and his wife, Ruby, also helped on the farm, in fact she preferred to be working outside than in the house.

They had seven children, all to become our good friends, as were Mr. and Mrs. Wise. Beryl was the eldest, then Audrey who later joined the A.T.S. Des was in the Royal Marines, joined I think at fifteen years and did "boys' service" before becoming a marine proper. He was a musician, played a cornet, and travelled the world. Next was Derek, known as Deg, Deggie or sometimes Dicky. He answered to all the above and still does. Deg is just a bit older than me, and so far we have enjoyed well over fifty years of good friendship. Joan is Stella's age and they palled up quite a bit; Enid a year or two younger, and finally young Geoff, who was only a little lad of four when they arrived.

Goodness knows how they all managed in the first place. There were three Hewitts and, I think, eight Wises under the one roof. Anyhow, manage they did, and they all got on well, which was just as well.

Quite soon after, Mrs. Hewitt died. I only saw her a few times. Some time later, Mr. Hewitt married again, and took on Blind Hall Farm where he went to live.

It was after Mr. Hewitt moved that we Webbs got to know the Wises better. My mother knew Jack Wise from sometime in the past, but I never remembered any details. The farmhouse was the great meeting house. Everybody seemed to flock there and we were all made welcome, although there was one person who just did not know when to go home. He had a bit of a "crush" on Enid, but all he ever got was "the cold shoulder".

Somehow or other Mrs. Wise could always provide a cup of tea. The family were always avid tea drinkers and Mrs. Wise could get more cups of tea out of a mashing than anyone else that I know. It was rationed, of course, 2 oz of tea per person per week, and naturally "weak" was the operative word – tea bags were not heard of then.

Again, somehow or other parents managed to provide some sort of a party for their offspring on their birthday and at Christmas. Our mother was no exception. Stella and I had a party at our birthday till we were about twelve, but the Christmas parties carried on into our teens, both of us inviting two or three close friends.

Mrs. Wise (Rube to Deggie) adored parties – any excuse for a get together, the dog having pups or the cat having kittens – anything. No need for excuses later on when they got married and then again later on came the christenings. More than once I was the only guest outside the family, which I looked upon as a real privilege.

Derek also worked on the farm, ploughing and working with "Tip" and "Taff", a pair of cart horses. Mr. Hewitt also had seasonal help from prisoners of War, Italians, and I think sometimes Germans. There were not a great deal of mechanised aids around Berkswell in 1944. The Wheatley estate probably had two tractors by this time, an Old International – it looked old anyhow – was their first acquisition, and it seemed to go on for ever. Bill Wilkinson was the driver. The next tractor to arrive was a Fordson, very basic, just three forward gears and a reverse. When the clutch was depressed it acted as a brake as well, therefore the driver chose the gear required according to the type of work being undertaken. It probably towed a two furrow plough in second gear and road work in top gear, which was I think about 5 m.p.h. The Ferguson System was still to arrive.

My father always helped Mr. Davies of Park Farm with haymaking and harvest, and as soon as I could use a pitch fork, I went along with him.

"Uncle" John Davies had arrived at Park Farm from somewhere in Wales quite a few years before the War (2nd World War), I understand. They brought their implements and possessions on farm carts all the way, and drove the animals – cows, horses, etc.

Mr. Davies was a typical Welshman, not very tall, wearing a trilby hat and a brown smock coat. His wife was a big lady and very much "in charge", behind the scenes of course. They had two sons. The eldest, whose name escapes me (David I think), farmed at Mercote Mill Farm, adjoining Park Farm. Trevor was still at home.

John Davies was a very good judge of shire horses and they had three greys, probably some Percheron in the breeding. They had a super device in the Dutch barn for unloading the hay wagons. A cable ran along the underside of the roof of the barn on pulleys. On the end was attached a huge two pronged fork which was plunged into the hay on the wagon. There was a locking device on the fork and when this was ready a "Right ho!" would be shouted. This was the signal to the kid at the other end of the cable. With a horse pulling the cable up went the hay and then along the barn as far as the rick, a smart tap with a pitchfork and down it came. A thin length of rope dragged the fork back for the next lot.

They gave me the job with Robin, the Welsh cob kept for the less heavy jobs on the farm, taking the feed out to the sheep in the fields, etc.

Trevor worked very hard; he had no choice. If, say, they were ploughing, and did so many bouts in a day, they would be counted by Mrs. D. and if the same number was not done the next day she wanted to know why. However, although she scared me somewhat, she was always nice to me.

Harvesting corn was also a labour intensive job. When the field was ready to cut with the binder a six foot "path" was scythed around the out-side of the field. The cut corn was tied into a sheaf with some of the lengths of straw. Then away would go the binder drawn by two horses. Cutting about six foot width of standing corn which was taken into the machine on an endless canvas conveyor, it was tied and discharged as a very neat sheaf, most of the time. Round and round the field until the centre was reached; sometime before the end of cutting, one or two, usually the farmer, would assemble with their shot guns. The rabbits would be driven into the remaining standing corn and then as the area got smaller they would make a bolt for it. This would provide a bit of sport for all, even the dogs enjoyed a bit of retrieving.

Then the next process began. I have enjoyed – yes – many hours "stook-ing", or "shooking", depending where one comes from. About six rows of sheaves were picked up and made into one row of stooks and so it went on till they were all collected. There were six or eight sheaves to a stook. It was said that the stooks needed to stand in the fields and "hear the Church bells" on three Sundays. The corn finished off the ripening process and also there was sometimes a lot of green weeds in the bottom of the sheaves.

If they had been stacked it would have heated up in the rick (internal combustion) and gone on fire. This was a common occurrence then, with hay in particular.

Stooking could be an unpleasant job. There was no spraying in those days and thistles could be growing in amongst the corn. Grab a handful and it made one jump and sometimes say naughty things – like bother! They were known to us as "Scotsmen" and Trevor Davies had more than his fair share.

Next came the "carrying". The farm wagons would be horse-drawn, only one big "hoss" at the Davies's, a big powerful grey, driven between two rows of stooks, a pitcher at both sides and one chap loading. It all had to be done properly, about two sheaves at a time, ears into the centre of the wagon, butts to the outside.

It was not long before I had the job of loading, always trying to build a neat square load, it was usually roped for the journey to the rickyard at the farm. Another job I liked was leading the horse to the rickyard and riding back on the empty wagon.

The horses were huge by the side of me when I was about thirteen. There was no problem as they knew exactly where they were to go, but, we did have to get as close as possible to the rick to make it easy for the bloke to unload. The unloader passed the sheaves, one at a time, to the rick builder, and that was it, a labour intensive job and hard work as well – not to mention the "Scotsmen". Really it was then only half way because at a later date it had to be threshed.

After the death of "Uncle" John Davies, Trevor took over Park Farm. He cycled miles to court Elsie, the nurse who became his wife. He was Welsh, she was Irish, and they were living in England. When their son was born he was christened Andrew and he had a severe speech problem, I wonder why? However, he attended a special speech therapy school and made a complete recovery. What a blessing. Now Andrew is the tenant of Park Farm. Since writing the above Andrew died a tragic death about 1998.

Father and I also gave Jack Dawson of Holloway Farm (owned by the Kerbys' at Binton) a hand from time to time and Jack and Trevor would help each other. At the end of the evening's work we were provided with supper which was very good and most welcome. The farmers had special rations to feed casual workers and those on overtime. During the War we had double summer time and it was light till about 11.00, but we knocked off at about 9.30 or 9.45. Normally I did not go much on cheese but those sandwiches of spam, bully beef and cheese, etc., together with hot, strong tea, went down a treat out in the yard at Davies's, but we had to go into the house at Dawsons. It was tired bodies that pedalled their way home afterwards to a good wash and shave out in the washhouse, and soon to bed. No bath or shower to jump into. Goodness knows what the B.O. was like before we did get a bath. We were all the same anyhow.

It was very seldom any harvesting was done on a Sunday. I don't think the Davies's were Church or Chapel-goers; having no vehicle they could not get to the nearest Welsh Chapel in Coventry anyhow.

Mr. and Mrs. Dawson were staunch members of the Methodist Church in Meriden. One exception I recall at Park Farm. One Sunday we were carrying corn from Cornets End to the farm and by this time Trevor had a nippy David Brown tractor. It had a bench seat for two. Jack and I were driving down the farm drive and onto the drive that led to Cornets End. It was supposed to be a private drive. However, as we went through the gate a chap on a motorbike came roaring up the bridle road, hit the front wheel of the tractor, headed to the ditch and managed to ride along the bottom of the ditch for some distance before coming off, landing in a heap with the bike close by, motionless. We stopped and rushed over just as his eyes started to blink open. Thankfully he was only shook – pardon the pun – up and his bike was O.K. He was soon on his way, albeit gently, but Jack was even less keen on Sunday harvesting thereafter.

In common with most of the other lads I had a go at smoking. The first time was when Georgie Wilkinson (Wilkie) produced some and we all lit up in the pig pens in the Slang. How grand we thought, or did I? Honestly, I didn't think much of it till probably when I was in the A.T.C. when they were all puffing away to their hearts' content and I started buying fags, eventually getting them out at home. My father was a heavy smoker, 40 or 50 a day, especially when he was in the Observer Corps during the War.

We all thought it was "big", puffing away at the pictures and so on – fools! With me, I was buying more and more. The "old man" was scrounging off me, also some of my mates, especially just before pay-day. It got that either I gave up smoking or the "flicks", etc. Thankfully, the habit had not got me hooked so I was able to pack up the ciggies. I think my mother persuaded father to cadge fags from me so that I would give up. It was interesting that very few girls smoked at that time, perhaps it was because most of their wages were much lower than the lads, but not in my case.

It was in 1945 when I was sixteen that Mrs. Hope started to teach ballroom dancing in the Reading Room at Berkswell. Mr. and Mrs. Hope lived at Meadow Bank opposite the Bear Inn on Coventry Road. Mr. Hope ran his builder's business from there. Mrs. Hope was a very qualified teacher of ballroom dancing. I understand she danced with and knew Victor Sylvester in her younger days. She was ably assisted by Mary Greenwell, now Mary Bateman.

I am not sure how the Reading Room was run before 1945 but it was in that year that the Wheatley family sold the Room to the Lant Trust. It was built at the turn of the century (1900) by Mr. Wheatley, for the benefit of parishioners. And I understand a Mr. Greenway paid for some or all of the furniture. Newspapers were provided for people to read and probably on certain days the newspapers would be read by a scholar to anyone that could not read – hence The Reading Room.

From 1945 The Room has been run by a committee and at the start funds were in short supply. Also, during the War, very little maintenance had been undertaken. That is how and why the dancing classes started. We paid 6d (2p) per evening, 8 till 10.30. There was tuition and practice then a break for a cup of tea, more practice and novelty dances and so on. Mrs. Hope's biggest and hardest job was to get boys to get up and dance with the girls. We all sat there itching to go, but no-one wanted to be first. I was very slow at coming forward then so it was rarely that I was first. It took a bit of getting used to but became really enjoyable for me anyhow once I got the hang of it and I must admit it was one of the best ways of meeting the girls. They, and the lads, were a nice crowd and we had a lot of fun. A bit different to today's so-called dancing. However, each to his or her own.

During the War there were lots of dances everywhere, including The Reading Room, and so it continued for some years till some time after Lonnie Donegan and Co. came along.

After I got a bit more proficient and, to some extent, braver, I started attending the dances. There would usually be one held at least once a fortnight during the winter months, also a few in the summer. After a while we started venturing further, to Balsall Institute (now The Village Hall) also owned by the Lant Trust. But I always enjoyed The Reading Room dances the best; it was like one big party really. We usually knew more than half of those attending and tried hard to get to know some of the others. There were some really good bands as well. Mrs. Hope ran a lot of the dances and most organisations had at least one "do" every year.

The bands did not arrive with loads of electrical gear, probably just one microphone for announcing the dances and tunes. They would carry their instruments in a case, but I always felt sorry for the drummer. He was always last to go.

One person that went on to become famous was Susan Maughan (Bobbie's Girl, a one hit wonder). She sang with Ronnie Hancox and they came to Berkswell once or twice. They were six in number, a bit too big for The Reading Room, but they were really good at The Fentham Hall at Hampton-in-Arden.

At the time there were no licensed bars at the dances – probably with a few exceptions – but we usually had a supper of some sort. If one wanted a drink we had to either go to The Bear first, nip out during the interval, or both. Some of the lads naturally liked to get the girls to go outside. They were not too keen as a rule, being well brought up young ladies. There were a few though. One excuse was to suggest a walk as far as the Churchyard to see the "Eggs and bacon" tombstone. This often worked, but usually it was too dark to see it anyhow. For my own part I always thought it a waste of good dancing time so never tried it on. Also, at the time I had no idea where the headstone was.

Venturing further afield some of us used to go to The Rialto Casino in Coundon, Coventry. It has been a bingo hall for many years now. Also, the old Drill Hall in Queen Victoria Road, bulldozed and gone now. We could go on the bus, first of all cycling to Youngs Garage at the end of Banner Lane, then taking the bus into town. Special late buses were put on at the end of the dance, but what a scramble, and the one from the Casino only went as far as The Phoenix pub on the A45 Coventry by-pass. We then had to walk back to Banner Lane. Most soon got fed up. I took my trusty bicycle which could be left quite safe chained to a drain pipe at the rear of the Casino and there was a passage we used at the Drill Hall, removing battery lamps and cycle pumps, etc.

The Big Bands came to the Drill Hall – Ted Heath, Joe Loss, The Squadronnaires, Oscar Rabin and Geraldo, to name a few. The Drill Hall was a dump, an awful place. We would trip over the knots in the wooden floor, but the music was terrific and the company good – two out of three can't be bad. No licensed bar here but we went to a little pub in Hill Street, The Newdigate Arms I think, not far to walk after dumping the bike and before the place "warmed up", which was usually an hour after the dance started.

The Casino was different. We paid to go in and the ballroom was upstairs, a purpose built-ballroom, chairs and tables on three sides with a carpet floor cover. A sprung maple floor for dancing with plenty of room – most of the time.

The band was of the Glenn Miller style, fifteen musicians, two vocalists, and Len Clarke conducting his "Rialto Casinians". Probably sounds very corny now, but the sounds to me were magic, absolutely wonderful; when they played a fast tune their stage shook and bounced as did the floor, tunes like "In The Mood", "One o'clock jump" and "At the Woodchoppers' Ball", all still great favourites of mine. I think I read somewhere once that the tunes of one's teens were favourites for life. This has applied to me so far, although I can listen to enjoy most music except the extremes. Anything to do with dancing is alright – excerpts from the ballet, Spanish flamenco super, Dixyland and Traditional Jazz, Swing, Rock and Roll and so on.

In addition to Mrs Hope's dancing classes I used to go to Keith Jones' dancing studios in Corporation Street, Coventry, with Derrick Wagstaff, who was the elder son of Mrs. Wheatley's chauffeur Bert. We cycled to Banner Lane, parked our bikes at the side of the garage, pushed 2d through the letterbox and took the bus 4d each way (less than 4p). The studio was upstairs in a building opposite where The Belgrade stands now. It was most enjoyable learning new steps in nice company, and it was a cheap night out. Funnily enough, I cannot recall any boys' names, but I do remember Mary, Norma and Jean. Dancing was to records. Sometimes Keith Jones came in and taught; he was a medallist and took part in all sorts of big competitions with his partner, Hazel Hathaway, who also owned dance studios, teaching all sorts of dance, especially for youngsters – Happy days!

Margaret and Home Life

Enjoying teenage life to the full, there was never a slack moment. Coming home from the nursery, having tea and then a playtime with little sister, Margaret – some fourteen years younger than me – the bombing, if you recall! Playing with Margaret often made me late going out to the pictures or whatever. I was always "on the last minute" anyhow. Nobody ever passed me on my bike, Derrick Wagstaff could "push 'em round" as well.

I always went dancing on a Saturday evening, even when we were harvesting at Trevor's. I would leave work soon after 7 p.m. A saucepan of hot water would be ready, half the water into a bowl and a wash down, feet in the bowl and wash up; shave, etc. then chop out the mud from the bowl (joke). Into my best suit and onto the bike. It took me twenty minutes to get to The Casino at Coundon, about the same time in the car today. Trouble was I was rather sweaty, but no-one ever complained, probably thought all the more!

Margaret had a pram cum pushchair and we pushed her miles in it all over the fields, taking care of course not to damage any crops. The fields were mainly down to grass for grazing anyhow. Up to the pit hole at the top of the "Slang", over the "Gypsy field", "Blackbridge", to the pits by the "Five acre". Coming back loaded up with firewood, Margaret just visible under the wood, which was mainly used for the copper fire out in the wash-house.

Mother eventually had an electric cooker, which was on hire from the Electricity Board at twelve shillings per quarter (60p), the electricity being paid via a meter under the stairs. The old black range was then taken out and replaced with an open fire with an open hearth, no metalwork at all, undertaken by the estate bricklayer. A poor old job, no finesse at all, however the fire went well and more time was spent in the living room thereafter.

The old range fire, although efficient, did not heat the room very well in the winter. It was the end of black-leading the grate and range, a job mother did once a week. That old range would make a lot of money as an antique today.

The next electrical luxury was a water heater, portable, but always used in the wash-house on wash days and for our bath, galvanised, for the use of. A permanent plumbed-in bath was yet to come, as was a flush loo and water on tap. Some progress had been made some time previously, a bucket lavatory, which I had to attend to from time to time. A handful of grass in the empty bucket made a good clean job when emptying – into a deep hand-dug hole in the garden.

In the summer water, or the lack of it, was sometimes a problem. All was well until one or more pumping stations were installed to satisfy increasing demands for water. One pumping station was installed at Mount Nod, near to Alderminster Road, Broad Lane. One year, the wishing well at Berkswell village went dry. Meriden Pool dried up as well. The shared pump in next door's garden just about provided enough water for drinking. Whether it would have passed today's standards is questionable. During those times it was my task on a Sunday afternoon to ferry water in a blow-up tyred butt from the farm (Home Farm). It was a forty-gallon butt, total weight over 4 cwt. Thank goodness for blow-up tyres said I!

Water was on the tap at the farm, maybe not mains water, however, to be pumped. Sometimes I had to do two trips. Still, mother usually had something extra for tea on a Sunday, a jelly or blancmange, and sometimes fruit. On those occasions 3d (1p worth) of cream from the farm collected in a jug was an extra treat. I also had to collect the milk on a Sunday sometimes. Before the War there were no charges for milk – part of a man's wage if you like, always paid fortnightly on Berkswell Estate. Later on the first two pints were free, thereafter 2d a pint, and later still it was all paid for but was cheaper than elsewhere.

We kids used to love going up to the farm often, as I have said before, with "Shep" Squires. Lambing time was especially nice. He had a big shed for a "Maternity Hostel" and often had to stay all night; there were lambs all over the place. Often there were kaid lambs to be bottle-fed, either orphans or, more likely, a ewe had three lambs and could not, or would not look after them all. Hens and sheep must be the most stupid things on this earth ("thinks" I'm not QUITE sure about that).

It was quite common for "Nan Nan" Squires to have three or four lambs on the hearth in front of the kitchen fire, all having to be bottle-fed, perhaps five or six times a day till they were strong enough to go back to the "lamb garten".

The Squires kept a lamb once when we, Stella and I, were quite small, a tup that was known as "Nibby". They had this yard for him and all went well till he grew bigger and started to throw his weight around. Apparently, he would try and butt anybody and any visitors that went to the back door. He had to go.

I have mentioned "Uncle Bill" before, also saying that I could not work it out as Dad was one of eight and Bill made nine. He was, I think, a bit younger than dad's brother Frank. He was married to Grace and lived in Berkswell Road, just below where Pettifor's coal-yard is now situated.

Grace and Bill lived in the same cottage as Mark James, grandfather of Arthur, who we will get to know better later on. I remember the garden was kept very nice and tidy. My father would take Stella and I there now and again on a Sunday morning. This was around 1936/37 time. Bill had a motorbike and sidecar, a B.S.A. Sloper, and would often be cleaning and oiling his "pride and joy". It was our pride and joy when he took us a short spin of a mile or two, dad on the pillion and us two kids in the chair, something to brag about next day at school.

Bill was not a big chap, but by all accounts a bit of a lad. He was in the Territorials and was called up for the Army I think, before War broke out.

Unfortunately, "the wheel came off" the marriage, and by this time they had Rona, a lovely little daughter. Bill was in the Army and Auntie Grace and Rona went back to Surrey. Woking was where Grace came from.

Some time afterwards they came to stay with us for a week. I thought Auntie Grace was nice, that's because she was nice. One day, Stella and I took Rona and Grace to the farm to get the milk. We almost always went over the fields, Slang, Gypsy field and Home Close. This day was no exception and all went well till we were on our way back. There was a flock of sheep in the field and, as on many occasions beforehand, we walked through the middle of them. Unfortunately, there was a "Nibby" (Tup) in amongst them and he did not approve of our presence. He started to charge and Stella was the unfortunate one to receive a butting, we others were not very gallant, anyhow I was carrying the milk, and scattered. I think Grace drove off the tup. Glad to say Stella was none the worse for her experience, but perhaps a bit wary of sheep thereafter. I often wonder what became of Rona and would like to meet her. It's up to me I suppose.

In the meantime, Bill went off to the Army to serve for the duration of the War. He was soon in France with the British Expeditionary Force and I understand was one of the last out in 1940, not from Dunkirk, but further south. He remustered at some time into the Commandos and became a glider pilot. I am not sure, but Bill returned to France either at Arnhem or Pegasus Bridge in Normandy. A useful bloke I would think at looking after No. 1 and most likely others as well. He came back in one piece and went to work at the North Warwickshire Golf Club, a nine hole course on The Straight Mile at Meriden (Hampton Lane).

So life went on. Although the War ended in 1945, rationing continued for years. Coal was still rationed in 1956. It was a much needed commodity to provide power for factories and industry in general to get Britain back on its feet. I am not sure if that project was ever completed.

My school bike was almost a wreck when I left school at Easter 1943 and as soon as funds permitted I bought a Phillips cycle from Young's Garage at the junction of Broad Lane and Banner Lane, Eastern Green. A bog standard "sit up and beg" utility job, no chrome, all painted black. I was a bit upset at the speed that I could get out of it, or in fact the lack of it, so I took it back to Mr. Young and he built a three-speed gearing into the rear wheel, then there was no catching up with me. The bike was £5.00 new and the three-speed cost £1.10.0 (£1.50p). My wage was £1.2.0 (£1.10p) per week. I gave my mother 10/- (50p) and I had the remainder. I bought all my clothing, maintained my bike and was expected to save at least a quarter of my pocket money. It proved to be a very good training for me, as I have never been without a shilling to spend. My mother always said "Take care of the pennies and the pounds will take care of themselves", and, "The first hundred pounds is the hardest". This, of course, is true and relevant today – just adding a few noughts on the end though.

It was not long after starting work that "The Man from the Pru" came knocking at our door selling endowment policies. I took one out costing 6d per week and some months later another policy costing 7d per week. To finance this, I saved all the 3d and 6d coins that came into my possession as change; therefore the Pru man was always sure of change after visiting the Webbs. I always found the best way of saving was by paying via insurance and the Pru played a big part in that right up until my retirement, and beyond.

Life for me was very full, working, entertaining sister Margaret, Air Training Corps; the cinema two or three times a week, and later on dancing classes – which was a nice social night out, once I got brave enough to ask the girls for a dance. Sometimes it was the girls that got me to my feet. I didn't mind as I was itching to have a go anyhow. Barbara Pope, she was a big gal to say the least but so light on her feet. Betty Haines, who I was quite fond of – and that's as far as it went, also Audrey Mears, Beryl Attwood were others that dragged me out of my chair.

I also helped out in the garden and eventually took over one half of the vegetable garden. Most country gardens were so different then, about half of country cottages were "tied", the occupier working for the owner or, in the case of a tenant farmer, on an estate. The farmer would pay rent to the estate for the cottage and a farm worker occupied the cottage as part of his wages, i.e. lose your job, lose your house.

Most cottages had large gardens, and most gardens were almost entirely used as kitchen gardens, vegetables and soft fruit in the main. Ours was no exception. We grew raspberries, black and redcurrants, also gooseberries and a loganberry. Mother seldom had to buy any vegetables but there were no fridges or freezers to store any surplus fruit or vegetables.

Our mother was a very good cook. Surplus eggs were put down in "water glass" and used for cooking, fruit was bottled in Kilner jars or made into jam. Onions or shallots were pickled and our piccalilli was very nice indeed with jacket potatoes and cold meat off the Sunday joint, a traditional Monday dinner.

We grew quite a lot of potatoes, which were stored in sacks in the washhouse, as were the Bramley apples which kept till the following May.

Dad grew a lot of parsnips and most were made into wine, boiled in the copper for starters and fermented in the big pantry. I never did get a sample of the wine, production of which had to stop during the War when sugar was rationed.

In the winter we had Brussels sprouts and Savoy cabbage. It all seemed to be more hardy than today, or is it my imagination?

CHAPTER 7

Life as a Country Teenager

Socially I was out most evenings, "pictures" at The Cameo, Balsall, or The Standard at the junction of Tile Hill Lane and Fletchampstead Highway (A45), dancing classes and a dance on Saturday evening. Sunday evening was the "pictures" at Balsall. My mother did not like me going to the "flicks" on Sunday but all the other lads went so she was on a bit of a loser really.

At the age of fifteen I stopped going to Sunday School. The teachers tried hard to persuade me to become a teacher, but (a) I had little confidence and (b) to be honest, I did not want to. I was prepared for confirmation by the Reverend Whittaker in 1944, who was rather confused at this time. He never really got over losing his son Peter, who was in the Merchant Navy. The confirmation service was held at St. Lawrence's Church, Meriden.

Work went on as usual. I really did enjoy my time working for Mrs. Morris. She treated me almost as a son. The Morris's had information at long intervals that son, Hugh, was alive and "well". In fact, I think he was just about alive. Eventually, he was liberated by our Forces, and received treatment and care.

He returned to this country and was demobbed and came home. That naturally was a great day for all concerned and I had the nurseries to myself. Hugh seemed quite fit and looked tanned and well, but he suffered from malaria and had attacks from time to time. Apparently he would perspire a lot and then go cold. Thankfully he fairly soon got over it, or seemed to be better anyhow. He found it difficult to settle down, I think, but was quite soon able to resume his love of ballroom dancing. I don't think he had any time at all for nursery work or market gardening. Farming was the "thing to be in". He convinced his mother of this and in January 1947 Mrs. Morris informed me that they were selling the nursery and going into farming.

Sister Stella and Margaret with brother John in A.T.C. uniform, 1946

Hugh's sister, Marjorie, was married to a farmer and Hugh's mate was Frank Barnacle who farmed just across the road from the nursery.

This was more than a bit of a blow for me and Stella who had also worked at the nurseries for a while. However, good fortune was on my side. "It is better to be lucky than rich", they say. I am not sure – Yes, I have been lucky but never rich – financially that is. Riches galore in other respects and one cannot have it all ways.

I do not know how it came about at all, but I was informed that help was needed on The North Warwickshire Golf Course. Bill Webb worked there; he must have called round. I was just two months away from my eighteenth birthday and was sure of being called up for National Service. Bill said not to tell the golf professional when I went for an interview, so I didn't. One was almost guaranteed getting any job then, no-one, or only a few, were interested in agriculture or horticulture, especially when wages in the factories were 75% or so more than the agricultural rates. Anyhow, I got the job and was due to start on the Monday morning.

It was towards the end of January and very cold, and I was not looking forward to working on a windswept golf course one little bit, but needs must. However, nature had something to say in the matter and it started to snow on the Sunday and did not know when to stop. It was one of the heaviest falls of snow that I can remember. 1940 was also a very bad winter for snow. Both times we must have had two feet of snow. It drifted and no-one could get very far at all.

In some parts of the country farmers had to walk along the tops of hedges to rescue their stock. I had to walk to work and snow was way over the top of my wellies. It was six or seven weeks before the thaw set in, then, guess what? Everywhere there were floods.

In the meantime, I had been notified of my pending call-up. I had to go for a medical examination, also to undertake various tests, presumably to see where I was best suited – poor things, they had no need of gardeners in the Navy, which was my one choice. There are no window boxes on air-craft, so the Air Force was out. In fact, they were not recruiting just at that time anyhow. So that only left the Army.

My idea was to try and learn something that would be useful when I came out, like driving or whatever. In the end it was "whatever". Whatever gave them that idea.

Back at the golf club the gaffer, who was a very nice bloke, went almost barmy when he learned that I would be leaving in a week or two's time. I made up my mind to work hard during my stay and he soon cooled down. Cannot think of his name, but he was six foot tall and came to work in a little Fiat 600 Bubble Car. When he was getting out of his car, it seemed to go on forever. How he got in I know not.

Once the snow and water had gone, work on the golf course was most enjoyable. Bill was the main worker. There was also an elderly man that came part-time from Hampton-in-Arden. Tommy was over eighty and still going strong.

The mornings were very busy for us three, and sometimes, the profes-sional. All the nine greens had to be brushed and rolled with a light roller. We had a big switch broom, a besom-type brush with only about five twigs in it. This was fixed into the end of a long bamboo cane. The end of the pole was under one's arm and the broom switched from side to side, pro-gressing forward, the action like a windscreen wiper on a car. This swept all the debris, i.e. worm casts, leaves and twigs, to one side, and was swept up with an ordinary besom, still today the best broom for the garden, in my opinion.

The bunkers were raked smooth and mowing carried on as required. We usually had this done before 10 a.m., before the course got busy.

In the afternoon we had jobs to do that kept us off the main area of play, and on Thursday afternoon, which was Ladies' Day, we found jobs in and around the tool shed, cleaning tools and mowers, etc. I was just get-ting into the swing of it all, even mowing the fairways with the tractor gang mowers, when my calling-up papers arrived. "You are hereby instructed to report to Budbrooke Barracks, near Warwick, between the hours of 10 a.m. and 2 p.m. on Thursday, April 26th 1947", or words to that effect.

CHAPTER **8**

You're in the Army Now

I did as was instructed and from then on I became a number for the next two years plus, 19160357, or sometimes "Webb 357". On arrival there was documentation. The army thrived on it. We, a whole company of three platoons, were kitted out, and had it drummed into us that we were responsible for keeping all kit clean and tidy. Having received our kit of two uniforms (best and working), underclothing, greatcoat, two pairs of boots, belt and gaiters, "eating irons" and mug, large pack and small pack, kit bag and a greasy rifle, etc. etc., we were escorted to a wooden hut which was our barrack room, which the occupants had to keep dusted, clean and tidy, each lad responsible for their own "bed space", taking turns to sweep down the centre every morning before parade and inspection.

Being in the A.T.C. was of great benefit to me. I had been to camp three times and was familiar with "square bashing" and was used to taking orders from N.C.O.'s and officers. I did not look forward to joining the Army – General Service Corps – neither did I mind going, probably just as well as I had no choice in the matter.

I was in "A" company. Our barrack room was quite good, plenty of windows, airy and light. There was a good atmosphere, lads all the same age but from different backgrounds, townies and country bumpkins. "April Showers" was one of the "in" tunes and Al Jolson was impersonated well, and poorly.

The first three days, Friday, Saturday and Sunday, were more or less used to settle in. Nevertheless, we were fully occupied. We marched to the dining room and walked back in our own time. There were facilities for washing our eating irons and mugs outside the dining hall. There were gaiters, belts, and two packs to be blancoed khaki. We had to buy our blanco. There were brasses to polish, buttons, belt and pack buckles and so on.

John with John Kirby, 1947

Our best pair of boots really had to shine. There were various methods of getting the wrinkles out of the toe caps and heels; rubbing with the back of the handle of a dessert spoon was one. It took a lot of "elbow grease" and time.

Monday saw the beginning of six weeks' training, marching, arms drill with rifles, fixing bayonets, etc. Quite a bit of physical training. A certain amount of classroom education. Route marches and obstacle courses, or assault course – which I loathed – but I never landed in the water, when "push comes to shove" one usually manages the task in hand.

We were taught how to dismantle, clean and reassemble an L.M.G. (light machine gun). The butts at Wedgenock were visited two or three times, marching there and back with our rifles. Everyone had to fire ten or twenty rounds (bullets) at targets. There was always a kitty into which we all paid (compulsory). The best shot took all. I was at a disadvantage from the word go, wearing spectacles, however, I was nowhere near the bottom of the class. Again, we had been to the butts at one or more of the A.T.C. camps. Then our rifles had to be "pulled through" and cleaned. The sarge said "Your rifles are your best friends now. Your mother can't help you here".

A "pull through" is a small weight on the end of a string which is dropped down the barrel of the rifle, on the other is a sort of plug which fits the barrel. Pulling it through once or twice cleans the barrel. Anyone found with a dirty rifle or any rust on it was "on a charge" straight away.

There were further aptitude tests early on; all sorts of tests to find out what one was most suited to doing, Chinese puzzles and so on.

Discipline was very strict, as one can imagine, and we were there for six weeks. No-one was allowed off camp for the first three weeks, then we were allowed out, if one could get past the guard-room. In any case, there was only time to walk to Warwick and back, three miles each way. I went once. We were only allowed out in uniform, including boots and gaiters. Shoes could not be worn. One had to present oneself to the guard-room by the gate, march in, request a pass-out, be inspected by the duty sergeant and, if he was satisfied with one's "turn out", away you went. I did get home twice, but it was a jaunt on public transport.

However, at the end of the day, life was pretty good. The weather was kind to us. I had some good mates and although discipline was tough, as long as one did his best, the N.C.O.'s were not too bad.

My mate, John Kirby, was called up just four weeks after me. There was an intake once a fortnight. He was in "C" Company.

He really was put through the mill. At the end of his six weeks General Montgomery of Alamein was going to take the salute at their passing out parade at the end of their training. Poor things, they did have to sweat and polish morning, noon, and night. We only met up once, in the N.A.A.F.I., during the two weeks our training overlapped. I must say he was much smarter turned out than me, and I have the photograph to prove it.

At the end of our six weeks we were pretty well knocked into shape and had our passing out parade. Then all of us were posted to our Corps training, departing Budbrooke for all parts of the country. The powers that were decided that I should become a clerk in the Royal Army Ordnance Corps, and me not knowing one end of a pen from the other was not very pleased. But one did as one was bidden and that was that.

About a dozen of us were posted to Hilsea Barracks, just outside Portsmouth. We were escorted there by an N.C.O. (non-commissioned officer). I was later to learn my father was there for some time during the First World War. He was in the Royal Field Artillery.

We were billeted in very nice looking brick built two-storey buildings. I was on the upper floor and for the Army we were quite comfortable. We did not see a lot of our billets, being kept on the go quite a bit. By the way,

Left: Showing off his stripes; right: 'Geordy' Townson and myself ready for a night in Benghazi

there were no bed sheets or pillow cases supplied by the Army and not many had a pair of pyjamas, including me. My shirt had to do, and it also saved time in the mornings.

There was still some square bashing and so on, but the majority of the time was spent in the classroom. We had a sergeant to tutor us and I like to think he was a good tutor. I found it all rather difficult. Some I do recall. The opening statement from 'sarge' was "The King (Geo.VI) is the Head of the Army". The Ordnance Corps were responsible for supplying the army with all its requirements, with the exception of food, water and petrol, which was the responsibility of the Royal Army Service Corps, also transport. The Pay Corps dealt with our pay, which was four shillings per day (20p) and our keep £1-8-0. per week (£1.40). There were stoppages of about one shilling (5p). I made a voluntary allotment of seven shillings per week (35p) to be sent home; this my mother banked for me after paying The Man from the Prudential, leaving me with a pound per week. Big deal. However, as I only drank a little, well nothing really, and did not smoke, I got by quite well, although I did overspend whilst at Portsmouth.

From various depots the Corps supplied vehicles, including armoured vehicles, clothing, etc. and ammunition.

On the Ordnance cap badge three artillery guns were depicted on a shield. In the centre with a row of cannon balls along the top, the words "Honi Soit Qui Mal Y Pense" which means "Evil to him who evil thinks", but our tutor had another interpretation which was "to the thunderer his balls"!

In the classroom we were taught the procedure for handling Ordnance stores, in and out of a depot; dockets and things in triplicate via various departments and offices. There were diagrams like family trees with strange-sounding names.

The usual spit and polish went on, as usual. The cookhouses needed potato peelers every evening and the slightest misdemeanour by anyone resulted in a couple of hours spud-bashing. I was only caught out once, and then there was a bit of a bonus. We managed to scrounge a bacon sandwich and a mug of cocoa from the cookhouse.

The food ration there was very poor, very small portions for eighteen year old lads. I reckon those in charge were flogging it off somewhere.

We were allowed more freedom after duties at Hilsea. There was the same procedure at the guard-room, but we were allowed to wear our own shoes, if they were highly polished. It was possible to catch a bus just outside the gate into Portsmouth, or further on to the beach at Southsea. There naturally was plenty to spend money on, one or two clubs for service personnel, probably run by the N.A.A.F.I. I cannot recall the names of any. At weekends, the weather being nice, we would go out after mid-day meal and do our homework sitting on the beach at Southsea, then probably push the boat out and have ham, egg and chips at one of the service clubs. Food and drinks were inexpensive, and I was always hungry.

I became friendly with a chap from Harringay in London and the last weekend in "Pompey" he took me home with him for the weekend. Train fares for service personnel were about one third of the normal price. We travelled up to Waterloo and to Harringay by Tube.

At that time, Middlesex were doing rather well at cricket with Edrich and the Compton brothers at their best, so cricket was the main topic of conversation. I cannot think of this chap's name, but he had a very nice sister, and the girl next door was O.K. too. I had a very nice weekend there and was grateful to be asked to go.

The weather was glorious whilst I was at Portsmouth. In fact, after the deluge of snow in January had gone, 1947 weather was good. We had a cross-country run one day, the whole lot of squaddies, "would-be" clerks, storemen, etc. with a promise of a weekend pass for the first twenty home. I thought of having a go at that. After the training I was quite fit, never felt better in fact, so did the others. It was quite a long run, probably seven or eight miles over all sorts of terrain, including a ploughed field. I came in about twenty-fifth, and only got a pat on the back. Unfortunately, our platoon had given blood during the morning. Did I suffer after the run in the afternoon? My legs were like jelly and were not right for some days. Some of us had a job to climb the stairs to our billet. However, I survived and the course came to an end with the usual "spit and polish" passing out parade and inspection by "the old man", i.e. the top officer of any camp was usually referred to as "The old man".

With hind-sight and a gut feeling, I think I failed the exams which we took at the end; however, there was no second chance – hooray for that – and we were all sent home on a week's leave. I had two rail passes, one to get me home and the second to get me to 25ASD (Ammunition Sub Depot), Gartmore, near Stirling, in Scotland. "Thinks" – that's what you get for not passing the course, gut feeling (I was never told).

We were sent on leave with all our gear, kit bag, large pack, small pack which I folded up and put into my kit bag which was made of grey waterproof canvas, round in shape, about fifteen inches in diameter, and three foot tall. With care, they could be packed quite well, clothing coming out without too many creases. Also, I had a rifle to be responsible for, feeling rather conspicuous travelling home "armed to the teeth".

The leave was good after ten weeks of being ordered around from pillar to post. However, I did feel very fit and even ready for a scrap, if it came my way. Pleased to say it did not come to that. There was very little feudin' and fightin' amongst teenagers, or anyone, at that time.

It was soon time to be on my travels and I was supposed to report to Gartmore during daytime on the designated day. This meant I had to travel overnight and I thought "What a waste". My previous travelling had been rather limited and I wanted to see where I was going. Looking at a map of Scotland I could not find Gartmore, so decided to take the day train to Stirling. It was a lovely hot day and we eventually arrived at Stirling railway station at about five-thirty – the train going on to Perth. Making enquiries at the station as to going on to Gartmore, no-one had heard of the place. Certainly no trains went there. "Why not go round to the bus depot and try that" said someone, so off I went, kit-bag over my shoulder, rifle at the slope, and sweating like a bull.

At the bus station desk, again, no-one had heard of Gartmore. Not very impressed with Scotland, thought I. Staff were running around disappearing into offices and making enquiries on my behalf. In actual fact, they could not have done more. Eventually, after what seemed hours, an inspector came along and said he thought there was a bus that would get me there, or almost anyhow. "You want the Aberfoyle bus" and the next and last one was about an hour and a half later. Not quite sure, I thanked him and headed for the nearest pub.

I had been sent on my way with a fair amount of food, but a pint of beer was called for. It was not far to go, thankfully, and I went into the pub through the wide open door, still clutching that blinkin' rifle, and ordered a pint. There was a middle-aged man sitting on a stool by the bar and he said "You look as if you've had a hard day", or words to that effect, and insisted on buying my pint. We had a good old chat and later I wished to return the compliment and buy us both another pint, but I was not allowed to. So, I began to think that Scotland was nay so bad after all.

Refreshed after a couple of pints and a hot pie, it was time to trundle myself and the gear back to the bus station. After trying to check with the driver and conductor, on board I hopped. They did say that there were soldiers on the bus from time to time. Soldiers indeed, never really sunk in that I was a soldier, despite what had been drummed in.

On our way at last, soon leaving Stirling behind, not a very big place anyhow. The roads were really quite narrow for a bus from time to time. On and on by what I am sure was not a direct route, in fact, the bus went as far as a lake once, then turned round and returned via the same route for some time. I was later to learn that the bus went to Loch Lomondside, to a village called Balmaha.

At Drymen some more soldiers got on, including a corporal and a sergeant, and were all chatting and matey together. "Thinks", a bit different to where I have been this last ten weeks. Eventually one chap asked if I was bound for Gartmore. "Yes" says I, rather relieved that someone actually knew of the place. "We are getting off there so will show you the way". By this time it was getting dark. After what seemed a long ride – that is because it was – we all got off, in the middle of nowhere. One chap said "It is a bit of a walk". Much to my amazement and surprise, the sergeant picked up my kit bag and carried it all the way. Someone else had my rifle, leaving me with my small pack. We all started to walk and after a few minutes passed through some open lodge gates and had a twenty minute walk

Christmas Day 1948. John with
mug – empty. Ray with bottle – full

up to Gartmore House, my
destination, although it did
not say so on my instruc-
tions which were "Report to
Gartmore, by Stirling".
Gartmore was twenty-five
miles from Stirling and a
very small village at that.

On arrival I was shown a bed, in a Nissen hut, provided with blankets.
I never had the luxury of any sheets in the Army. I was instructed to be
breakfasted, washed and shaved, and to be on parade with the others at
eight o'clock next morning.

By now most of the other occupants of the hut were in bed. Mine was
soon made up and I was in it. I had arrived.

Next morning on parade at eight, nothing was said about "a late arrival".
New postings were ordered to report to an office after the morning parade
and inspection.

I think there were four of us for documentation, and I got rid of that
blinkin' rifle, which ended up in the armoury. Then came instruction on
what was desired in the way of laying kit out in the mornings. Not quite so
elaborate as Budbrooke or Portsmouth, but the three "biscuits" (mattresses) had to be stacked at the foot end of the bed, blankets folded on top,
eating irons and mug on top of the blankets, all before parade at 8 a.m.
Beds could be made up any time after the mid-day break.

It was then that I was introduced to the workplace, an office in the
main house, where I think I was expected to know the procedure for
receiving and despatching (movement) of ammunition stores. This office
procedure was different from other ordnance stores, and that was just
about all I knew about it.

Gartmore was the H.Q. of 25 A.S.D. There was a detachment at
Drymen, near Loch Lomond, located at Buchannan Castle, and another at
Doune, some nine miles from Stirling.

The ammunition was stored in the main in small Nissen hut-type sheds,
half round and about six foot tall at the centre top. The huts were in the
fields and woods along the sides of the roads. The depot stretched from
Milngavie (pronounced Milnguy) and Kilsythe in the south to Loch Earn
in the north and Loch Lomond in the west to the outskirts of Stirling,
Dunblaine and Creif in the east.

At the end of June 1947 a lot of the ammunition was being disposed of, being taken by Army lorries to various railway sidings on the Stirling to Perth line, loaded onto railway trucks for its journey down to Stranraer, where it was loaded onto old or Wartime redundant boats. I think they were supposed to go out into the Atlantic and be scuttled. I wonder now if some of this debris being washed up is "our" old ammo. That probably got no further than the Irish Sea.

However, back to the office, groan and groan again. I often wished I was a storeman going out on the depot every day, but when they came in often soaking wet, I was not so sure. All the best clerks were kept at H.Q. They were the types with their heads down and dead keen, not like me, chewing the end of a pencil and nipping off to the loo as often as I dared. The problem was no-one could be bothered to help me along or show me the job, so I really just drifted along, doing odd jobs and probably getting in the way. I was disillusioned and just a bit fed up. Occasionally I had to go to the Post Office in Gartmore village, which in common with other Scottish villages had a very wide main street. That took quite a while. It was a long walk, the scenery was very nice, when the sun shone.

We had a long weekend once a month, at the discretion of the Commanding Officer (the old man). The weekend began after duties (5.30 p.m.) on Friday, till 8 a.m. the following Tuesday. One had to be back for the inspection and parade roll call on Tuesday a.m.

My weekly pay was £1-0-0 per week and the train fare was almost £3.00 return, so that left me with 25p to spend each week. It would buy a bun and cup of tea six days a week and about the same in the small N.A.A.F.I. in the evenings. When at home, I dug into savings now and then to pay for any extras.

By the time my first weekend was due, I had got to know the ropes a bit. We had to apply for leave in writing to the old man – Sir, I submit this my application for a long weekend from, etc. It was always granted, he was probably glad to see the back of me, although we only saw him now and then.

There was an inspection of the barrack room on Saturday mornings, followed by parade and perhaps drill or P.T. The barrack room was liable to be inspected any morning except Sunday, when one could stay in bed all day if one liked – some did.

We never knew if the old man would inspect in the week or on Saturday, so Friday evening was often spent polishing one's brasses, blanco-ing packs and gaiters, etc., just to be on the safe side.

On my weekend off my pack would be ready and I would disappear immediately after mid-day lunch, down the drive, hoping no officers would come along. It was fairly safe, we were told they were usually in the Mess on the booze at that time. The bus came at about 2.30 p.m. bound for Glasgow. It was quite a long wait till the train left at about 9.30 p.m. but I used to wander round the shops and have a fish and chip supper. Anything was better than being in camp. Also, I had not got a rifle to hump around. The train got me to Birmingham and I was home for a good old breakfast of home-cooked bacon and egg, plus whatever else was going at the time. Three whole days to be at home and do as I please. Also, get my washing done.

Back in the old routine, digging into reserves for the dance on Saturday evening, "pictures" on Sunday, leaving home on the six o'clock bus on Monday evening, and spending about an hour and a half at Keith Jones' Dancing Studio before catching a Midland Red to Birmingham and the night train to Glasgow. I used to get back to Gartmore on the first bus, about 9.30 a.m. Nothing was ever said or queried.

Not surprisingly, it was not all that long – about six weeks – when I was dispatched to the detachment at Deanston by Doune. I was billeted in the house on the second floor in what probably was the master bedroom, very large, there were about eight of us in there. It had a big bay window with a window seat all round under the windows, very useful hidey-holes. The few officers and N.C.O.'s were on the ground floor, as were the offices. The parade ground was the forecourt in front of the house where we paraded for roll call and inspection every morning (except Sundays).

The whole place was more relaxed but the same problem existed, again, no-one would show or help me with a job and, once again, I became a square peg in a round hole. No-one seemed to bother, so why should I? One thing I did do was telephone operator; we had three lines in Doune 291 and about ten internal.

The food at Gartmore was on the whole not too bad. It was useless complaining anyhow.

At that time farmers could apply to have personnel released for agricultural work, especially harvesting. I thought this was a good "skive" and Trevor Davies applied and got me off for a month. The regulation was that a 48 hour week was to be worked, make one's own way home and back to the unit, no army pay, usual stoppages (National Health Stamp, etc.).

It was good to be doing something useful for a change. The harvest was fairly early that year, so after we finished corn carrying I spent a lot of time on the tractor (David Brown) scuffling fields in order to expose weeds to be killed off by the sun, prior to ploughing for next year's crops.

Some of the corn was soon threshed. This was a major operation. To run the job efficiently we needed eight workers. Rupert Arnold, or his man/men, would arrive with the threshing drum towed by a powerful tractor. In the early days he had two sets of equipment and two steam-driven traction engines that used to snort and hiss their way around the local area. It is nice to know that one of the engines has been fully restored and has made at least one appearance in Berkswell.

The drum would be drawn close up to the Dutch barn or rick, and a long

Arrival in the Suez Canal Zone, Egypt 1948

belt from the tractor pulley would extend to a large drive wheel on the threshing machine. Two men were required on the rick to pitch the sheaves onto the top of the threshing drum; one man would pass the sheaves – the right way round – to the bond-cutter, who cut the string holding the sheaf of corn together and then feed it into the drum. One man had the job of looking after the corn that came down chutes at the back of the machine, another bloke removed the chaff i.e. the corn ears after the corn had been extracted. The straw was fed into a separate machine where it was bundled into a large "sheaf" known as a bolting. A dusty old job which sometimes got exciting when we arrived near to the bottom of the rick.

Some farmers would surround the rick with wire netting in order to prevent rats and mice from making their escape. This is why some workers wore "yorks", leather or string tied tight below the knees to prevent vermin running up a trouser leg. Trevor Davies had his share of rodents and I have seen the unthreshed corn heaving up and down just before the last two or three courses of sheaves were moved for threshing. Catching rats, etc. could be a "free for all". Dogs would be put inside the wire netting and men would arm with sticks. I think the dogs had the most fun. The chap that was responsible for the threshed corn had the hardest job. Some of the sacks held two and a quarter hundred weight. There was a device for hoisting the sacks up to "back level".

The agricultural leave was O.K. and eventually I returned to Doune and 25 A.S.D., together with the usual grind.

Winter was coming up and we did have a ration of coal for the fireplace in our large room.

One day, I had a stroke of good fortune. From somewhere I found a saw, a chopper and also a hessian sack, plastic was still a long way off. The grounds around Deanston House were quite extensive, lots of spinneys and woods. There was an ornamental lake lined with concrete. This was dry and the place where we had our drill on a Saturday morning. We worked – some did – a five day week and Saturday morning was regimental kit laid out for a probable inspection by the old man. Brasses had to be cleaned and so on, but thankfully no rifle to bother about. There was some square bashing (drill) and other minor events. In the main, a low-key morning designed probably to keep personnel occupied and out of mischief.

On some days during the week I would put in an appearance after dinner time and after a time I would execute a "disappearing act", collect the saw, chopper, and sack, hidden in the woods. There was a load of dead wood to be tackled. A sackful would be sawn up and bagged up and hidden, to be collected after duties and before the evening meal. The sawn wood was stored under the window seats. We always had a good evening fire, the only problem being other blokes came into our room and were sometimes reluctant to go when we wanted to turn in. They were sitting on our beds.

Time went on and we had a week's leave for Christmas. Most of the lads were Scots and they had their leave at Hogmanay. Christmas at home was very good as always, but it was soon over and I was on my way back to Scotland once again. Fortunately, as a result of agricultural leave I was a little bit better off financially.

We decided to go out on the town on New Year's Eve. The plan was to walk up to Doune, just over a mile, have a couple of drinks, then get a bus into Stirling to a dance. However, having got into the pub, some were reluctant to leave, and with hindsight staying put would have been the best option.

Eventually, we caught a bus and arrived in Stirling but all two of the dance halls were full. We were advised to go to Dunblane, the next place of any size. Away we went, and it must have been getting on eleven when we arrived, and got in. It was a very good hour or so. Everyone by that time had given up the beer and was knocking back a wee dram or three. I liked a drop of rum as a chaser at the time.

I was quite looking forward to the magic hour of midnight in Scotland, and what a letdown it was for us. A shabby old piper came in, piped his way round the hall and could not get out quick enough. The band was knocking back the hard stuff like there was no tomorrow and 90% of the dancers disappeared never to be seen again – by us anyhow! The band did start to play again but it was pretty awful so we decided to call it a day. We had a walk of almost four miles to undertake, over mostly moorland. It didn't really matter because the fog had come down and we could only see a few yards. It was fortunate that one of the lads were a storeman and knew the area well.

We arrived back all O.K., but very tired, never bothered to get up for breakfast as it was a holiday anyhow. So much for a Scottish Hogmanay. I bet they had a great time in the pub at Doune.

Occasionally at Gartmore and Doune there was a "liberty truck" laid on to take personnel for a night out in Glasgow or Stirling. I did take advantage of these trips about four times. When in Glasgow the Barrowland Ballroom was the attraction for me. The famous Jimmy Shand

and his orchestra played there. It was very good indeed and time to depart was always before the end of the dance. All the patrons, male and female, were a friendly crowd, as were most of the Scots that I came into contact with.

Just about two weeks after New Year I was on my way home again. They had not got fed up with me – "thinks", perhaps they had. It was a week's embarkation leave and, in fact, my last leave before demob. some eighteen months later. We had no other information, just that we were going abroad. As usual, it was a very nice leave and my mother "pulled out the stops". Lots of items were still rationed, but Mother could always make a feast out of ordinary fare. By this time, we had an all mains radio, a small model by Bush built into a circular case. Another improvement, probably a luxury, was an electric cooker, a very basic job on permanent hire at 12/- (60p) a quarter from the electricity board. There were two hotplates, a grill/hotplate and oven. One consolation, there was no range to blacklead and keep clean when it was eventually taken out and replaced with a well grate and hearth. The fire was made in the hearth at floor level; with nowhere for ashes to fall it did mean that the fireplace had to be cleared out daily.

Reporting back to Scotland saw about eight of us preparing to depart for Stirling Station on to London, Euston and transferring by underground to R.A.O.C. Headquarters at Feltham.

We were at Feltham for about three days. There were vaccinations and innoculations in both arms. I had a job to lift anything for a while, but by the time of departure, it was not too bad.

We were kitted out with all sorts of new kit, including shorts and light-weight underwear, indicating a posting to somewhere warm. My folks could not understand why we were not told of the destination and neither could I, the War being over some two and a half years previously.

We went again by train down to Southampton and on board the "TAOS VICTORY". I understood this was a liberty ship of about 7,500 tons. These ships were built by the Americans for the War effort, welded together and not riveted in the usual way. Anyhow, it held together for us but I never heard of it again. We all sailed away in the middle of January and all was well until we arrived in the Bay of Biscay, a notorious place for bad weather and heavy seas.

The food on board was superb. The bread one could eat on its own, white as snow and lovely crust. Our meals were nicely served sort of cafeteria style, picking up a tray with indentations in it, one dent for cereal, one for cooked breakfast, and another for the marmalade and so on – honest!

Things got very rough in the Bay and as mealtimes came around, there were less and less takers. Myself, I did not miss a meal and wrote home to say so. I also wrote to John Kirby who was by now in the Royal Army Service Corps, teaching "squaddies" to drive Army lorries. Why couldn't I be one of those? – eye-sight no doubt. Even to this day I am often reminded by John's

Mum about me going for seconds during our voyage through the Bay of Biscay.

There was still no news as to our destination as the ship passed into the Mediterranean Sea where the sea was calm and all quickly recovered from seasickness. It was so rough that we were not allowed out on deck at one time.

The only time land was seen was Cape St. Vincent in Portugal. Until low on the horizon, when we could see a long thin strip which turned out to be land. The sea turned from blue/grey to a sandy colour, which indicated shallow water. It was the "old sweats" (regular soldiers) who said it was Egypt as Port Said eventually came into view.

The ship sailed into the entrance of the Suez Canal past the statue of the Frenchman who built it, Ferdinand de Lesseps.

The time was about 2 p.m. when we disembarked and were herded into a waiting train, more like a cattle truck in fact, with wooden slatted seats which got very hard. All personnel had received a lecture prior to leaving the ship and told about the train journey. "It will stop from time to time" says the officer "and you will probably be accosted by traders on the platforms and maybe on the train. Do not buy any of these wares and take good care of personnel property and your kit. You are responsible for your belongings".

This information was very soon proved to be good advice. It was a long time before the train departed and, in the meantime, these Egyptian tradesmen were everywhere, almost in the luggage racks, selling trinkets of all sorts, ice cream, and drinks. Talk about the "Old Bazaar in Cairo". They would take English money and some of the lads were tempted. It was not till we were finally on our way that some blokes found things missing, watches, etc. They had been warned.

Ray and John outside Alakiefic Villa, our Egyptian home, 1948

No-one knew where we were going, in fact our route was more or less alongside the Canal down to the Suez area. The train stopped two or three times to drop off personnel at various other camps in the Canal Zone as it was known. And again, at all the stops we were invaded by "wogs" on the flog – and pinch. The Egyptians we came into contact with were known to us as "wogs" (W.O.G.S.). Some working for the Army had the letters printed on clothing they wore. It was said it indicated they were Working on Government Services, never confirmed to me. By this time it was getting dark which made security of possessions all the more difficult.

We eventually arrived at what I think was the end of the line. We disembarked in the dark, although there were a few lamp standards. We formed up into ranks and were marched the rest of the way into a transit camp, just about the most awful place I have ever been in before, during, or since Army days.

We marched straight to the dining room and guards were put on our kit, which was left outside. The food was quite good, as a matter of fact. After our meal we were marched off to our billets, lines of tents each sleeping about twelve blokes. Most of the beds were on nine inch legs, just off the ground in fact. Blankets were issued and we were all whacked out, so we soon had beds made up and settled down for the night. I thought it rather odd that the tents had no sides (or walls) but we were far too clapped out to bother about such things.

Parade was eight thirty in the morning, after ablutions and breakfast. I had no idea where to find the wash-houses or cookhouse. We were all up in good time anyhow, no laying in after the wakey wakey on the tannoy.

After breakfast there was the usual inspection and roll call. All the officers and N.C.O.'s at this transit camp were the most officious regimental b.....ds I ever came across – with the odd exception.

At the inspection the sergeant found something wrong with at least half of us. "Get your hair cut!" "Camp barber today!", "Take his name and number Corporal!", "Get those brasses cleaned you 'orrible little man!", "Get that webbing blancoed", and so on. It was worse than training and I was not used to it. Those that had their names taken were put on fatigues, peeling spuds, cleaning latrines, etc. All the others were found various jobs to do.

There were fire picket duties round the clock, firewatching in other words. The camp was very large, covering many acres or so it seemed. There was a ten foot chain link fence all the way round with the usual gate and guardroom, also a hut for those not actually on guard duty.

Some of the lads that had been out there before told us hair-raising stories about the Arabs – wogs for short. They would take most or all of their clothes off, smother themselves in grease, so that they could slip through the smallest hole, or under the wire fence, also one could not get hold of them.

During the first day we were all kept on the go almost at the double. After duties we realised that the tent "walls" were rolled up to the corners and, after being unrolled overnight, they had to be rolled up again before parade the next day. As my luck would have it, I found myself on guard duty on the first night; two hours on guard and four hours off, i.e. two stints of two hours each. There were two or three guard commanders who marched us to our posts and relieved us two hours later. Off duty, we could sleep in the guardroom hut.

So, before I knew it, I found myself guarding a length of perimeter fence, which was floodlit on the inside, and pitch dark outside the wire. I had a rifle and five rounds of ammunition in my pouch with instructions "not to fire without permission". The area was undulating, rocky and dusty underfoot. After the party moved off there was nothing in sight and the place was as quiet as death itself. We were ordered to patrol in a smart and orderly fashion up and down the fence, the length of about 400 yards up and down between two marker posts. Not at all like the Grenadier Guards outside Buckingham Palace.

It was very soon after that the stories of the antics of the wogs came flooding back. It was deadly quiet, but I heard noises at the side of me and behind all the while, but on glancing round there was nothing there. During the two hours, which seemed like all night, I saw the other guards once, once each that is. As one of them approached over the hill about 100 yards away, he scared me to death. However, the duties went off uneventfully for all of us and that was one of two nights I was kept from my little bed.

All these duties and fatigues were really just to keep people busy. Most of the lads were soon posted to units. There was a huge R.A.O.C. depot at Tel El Kabir, known as Tek for short. This base had supplied the Army in the Middle East with most of their requirements.

In 1948, the British Forces in Egypt were confined to the Canal Zone, a strip of land on the West bank of the Suez Canal. I do not think there were any troops on the other side of the Canal. However, there was access overland via the Sinai Desert to Palestine. There was a lot of trouble there at the time and the whole country was evacuated shortly after my arrival in Egypt. Being no historian, please find the facts in some other book. King Farouk and Queen Farida were on the throne of Egypt, "thinks" – they are welcome to it. However, the Egyptians wanted us out – only six years after our blokes saved their skins at El Alemein and many places to the West. Just to get our own back, we sang rude songs about Queen Farida, starting off "Queen Farida, queen of all the wogs". It is convenient that the rest is forgotten. Farida, if my memory serves me right, she was a nice-looking "bit of stuff".

Back to business, and, finally after almost a week, four of us were posted. I think the powers that be were looking for a round hole to put a square peg into. So it was that Jock Campbell, Eric Tyreman, Ron Brumly and yours truly were posted about fifteen miles on past Suez to a port detachment at Addabiya, actually on the Gulf of Suez. The detachment was attached to G.H.Q. Medical Store for the Middle East. We had a row of tents at one end of the camp and were quite separate from the Royal Army Medical Corps lines, although we did share the dining room, etc.

We were billeted in tents about fifteen feet square, four to a tent. They had another "skin" over the top, making it a double tent in effect. This kept it cool in the daytime and warm at night. The weather was often very cold at night; perhaps it felt more so after a very hot day. There were perspex windows in each "wall" and the whole thing stood on a concrete base. We had a proper wooden door and our tent had the name of Alekefic Villa (Alekefic is Arabic for "could not care less"). Next door was "Nil Carborundum Ignightum". The motor transport (M.T.) drivers and despatch riders dwelt therein.

Overall we were very comfy, much better than TEK I was told. We still had to lay some kit out and fold all blankets as before. This did mean they had a daily shake. As some of the blokes were demobbed we new ones took over their cupboards so we had somewhere to stow our gear. We were also permitted to display photos on the top. In fact it was quite homely.

From time to time we had uninvited "guests" in the form of beetles or cockroaches. They were huge, over two inches long and an inch across. They stayed at ground level and were harmless. For a bit of sport a boot would get thrown at one, then another, till there was a direct hit, then, as if by magic, out would come the ants to "cut it up" and drag it away, all in the space of about five minutes. One never left sweets lying about, because all that would be left was the wrapping, all nicely cleaned out.

Our beds were quite comfortable, and to keep nasties away old boot polish tins and lids were kept. The M.T. lads provided paraffin and each bed leg was placed in a tin, topped up with paraffin. I only had a problem once. Getting up one morning and stacking my blankets and biscuits, etc., I discovered a yellow scorpion under the pillow. He ran for it, boots came flying from all directions. One was well directed; it also was left for the ants to dispose of.

The detachment, as 25 A.S.D., was a working unit; therefore we had very little in the way of "regimental", apart from the usual Saturday inspection. It was not often the "old man" bothered, but one could not take anything for granted – cunning devils those officers.

The camp was at Attaka and Addabya docks were three miles down the road. There was only a track beyond this place, the end of the road and railway built by the British to service the military docks.

At the time a tremendous amount of ordnance stores were being despatched from Egypt to various destinations East; West bound went via Port Said.

Our job was to ensure all the stores arrived and were put on the right ship. Occasionally some stores would be imported but very small amounts. On these occasions lighters were sent out into "Suez roads" to meet the ship. Stores were loaded or off-loaded by ships' derricks. The stores would arrive by train, diesel driven; all the labour was done by local wogs. I did feel a bit sorry for these men, most were barefoot and only wore rags, but on the whole they seemed quite cheerful. They were controlled by their own foreman (Rice in Arabic). All the checking was done by other Egyptians, better dressed and better educated; they could add up anyhow.

On arrival my job was to be on the quay and check the checkers. In actual fact, a complete waste of time, but I did enjoy, up to a point, being on the docks.

We had a captain in charge, Capt. Anthony Roache, Tone for short – I don't think. There was a regimental sergeant major and a sergeant major. In the Ordnance Corps, just to be different they were known as Conductor and Sub Conductor respectively. Two or three staff sergeants, five sergeants, six or seven corporals and the same lance corporals and about fourteen privates made up the detachment. Numbers varied from time to time. There was a very high percentage of N.C.O.'s. Goodness knows why such a complement was needed and I cannot remember what they all did.

We started work at 8 a.m. on the docks in the winter months; that was after the usual ablutions, cleaning out the tent, laying out kit, having breakfast, plus parade roll call and inspection – five days a week. Work went on at weekends if there was a boat in. We did very little in between boats so it was swings and roundabouts.

The "old man", who had a tent to himself just up from us, arrived about 9 am and was usually gone about 12 noon. The Conductor, who lived in married quarters near Suez, arrived about ten to nine and he departed soon after the old man.

That left Sub Conductor Nicholson, I think his name was. Anyhow, he was always referred to as "Neep" or "Old Neep". He was one of the old brigade, must have done twenty years or more; a big bloke with a big voice and, after 12.30, "I'm in charge" attitude. I didn't like him much, and he didn't go a bundle on me either. I just tried to keep out of his way. I don't think anybody liked him really.

We had a big building close by called the Lock-up to hold onto stores inward or outward awaiting transport or shipment. If we were not busy that was a good place to skive off to. He knew where we were, but at least we were out of the way.

It was quite good now and again to go out into "the roads" on the barges to meet a ship. The highlight was to be invited on board and provided with a meal and a bottle or two of beer.

One day I was issued with a rifle and five rounds of ammo. I set off from the docks with a civilian (Egyptian) driver next morning in a 15 cwt truck with this big box in the back. The driver could only speak a few words of English and me a few words in Arabic – including a rude song about Queen Farida. However, I was told the driver knew exactly where he/we would have to go. We had rations for the day and provisions for an overnight stay.

All was well till we got to Suez when he drove straight into the out of bounds area and despite my anger and protest, he just carried on "Marleash effendi" – "Never mind my friend" says he. I was more than a bit concerned. However in about ten minutes we were out of the town and heading north.

It was very interesting passing through some of the villages with glimpses of the Canal from time to time and sometimes alongside the Sweetwater Canal. It was said if a squaddie fell in he needed all sorts of vaccinations and innoculations. It looked a bit grotty but folk were washing clothes in it here and there. And I must say the foremen (Rice) on the docks wore snow white gallibeers (nightshirts for short).

The Suez Canal goes south from Port Said and then enters into the Great Bitter Lake at Ismailia. Then a short canal went on to the Little Bitter Lake and then the final leg of the canal to Suez and Port Tewfic. Ships travelled in convoy most of the time, I understand, and on that journcy I saw six ships of various sizes sailing south. It was a strange sight. From about 500 yards away it looked as if the ships were sailing through the desert. I could only see a part of the boats below the superstructure and hear no sound at all, almost eerie. The rest of the trip was uneventful, a nice two days away.

We had a N.A.A.F.I., but can't recall using it that often. I did not like the beer, it was made from chemicals and called Stella. There was a "wog shop" selling confectionery which was patronised quite well; coconut bars and toffee and nut bars appealed to me. The ice cream man came round now and again, "Icy, you likee, two akher slicee" was the cry. Sweets were still on ration at home but I think ice cream was to be had, especially at the cinema when, during the interval, the usherette would have this tray in front of her selling monkey nuts, popcorn and ices.

There was the wog laundry known as the Dhobi and the bloke in charge was the dhobi walla. I used to take shirts and shorts in the summer. Smalls I took to the shower and trampled them underfoot and rinsed in the washbasin.

It was quite entertaining to watch the launderers at work. They had two army tents joined together and a big table for ironing and pressing. The place was lit with Tilley lamps and was very bright. They mainly worked in the evenings as people could take or collect laundry in off-duty hours; also, it was cooler for working. The "pressing department" always amused me – shirt collars and shorts were always starched. The liquid starch was in a basin and the dhobi walla would take a mouthful and spray it between his teeth onto the garment, never missing his aim, and then to work with the iron.

On arrival they marked each garment with a blue pencil and never got any items mixed up. I never did work out their system.

The blokes on the unit were a super lot and it really was a good place to be. All the N.C.O.'s were mates. We did not see much of the sergeants as they were using the Sergeants' Mess when off duty.

My best mate soon came upon the scene, Ray Wallis, who transferred down from Palestine. We have remained good friends to this day.

Probably the next event was me being promoted to Lance Corporal. The stripes were dished out with the rations at this place. I had no option, being marched into the old man's office and given the news.

I was soon to be in minor trouble on going back to work after Tiffin (no lunch here, it was tiffin – so there!). Old "Neep" wanted to know why my stripe was not sewn on. "Be properly dressed in the morning" bawls he. They put them on for me at The Dhobi.

There was a bus service into town in the evenings and at weekends. The "bus" was a canvas-covered lorry with seats in. It ran to Suez and on to Port Tewfic, which was on a sort of peninsular and was at the southern end of the Canal.

On occasions we would go into Suez, but it could be a bit rough and there were areas out of bounds to all service personnel. Apparently there were a few stabbings from time to time.

We were allowed to wear civilian clothes off duty and it was considered the thing to do. I took no civvies with me except a pair of shoes. As funds permitted a pair of slacks and a couple of shirts were soon hanging up behind the bed on the same hanger and underneath my best uniform.

Port Tewfic was a popular destination for us. There was a very nice open-air cinema where one could sit at the bar and watch the film; our pay did not often run to both. A lot of French people lived there and visited the cinema. The ladies were very fashionable and smart. I do not remember about their escorts.

In the summer there was a place to swim in the sea. It was quite a walk and I only went a few times. I almost learnt to swim; quite a bit of ducking went on and I was not too keen on that.

Another interest loomed up for some of us, a club for photography. I had bought myself a box "Brownie" camera of which hundreds of thousands must have been manufactured. Eric Tyreman had a super camera and knew how to use it. He started the club; he was a corporal by this time. Being attached to the Medical Corps, arrangements were made via the old man to obtain the necessary chemicals for developing and darkroom equipment. A small spare room was made available as a studio and a darkroom attached. We were instructed on taking photographs, although the scope was limited and film expensive; also developing and printing and glazing photos. It was all another interest. I bought the camera from a bloke who was "hard up". There were a few of them around, but fortunately no

British Military Hospital, Benghazi. My Mauritian friend Roland – I had yellow jaundice

thieves. It cost me £1.10.0 (1.50p).

One Sunday a group of us decided to explore in the Attaka mountains. They were quite high and rose quite quickly about two miles inland from the sea (Gulf of Suez). It was hard going as we made our way to a gully that looked promising. There were all sorts of tales about the mountains and possible inhabitants; wild cats and other beasts, hidey holes for robbers, etc., even talk of a residence for some posh Arab.

We took rations from the cookhouse and set off, getting quite high up and we were able to look down on parts of the coastline. The only other signs of life were a few birds, but we all enjoyed our unusual day.

During my time overseas, I had no leave. There was a trip being organised to Cairo, and my name was down to go. It was all cancelled and that was that.

There were lots of changes of personnel over the months. Our Conductor left, "Neep" departed (Hooray!) and Captain Roach became a Major. A snotty young Second Lieutenant was posted to the detachment. He had more bounce than a tuppenny balloon. He was about my age, and still wet around the ears. He had the idea of smartening the place up and us as well. "We will have some square bashing in the mornings before work" says he, "and I will call the roll and take the morning inspection".

Square bashing was at 5.30 am on the "Medics" parade ground. It was a bit of a "shower" that turned out that first morning, all having agreed not to put too much effort in and so on. The bright sun was just coming up good and strong and we were looking straight into it. I was squinting somewhat. "What are you laughing at Corporal?" says he. When I realised he was talking to me, I said "I'm squinting sir. There is nothing to laugh about".

The whole parade roared with laughter. Had they not, I may well have been on a charge. In the event, he could not put everyone on a charge. A person put on a charge for any offence had to be marched before the C.O. to answer the charge and found guilty or otherwise.

Fortunately I was never on a charge, or "fizzer," as we knew it. It was most pleasing and gratifying that our new boy soon got fed up and things got back to normal.

In the summer months when it was very hot, we started work at 6 o'clock and worked till tiffin. If the docks were very busy, there was another shift in the early evening.

And so life went on and we were all a very happy and mostly contented bunch.

It was about November when they decided to give me another stripe to put on my arm. Naturally, there was a bit more responsibility and there was also a bit more pay, which was very welcome. I always made my pay last the week, now we could draw what amount we needed, as long as we were in credit. I was only broke once for two or three days and it was an awful feeling. By the same token some of the lads sat down to play cards on pay night – not even going for their evening meal, and some were "cleared out" by the time I returned from the dining room – and it was more or less always the same ones.

I was now in charge of our tent, making sure it was clean and tidy before parade in the morning, calling the roll, and handing over to whoever was duty sergeant. The old man only appeared once in a blue moon.

Soon after there was another posting. About eight of us were posted to Benghazi in what was then Cyrenacre (Libya). Ray Wallis, "Geordie" Townson, myself, and Sergeant Geoff Larn, were part of the group. We were going to 624 Ordnance Depot at Duc a de Aosta Barracks about two miles from the centre of Benghazi town.

We went by train up to Port Said and went on board a tank landing craft called the "Evan Gibb". Tank landing craft are not the best ships to travel in, having a flat bottom, but we were in the Med., therefore there were no problems. The craft chugged along at a very slow rate and took three days to get to Benghazi.

The harbour was still littered with sunken ships that were bombed or shelled during the Desert War, their masts sticking up out of the water like dead trees. It was a short ride up to Duc a de Aosta. Quite a large camp after our cosy stay at Attaka. The place was an old Italian barracks and I don't think much had been done there since they left, probably in a hurry.

I found myself in a huge barrack room with seventy beds, a great long concrete "box" type building and no creature comforts to speak of, or write about.

The way of life was as before, but a lot more blokes. I don't think I would even have had any promotion here and, as before, the extra pay was most useful and corporals' duties were not all that demanding.

The food was not bad but not good. I suppose it was good food ruined by the cooks. "Who called the cook a twit?" answer, "Who called the twit a cook?"

The Ordnance Depot was about some two or three miles away, I think, on the outskirts of the town. We were transported to and from there twice a day. My memory fails me as exactly where to. We were in the back of a covered army lorry anyhow.

The depot held all sorts of stores with a Motor Transport (M.T.) Depot adjoining. I understand there were all sorts of vehicles stored there, tanks, lorries, you name it.

There had been a lot of thefts and pilfering from the whole depot, and the idea of our group being posted there was for us to do a stock take. However, when we arrived, it had been carried out, presumably by existing personnel so that their thieving activities could go on – who knows? Apparently, I/we found out later, the thefts still went on, mainly motor spares and chiefly tyres. After the War that sort of thing was in very short supply.

Our little group was distributed around the various offices and I had a job in "Provision". For the first time I had a proper job.

It was my task to go through the stock sheets which kept the records of what was in the stores; no mechanical or electrical aids then, or computers and the like. Some of the blokes did bash old-fashioned typewriters; there were no quill pens around though.

I was mainly on clothing and the like, checking what was in stock and ordering replacement stores. Quite easy, but I did slip up once, being called before the officer in charge of the department. I had got the order for Boots, Army, for the use of: Question from Officer I/C: "What is the most common size of boot would you say, Corporal?", "Size eight, sir" says little me, that's how I felt anyhow. "Why have you ordered so few then?" says he in the peaked cap, "Because we already have a lot in store sir" was my confident reply. It did not go down very well with "his nibs". But he had his say.

When off duty we often went into the town of Benghazi. We could walk. There was some sort of bus service, but my memory is a blank beyond that. There was also the Arab "garry" to come back on, a horse-drawn four wheel carriage. The old Arab drivers were not always too keen to transport some service personnel because sometimes the blokes would pile out and run for it without paying. I think that was how some of them learned to swear in Arabic.

There was a Salvation Army place about twenty minutes' walk away, on the road to the town. That was quite nice to visit for a supper of ham and eggs and the like; no fish and chips. It was good and cheap and the place had a nice atmosphere.

There was the Globe cinema in town showing quite modern film releases and The News, which interested me. The signature tune at the Globe was "Japanese Sandman" and it took me years to find out the title of this song – a very nice picture house.

There was also a very nice club called The Wavell Arms (named after General Wavell) where there was a library, quiet rooms, a restaurant and bar, and, I seem to recall a games room. Ray Wallis still blames me for getting him tipsy there one night. A number of us had indulged in a very nice supper and one of the party, John Meikle, a Scot, suggested we had a liqueur. I only just about knew what it was, but we all agreed it was a good idea and a tray of small glasses arrived with clear water-like liquid in them, about double the measure that would be served here. A lovely orange sort of taste – moreish. I learned a long while after it was cointreau. Anyhow, we had a few with mixed results and "old" Ray wasn't quite himself.

Benghazi still had the look of being knocked about a bit during the War. It had changed hands a few times. The harbour was still full of sunken ships with masts and funnels sticking up out of the water. There were lots of gaps along the streets where property had once stood, but most of the rubble had been cleared away.

Time went on and Christmas came. Our Scots mate found an Arab shop selling all sorts of booze so a whole gang of us went Christmas shopping. I remember buying a bottle of cherry brandy, also nuts, dates and fruit. Most of it had gone by Boxing Day. I didn't want the ants to have any of it, although there were very few in our massive billet.

All the interiors of the camp were plain and dull. There was nothing we could do to brighten the place up for Christmas.

I did go to breakfast, which was a full cooked job. The poor old Catering Corps had a busy time over the holiday. The dining room was decorated up somewhat at lunchtime (tiffin), when the officers waited on us hand and foot with a full Christmas menu and Stella beer, which I did not much care for. However, I did indulge in a couple of pints. We had all the trimmings, plum pudding, mince pies, nuts and fruit. Not bad at all, then the officers went off to their do, not to be seen again for two days.

As personnel got demobbed, I was now in charge of this billet, over seventy blokes, and getting all the bed places brushed out and the duty blokes to sweep out the centre was a bit of a nightmare. Brooms were always in short supply so I took to having a wander round the other billets some evenings and pinching any broom that was lying around. I gave them to reliable chaps at strategic places up and down the billet. It worked for a few days, but there were always others on the clifty (clifty – Arabic for thieving).

Being a corporal, I had to take my duty as guard commander from time to time. The guard room was between our depot and the M.T. depot. I think our guard was from about 7 p.m. till 7 a.m. There were foot patrols in the depot and the guard was changed every two hours. I could not sleep but the others could, between duties, i.e. two hours on and four off.

The M.T. depot was guarded by a Mauritian company and they had their own commander who reported to me every two hours. One night, I was having a job to keep awake when I was soon very much alerted by shots being fired in the M.T. depot from a Sten gun. Due to a lot of theft of vehicle parts, the Mauritians had live arms, "up the spout" as well, ready to fire.

There was a clatter of army boots running towards the gate. Their guard commander and a guard with his Sten gun. Four of us went on a tour of the depot but anyone could have hidden anywhere. There were old Army trucks and M.T. stores piled high all over the place, all in fairly neat rows and various degrees of decay.

It was a bit scary, but nothing like I imagine the War would have been like, with the enemy probably not far away. However, nothing or no-one was found and there were no more problems that night. I prepared a full report for the orderly officer on duty, who I did not see, and never heard any more about it. I did learn not long before I was due for demob that the whole "ring" of thieves had been caught. Apparently, it involved officers and men of our depot and local people, Arab men. I did wonder if the orderly officer of that night was one of them.

It was about the end of March 1949 when I awoke one morning feeling very unwell. I did not go to breakfast and for the first time since joining the Army, reported sick. This meant a trip to B.M.H. (British Military Hospital), Benghazi by one of our lorries fitted out with seats, etc.

I duly arrived, was examined by a doctor and admitted, not being told what the problem was. I felt awful and I think slept most of the next twenty-four hours, when I was visited by a "posse", including a starchy old matron, apart from two ladies at the "Sally Bash", the first female I had spoken to in fourteen months. She said that I must go back to my unit. My reply was something like "you will have to carry me then". I had a job to get to the W.C. at the end of the ward, which, by the way, was a Nissen hut. "Oh well" says she, "We will let you stay for one more day". When they came round next morning I was as yellow as a canary – yellow jaundice. The matron did apologise. She said "We thought you were malingering".

My stay there was about six weeks and it was very good; very nice meals, also radio and books and newspapers. Some of the blokes came visiting. The only worry I had there was one day all the bathrooms were busy, so I sneaked into one belonging to the next ward, only to find out it was full of V.D. patients!

My fellow patients in our ward got me worried, I can tell you, and I did not dare say anything to the doctor or matron when they came round. Anyhow, all was well. My fellow patients were a nice crowd and the chap in the next bed was a Mauritian, one of the M.T. guards. His name was Roland and he spoke good English. We hit it off really well.

Some of my mates from the depot came visiting from time to time, including Ray Wallis, who was getting excited at the prospect of demob. He is just a month or so older than me and therefore had a lower demob number.

Eventually I was discharged back to my unit and was more than a little angry to find no-one had put my belongings into store for safe keeping. Some of my kit had been stolen as there was no means of locking anything away. I had also bought some carved wooden picture frames for photos from home, etc., also other bits and pieces to treasure; these items were made by German P.O.W.'s who were billeted in a camp near ours in Egypt. They were just about repatriated when we left, and now they were all gone and there was nothing to be done about it.

I was discharged with light duties, which meant work as usual, but no guard duties. All I had to do now was wait for my number to come up – No. 108. The National Service intakes started at 100 in January 1947, and I was in the 8th fortnightly intake.

The good news eventually came and some gear was handed in. One lovely morning, we, about twenty of us, jumped into the back of an Army lorry and set off for Tobruck. Our journey took us inland for a while, calling at an Army base at Barci, and then on through interesting countryside for an overnight stay on the coast at Derna, a small town that got knocked about a bit during the Desert War.

Although it was known as the Western Desert, it was not like the Sahara. It was for most part undulating with scrublike bushes. They looked prickly as well. Some parts were flat and one could see for miles. We went through a pass on entering Derna; steep hills up and down with hairpin bends. The transit camp was rather basic to say the least.

In the evening we had a walk into town, shopping for things to bring home as gifts. The only thing I can recall buying was a length of dress material for sister Stella.

I had a bad night's sleep in Derna on one of those beds that was only about nine inches above the ground. A lot of us were bitten by bed bugs. They are a grey colour in the evening, so I was told, but in the morning they were red, full of my blood. The itching wore off by lunchtime. Some of the lads had a bright idea and just before we departed, all the beds were piled into a heap, the mattresses ripped open, and the straw stuffed between beds and put on the top. A match was put to the straw, which burnt the little devils that lived in the bed springs. This did not please a sergeant, but we had to go – there was a boat to catch.

On we go, mile after mile along the coast road, and I did wonder what could have been told about the place which changed hands a few times during the desert battles. The surrounding countryside was still littered with burnt out vehicles and guns, although I think a lot had been cleared away.

One vivid memory that will last with me forever is the War Cemeteries where Italian, German and Allied service personnel are buried. Huge areas with acres of white crosses stretching as far as the eye can see as we approach Tobruk, all so neat and tidy. I expect they are still as immaculate today, looked after by the War Graves Commission.

We drive straight into the docks and transfer to lighters (barges) to take us about a mile out into the bay where the "Empress of Australia" is anchored. Only vessels with a shallow draft can get into Tobruk habour. There were many more masts and funnels sticking out of the water here

Bon Voyage to Benghazi – Ray Wallace (2nd from left), and me (fourth from left)

than in Benghazi.

Out we sail, slowly to the waiting ship that seems to get much longer as we approach, alongside and up the gangplank to be shown our deck. Thankfully we had bunks and not hammocks.

There were a lot of other service personnel on board; mainly R.A.F. and we were all surprised to learn that the next port of call was Port Said, so we were going further away from home. It did not bother me unduly; a cruise at the expense of the British taxpayer was O.K. by me. It was only two days to Port Said on this troopship and soon came the time to disembark, humping all our gear in kit bags, etc. Down the gangplank into a big lighter, when over a loudhailer came the order for two sergeants and twelve corporals to report back on the ship. Some officer was bawling "you, you, and you", etc., so back up the gangplank goes I and my kit. They wanted personnel for an officers' baggage guard on the ship for the duration of the ship's stay at Port Said, which turned out to be three days.

I was the last to be "chosen". Yes, I did have a choice. There were corporals all over the place. The officers' baggage was in a store behind a huge iron grille-type door and we had just to be there. I think it was two hours on duty and six off.

After sorting our duties out, with two sergeants in charge, we had the pick of the bunks, so we elected to go forward on E Deck, the very best berths for "other ranks". It was a very cushy number. The ship was berthed opposite all the main buildings along the waterfront which was, in fact, some way into the north entrance to the Suez Canal. It was busy from time to time with various ships usually in convoy entering or leaving the Canal.

The food on the boat was the best I had enjoyed in the Army, and nicely presented as well, still on the stainless steel trays with a depression for the various courses and one for a mug.

Eventually, the homeward-bound mates embarked once again. They had had a dreadful time in the transit camp not far away, chivvied about and found lots of irritating things to do, when all they wanted was to get home.

We set sail and waved (sort of two finger job) our goodbyes to Egypt. At long last we were sailing westward. No more duties for the baggage guard; just a nice easy cruise home.

We called at Tripoli (the one in Cyrenacre, now Libya) to pick up some personnel, only anchoring in Tripoli "roads" some one and a half miles off shore. Soon under way again for the next port of call, Malta. We sailed into the huge natural harbour of Valleta and berthed stern onto the quay, next to a posh yacht which we were informed once belonged to Adolf Hitler. True or not, I know not. We were there about five hours and very soon the Maltese traders were alongside selling their wares. You name it, they had it. The merchandise was put in a basket, hauled up on a rope for inspection, and either the goods or the money was returned likewise. Sad to say, more than one item was kept and not paid for, the thief rushing off to hide his ill-gotten gains amongst his kit.

This was the last port of call and we were soon on our way once more; an uneventful trip, apart from getting up in the early hours one morning to see Gibraltar all lit up. I could just make out the famous rock silhouette fashion.

We eventually arrived at Southampton, disembarked, and onto a train, a special troop train bound for Aldershot.

We were pushed from pillar to post, handing in part of our kit. I hoped to keep my greatcoat but was not successful. There were no demob suits for National Service men, but we kept our best uniform. Well, we had to go home wearing something, did we not?

It is a fact that in the Army one sometimes uses language that is not normally used; swear words actually and one of the parting shots from one bloke was "Well mates, when you get home, don't say will you pass the "b....y" salt".

There was quite a lot of documentation, as one can imagine, including settling up the pay. I think we were paid for one or two weeks after demob, and I picked up about £50.00 in credits for wages or pay not drawn.

The final item was a travel warrant to get me home, well, to Coventry railway station anyhow. It was all a bit of a blur after that. I think I 'phoned someone to say I was on my way. There were very few 'phones about then, but I think the Wises had one, put in by Harold Hewitt, who had now remarried and was living and farming Blind Hall.

I arrived at Coventry station and got myself to Pool Meadow bus station, complete with a big kit bag on my shoulder, and caught a Midland Red bus to Meriden. For once in my life I went all extravagant, walked along to Shirley's Garage in Meriden, and hired their taxi to take me the mile and a quarter home. It cost half a crown, or 12p.

I really did not know what to do first, but as it was almost tea time, a bit of home cooking, etc. and a real cup of tea, or three, was just what the doctor ordered. There was home-made cake and raspberry jam and a lovely salad. All five of us sat down to do it justice. And just before starting mine, I enquired if someone would pass me the "so and so" salt. Well, did you ever? But all was well after a short silence. The meal progressed,and that was the only time I slipped up. I do remember how nice it was to be in my own bed again, with sheets and pillow cases, which we did not have anywhere during my two years plus for King and country.

My mother had written to me at least once a week and sometimes more often, and I like to think I was good to answer them all within a day or two. I knew all that was going on and what everyone was up to, etc. News of John Kirby and so on. He (J.K.) I think finished up as a sergeant in the Royal Army Service Corps. He could drive before going into the Army but was not allowed on the road. However, he was taught to drive in his early days and spent some time teaching others. He was also involved in training new intakes. He was demobbed some time after me. He had pressure put on him to sign on for an Army career.

In her letters my mother had told me of a new dancing venue that had opened up – The Matrix on the Fletchampstead Highway, quite close to the Standard Cinema (now the gambling casino).

Apparently, all and sundry were flocking there, so that was my destination on my first Saturday night. "Old big 'ead" went in his uniform (the last time I wore it). It was hot, but I had not been shopping for new civvies. The Matrix was the works canteen for the Gauge and Tool Works, and probably then was Matrix Machine Tools, later to become Matrix Churchill, the firm involved in the supply of arms to the Middle East, which included the barrel of a huge gun. The dust has not completely settled now in 1998.

However, to The Matrix I toddled on my bike, and yes, it was very nice. Jack Owens had an orchestra of fifteen musicians, five saxaphone, four trumpet, three trombone, piano, drums and double bass. Two vocalists sang, Ann and Hughie, as Jack waved his baton about.

The place was packed and we used to stand up all evening there. The band usually played three tunes per set, i.e., three waltzes, quicksteps and so on. After the first number, ushers would push the crowd back to one end to make more room for the dancers. All the staff were very nice, as were the dancers. Without sounding "toffee nosed", it was perhaps a cut above the average. We paid three shillings and sixpence (17p) admittance, which was a bit more than one would pay in town. In those days there were probably six or more large ballrooms (or dance halls) in Coventry. There was the Drill Hall, Queen Victoria Road, the G.E.C. in Stoke, the Rialto Casino in Coundon and also, Courtaulds, the Liberal Club, to name a few.

The Matrix became a firm favourite and the first big hit was "12th Street Rag" in June 1949.

There was no bar, in common with lots of dance halls, so, one either went without or had a drink before going in. I usually chose the latter.

Cranes had a shop and, I think, the post office in Stoneleigh. They were the caterers where coffee and tea was available, also sandwiches and cakes.

CHAPTER 9

Back to Civvy Street

One of the first things to consider, naturally, was getting a job, and at that time there must have been very little or no unemployment. Just four years after the end of the war, lots of things were still rationed; I cannot recall what was or was not. However, coal was still rationed until the said 1950s, as priority was given to factories and manufacturing industries. Europe was still recovering from the ravages of war, yes, and who made the best job of that? No hard feelings.

One could just walk into most jobs, and I applied for and got a job in the Parks Department of Coventry Corporation. The parks and gardens in Coventry were maintained very well in those days. Wages offered were £4.15.od (4.75p) per week, for a 48 hour week, the norm. However, one evening before I started, a Mr. Goode called to see me. He was head gardener at "The Moat", Coventry Road, Berkswell. Mr. and Mrs. Jarrard lived there and he was the chief solicitor at Rotherham and Co of the Quadrant in Coventry. Mr. Goode offered me £5.00 per week for the same hours and it did not take me long to decide to go and work there. Once again, yes the bench was still in the potting shed, but I was not caught out a second time.

Under Mr. Goode was Les Clarke, who lived at South Lodge, at the end of The Moat Drive opposite Baulk Lane. Betty Edge cycled out from Widrington Road in Coventry, and I made up the work team.

There had been a lot of changes at The Moat; the gardens were still very nice, but nothing like pre-war, and the days of our visits to the swimming pool.

We had to look after the gardens round the house. The huge kitchen garden was still there, looking tired. In addition, there was a six acre field used as a market garden where all sorts of crops were grown, salads, early potatoes, runner beans, cabbage, cauliflower, and sprouts, to name a few.

Mother, father and sister Margaret in our garden, 1948

The field was irrigated and the old swimming pool used as a reservoir.

I cannot remember where the produce went to; perhaps the wholesale market or a factory canteen. Mr. Jarrard was a shareholder in A.C. Wickman who made and restored machine tools in the factory next to Massey-Ferguson on Banner Lane.

Not all that long after I arrived, Mr. Goode left and Les Clarke took over as head gardener. Ted Treadwell arrived on the scene; no disrespect, but he was a ham-fisted farm labourer and not much of a gardener. I enjoyed my time at The Moat, although sprout picking and other jobs in the winter did not always go down well.

A day or two before starting work, I went to the Royal Show. Ron Webber, who was bailiff at Wheatleys' Home Farm organised a coach to the Show which was held at Attingham Park, near Shrewsbury. The Royal Show was held at different venues around the country until it came to Stoneleigh in 1963. My father and I were joined by Ted Dawson, who was only about fifteen years' old at the time.

However, we did very well, as Ted's father, Jack, had instructed Ted to visit all the trade stands of the firms of whom Jack was a client; so we visited a seed firm, also a fertilizer company, and so on, ending up in the hospitality tent, and supplied with beer, refreshments, and even lunch on one stand. All very nice, including the weather, which was hot and sunny. We kept in quite high spirits all day, and it was the custom then to stop at a pub on the way home. Ron Webber had quite a job getting us out of the pub and onto the coach again. Happy days!

By now, of course, my little sister, Margaret, was growing up; six years' old and getting on well at school, and Stella was working at a laundry in Coventry. Mother was, as always, a very hard-working and busy housewife, also a member of the Mothers' Union and Women's Institute. My father was ALWAYS the same, as long as he had his three square meals a day, his old Woodbines, and a pint or two now and again, he was happy and contented.

At the time, there was a lot of big band music on the radio, often at teatime, which I had on; he did not go on that very much, but he put up with it without too much complaining. There were lots of big dance bands then; Ted Heath and his music, Geraldo, Ambrose, The Squadronnaires (R.A.F.), The Blue Rockets (Army), Harry Gold and his Pieces of Eight (Jazz) and Oscar Rabin, to name a few.

Some short time after coming home my mother suggested I treat myself to a new suit. I did need one. Also, why not a new push bike? perhaps a racer. This I did, and she went with me to Haywards at the bottom of Hertford Street to choose material and for me to be measured up. I ended up with a very nice two-piece single-breasted blue suit and it cost me nineteen guineas (£19.95p), almost four weeks' wages

Then, I went out and bought an Elswick cycle, with dropped handlebars and three-speed Derailia gears. Back-side in heaven and head in hell type of thing. That was my credit money from my Army days gone, but there were no regrets at all. I could, and did, go to all sorts of places in my suit, and always felt at home, and with my new bike, I had the means of getting there.

John Kirby eventually came home and we spent a lot of time in each other's company, although he was a bit "Will o' the wisp" and sometimes unreliable. He went to work at Standard Motors and he soon had a motor bike. I heard his bike go past The Moat long before my knocking off time. He did start work before me in the morning, but truth to say, I was sometimes envious of him. He lived at Banbury Cottage, opposite the school in Berkswell Village and I would sometimes call in on my way home from work and arrange to go to Balsall pictures, nip into the 'phone box and book the seats, and call for him later on, only to be told by his mum that he had gone out with Eddie Horsley, who lived opposite at Grove Cottage. But such was his personality that I could never fall out with him.

Times then I thought were good. I was either working, sleeping or playing. There were lots of mates, all the Wise family just up the road. Beryl, the eldest, then I think Des, who was a "regular" in the Royal Marines. He played a cornet in the Marines' Band, then came Audrey, who joined the A.T.S., The Women's branch of the Army known now as W.R.A.C. (Women's Royal Army Corps). Derek is my age and worked on the farm for Harold Hewitt, as did his father, Jack Wise, the cowman. Joan was Stella's

'Grandad' and 'Nan Nan' Squires, April 18 1948

Nellie and Albert with Margaret 1948. Father loved his Woodbines

friend and then came Enid, and last in line, Geoff, who when they came to Four Oaks Farm was very young, not started school.

Four Oaks Farm was "Open House". One of those places where the house was always full of teenagers and we were all welcome, as long as we went home at a reasonable time. One bloke did not always know when to depart; he is still talked about today, in fact, he is often still last to arrive and last to go.

Kirby's house in the village was similar, always full of visitors, lots of them young ladies, probably chasing John, who was a great favourite with the girls.

The Wises all loved their cup of tea. Very little coffee was drunk then. Tea was on ration, but Ruby Wise made the tea go a long way. We all had a cup.

There was always something going on in the village from September to June. There was usually a dance in The Reading Room about every fortnight in aid of various village organisations or probably The Red Cross or St. John's Ambulance Brigade. Again, no licenced bar; liquid refreshments at The Bear beforehand, during the interval, or both, depending on the state of one's pocket usually. Organisers had to be careful which band was booked. More than once they had to be dragged out of The Bear at the interval. However, they would often play for an extra fifteen minutes, except on Saturdays when everything stopped at 11.45 p.m.

There were no electronics, often not even a microphone. The musicians carried their instruments and music in under their arms, except the drummer. There was usually a quartet, quite enough for The Reading Room, hardly ever a vocalist or guitar, but often a double bass.

There was always a dance after the Church Fete in June, organised by Mrs. Kenneth Hope (Joan). People had more energy then and would be involved at the fete and then dance till 11.45; also probably prepare refreshments for the interval. Also, a lot of the menfolk would be at work till dinnertime.

There was always a dance at Balsall Institute on Saturdays (now the Village Hall on Station Road). Jack Pierce and his "Modernaires" would play. He was also the local electrician and later on had a shop in Balsall

Common, selling all sorts of electrical appliances. I can see him now, puffing away at his ancient, it looked it anyhow, saxaphone. As the evening wore on his face went from white to pink and then red. He was assisted by a pianist and drummer.

Stan and Eileen Fisher were almost always there. This brother and sister would take the floor for a tango. Not many people could manage the tango, and I was one of them. But Stan and Eileen would put a real show on, scattering anyone that got in the way. Quite an amusing interlude. Stan would also have a go on the drums now and again.

I would only go to Balsall if there was no alternative. The dance did not liven up till well after 10 p.m. when most folk came in from the local pubs (they closed at 10 p.m. at the time). There was just over an hour of real good fun, and that was it; also, the R.A.F. lads came in from their station at Honiley and some of us lads never got much of a look-in. John Kirby always did alright.

Sunday afternoons we often went to the pictures (cinema) in Coventry. Quite a crowd of lads and usually just one girl, Mary Shilvock. We caught the 1.45 bus, which got us into town in good time to get to the Opera House in Hales Street. It had been an opera theatre once, with stalls, circle and upper circle or "the gods". The place was an awful dump but we went almost regardless of what film was being shown, all of us trying to sit by Mary.

After the performance we just had time to catch the bus back to Berkswell. Mary would go on home to Beechwood. All or most of us lads would go home for tea, then congregate again either at our house or Wises to play cards – often Pontoon – for matches.

The first summer back home (1949) I did quite a lot of cycling. We were too far away from Coventry for me to join a club so many nights I would set off on my own, probably about 7.30 and bike to Evesham and back by a different route. It was very seldom anyone passed me on a bike, but Derrick Wagstaff could give most of us a run for our money.

Towards the end of 1949 I decided to join the Balsall and District Horticultural Society. Being me, I chose the wrong evening. It was the A.G.M. and I went home as a committee member. I had not been on any committee before and found it all very interesting; it was nice to be involved. Other committee members were the President, Mr. Jarrard, my boss at The Moat, Mr.F.W.E. Seeley, Headmaster of Balsall Street School, Charlie Nutt, who ownd the transport cafe where Arden Close is now (next to the Shell Garage). Albert Reeves was Secretary and he drove the railway lorry delivering goods from Coventry station around Balsall and the local area. Arthur Wilkins and David Crosswell were great rivals at show time, as were Mrs. McLaren and Mrs. Savage in the flower arranging classes. Committee meetings were held in the cafe and later on in a room at the newly-built Methodist Church in Station Road.

Christmas 1949 was looming up and my mother suggested I make holly wreaths for a bit of extra cash. The question was, where? In the end, we put old sheets down on the floor in the front room, a trellis table was rigged up, and I went on from there, acquiring moss for the frames from down in the woods and holly from Mercote Hall, by permission of Captain Wheatley-Hubbard of Berkswell Hall.

The frames and wire, etc. came from Coventry Wholesale Market in the Barracks Square, Coventry, where Shelton Square is now.

The next job was to get orders and again Mother suggested Mrs. Pope who kept the shop in Berkswell village, so off I went and enquired if she would buy my wreaths wholesale to resell. She declined and said that if I liked to take in a sample she would take orders. This I did and that Christmas I made about thirty wreaths, a lot of which people collected from the shop.

The problem getting them to the shop was solved by threading the wreaths onto a clothes prop with Father and I carrying one end each. We probably looked a funny sight on a dark Sunday evening while all the "good folks" were singing away in Church at the Carol Service. Wreath-making at Christmas was to go on until 1996. By that time I had made in the region of 25,000 holly wreaths.

It was about this time (1949) when it was decided to form a Rover Scout Crew, senior scouts in other words. Harold Hewitt who was farming Four Oaks Farm, which he owned, was a tenant farmer at Blind Hall where he lived. Before the War he had been involved with the Coventry 38th Group. I think it was at Sibree Hall in Warwick Row. However, he volunteered to steer us in the right direction but did not wish to be involved too much.

Quite a few joined – Bill Green, George Teague, Scoutmaster of the Berkswell Troop, Derek Wise, Trevor Lowe, Bob Thompson, Derrick Wagstaff and a few others. Captain Wheatley-Hubbard provided a place for us to meet which was an old grain store in the stable yard at Berkswell Hall. One entered a room about twenty foot square by climbing over a three foot wall, persumably to keep vermin out of the grain. There was a door above the wall.

We acquired a coke stove and set it up in one corner with a metal chimney going out through the wall and into the kitchen garden. George Teague provided a metal work bench and all sorts of equipment arrived from all sorts of places. After a coat or two of paint, the place became quite respectable

.We met up once a week on a Thursday evening. I had the job of going down and lighting the stove on my way home from work. No-one else would volunteer. In actual fact, the Rover Crew never actually got round to much scouting activities, but one or two "good deeds" were undertaken.

A major project was levelling the village green in Berkswell, under the expertise of Ron Hurford, but the actual seeding work was disappointing.

Six of us went to the Chelsea Flower Show and on our return the seeding had been done by Gordon Thompson, working for Mr. Kenneth Hope. As a parish councillor, I think he must have had the grass seed which was harrowed in with a horse-drawn harrow, which left huge hoof marks all over the area. We were not too pleased, but it must have been Ron who raked out the hoof marks and the result is for all to see. Some time later the Green was surrounded with very nice stone kerbs. All's well that ends well.

One Sunday we arranged a hike, which was a bit ambitious, but we were all reasonably fit and young. However, we met at the Rover Den about 10 a.m., bringing a packed lunch and something to cook on our return. Bill Green was to blame for the planning and we set off up to the Kenilworth Road at Balsall Common, taking to the footpath that went via Needler's End and past the Saracen's Head pub on Balsall Street to Fen End. Then, on to Chadwick End and Baddesley Clinton. We then set off cross-country for Kenilworth and returned to Berkswell via the disused railway-line.

I am not sure how I and some of the others made it back, but there were some bottles of beer waiting, and after getting the hotplates going (we had some means of frying and boiling kettles, etc.), a real old fry-up soon put us almost right again, but I was still a little stiff next morning.

In the early days we (or rather I) ran a dance in The Reading Room to get some funds together. It was like getting "blood out of a stone" getting very modest "subs" out of some blokes; also the same problem getting help to do things.

Anyhow, I booked the room and a band, who were four players from Jack Owen's Orchestra, who played at The Matrix. I called them the "Jack Owen Quartet". Fancy names were not yet in vogue. Tickets were printed, also posters put up all over the place.

Les Clarke manned the door for us and the whole event was most successful, which was just as well, because our total assets were just 12p at the start of the evening. That was the first event that I had organised.

Back to our "country bumpkin" trip to Chelsea Flower Show, I think in 1951, with Ron Hurford and Jack Smith from Tile Hill; Bill Green, also Jim Eppey, who was a maintenance man at The Moat, a Cockney and good at drinking beer. There was also me and A.N. Other, whose name escapes me.

We caught an early train from Coventry Station and arrived at The Show at about 11 a.m. We had a good look round The Show, keeping off the beer because it was very expensive on the showground. Leaving the Show at about 4 p.m. we were at the mercy of Jim Eppey who knew London very well.

We all got into a taxi somehow and went up West. First port of call was a wash and brush up, then into where I think it was The Dorchester, in Park Lane. The carpets were over the top of my ankles, well almost. We were shown a table and enjoyed afternoon tea of scones and jam; also toasted teacakes and fancy cakes. An orchestra – well, a group of musicians –

was playing Palm Court type music and, yes, it was oh so grand. I did feel a bit out of place but Jim said "Our money is as good as anyone else's", and, of course, he was right.

After a pleasant hour or so, Jim booked seats for the "Follies Begére" at The Windmill Theatre, second house. "Now for a drink" says he, Jim. We went on a real old pub crawl, I know not where, and was soon past caring anyhow. We did get to the theatre in plenty of time. It was a bit risque for those days with nudes on stage, but they must not move, not even a muscle, or even wobble.

We did almost get thrown out or requested to leave. A very attractive female came on in a skimpy red two-piece outfit, all covered in sequins and spangles – the lot plus! – and hanging from her bra, which must have been of very good material, hung two huge gold and red tassels. Well, they swung to and fro, then up and down; next they were whizzing round clockwise, then the other way. There were eyes that were about to pop out of heads when this clever little lady got one spinning one way and one in the opposite direction, like the propellers on an aircraft in fact. It was at this moment that Jim stood up on his seat and shouted out at the top of his voice "How's that for muscle control?".

After the show, we made our way back to Euston Station and caught the midnight train which went via Northampton and arrived at Coventry about 3 a.m., clapped out and broke – us – not the train.

The Rover Crew did a little entertaining now and again. One evening, the Rector, Rev. Henry Bursell, was one of our guests. It was my lot to do the inviting and he duly arrived. We discussed all sorts of topics, but Jim Eppey (who was older than most of us, married with three children) got into a very heated argument with the Rector and they were going hammer and tongs at each other, much to my embarrassment and others too. Anyhow, it all ended O.K. and we all departed, but I felt a need to go and apologise to the reverend gentleman, which I did. He was most gracious and said it was the best discussion he had had for years and could he perhaps come again. He never did.

One game we played was Tippit. Three players sit each side of a table. One team has a small coin and six hands go under the table. The coin is placed in one hand. On the command of "Hup" six clenched fists are placed on the table, then one member of the opposing team has to locate the coin; two points for a guess in one, one point for a correct second or third guess. All the team have a go and then the other team do the guessing.

There are all sorts of devious tricks to try and kid the opponents. One trick is to clench the fist tight and make the knuckles go white, to make the guesser think the coin is held within.

This all may sound a bit simple, but after a beer or two, it can become hilarious, or is it that "little things please little minds". I think not, as we used to challenge the Twelve Club to Tippit evenings. What on earth is

the Twelve Club one may ask. "A very good question" says I. The Twelve
Club (now defunct) was started from the residue of the Home Guard.
When the Home Guard was disbanded, some of the members decided to
form this club. It consisted of just twelve members meeting once a month
on the twelfth, or on a Monday if the twelfth came on a Saturday or Sunday.

They met in a small reserved room at the Brickmakers' Arms in Station
Road. Each member took a turn to organise the refreshments and invite
any guests. Original members I can recall are Les Clark (ex sergeant),
"Bunny" Hare, an officer, Bob Jennings, Eddie ("Willy") Williams and Jim
Heartfield.

The club did one or two good turns in the parish. One was to provide a
seat on the village green. It is still there and often used by the occupants of
The Flats, formerly The Almshouses. I do think it about time that building was given a decent name.

As members died or moved away, others were invited to take their
place. George Teague was one.

Time went on, and I still kept in touch with my Army pal, Ray Wallis,
who lived in the village of Bonsall, just north of Cromford, near Matlock in
Derbyshire. I did cycle up there once or twice and was made very welcome
by Ray's parents. I would explore the area whilst Ray was at work, and
enjoy evenings together. He has a brother, Brian, and sister, Vera. They
have all been to Berkswell at different times.

I still had the odd spare time job here and there. Ron Hurford had an
area of ground in Cornets End where he grew all sorts of shrubs and perennials to use in his work as a landscape gardener after being demobbed from
the R.A.F. I used to go to his garden when I had some spare time and spent
time hoeing and weeding.

Ron was one of the few that tried to get on to the District Council –
Meriden Rural District Council as it was then.

He began married life in one of the Almshouses in Berkswell village
and by this time had a wife and two daughters, with not much prospect of
getting housed by the Council. He did not win the election, but was housed
fairly soon after at Benton Green Lane, where he and Pat still live.

Really at this time there was hardly a dull moment. Thinking about it,
that is how my life has been, a lot of work and a lot of play. In fact, I should
probably have spent more time at home, being off out somewhere most
evenings.

I had not been long out of the Army when Les Clark, the head gardener at The Moat, asked if I was interested in buying a greenhouse. I suppose
really nothing was further from my mind, but my mother has always
encouraged me to think about it as a means of making a "bit on the side".

Mr. Pope, who was the farm bailiff at The Moat, wanted to get rid of
this greenhouse which he had bought for his daughter in 1939. I went to
have a look and, being only about eleven years old, it was in very good

condition; measuring twelve feet by eight feet with wooden ship-lap boarded sides, complete with staging and a boiler and four inch hot water pipes for heating; also, a quantity of seed trays and clay pots. No plastic then.

I was hooked and paid Mr. Pope £35.00 for the lot which he had delivered to our house in Meriden Road by one of the farm wagons. The cost amounted to about nine weeks' wages and made a big dent in my savings. The only thing now was to get cracking and make the investment pay. With hindsight, that greenhouse was one of the main reasons why I eventually took the decisions I did in later life.

I grew tomatoes, bedding plants and pot plants, not having a lot of trouble selling the produce. Again, my mother was a good salesperson, which did help a lot.

A few lines now on a few characters of that time, the early fifties.

Jack Fennel lived at The Spring in Cornets End. Before retiring, he was chief tester at the Daimler Car Factory in Coventry. One of his jobs was to deliver new Daimlers to the Royal Family at their various palaces and houses. He liked a pint, especiallywhen someone bought him one. He kept quite a few pigs and collected "swill" from one or two factory canteens in an ex Army truck with dustbins for the "swill". It didn't half pong, especially in the summer.

Another claim to fame was that Jack celebrated two Silver Weddings. His first wife, Kitty, died of cancer, a very nice lady indeed. Later he married Betty Price, who is still living at The Spring.

Teddy Barr lived in the cottage next to the well opposite the school in Berkswell village. He was a big, big man, twenty stone plus I would think, and most of it muscle, with some beer. He worked on Wheatley's Berkswell Estate as an estate worker, specialising in timber felling and tree work. My father and Ted worked together for a long period during the War felling trees on all parts of the estate, the timber being used for the "War effort", a well-used phrase at the time.

One of their projects was to fell all the useful timber at Rough Close, a forty-two acre site near Tile Hill. The site was later sold to the Coventry Scout Association. It was opened by Captain Wheatley-Hubbard in 1949 or 1950. He was Mrs. Wheatley's son-in-law and was the District Commissioner at the time.

Teddy Barr would also help out at Davises at harvest time. A stook usually consisted of six sheaves and Ted would stab his pitchfork into the stook and usually the whole lot came up in one forkfull, almost knocking me off the load with the force. For all his size and strength I always thought of him as a "gentle giant". I was far too young to be in his company at the pub, which is just as well. He could put huge quantities away, so I was told. Apparently, he was challenged to a drinking contest to be held at The Bear Inn on Sunday at twelve noon. The aim was to consume twelve pints while Big Ben was chiming and striking twelve. The story goes that Ted was

The first combined harvester in Berkswell. Harvesting cocksfoot (a variety of grass) for seed on Harold Hewitt's farm.

Carrying in the harvest at 'Home Farm', 1948. Note the new Fordson tractor. Teddy Barrs is nearest the camera

Trevor Davies, son Andrew and my sister Margaret on board the old David Brown

missing, but on enquiring, the gathered company were told Ted would be there on time. He had called in at The Railway Inn to practice. Not so sure about the story, but there was a contest – result unknown.

John Gaitly, known as "Irish Jack" or "Navvy Jack". He lived rough in Rupert Arnold's barn in Back Lane. Rupert was a bit of a character as well. He had a steam traction engine and threshing tackle (a threshing machine known as a "drum"). The tackle went from farm to farm threshing ricks of corn before the days of the combined harvester. It was in fact 1948 when Rupert bought his first combine harvester.

However, back to Jack, who followed the drum from farm to farm and usually spent his day "bond cutting". He would be on top of the threshing drum cutting the string bonds of the sheaves and feeding it into the drum. After work he would go directly to the pub, The Bear in fact. He sat by the fire in the corner of the little tap room till chucking out time at ten o'clock and walked the mile and a half to Rupert's barn. He caught up with his washing on a Sunday and came to The Bear in the evening in his better corduroy trousers, but still in his "Yorks", strapped below the knees, and his hob-nailed boots. We could put the clock right by Jack's passing the house, cerlump, cerlump, cerlump, cerlump. He was a perfect gentleman and was thought to be quite well educated and probably jilted earlier in life. It was rather sad that he ended his days in what was the workhouse in Meriden.

Jimmy Rice lived in a tiny cottage in Back Lane, Four Oaks. His wife died and I think he tried to drown his sorrows, with beer. I understand he frequented The Bear and often had quite a problem with his bike. They often parted company on the way home. On one occasion he was lying in the ditch at the side of the road and offered a £5.00 note to anyone who could show him his own front door! Soon after, he took to going into Coventry on the bus. He frequented The Olde Dyers' Arms in Spon End.

He naturally was known to the drivers of the buses, also the conductors – we had conductors then – who were in charge of the bus, took the fares, and generally assisted their passengers. They all knew if Jimmy had gone into town and if he was not at the bus stop for the return journey, the conductor would hop into the pub and fetch him out. Also, on some occasions they would escort him off the bus to his front door and see him safely home, much to the amusement of the other passengers no doubt.

Jim Squires lived next door to us in Meriden Road. He was like a grandfather to Stella and me. He was the shepherd on Wheatley's Home Farm. He could and did tell a good tale. On the rare occasions we went anywhere on the bus or train, he always said "You will never get there; there's a pig on the line", or things just as daft, then we would run home and relate the tale.

On a Sunday afternoon we would often go with him and his dogs round the sheep, feeding and counting, to make sure they were all there.

On nice Sunday evenings, the Squires' often went for a long walk, perhaps ten or a dozen of us quite often. We got off the beaten track most times. Son Bill would challenge us kids to find birds' nests, offering 6D (2p) if anyone found a nest before he did. His sixpence was quite safe in his pocket as no-one could beat Bill at "birds nesting".

Harry Taylor was the village butcher and lived and had his slaughter-house and shop opposite The Village Farm in Spencers Lane, next door to Ken Woolley's blacksmith's forge. The butcher's premises were up the yard at the rear and old Harry usually had a fag in his mouth. He was quite liberal in sharing the fag-ash with his customers. He also liked liquid refreshment and during a quiet period would pop along to The Bear for a swift half, to chase the drop of rum, you understand.

Harry's wife died and eventually Harry began a courtship with Miss Ivy Wood, who, I think, was related to Alf Winters, landlord at The Bear. Anyhow, Ivy lived in and was a cleaner and general factotum there.

The Bear belonged to Berkswell Estate and was a free house, not tied to a brewery, and could sell any brew they chose.

There are various tales about Harry and Ivy's courtship. On at least one occasion she was heard to say "Oh Harry, I like it, do it again". This was heard under someone's bedroom window one evening, whether by design or accident I know not. They never did marry and when The Bear was sold to Manns Brewery Ivy moved into an almshouse in the village.

Another character of schooldays was Ernie Jarvis, sometimes known as Ernie Renshaw. He arrived in the village at the age of eleven or twelve and lived with a Mrs. Jarvis in the almshouses and called her "Mum". He was a big rough-tough lad who pushed all the other kids around. He was a duffer at school and caused mayhem wherever he went. He even interfered and disrupted the scouts' meeting on a Friday evening. He really was a problem in the village, but after a year or two disappeared as mysteriously as he arrived. More on Ernie later on.

On a Saturday evening a certain clientele always went to a dance, not necessarily the same one, all on our push bikes of course. For me it was usually The Matrix, until the summer recess, that was from June till September. Other ports of call were The Rialto Casino in Coundon or, if there was absolutely nothing else, Balsall Institute (as it was then) now the Village Hall. However, after the dance we would all, or a lot of us, congregate at the Berkswell crossroads by The Bear. There used to be a huge tree on the corner by the spinney, with a seat underneath, and we hung around there for ages sometimes.

Mrs. Leeson, who lived at the first house in Meriden Road, would stick her head out of the window and enquire if we had any homes to go to. We were all lads and lasses together and really did not make a lot of noise. Two of the girls were Betty and Flo from Meriden. Their father was a gamekeeper on the Packington Estate and they lived on the corner of Maxtoke Lane and the A45; the Little Chef is close by now.

Betty was a very good dancer and would cycle miles to a dance. I escorted her home one night from Berkswell, after Flo had gone on in front. This led to a few dates, mostly dances, and now and then to the pictures, usually on a Sunday. It was not really a courting arrangement. I don't think so anyhow, till one Saturday we all went to The Balsall dance. On this particular evening there were quite a number of R.A.F. lads there from Honiley and as the evening progressed, so did the R.A.F. Most of the girls, including Betty, had been commandeered by the Air Force. Well, for a start off, they had a uniform. However, this evening Betty was being taken home by one of these lads. It did not bother me unduly and one or two of us set off for our usual meeting under the tree on Berkswell crossroads.

On my arrival there sat Flo, and I like to think we made a nice twosome on the bench; in fact, it was the best part of the evening. Eventually, Betty turned up with Mr. Airforce who refused to go any further and he pushed off, literally.

I was rather "tied up" at the time, when Betty came over and said "You can take me home if you like John". She was politely told "No thanks". "Push off" and "Get lost" had not been invented. However, the two sisters eventually went home together. I waited till they were well on their way and toddled off home to have half an hour's radio with the American Forces Network, A.F.N. from Munich. I think the compare was Roger Moffat, but his radio name was MUFFAT MOFFAT. They played all the Big Band music of the day till two in the morning. And that was the end of my first boy girl friendship. I can't call it a romance. Betty was very nice and we remained good friends.

Opposite The Bear stood the Cafe, run very well by Mrs. Hadley. As well as catering for teas on a Sunday afternoon, she catered for most of the village events and happenings – Weddings, Christenings and Dinners; The Bear Inn "Sick and Dividend Society's Annual Dinner for one. Members paid in so much per week and received a payment when off work sick. Monies remaining at the end of the year were paid to all as dividend. They ran a summer outing and an annual flower and vegetable show.

The Berkswell Association for the Prosecution of Felons held their annual dinner there as well. This organisation was always a bit of a mystery to me, but all became clear much later on, so you must keep reading if you want to know.

Then, there were no doubt, the tennis, hockey, football and cricket clubs.

Mrs. Hadley also produced a Pantomime every year in The Reading Room. The youngsters from Berkswell School were the stars, all under twelve. They were all first-class shows. She had the knack of bringing out talent in lots of youngsters, as did Mrs. Kay Fensom and Mrs. Claudine Jagger later on. They had all been involved in The Theatre earlier on in their lives.

It was in September 1949 that I started going to "night school" at the Coventry Technical College at The Butts. The idea was to learn a bit more about the gardening profession. In actual fact, it turned out to be a weekly lecture on all sorts of horticultural subjects and was very informative. The lecturer was Miss Cluly, daughter of a nurseryman in Jobs Lane. The nursery has long since disappeared under bricks and mortar.

She was a very learned lady and put the subjects over very well, sometimes with practical demonstrations. I found it most helpful. Not a youngster, she married a senior manager from the Coventry Parks Department. I went there for three terms, on my bike of course. Then at nine o'clock would cycle up to the Mallards (from the Blitz days) and Stevenson Road, Radford, for a coffee and chat; then bike home.

I was quite happy getting around on my bike, but sometimes, after a day at work and an evening's dancing, the last mile or two home were a bit like "the last straw". This was especially noticeable after I had been out with John Kirby, who now possessed a motorbike. I rode pillion a few times and found it a bit strange. It was difficult for me to lean over into a bend, so much so that we came off one night in Back Lane. Fortunately, no damage done, both landing in a dry ditch, the bike coming to rest up the road a bit. The only problem I had – lost my spectacles and try as we did, they could not be found. John was not very happy with the whole episode, and told me so. I got up early next morning and returned to the scene to find my specs all intact – all's well, etc…

CHAPTER 10

Acquiring 'Wheels'

By this time, quite a few of the lads had motorbikes, Georgie Wilkinson, Derek Wise and Trevor Lowe, to name a few. And I thought why not me? I made a few enquiries about the cost and running costs, etc. Ron Hurford had a big Triumph with a box on the side. He was landscaping and this was very handy for him. His side-box was known as "the coffin". He gave those who dared a ride in his "coffin". At the time he was still living in the village with the Kirbys just round the corner.

One evening, John Kirby got in the side-box, but no-one knew his mother was watching. Ron's trick was to roar up the road, slam on the brakes, and by steering the bike in a certain way, the whole thing would take off, turn round, and set off from where it had started from. Apparently, Mrs. K was heard all over the village screaming and yelling "My John, oh my John, what have you done?" She took some time to get over that.

Eventually, I decided I would like a motorbike. As I was, and still am, a non-mechanical animal, I was a little bit unsure. About all I could do was blow the tyres up, I think.

John Kirby took me on the pillion of his bike to The Coventry Motor Mart, on the London Road, Coventry. The shop was between the cemetery and the traffic island on the Coventry Ring Road. John, and others, did not recommend a used bike as it would probably have meant buying someone else's problems. In the event, the only new motorbike they could offer without a long wait was a 250 cc B.S.A. In 1950 the country had nowhere near recovered from the War. Many products were still utility in name and nature. Export was the order of the day.

I did decide to buy the B.S.A. 250 cc bike. The Motor Mart arranged a twelve monthly hire purchase agreement and, after paying the deposit, etc., I collected the bike one teatime during the following week.

Prior to that, although I was over twenty-one, my parents' agreement was sought. My mother said she had known that is what I would want and would not stand in my way, subject to the usual requests of taking care of this bike and to be careful. Also, she was not too happy about H.P. as they, my parents, had never had what they could not pay for.

The only experience of riding was being a passenger on John Kirby's bike. Also, Trevor Lowe had a B.S.A. 250 and we went for a spin round the lanes one evening, with me actually driving for a mile or two.

So it was I collected my bike and drove it home, very carefully. I never did tear about on it anyhow, as I could not afford repairs or another bike; it would only do 70 m.p.h. flat out, down hill, with a tail wind anyway.

Around about this time the local lads were invited to a dance at the Girls' Teacher Training College in Charter Avenue, Canley. This is now part of Warwick University; the dance entitled DRA. HI. SCI. MU. (Drama, History, Science and Music), so I learned later.

There was quite a bit of excitement amongst the lads at the prospect of being let loose in an all-girls college. In the end only two went, John Overton and me.

What a "do" they put on; a lovely decorated hall, the dining room I think, a super band, and piles of mouth-watering eats, all free. And, to top it all, a huge bevvy of young ladies, all dressed up for the asking – to dance that is. There was again no bar, but who wanted a bar with such glamour and talent about.

I usually looked for a tall girl for a dancing partner and had no problems on this occasion. It was not too long before I was dancing with a Miss Margaret Wheatley who came from Neasdon, near Wembley, in London. We got on very well, a very nice personality, good host at refreshment time, the interval. I felt a bit sorry for John Overton, who was a bit neglected by me, but "he who dares........".

At the end of the dance arrangements were made to meet again and so began a steady friendship. Margaret came to our house at weekends, perhaps for Sunday tea. One day, four of us went to Stratford. It must have been by the Midland Red bus, because no-one had a car. Margaret's friend was the niece of Emmanuel (Manny) Shinwell, the M.P. and Cabinet Minister; Ray Wallis escorted her. He was spending a few days' holiday with us.

We had a rowing boat on the river. No-one could row, but we did make progress up and down the river but all ended up soaking wet. Fortunately it was a nice warm day and we soon dried out.

Once or twice at holiday times I visited the Wheatley home in Mallard Way, not all that far off the Edgeware Road. We went dancing at Wembley Town Hall and Mr. Wheatley treated us all to a trip "up West" to see "Carousel" in fact. They, the Wheatleys, were very nice people and kind to me. Mr. Wheatley was employed by De Haviland who built aircraft. I don't

Back to 'civvy street' and work
at The Moat Berkswell, 1949

think I made a big hit
with brother Ken who
was a couple of years
older, had a good job,
and a car. To be honest, I
was a bit of a "country
bumpkin" compared with the more street-wise Londoners. He was alright
though.

I really cannot be sure how long our friendship had been going on, but
on leaving to come home one Sunday evening from London, Margaret told
me it was all over, straight out of the blue as they say. To say I was shat-
tered and upset was putting it a bit mild, but these things happen. We
never fell out, or anything like that, so I had to grin and bear it. I believe
my mother and Mrs. Wheatley corresponded for some time after, but it
was the end of a very nice friendship for me. I seem to recall Margaret
eventually married an ex boyfriend, one she had before I came on the
scene. However, with the busy life that I led, both at work and after work,
I decided not to indulge in any more serious dating, but simply to enjoy
the company of whoever I happened to be with – full stop.

Generally it was not a good time for me because John Kirby applied,
was accepted, and went to Malaya (as it was then), joining the Malayan
Police Force. I never knew very much about his work there, but he was an
officer in charge of native policemen, after training I presume, although
his Army record would have been a good asset in obtaining the job and
provided valuable experience.

I recall his address was SUNGI BESI, not too far from Kuala Lumpur,
the capital. At the time it was not a safe place to be, with terrorists in abundance.

During his time there he was awarded the Colonial Police Medal. This
I understand was an award for bravery. I am not sure what it was for, but
was told he saved some local people, maybe policemen, from crocodiles.
He came home on leave after about three years, and stayed in Malaya until
the country became independant.

Work at The Moat was going along alright and after twelve months there
was no sign of a pay rise, so one morning I plucked up courage and mentioned the fact to Mr. Jarrard, the boss. He promised to consider this and
let me know in due course. This he did and a few days later told me that I
would receive a rise in pay, on condition that I did not tell anyone about it,

as I would be getting the same as the head cowman. Mind you, the cowman did also have a rent-free home and free milk, also probably other perks like a row of potatoes from the farm. This was a common perk on some farms, if they grew spuds. Some years, my father was allowed a row on Berkswell Estate. The potatoes would all be grown together, then when it was time for them to be dug up, in October, all the interested parties would assemble in the field on a Saturday afternoon. The potatoes would be dug out with the farm machine one row at a time, with all having a section to pick up and put the spuds in hessian sacks. When they were all bagged up, bags were counted, divided, and delivered round on the farm trailer.

I digress. I received my pay rise O.K. but really I was not too contented working there, not learning very much and not a great deal of job satisfaction. It was Mr. Norman (Gubby) Taylor, of Ye Olde Berkswell Stores, who provided the answer. He told me one Saturday lunchtime as he was writing down the grocery order that his brother-in-law, who ran a nursery in Kenilworth, was seeking an assistant.

The nursery was owned and run by Bert and Harry Douglas, Douglas Brothers,and was in Whitemoor Road, Kenilworth. It was at the rear of Elmdene Nursery and another nursery owned by the Grinrod brothers. I went to see what was on offer and discovered most of the work was under glass, which meant no more sprout-picking and cutting savoys and cabbages with snow and ice on.

I was offered a little more money for the same hours, so I accepted. There was no prospect of promotion, but I may learn a little more, so I took the job and worked eight till five with a half hour lunch break instead of an hour, which meant a packed lunch.

The work was very interesting. Most of the produce went straight to shop customers, florists and the like. I called the brothers "Mr. Douglas", and we all got on very well. Bert's son, John, had bought and moved into Elmdene on the front, and I was his replacement.

We grew, or forced, a lot of bulbs, daffs, tulips, hyacinths and irises for Spring trade; the indoor azaleas (Indica); asparagus fern for brides' bouquets, which were huge bouquets at the time; some bedding plants and pot plants. Greenhouses were full of early lettuce and tomatoes, also five thousand late flowering chrysanthemums which flowered from October till well into January; perhaps twenty-five or so different varieties, all requiring different "stopping" dates (i.e. pinching out the growing tip to make them bush out).

One of my jobs was to look after and pot on the chrysanths. The final potting in July was into eight or ten inch clay pots. We made up our own compost to the John Innes formula, i.e. 7 parts loam, 3 parts peat and 2 parts sharp sand. A base fertilizer was added to that and all mixed up with the help of a rotavator machine. This formula has stood me in good stead ever since, more or less.

There were about fourteen greenhouses altogether, most of them about 100 feet in length, with various widths and heights. Bert Douglas was a very good grower and could time the flowering of the bulbs to perfection; Mothering Sunday and Easter for the bulbs and Christmas for the chrysanths. He took all the cuttings, but after tuition, I did sow and look after the bedding plants which again was to be very useful to me in the future.

Holidays at the time, early fifties, were Good Friday and Easter Monday, Whit Monday – not to be confused with today's Spring Bank Holiday – the first Monday in August, Christmas Day and Boxing Day and one week's annual holiday. I worked on Saturdays from eight till one, so that meant nine days' holiday, plus a Saturday morning.

For my first holiday, apart from short trips to visit my Army pal, Ray, near Matlock, I had a week at camp with the Berkswell Scouts. This camp was at Bowleze Cove, near the village of Preston, about three miles to the east of Weymouth.

The main party departed by train on the Friday evening and arrived at Weymouth station at about 4.30 a.m., and after loading all the gear – tents, etc. – onto the trek-cart, clattered off through the streets, making the dogs bark and creating mini-mayhem as they walked the three miles or so to Bowleze Cove.

The party was led by Bill Green. George Teague, the Scoutmaster, combined the camp with a family holiday. He had an ex W.D. (War Department) ten hundredweight vehicle, a pick-up type with a khaki canvas cover. He towed a small caravan for his wife, Evelyn, and young son, Paul, also daughter Gillian and my younger sister Margaret. Sons Lawrence and Ken were with the scout troop.

I had to work on the Saturday morning, so I started at six o'clock and was on my way home at eleven. Once at home, I loaded up the panniers on the bike, had some dinner, and collected Derek Lambley. We were soon on our way. We arrived all O.K. to find the camp set up and running but no firewood, so I emptied my panniers onto my allotted sleeping place in a bell tent and set off with Bill Green in search of firewood.

Heading off inland we soon found some dead fallen branches and filled the panniers with wood sticking up four foot or so into the air. It must have presented a funny sight and we did get a few strange looks on our return, but we had fuel and could get on with cooking the evening meal. Nowadays the troop uses a calor gas arrangement for heating water and cooking.

I recall we were quite fortunate having good weather and although the camp site was not ideal for scouting, we had a very good week. There were cooking and camping skills for the younger ones, a day's hike on Portland, and Bill and I had a day out on my motorbike to Lyme Regis.

But all too soon it was back to the old routine of work, also helping with the harvest at Trevor Davies's and Jack Dawson's at Holloway Farm, Cornets End.

One year the weather was very bad and it took a long time to get all the corn dry and into the barns or ricks. One weekend it was decided to work on the Sunday, something that had never happened before, apart from essential work, like feeding and milking, both a 365 days a year job to Trevor or Jack.

We were carrying corn to Trevor's rickyard from Cornets End via the bridle path to Mercote, where no traffic should be. Jack was driving the tractor down the farm drive and out onto the bridle road when a motorbike came hurtling up the track, hit the tractor a glancing blow and ended up, bike and rider, in the ditch. We stopped, ran over and pulled rider and bike out. Fortunately, no damage seemed to be done to man or machine and he was soon on his way again, albeit a little more slowly. I seem to think that was the end of Sunday harvesting, Jack being a staunch member of the Methodist Church, and Trevor attended a Welsh Chapel in Coventry when he was able to get there.

Then there was a wedding in the family. Stella got married to Bill Forrest from Elm Tree Avenue off Broad Lane. The ceremony was at Berkswell Church, with the Reverend Bursell officiating. I canot recall the reception at all and no, I was not "de lux" (drunk). Stella and Bill lived in the front room of our house as they had nowhere else to go. Accommodation was expensive with nothing available in Berkswell.

By now the Matrix had opened up again for the dancing season. I would work till about seven on a Saturday evening, go home to a bowl of water to wash down, then I put my feet in and washed up. After a shave and

A dance at Banner Lane factory. Left to right: Bert married Anita; John and Stan; John Kirby married Pearl; Eddie Horsley

"togging up", I was on my way.

I parked my bike in the car park, still with the "L" on and then walked down to the "Fletch" (the Fletchampstead Hotel) Pub in other words. Quite a gang used to gather there prior to getting into the dance about 9pm.

In the winter I would be in the pub at 6.45 and have a real session of a few pints and a good old chinwag. They were a good bunch of blokes, including "old Sam" Wakelam, a farmer's son from Fernhill Lane, off Balsall Street, and often Bill Green. Sometimes I would go in there and never buy a round, but it was my turn the next week and it didn't half make a hole in my wages. It was a Mann's (Brewery) House and we would drink "black and tan" – a half-pint bottle of stout topped up with mild beer. By this time, I had got to know quite a lot of people. The stewards on the door and in the ballroom were ex Coldstream Guardsmen. I think we all had regular dancing partners. I remember a Barbara. Tess was a nice blonde and her sister Jean (their big brother kept an eye on them from the other side of the ballroom). There were two others. One had a relative living in Berkswell, and the other was a Miss Olive Holmes. For a start off, I got the two mixed up. I still get people mixed up today!

I seemed to be dancing more and more with this Olive, and we were soon having a cup of tea together. The band would always play a Latin American section, i.e. Tango, Cha Cha Cha, Samba and Rhumba. As I was no good at any of those, except dancing on my own, it was my cue for a cup of tea and a sit down. We always stood in the crowd at the dance and at the bar in the pub, so I was ready for a squat.

This casual acquaintance went on for some weeks. Olive did not go to the Matrix every week anyhow, and I was not too keen to get too involved either, as it was not all that long after my other experience when perhaps my confidence or ego, call it what you like, was dented.

However, time went on and one Saturday I asked if I may take Olive home. She only lived less than a mile away at No. 2, Glendower Avenue, off Broad Lane. I cannot remember the exact reply, whether it was "Oh yes please, Yes, or If you like", but I did take her home on the pillion of my motor bike, with "L" plates removed.

That was the start of a forty-eight year friendship, marriage, parenthood and retirement, with no regrets whatsoever.

Regular dates followed; the cinema as well as the Saturday dance at The Matrix. Nevertheless, the usual trip to the "Fletch" still carried on. As Olive was earning as much as me she took herself to the dance and I tried to be there for nine o'clock. I did not always make it. Well, one knows how one can be delayed occasionally, especially when another pint is put in front of one. Being punctual was not and never has been one of my strong points.

Soon I was meeting Olive's parents. She was the youngest of seven and they were no longer youngsters. I was always made very welcome and was invited to Sunday tea. As far as I am aware, there was no entertaining at lunchtime then. Olive's mother was, I suppose, typical of the housewives of that era, completely in charge of all they surveyed. Mr. Holmes had taken early retirement through ill health, but was still doing some gardening at home. Then came the "return match" at our house. I cannot remember it at all, but my mother had met Olive at The Reading Room when I was involved in running a dance, probably for the Rover Crew funds.

My mother loved catering and cooking and was one of the organisers for the refreshments. Poor Olive had to meet the dancing population of Berkswell, and no doubt tongues were wagging as to Webby's new girlfriend. I know, I've done a bit of tongue-wagging myself. Sufficient to say we all got on very well, boys and girls. Also, lots of people of all ages attended dances then, the bands playing a real mixture of dances to suit young and the not so young. In fact, the guitar era was just about to descend upon us all and, in my opinion, was the ruination of dances as we had known them. Folks like Lonnie Donegan and Skiffle came in first, as I recall it.

Olive and I used to meet up only about once a week for the "pictures" and then on Saturday and Sundays, Olive mostly coming over to Berkswell on the bus which arrived at our house at about 1.40 p.m. We were often still having our Sunday roast. At this time I often went to The Bear with my father riding pillion.

In the meantime, I had taken and passed my motorbike riding test. The test was booked and I presented myself at Manor Road Test Centre, close to Coventry railway station. The examiner stood on the corner of a crossroads and I was instructed to do a "figure of eight", round two blocks, left-hand and right-hand turns; also there was to be an emergency stop at a given signal, after which I drove the short distance back to the Centre. After some questions on the Highway Code he informed me that I had passed. That was quite a relief, as passing any test always is.

My next holiday was to be really extravagant, a tour of Devon and Cornwall on the bike, together with Colin Steventon from Meriden and Derrick Wagstaff who would ride pillion on Colin's bike and I would have most of the luggage on the back of mine.

We set off on the Saturday, long before any motorway was heard of, down through Bristol

Camping with the Berkswell Scouts, Bowleze Cove, near Weymouth, 1952

and over the Avon via the suspension bridge, and on for our first night at Highbridge. Next day, on to Cheddar Gorge and then over Exmoor, having to find B and B every evening, the job usually delegated to me.

Eventually we arrived at Ilfracombe and spent quite a long time there. It was getting on into the evening before we decided to find our B and B, with the result there was just nothing available, not where we were anyhow. Perhaps it was not the best idea, but we set off towards Barnstaple.

We were some four miles out of Ilfracombe and I was in front when a B and B sign loomed up. It was outside a very tatty-looking smallholding with poultry and little pigs running around the yard. As beggars cannot be choosers, I picked my way through the p and p (poultry and pigs) plus what they had discarded, and knocked on an old door that had not seen paint since it was hung there. A little elderly lady came to the door (she was more likely younger than I am now) and said she had a single and a double. We said that would be fine, we were dog-tired.

The place was rather old, from what I could see in the gathering darkness. We were led up creaking spiral stairs into a very plain room with a double bed, wardrobe and washstand, with the usual bowl and large water jug thereon. After sorting our gear out and a quick wash, I was soon in my half of the double bed and "Waggy" in the other half. I had not heard of queer men and their funny ways then, having perhaps led a rather sheltered life.

However, I was soon asleep, but the next thing I woke up and it was pitch dark. There was a creaking on the stairs, slow creak, slow creak. Then, a shaft of light appeared on the ceiling and slowly went round the room as the creaking continued. All of a sudden, a door slammed and the light went out. By this time Waggy and I were completely mystified, but we worked it out next morning that it was the old dear coming upstairs with a candle and retiring to her bed, and not a ghost after all.

Although the place was old, with no mod cons at all, we had a good breakfast next morning and were soon off on our travels. On towards Clovelly and just before the turn-off, I spotted a sign on the right which said "Hobby Drive". This turned out to be a private drive entrance to Clovelly. We paid a small fee to bike down this long woody drive to arrive at Clovelly church. We parked our bikes at the end of the drive and walked down the steep cobbled street – more of a wide footpath really – traffic-free – all deliveries undertaken by donkeys, including coal. There was a pub at the bottom at the harbourside.

Rowing boats were there for hire and, although no-one could row, we had to have a go. All went well until we got out beyond the breakwater when the sea became quite rough and the boat began to buck and bob; no life-belts, no-one asked any questions when we set off. It took some hard rowing to turn the boat round and steer a zig-zag course back to the harbour.

On to Newquay, and then the coast road down to Lands End; all free, nothing to pay to visit or park. We climbed down the cliff and struggled up again. Back along the south coast to Penzance, Falmouth, and Torquay. Then heading north and home. Quite an adventure for me.

And so it was back to the old routine of work, play and more work, which I enjoyed. Chrysanths to look after and getting on for two tons of Spring bulbs to pot up and box up for the Spring trade, also Mothering Sunday and Easter.

Still "going out" with Olive and getting to know her family.

Olive's eldest sister, Vi, was married to Charles Jarvis, a Berkswell man. He lived in Back Lane as a single man but was now a farmer at Cragg in Yorkshire.

Next was Gilbert, who I never met as he had met with a fatal accident during the War. Then came Lily, who was married to Alf Garlick and lived in Wallace Road, Radford, Coventry. Lily also became stepmother to Brenda whose mother had passed away some years before.

Olive had a brother Ernest, but he sadly died aged eighteen months' old. Ida was next on the scene, married to Alec Harris. They had four children. My first encounter with the Harris's was when Alec was in hospital for a spell and Olive stayed with the youngsters, Ray, Beryl, Brian and Sylvia, while Ida visited Alec on a Sunday afternoon. I went on my motorbike to Brightmere Road, Coundon, and stayed for tea and the evening. The four youngsters all sat on the settee and looked like four birds perching on a wire.

It was during the first evening that Brian called me "Uncle John" which caused great amusement all round, Ray and Ida laughing out loud and the two girls just looking at each other. At the time, I had no real thoughts of becoming Uncle John, but Olive and I got on very well together, she being easy to please and nice to be with.

We were both earning about the same money each week and now the Matrix was more or less the usual Saturday night venue. I still went to The "Fletch" with the lads but Olive did not come because she could not put up with the clouds of tobacco smoke in the public bar. At the time all the pubs were the same. The longer the evening went on the thicker the smoke became.

The arrangement was to meet inside the dancehall at nine o'clock, each paying our own way, and this worked very well. "Alright for you I hear the cry", well, "Yes" has to be the reply.

Visits were made to see Olive's sister Lily who had not been married to Alf all that long. Alf became a widower and Lily went to look after Alf's daughter Brenda and a good job she made of it too. They lived in Wallace Road. Lily is still there.

Alf was a staunch and loyal member of the Radford Congregational Church which was in Radford Road on the corner of Villa Road. He worked for many years for the Electricity Board as a jointer, spending many hours in a tent over a hole in the road.

Olive's eldest sister, Vi, lived in West Yorkshire and was married to Charles Jarvis. They had a smallholding or small farm near to Halifax. Brother Bert lived in Essex and we never saw him. It was not easy to get around; no motorways and no cars to drive on them. Also, there was not a lot of spare time or money.

By this time I think the five day week was just beginning to come into being, but that only applied to industrial workers, i.e. car manufacturers and probably office staff. My £6.25 for 47 hours' work did not go far. My mother was always very generous regarding the amount I paid for my keep. After paying that I had to provide all my other needs, clothing, maintenance of cycle or motorbike, and so on.

I undertook to dig and plant one side of our large garden from aged about sixteen. The expenses of seeds were shared. Other jobs were also "found" for me. All these arrangements were very good for me, teaching me to look after money and take care of possessions. The motorbike did get neglected, sorry to say. I "fell out" with spanners, screwdrivers and oil at a very early age and have not changed.

We had a shed in the garden, not very well sited. It blocked the view across the fields from the living-room window and the back yard. The builder of the shed sank four (or maybe six) posts into the ground and nailed shiplap boards to these posts. There was a pitched roof of corrugated iron and a sturdy door. I remember this shed as an upright and sturdy useful building, housing all sorts of things. One relic was an adult's tricycle belonging, I think, to my Grandfather Webb. I longed to get it out, but it was hung up and there was no way of having a go on that. I never did know where it went to.

The firewood was kept in the shed, also a couple of pushbikes, until it started to lean like the Tower of Pisa. The wooden posts holding it upright were rotting away. I suppose with hindsight godfathers could have been put in, but my father was not much of a handyman and materials would have cost money. In the end it was almost impossible to get into the shed and one day I decided to do something about it – like knock it down!

I am not sure what I was doing at home, but by dinnertime all that was left was a pile of wood and a heap of old corrugated iron. The old man was not amused one little bit when he came home and took a long time to recover. I was far too big to go over his knee or feel his leather belt which I had been threatened with many times but NEVER felt it.

He came round in the end, not quite admitting that the view was better, or the resulting flower bed. Mother was pleased. The wood did make some super firelighting sticks and firewood. All the rubbish went up The Slang and into the pit hole tip used by all the locals.

As I may have said before, Stella and I were encouraged to save from an early age and very soon after leaving school, the "Man from the Pru" came calling. They had a campaign in the area on school leavers, and we were all in work. I was talked into saving one and threepence a week (15p), one seventh of my wages. This I doubled in less than twelve months, but after a wage increase. I had a small collecting box and saved every threepenny piece and sixpenny coin, regardless of the state of my pocket.

This method of saving stood me in good stead until retirement, fifty years later. And, the Man from the Pru always had plenty of change after calling at The Webbs.

Life went steadily on, Olive and I getting around on the motorbike, visiting Ray and his parents at Bonsall, near Matlock.

One Whitsun weekend we went to North Wales and stayed overnight in Llandudno, after having a slight problem of finding two single rooms. All was well till we got back to the Birmingham area – again no bypass or motorways. Somehow or other I took a wrong turn, ended up in the city centre and eventually found the way out through Digbeth. That is when the chain broke and I had no spare link. I don't suppose I could have executed the repair even if I had. Called the R.A.C. of which I was a member, no luck at all, no-one wanted to know – Bank Holiday Monday at about 8 pm.

We were stuck at the railway bridge over the main road at Bordesley Green. Eventually, I approached a patrolling policeman and he advised me to go to Dowding and Mills, a premises that had men on duty 24 hours every day. I think they had something to do with "electrics". Anyhow, into the premises I pushed the bike, to be met by a maintenance man and he set about making and fitting a chain link out of ordinary steel. Not the right material at all. This all took quite a long time to do, but, with instructions to let the clutch in very steadily to eliminate any jerking on the new link, we set off for home.

There was no telephone at either home, so we could not make any contact. It was decided to go to our house first – we were a bit peckish by now. Nevertheless we arrived at Meriden Road all O.K. with twenty fingers and toes crossed. We were soon refreshed and Olive stayed and slept in my bed. However, I was downstairs in a chair that opened out flat; the same chair that Lewis Boland slept in some ten years previous.

On our return, funny little noises were coming from the front room occupied by Stella and Bill. We soon realised that baby Peter had arrived, my nephew.

There was always something happening. Joan Wise married Ted Corbett about the time of Stella's wedding and they also had a baby son born about the same time as Peter. Someone was a copycat!

After collecting my working clothes from my room, we all retired. I had to be at work at 8.00 the next morning. Olive always had an extra day off at Bank Holidays. The bike got me to work and back O.K. and I went to Alec Staddon's (now Gambles) garage where a new link was put in for me. I was a regular customer there, being useless at anything to do with motorbikes. "Bunny" Poole was nearly always there as Alec and Bunny were motorbike mad. Alec used to race bikes somewhere, I know not where. Bunny Poole, a few years older than me, was in the Berkswell Scout Troop when I was a cub. He was one of quite a few that helped out with the troop when there was a shortage of leaders during the war years, till he got called up during the war, for the army.

There was never much work done at the garage in the evenings when I was there, not my fault I hasten to say. But they always sorted out my bike problems, showing me where to put the oil and grease. I did know where the petrol went in. We had many a laugh there I can tell you.

It must have been September 1952 when Olive and I decided to have a motorbike tour of Scotland. I had not had a holiday so I was a bit flush with money earned helping out with haymaking and the corn harvest.

We set off in September early on the Saturday morning. As usual for us, the weather was not good, low cloud and drizzling rain. We had got fairly good clothing to try and keep out the elements. Trevor Davies had given me a coat made of chamois leather, in fact, a coat worn by air crew of the twenties. It was tattered and torn, but "beggars cannot be choosers" it is said. However, it did the job and it did go into quite a few posh places, plus my wellies and crash helmet, with a pair of shoes in the pockets.

Olive had a nice leather-type coat off Enid Wise, plus wellies and a white helmet – looked a little bit like a snowdrop.

We went via Lichfield, Stone, Stafford, Warrington and Wigan, arriving in Kendal at teatime 5/6 p.m.; found our B and B and hoped for better weather for the next day. If it was nice, we were going to stay in the Lake District.

It was not nice, so on northwards we went, along the A6, which began with a long climb out of Kendal up to Shap. We made Carlisle by dinnertime and after fish and chips, quite a treat for me as the nearest chip shop to Berkswell was on the outskirts of Coventry.

I cannot recall all our stops, but sufficient to say, our route took us north between Glasgow and Edinburgh and on to Loch Lomond at Balloch. From there, up the west side of the loch to Tarbet and Crianlarich and Tyndrum.

The weather was not bad, but we arrived at The Tyndrum Hotel at lunchtime in a real downpour. Then there was nothing there apart from this huge fortress-looking hotel. Now it is quite a big village.

It was dinnertime so in we filed and me in wellies and tattered old coat! It made no difference and we sat down to a nice lunch. The weather better, we set off again for the Bridge of Orchy and Ballachulish. The choice then was a ferry across a narrow strip of fast-flowing water out of the loch into Loch Linnhe. There is a bridge over this channel now.

The alternative to the ferry was a sixteen mile journey round the loch via Kinlochleven, and I cannot recall which option was taken.

Onwards to Fort William and via Loch Ness to Inverness. Then we

Miss Olive Joyce Holmes comes on the scene, 1951

turned south towards home via Royal Deeside, Balmoral, Crathie and Braemar, also Tomintoul, the highest village in the Highlands. That was a bit remote. Lots of roads in that area were just two strips of tarmac with grass in between; black grass here and there where vehicles' undersides had left a deposit of oil.

Eventually we had a day in Edinburgh and made our way home via Carter Bar and the A1 to Newark and Leicester. A very enjoyable holiday and the only problem was getting single rooms every night, but I think owing to it being the end of the season and calling late afternoon; it was not a great problem.

It was vowed to return to this land of lochs and mountains when time and funds permitted.

On board our speed machine, a 250cc B.S.A. 70mph flat out downhill –
with a following wind, 1951

Another event at the time was George Wilkinson's twenty-first birthday bash. Most of us others had passed twenty-one by now. Olive and I were invited by George who lived at Wilmot Cottage, just along the road about one hundred yards from our house to his party at home.

He lived with his gran, known to us as Ellen Wilkinson, after the Labour M.P. at the time, and his grandfather, Bill, who was head wagoner on the estate farm. Their son, Arthur, lived there as well. He was a bachelor. He also worked on the farm, a champion ploughman, first with horses then later on with tractors. Ploughing had to be done properly then, a ridge set up to start and a neat furrow to finish, both to be as straight as a gun barrel, and they usually were. Today it seems to me as long as the soil is turned over that is good enough, and really I suppose it is.

Back to the party; guests included Derek Wise who was courting Eira, the dairymaid at Home Farm, Trevor Lowe, who was a lodger with the Wises and was courting Enid (she did not want to go), also Olive and I.

The elders were all going out down to The Bear I think, Mrs. Wilkinson (Ellen) worked behind the bar. Mrs. W. had a nip of whisky out of a full bottle, and we were left to our own devices.

Sufficient to say we all had a good time with Trevor and I getting stuck into the Scotch. George did have some. At the time the party broke up, Derek would not take Eira home to the hall where she had a flat, so Trev had to go as well. Olive refused to let me take her home on the motorbike, which was a very wise decision. She ended up in bed with my sister Margaret so that I could sleep it off in my bed rather than the old chair in the kitchen.

During this time, there seemed to be lots of weddings and at the Wises a few christenings, not at the same time I hasten to add.

Beryl married Bill Ritchie, he was an R.A.F. airman stationed at Honiley aerodrome. It was a base for nightfighters and "Beaufighters" were the aircraft in operation at the time of the War.

Audrey married Sid Beckett, a Londoner who worked in Billingsgate Fishmarket at one time.

Then Trevor married Enid and Derek (Deg, Deggy, Dicky) married Eira Jones. Her father was a Reverend with the United Reformed Church in Holyhead Road, Coventry.

And, quite naturally, the same as Stella and Bill, they all began to have families. Olive and I became "Auntie and Uncle" to quite a few in a comparatively short time.

Many things were still on ration, getting better all the time though. Mrs. Wise (senior) loved having parties and no excuse was missed for a gathering – weddings, christenings, the cat having kittens, you name it. Naturally, they had a houseful of family and there were times when Olive and I were the only guests outside the family. We are just as welcome to this day.

Olive and I must have got around to thinking why not us getting married? The big problem was where to live. I did not wish to live with Olive's folks. There was plenty of room, but one or two reasons agin. They were not youngsters and deserved a quiet retirement, probably desired one too, and to be perfectly honest, I could not have lived there. It would not have worked out.

Mr. Holmes was a very quiet and I think contented man. Olive's mother was a more dominating person, always very kind and helpful to me and, in fact, everyone she knew. A very hardworking lady, always on the go, and probably found it difficult to relax, always thinking about the next job to be done; a very clever person with pins and needles, she had spent many many hours making and mending for family and lots of others.

When I met Olive her father had retired on health grounds. His last job was as a gardener/groundsman at the Standard Motor Co. on Tile Hill Lane. They were still buying their home in Glendower Avenue. How they managed I do not know. A pair I looked up to and admired and who set a fine example to their family and others, but it would have been a disaster for me to have tried to live there. I suppose I like my own way as well, to a certain degree.

However, we decided to become engaged at Christmas 1952. Nevertheless, I believe a couple become engaged WHEN they decide to become married, i.e. when the girl, or lad, says "Yes". In our case this was a week or two before Christmas.

There was to be a Christmas dance in The Reading Room a day or two before Christmas, mainly run by me, and I was getting good at it now. My mother was in charge of catering, together with her helpers, providing tea, sandwiches and cakes served from a scruffy kitchen at the rear of the room where the toilets and storeroom are now situated.

Olive and I had arranged to go on the bike to Leicester to buy the ring and do some Christmas shopping on the Saturday before Christmas. As I had to work till one o'clock in Kenilworth, come home, wash, change, etc., it was getting on before we set off on the 22 mile trip; no M69 then, which meant chugging through all the villages, also I did not really know the way, not having been that way before. To make things worse, it started to snow but we carried on not quite regardless. Parking the bike we were soon at the shops and eventually found a jewellers where Olive chose her engagement ring which was one of the best "deals" I ever made.

In the shopping area the weather was forgotten but on returning to the car park the bike was covered with over three inches of snow, and it was still coming down. As I said before, we were well kitted out, although keeping my hands and feet warm was a problem.

We set off for home, me telling Olive to sit still and not to move a muscle. The journey was slow. All the signposts were obliterated with driving snow. Not many other idiots on the road though. We got back all O.K., albeit a bit cold, but we were going to the dance – well I was anyway.

When we arrived at No. 2 Glendower Avenue, I took out the ring on the front doorstep and officially asked "Will you marry me?". I did not get down on one knee in the snow but was accepted. I also said that Olive deserved the ring there and then. That offer, or idea, was declined and we stuck to the original arrangements, to become engaged at the dance. I would like to say it was a happy evening – a very nice dance and so far they have lived happy everafter.

Christmas came and Christmas went, also the New Year. There was always a dance at The Matrix on Christmas Eve and it was always a rush for me. I seldom got away from work till 4.30 at the nurseries in Kenilworth. On Christmas Eve and Saturdays I had to ensure there was a good supply of fuel, coal and coke, at all the greenhouse boilers in use, probably four. Materials were moved around the nursery on a Wrigley three-wheel motor truck, the engine mounted above the single front wheel which would pivot a complete circle 360 degrees, a very useful device.

I was usually given a small bunch of small chrysanths that had not made the shops for a Christmas box – no comment – but they looked quite nice on the sideboard at home.

Anyhow, once away meant a trip to The Matrix to buy tickets for the dance to make sure of getting in. I think I actually took Olive in on this occasion, newly engaged and all that. She might have even gone to the Fletch as well, but it would have been in the lounge bar. I forget.

I know the dance was great; a super bunch of friends with their congratulations and Christmas good wishes.

A Christmas dance at The Matrix, Fletchampstead Highway, Coventry. We had just become engaged. 1952 (Fashion note: ladies wearing 'The new look' after the war years and after austerity)

Christmas was spent between Meriden Road and Glendower Avenue, lunch at one place, tea at the other, and I like to think a good time was had by all. Not really much different from today, although for my part, Church did not play much of a part in my Christmas at that time. I only had two days off and I am fairly sure that if Christmas Day or Boxing Day came at a weekend, there were no days off in lieu, not for me anyhow.

Next was New Year's Eve and most folks went to bed as usual. New Year's Eve, Mother's Day (Mothering Sunday), Father's Day, had not been invented; Valentine's Day plus Tinsel and Turkey and so on were non events; no-one went out during the evening or out for Sunday lunch; no places were catering then, or very limited and not many could afford it anyhow.

New Year's Eve – Oh yes – there was always a dance in The Reading Room organised by Mrs. Joan Hope. Reg Harris, a four piece, usually provided the music. It was always a crush which made it cozy, if you know what I mean.

Quite a few of the senior members of the parish would turn out on this occasion. I recall the raffle always took a long time and someone would produce a prize to be auctioned or give a prize back. These senior parishioners, most of them "tight and mean", would show off and bid against one another, great for the funds, but I wished to have the lights dimmed and get on with the dancing. Work next morning as it was some years before New Year's Day became a public holiday.

CHAPTER **11**

Getting Wed

I have no idea where the idea came from but the thought of living in a caravan was put to Olive and me. A few enquiries were made and Roger and Amy Simpson had started married life in a caravan. I bumped into him one day and asked him what it was like. His reply was "It's fine, O.K., but make sure you get a big one, as large as can be afforded". Apparently theirs was quite small. They did tend to get in each other's way.

Roger and Amy eventually bought a plot of land in Alder Lane, Balsall Common, and he built a house there himself. They still live there. Roger and his brother Walter were both in the Air Training Corps at the same time as me. They were older and both eventually joined the R.A.F.

On a cold Saturday afternoon, armed with a little knowledge, Olive and I went to see the caravans at the sales park in Meriden, owned then by Bayliss'. We were quite impressed with two or three on view and two in particular. The salesman appeared and gave us the "lowdown". One was brand new, a Fairholme I think, the other second-hand or used, a Berkeley "Ambassador". There was not a mark on it. It looked brand new but a far superior van and the price was about the same as the other new one, which was over two years' of my wages to pay for it.

This van had the lot, for its day, that is. Twenty-two foot in length, that was as big as they came in January 1953. The floor was covered in quality cork linoleum, venetian blinds at all the windows, a solid fuel stove, with airing cupboard, above all, properly insulated. The built-in furniture was genuine light oak and the walls were panelled to match so far up; a settee at one end which opened up to a double bed, and another double bed which folded up in one piece into a recess; a dividing screen (i.e. two rooms), two fairly spacious wardrobes, and quite a few drawers, also hot water from the tank above the stove.

Valerie's Christening, she's nowhere to be seen! Left to right: Mother, Olive, Stella, Father. Nephew Peter and Margaret seated

The kitchen was fully fitted with formica work-tops, a generous sink and draining board, full-size oven grill and four rings on top. There was a small – very small – bathroom, the bath reared up against a wall, plus another wash handbasin. Lighting and heating, apart from the stove, was by calor gas, a cylinder which lasted on average six weeks, but I am over-running the story. There were two doors and the gas bottle was stored inside via a trap door from outside. There were other useful refinements.

This all looked and sounded very good, especially when the salesman said there was a caravan site on Broad Lane (Coventry) opposite the Hawthorn Tree pub. Another bonus, because Olive worked at the then Standard Motor Company at Banner Lane, just ten minutes' walk away. The factory made aero engines (Rolls Royce "Merlins") during the War, in latter days for the "Mosquito". They then made car engines for the Standard eight and ten. They went on to building the Massey-Ferguson tractors in about 1947.

Were we being shown the way? Who knows? However, we put a £2.00 deposit on the Ambassador, went home and informed our respective families what we had been up to.

It was the 24th January. I could not remember, so I worked it back. We went to The Matrix that evening very excited. It was not good for me.

So, with a roof over our heads there was no need to wait any longer and wedding plans commenced there and then. We, Olive and I, got together with both our folks and it was decided that Saturday, April 4th 1953, would be the day, less now than ten weeks away. Easter Saturday in fact.

We met the Rev. Williams, Vicar at Westwood Heath, and there were no problems there. Twelve o'clock midday was to be the time. The reception was fixed to be held at The Cafe opposite The Bear Inn in Berkswell Village. Mrs. Hadley catered for many weddings, christenings, and various village organisations' annual binge, the Sick and Dividend Society, Tennis Club and "Felons" dinner, to name a few. Then came the many other arrangements, nothing like today's proceedings though.

However, there were two bridesmaids, my little sister Margaret who was ten and Olive's niece Beryl Harris. I chose Bill Green to be my Best

Man. He was and still is a steadying influence and level-headed. Only once did he falter to my knowledge – more later.

Olive's brother, Bert, offered to take the photographs. He was at one time previous editor of the publication "Amateur Photographer".

Then there were dresses to be made. Olive and her mother made the bridesmaids' dresses, also her own, and they really were nice I was informed by Olive; probably would not have taken any notice of anyone else.

I really could not afford a suit but we went to Fred Mayne in Fleet Street, Coventry, and came away with a brown double-breasted pinstripe three-piece suit. Nothing to do with the wedding, but I never did like that suit, never felt really at home in it. Many years later I was still trying to wear it out.

One Saturday afternoon, I wore it to go shopping with Olive in Coventry. We were minding our own business in a big store when three young chaps aged about twenty and a "Dulux" dog came up to us ("Dulux" dog – Old English Sheepdog). Says number one "Could you please tell me where you got the suit from, it's fabulous?" and so on and so forth. I thought it was "Candid camera" or another TV stunt but no, fashions must have turned full circle and yours truly was for once – probably the only time – dressed in fashion and style.

I told them the tale. The shop and Fred Mayne had long since gone, but I did offer to swop my suit for their dog. Thank goodness, common sense prevailed. I kept my suit and they had to keep feeding their dog. He was nice, though I never saw his eyes.

Nothing ever got back to me then or since but I bet a few tongues started to wag – old "Webby" getting himself married in a few weeks' time. That usually only meant one thing. If there were any wagging tongues, the owners probably were disappointed.

Funds – our folks' funds – did not run to a big affair, which suited both of us. Nevertheless there were over thirty people at the reception. The wedding, I think, was timed so that people could get to Westwood Church on the bus. A single-decker was hired to get people to Berkswell Village, then there was the bus back to Coventry from there, all clever stuff as very few people had a car in 1953. Television sets were few and far between as well, with only one channel and probably about six hours' viewing daily.

Times were very exciting because at the same time as we bought the caravan I saw, or was told about, an advert in a local newspaper roughly as follows:

"Wanted gardener to organise and grow large quantity of summer bedding plants. Good pay to right man", etc.

So, with nothing to lose, I made contact and arranged a meeting come interview with Jack Barton.

As it turned out, he was a grower of exhibition chrysanthemums and sold chrysanth plants to callers and mail order in the Springtime, well February to end of May.

The nursery was in Brown's Lane, Allesley, between the two entrances to the Jaguar Cars factory. I went along to the house, a semi-detached, and met Jack and his mother, Elsie; I always called her Mrs. Barton. Jack used the greenhouses in the autumn to grow and flower the indoor or late varieties and he only required a small greenhouse to root the chrysanthemum cuttings, starting in mid-December. So, he wanted to utilise the space growing bedding. There was a big demand for bedding plants then and his idea was to offer plants to all at wholesale prices. He said he would organise soil, peat, etc. for compost, also staff for pricking out. Would or could I undertake the job?

I was honest and said that I had not handled that quantity before but was confident I would cope and, as I am sure I was the only applicant, I was offered the job but not before we talked about wages. Jack asked me what I thought would be acceptable and I said £7.00 a week. Much to my surprise, he offered me £7.10.0 (£7.50p) and I finished at 12.30 on Saturdays. But there would certainly be some paid overtime during parts of the year.

I accepted the job. We shook hands, including Mrs. Barton, as I am sure she still had a say as to what went on in the business. I went off home with a seed catalogue under my arm. We were to compare notes in a few days' time in order to get the order for seeds in without delay.

Next day, I handed in my notice to the Douglas brothers and started work for Jack when my notice of one week was worked out.

There was one other fellow employed at Brownsland Nurseries. Stan Pope was a very street-wise young man. He really knew the ins and outs, which is probably the norm today. He also claimed to know quite a number of "important" people, including "Jane" of the Daily Mirror newspaper. For those that do not know, Jane was featured in a daily cartoon-type strip and strip was the operative word. The poor girl was always losing all her clothes, well almost all. Talk about embarrassing moments. Quite a daring column really, as one never saw a picture of a nude anywhere, well perhaps in one publication called Men Only.

Jack lived some way away and had a caravan. Mrs. Barton did a lot of light work with the chrysanths.

The nursery consisted of quite a few back gardens. The houses on Brown's Lane were semi-detached and the plots only about thirty foot wide. The back gardens were very long and narrow and went as far as the Jaguar factory at the bottom end. The Bartons had purchased quite a number of rear gardens and the nursery was about an acre. There were two or three small greenhouses about twelve feet wide and forty feet in length, one very large greenhouse for the chrysanths in pots, and a Dutch light house.

All materials had to be wheeled in from the road where it was tipped by the delivery lorry. Soil, peat, and sand, also coal and coke for the greenhouse boilers. Coal was still rationed to householders in 1953, eight years after the end of the war.

We had a two-wheel truck for getting in the materials and we put perhaps six or seven hundredweight on this. One pulled and the other pushed. Fortunately it was downhill but I thought highly dangerous if the one in front ever slipped.

After I had been there a while I asked Jack if he would consider buying a Wrigley motor truck like we had in Kenilworth and in due course one arrived, which made the job easier, quicker and more safe. The only problem was I often had the whole lot to shift on my own. I did not really mind.

At the start I began riddling soil for the growing compost, fixing up some staging with Jack in the warmest part of the big house. The seed arrived and sowing began in a big way, using the John Innes formula that we used at Kenilworth, four parts soil, two parts peat, and two parts sharp coarse sand for seed sowing and seven parts soil, three parts peat and two parts sand for the pricking out. All plants were pricked out sixty to a seed tray, all wooden trays, no plastic then. Antirrhinums, lobelia, ageratum and salvia first, then stocks, asters, nemesia, petunia and so on. Last of all, the fast growers like marigolds and alyssum.

It was a real challenge. 4,000 boxes was my brief and I am pleased to say we made the target and sold out in early June.

At the same time, all sorts of other happenings were taking place. Olive's sister Lily and Alf had adopted Delia and we became Godparents. We also became Peter's (my nephew) Godparents.

Most importantly, our wedding plans were all falling into place, with a lot of sewing taking place at No. 2 Glendower Avenue. I was very fortunate during our courtship to have a night out with the lads now and again, well sometimes once a week. It nearly always was a pint or three somewhere, in whatever direction we were going. I went to dances in Warwick

Brownsland Nurseries chrysanthemum exhibit at a show in Sheffield

and Leamington with Eddy Horsley, then started going to Hinckley with the Saturday crowd from the "Fletch". I would meet Sammy Wakelam by or inside the Bear Inn. Sam was about twelve years my senior, a farmer's son from Fernhill Lane, off Balsall Street. He had an old car, kept together with binder string and bits of wire. We picked up the others at various points and then off to Hinckley and The White Hart.

They got to know us very well at the pub where we holed out till getting on for 9.30. We left Sam's car at the pub, crossed the road and into the dance hall where there was always a nice crowd, a good band, and a bar upstairs. As far as I was concerned, it was all harmless fun – honest. We danced the night away, till 11 or 11.30, had a good old chinwag, another drink during the interval and then home again.

When it came to my "bachelor night out" before the wedding, there was only one place to go, Hinckley. I met Sam in The Bear and we had a couple of pints of black and tan, a half pint bottle of cream label stout topped up with draught beer. We picked up Bill Green, Brian James and Jack Payne and off we went. At The White Hart we all bought a round of black and tan, then just before leaving, Bill Green ordered whiskeys all round. I did enjoy a drop of rum in those days. We filed into the dance and it was very soon the interval, the signal to visit the upstairs bar, and we all bought a round of half pints of beer and whiskey or rum chasers. As I said before, we had got to know the barman who knew what we had had and why. On leaving he said to me that if I could get back up the stairs from the ballroom I could have my choice of drink on the house!

We all trooped downstairs and I had a dance. On my return to where we all stood, Sam was there on his own. After the next dance I was on my own. Sam had disappeared. I could not work it out – I felt fine. I did find some of them in the toilets and apparently one or two were outside. I went back to the ballroom and the next set was some Olde Thyme dances or sequence dances that I did not know, so what else, up the stairs for my free drink. I had the same again, a beer and rum chaser, shook hands with the barman and spent the last half of the dance on my own. Then I had the job of rounding them up to go home. I more or less got them all together, went to look for the last one, got 'im, but by the time I got back another one had gone. However, I knew where he was. Eventually we got loaded up in the car and started for home. Thankfully old Sam seemed to be O.K., although this was long before the breathaliser rules came in.

There were a few comfort stops on the way. I never felt better, or so I thought. Again, it was long before I got round to learning to drive. Never given it a thought in fact; no need. Sam was the only driver amongst us.

We dropped off Jack somewhere near the Forum on Walsgrave Road and Brian was next. He and Bill were now asleep in the back. I sat in the front with Sam. Instead of dropping Brian off in Hearsall Lane, he insisted on taking him into Earlsdon Avenue and then into Bristol Road. Brian got out and vanished and Sam began a three point turn, but half way through and in the middle of the road, passed out. I shook, punched and kicked him. He was breathing O.K. It probably only lasted a couple of minutes but to me seemed like two hours when eventually his eyes opened. I could just see him under the street light. He had a mumble, shook himself, and away we went, much to my relief. I don't think Sam realised what had happened and Bill, my best man, was spark out in the back. As we went over the Hearsall Common towards Tile Hill Lane and to the A45 I was trying to waken Bill. By the time we got to the Fletchampstead Highway Bill was sort of mobile. We stopped, he grunted and was gone.

On to Berkswell crossroads. I got out, wished Sam a goodnight – what was left of it, walked the three quarters of a mile home, let myself in home, and went to bed. I slept like a log all night. Phew!! What a night!

Up next morning, as usual, to a hot breakfast of bacon and egg, etc. Mother saying "Did you have a nice evening then?". "Yes thank you" says I, wondering what was coming next. It was a job to hide anything from my mother, not as I ever tried you understand.

She said "I heard you come in; a bit late wasn't it? But I knew you were alright, hearing your steady footsteps on the road". Oh well, all's well that ends well. She did say something about "I bet Olive had been in bed for hours" – right again you see.

That was my final visit to Hinckley and really have not missed it one little bit. Thank goodness it was on the Wednesday and not the Friday evening, as most bachelor nights were. I never have understood why I felt very little effects of alcohol on that night. Bill Green has been more or less tee-total ever since; he apparently suffered for days and said and meant "Never again".

It was work as usual for me the next day. We were very busy at work, me with the bedding plant programme, a challenge I really enjoyed, and the others with the propagating and dispatching of rooted chrysanthemum cuttings.

The cycle of the main business was chrysanths. Just after the war there was a big demand for quality plants. Brownsland filled the bill. Every year Jack Barton would purchase new varieties. The blooms of all the new varieties would have been on show at the Horticultural Halls, Vincent Square, Westminster, the early varieties at the September Show and the "lates" in November. Jack would probably buy in ten or so new varieties, the ones he thought had the best potential to grow on and produce good varieties for showing. These would be grown on and the resulting blooms showed at the next year's shows. Orders were taken at the shows and a catalogue was produced; more on that later – I have an important date next Saturday.

I had to work on the Good Friday and was off till the following Wednesday.

In 1953, as far as Olive and I were concerned anyhow, getting married did not seem to me as big a rigmarole as it is today, but I was only the bridegroom.

Goodness knows in fact what was going on at Glendower Avenue.

My workmate, Stan Pope, made the bouquets, ladies' sprays and button-holes for the men. He came to our house and must have delivered same to Olive's home.

The big day arrived. I had a few errands to run. We were spending the whole time at the caravan, only no-one knew. For two reasons, we could not afford to go away, also I was broke. However, we had bought a small portable radio and I took that to the caravan, together with some last-minute provisions. Olive had done the same so we would not starve.

When Bill Green arrived I was still in the greenhouse. Where else? all those who knew me would say. However he chivvied me up. I had had a bath the night before in the old tin bath in the wash-house. I was ready in good time and off to St. John's, Westwood Heath, with Bill in a Standard "Vanguard" – Shirleys of Meriden Taxi.

Easter Saturday and a glorious day. The Church was all beautifully decorated for Easter. We did not have to supply any flowers. We had been to see the Reverend Williams previously and he was there to conduct the ceremony. Shame on me, but I do not recall the service in great detail; the flowers in Church and Uncle Bob Hammond playing the organ, yes. I know it all went well. Olive's brother Bert took photographs at the Church and later at the reception.

Olive and I sped off in Shirley's Vanguard to the Garden Cafe at Berkswell, opposite The Bear Inn. It is now known as The Malt House, greeted by Mrs. Kirby, mother of John, who helped out very often at the Cafe run very well by Mrs. Hadley. More or less everyone else followed on in a hired Coventry Corporation single-decker bus. The only car there belonged to Sam.

There were about thirty guests and I enjoyed it all immensely. The only disaster was the bridegroom's speech, "not being accustomed" and with no previous advice or planning. I was tongue-tied, just about able to stammer a few thank-you's on behalf of my wife and I.

Then came the going away, everyone wanting to know where, was it Southsea, Weston-Super-Mare, or Skegness? Only my mother knew the answer and she did not let on.

The Vanguard duly arrived. Alf and one or two others tied National Dried Milk tins on the back and off we went in all our wedding attire. Fortunately, no-one followed. Only Sam could anyway and he would not have thought of such a thing.

The plan was to go to Olive's old home where she would change. I would take off, wait for it – my buttonhole; meanwhile the car waited round in the next street. The driver then took us to Pool Meadow bus terminus where we decided to get on the first Midland Red bus we saw. It could have been Rugby, Nuneaton, Birmingham or Stratford, but in fact we went to Leamington.

We had a wander round and had some tea in one of the big stores, then set off for our new home. It was getting dark when we arrived at No. 11 Farcroft Caravan Park. It had just started to rain as I carried Olive over the threshold (as one should).

Next morning we woke up and it was still pouring down as it did all day Sunday and Monday, finally clearing up in the afternoon of Tuesday.

After all the rush and bustle it was nice to take it easy, get up late and so on, something I had not been able to do for a long time, apart from a bit of a lay-in on Sundays.

There were quite a lot of thank-you letters to write. Our relatives and friends were most generous towards us and as I write, forty-five and a half years on, some of those gifts are still in everyday use.

Speaking to the lads at the wedding, mainly about our night out, they all said "Never again". Bill said he did not recall anything after leaving the pub till he woke up the next morning all as usual, in his own bed, at home. His clothes were all put away, suit hung up all neat and tidy.

We soon settled down into quite a good routine. I was up first and cooked my own breakfast and, with a few exceptions, I have got my own breakfast ever since. With reference to the saying "Start as you mean to go on", there is of course a bonus side to that and that is one has what one chooses and not what one is given.

Olive went in early as overtime. She assisted with opening the mail. I had to be there at eight o'clock and worked till five with a half hour at one o'clock for lunch, in the warmest greenhouse when chilly and a seat out-side on the better days.

During the time we were selling bedding plants I very often had to get up and serve customers; I did enjoy it all though, we all had a lot of fun – most of the time.

Friday evenings the washing was done. We had a toilet block close by with cold water sinks for swilling, also hoppers for disposing of waste water from the kitchen. It was quite a little walk to the toilet. I had been used to going outside to the privvy, but not Olive. But we were young weren't we? No problem.

The only sad thing about our caravan was that it was all wired up for electricity but although we had lights all round the park there were no hook-ups. The park was quite new when we went on and there was quite a good camaraderie amongst the "early settlers". They all turned out to site an incoming van, Tommy Morton and Tommy Hill to name two.

Bayliss delivered the caravan for their clients and that was it. It was preferable to jack up the 'van and get the wheels just above the ground, so that they would turn round. This was to protect the tyres as much as possi-ble, exposing them to fresh air all round, also take the weight off.

The van was levelled by adjusting the four jacks on the corners. It was important to have the van level otherwise interior drawers and doors would probably warp, especially on cheaper model caravans.

Olive's parents bought us a nice size shed – maximum size allowed – as a wedding present. We bought some paving slabs and the weekend work-free helped me put them down. It was my turn to help others later on. We were No. 11, we had a choice of site, and there were only about fifteen vans on before us. There were well over 120 before we left.

So began a very happy married life. We were cool in the summer time and cosy in the winter when we had to take care not to let the calor gas bottle freeze up. It was inside a trap door anyhow. Also, the waste water could be a problem. The rent was fifteen shillings per week (75p) which was a bit above the going rate but we were satisfied.

In addition to my work, I was growing bedding plants in my greenhouse at home, also trying to cultivate "my" side of the garden. It did get a bit of a problem because when I was busy at work, jobs needed to be done at Meriden Road. My folks did their best, however, and all was not lost.

One or two other things happened in 1953. There was to be a Coronation on June 2nd. Queen Elizabeth II was to be crowned and Philip became the Duke of Edinburgh.

1953 and television was beginning to become very popular. Mr. and Mrs. Fletcher (the people I used to take eggs to in the village – he was the retired butler from Berkswell Hall) now lived next door to us in Meriden Road. They had a telly with an 8" screen and we were invited to watch the Coronation ceremony on their television. Mrs. Fletcher was very nice but very prim and proper, so togged up a bit and went along. It must have been our first experience of T.V. and was to be a long time before we had one.

There were the usual village celebrations. First of all, in the afternoon, a parade of floats, all village organisations invited to take part. Decorate a tractor and trailer, or whatever, with a theme, all dress up and make merry. The Rover crew was still stuttering on and together we decided to be "The Giles Family", a daily cartoon strip from one of the daily newspapers. Guess who was Ma Giles? My husband, Mr. Giles, was Bill Green. I borrowed one of Olive's mother's dresses and all sorts of other clobber, including a straw hat. We put a big "baby" scout in a battered old pram and he hung over both ends, holding a big beer bottle with a teat on the end. All the rest of my ruffian family running around and getting into all sorts of trouble.

We assembled at the Reading Room for the judging and the prize went to Berkswell Women's Institute. The trophy hangs in the Reading Room still. The parade moved off through the village, along Old Lane (now Lavender Hall Lane) towards Balsall, turning into and through the spinney into Wheatley's Long Meadow at Butcher's Barn, some three hundred yards from the village green.

There were all sorts of races for young and others. Sideshows and so on. The Rover Crew and scout leaders had the job of letting off the fire-works. There was also the big bonfire, built and looked after by the estate workers, my father included. The bonfire and fireworks were on the far side of the brook which runs through the meadow.

Naturally, there was a beer tent which was well patronised and we were all well "lit up" long before any fireworks were let off – not incapable, mind you, although one of two rockets were let off on a slight angle to go over the spectators, a stupid thing to do, but I suppose boys will be boys. There were no casualties, the rockets all landing well away from people, also there were no complaints, but we have never been asked to let off the fireworks since. It is probably because there has never been a Coronation since.

The day ended with a dance in the Reading Room, which was packed to the rafters.

The scout group was still going strong but the Rover Crew ceased functioning soon after. The fact that one or two of us got married, some had got called up for their National Service did not help matters. At the time, we had started a project to provide the village with a new and much needed notice board. Harold Hewitt, the farmer at Blind Hall and once upon a time a builder, carpenter and joiner, provided the wood – I think. There were two stout uprights to go into the ground, a heavy wooden frame to hold three panels of thick chipboard for pinning the notices on. The whole had a lych roof sloping down over the notice board and the roof was clad with shingle. It was to be erected by the crossroads. I think Harold had the job of finishing it off and it was erected by the Churchyard gate by the men from the Berkswell Estate – my father, Jack Woolley and no doubt supervised by the Estate foreman, Billy Tranter.

I do not think I mentioned it before, but Billy Tranter lived just down the road from us, near to the drive up to Home Farm, which was always known as Chapel Hill. He gave me my first haircut. One Saturday afternoon after dinner my father took me down to Tranter's. We went round the back and onto the back yard and stood me on a dining chair – me holding onto the back. On went the cloth and I was not too keen as he started snipping away. I was a bit meek and mild then and dare not protest. All the time he was reassuring me and saying things like "how good I was".

Billy and his wife Gertrude (always Mrs. Tranter to us kids, and our parents for that matter; one did not hear many first names then, always Mr. or Mrs. so and so) never had any children but they always thought a lot of Stella and me. They would come to the garden gate or pop a head above the hedge if they heard us passing. They had a big garden and it was all cultivated. He grew a huge patch of daffodils, which they cut and sold and gave all the proceeds to the Red Cross. Oh, by the way, I had my hair cut many times on Billy Tranter's back yard. When he had done mine it was Father's turn and the cost was one Will's Woodbine (cigarette) per head so, because I did not smoke then, it was free for me.

Another character that worked on Berkswell Estate was Alfie Carter. He also was capable of "gents' hairdressing". He lived down at "The Nuek" by Barnacles Farm at Bradnocks Marsh, just over the main road in fact from where I first started work for Mrs. Morris.

I first remember Alfie (Mr. Carter to me) when I first went to school. Carters had the shop in the village. They had three children, Edgar, Roland and Maud. Mrs. Carter ran the shop, Alfie worked during the day, and spent many hours repairing boots and shoes in the evenings.

The young Carters were all older than me, and eventually they left the shop and the village to live at The Nuek. It is said that due to their young-sters helping themselves to sweets and goodies from the shop was the main reason for their departure.

Alfie Carter stood less than five feet tall, always smartly dressed in boots and leather leggings (a type of gaiter) worn over his corduroy breech-es, a jacket and always a cap at a slightly jaunty angle. An avid pipe smoker (I don't know what it cost for a haircut) with clouds of smoke when he lit up. There was no job on the Estate or farm that Alfie could not do and, what is more, he made a perfect job of whatever he was given to do.

During the War the farm was desperate for some help with the corn harvest and the Estate men were called in. They worked separately from the farm men and set about "carrying" corn – that is to say carting the sheaves of corn and stacking it in this case in the corner of the field.

Alfie built the rick and it was a masterpiece, not your ordinary oblong square-sided rick. This one started quite small at the bottom, straight sides, and the ends were a half circle; as it went up so it went out – the ends more than the sides – and ending looking rather like a ship. When it was fin-ished Alfie thatched it as lots of ricks were then, with fancy edging and tufts at each end on the top. The farm men were most upset as their ricks were quite inferior to Alfie's and it was thought at the time that it was jeal-ousy that caused that particular rick to be threshed first.

Another of Alfie's talents was as a mole catcher. There were a lot of moles in the area where they lived and I understand he was up at the crack of dawn to go round his many traps on the local farms. Having caught the mole it would be skinned and the pelt stretched out on a board to dry off. I think he rubbed saltpetre onto the inside of the pelt to assist the process. He got sixpence per pelt (2p).

He also was a champion hedge cutter and could trim a hedge with a brushing hook as neat as a pair of shears and much quicker. A brushing hook is almost five foot long with a straight wooden handle and a curved metal hook for cutting, sharp as a razor – also known as a slash hook.

One final little story regarding Alfie, then I will let him rest in peace. Sometimes after knocking off time (12.30) on Saturdays, one or two blokes on the Estate would drop into The Bear for a drop – if you follow. I was only a naive young lad at the time and when Father came home (and he would always have more to say after a couple of pints of mild), Mother would say "Alfie at The Bear?". Father's reply: "Yes". Mother: "Is he going gardening this afternoon at Miss Records?" "Oh ar, he's going to touch Pol's front up this afternoon". At which they both were in fits of laughter and great merriment. It took me a long while to work that one out and, as a gardener I always had to be careful when working in a front garden. R.I.P. Alfie.

It was just before the Coronation that one evening after work I popped over home on the motorbike to have a look at the newly- planted tomato plants and so on, walked into the house, and there sat this sailor. I knew he was a sailor by his uniform. He had his cap on one knee and I spotted the word "Sydney". Mother says "I bet you don't know who this is?" "Thinks" – it must be David or Alan from Australia and I said "David". Hole in one! We had had no news from our Uncle and Aunt or four cousins in Australia and they had no news of us, as far as I can recall, although I think Mother's sister, Ruth, wrote now and again to her brother Harry.

Well, there was no gardening done that evening. It turned out David was a crew member of the aircraft carrier Sydney of the Australian Navy. The ship had brought contingents of Service personnel to take part in the Coronation procession and celebrations – personnel from Australia, New Zealand, Fiji and one or two other locations in the Pacific.

They were in England for quite a while, six weeks or more. I took David out and about a bit on the back of my bike. He wanted to swop places but there was no way that was going to happen.

He was not very interested in our ancient buildings or places of interest. Women and a pint or two was his main object. I think it was a good job I was newly married, otherwise he might have led me astray. His mother had given him quite a list of relatives to look up. Some were distant cousins about five or six times removed, but Aunt Marie (Marion) had kept in touch with some of them. We did attempt to look one or two up at Great Alne and others between Coventry and Rugby, without much success I'm afraid.

We took David to one or two dances but cannot recall how we got him there or back home. Bill Green remembers David just a bit "de lux" on our beer on at least one occasion. However, it was good to learn a little about our relatives down-under and was the first encounter of quite a few with Cousin David. After their wedding at Freemantle, in about 1926, Uncle Harry and Aunt Marie went to live at Nannup, which is located about 150 miles south of Perth, and 40 miles or so east of Busselton, on the coast of West Australia. He became a dairy farmer, and when the farm was sold, many years later, it was over 90 acres which he had "claimed" from the bush.

The scrub was cleared off first, and I understand large trees were ring-barked and from this treatment they died, very little mechanical aids then, but cable winches were used. At first they lived in a home-made wooden shed type structure, and later a better wooden bungalow.

They had a hard tough life, in common with many others. Times were especially bad in the early thirties when the depression was at its worst, apparently there was very little money about, and lots of people, including Harry and Marie survived by bartering milk, eggs, etc.

As time went on things got better, but it was no doubt a struggle to bring up four children, Betty, David, Alan and Esther.

Aunt Marie did return to England once in about 1930, bringing Betty with her, the next visit was in 1954 when she and Harry came for about seven months on an extended visit – all by sea, of course, taking about four weeks one way.

Our belated honeymoon was Devon and Cornwall on the motorbike in early July, for the first time ever, two whole weeks. We nearly did not make it. I used to go to work via Lower Eastern Green and through a very narrow lane called Park Hill Lane. About three mornings before our planned holiday, I met a small lorry on a bend in this lane. I think we were both going too fast and there was an awful crunching sound. After I got up and decided I was O.K., it was time to have a look at the bike, which was just about alright, except for a smashed headlight. The ignition switch was built into the headlamp and although bits were floating about and all floppy-like, it worked. There was no damage to the lorry or driver so off we went. I got to work and at lunchtime we taped it all together with insulation tape, and off I went to Alec Stadden's Garage in the evening. He made a better job of the taping up and said he would get a new headlamp the next day. In the meantime I had no lights, which was not an offence then. By Friday evening no new headlamp was to be had from anywhere so we decided to go without it, setting off about nine o'clock on a nice dry sunny morning.

We got as far as Moreton-in-Marsh and the clutch cable fell in half. A good motorcyclist would have had a spare all threaded through just to hook up at each end. Needless to say, I was without; however I was in the R.A.C., and as it was quite early in the morning, no problem thought I.

We went to a large garage in Moreton, which was proudly showing off a big R.A.C. sign outside the premises. Inside, no-one wanted to know – just another motorcyclist – too bad sort of thing. Today I would hit the roof, but had to accept the fact that no help was forthcoming. We stood on the side of the road for a long time, hoping a patrolman would come along, no such luck. In the end I pushed the bike – loaded down with all our gear – up onto a bridge which took the road over the railway. We both got on and I kicked up the bike, glided down the hill, and gently "slid" into gear.

We went all the way to Cirencester in this fashion, carefully timing the traffic lights at Northleach and roared over on the green. We did not quite make it up the other side so I turned the bike round, instructed Olive to walk to the top of the hill and hop on as I came past in bottom gear. Down the hill a few yards, engine running, slipped into bottom gear (of three), turned round in the road, made the top O.K. Olive nipped on and away we went.

I was directed to the premises of a motorbike mechanic – a bloke who mends motorbikes – he would fix it, but not till Monday morning. He had to get the new cable.

We found two nights' B and B close by and when we woke on the Sunday morning it was pouring with rain and kept on all day. What to do was the problem. In the end we went to Bristol on the local bus. At least we kept dry. Had we been on the bike goodness knows what we would have been like.

On our way soon after eleven, with not a big expense for repairs, and a nice morning as well. We based ourselves in Ilfracombe for a few days, then went on to Newquay in Cornwall where our landlady was very worried if we were not in well before lighting-up time. We were a bit on the last minute more than once.

The rest of the holiday went well, although due I think to neglect, the bike did not like the steep hills in Devon. We had to choose a route home trying to avoid big hills. This we managed more or less alright and after a very nice holiday overall, it was back to work on Monday morning.

Most of the time now was taken up growing the chrysanthemums to show in September for the earlies and November for the lates.

My job was mainly with the early varieties growing in orderly rows out-side in the nursery. There were three main types, reflex with petals hang-ing outwards and down, like a mop; Incurving, with petals mostly curving upwards and inwards in a fairly loose habit, and the incurves which had all petals curving inwards and the bloom finishing up in a complete ball shape. All the varieties that made the show-bench were classified into various groups and every class at a show was for so many blooms of a particular classified group. Sounds complicated, not so after a short time.

We could identify many varieties by the foliage, as a shepherd knows his sheep. So there I was, hoeing, tying up, and later on dis-budding; the centre bud was retained and all other buds and shoots on that stem were removed so that the plant put all its energy into the terminal buds of which there were about four per plant. When the buds were about half open, the blooms were then "bagged"; we used brown paper grocery bags, blew them out and slipped the open end over the flower and tied it tight, just under the bud. This was to protect the bloom from bad weather.

Getting the plants to flower at the showdates was crucial. This was mainly controlled by the date the plant was "stopped". This was usually in the middle of May when the plants were about ten inches tall. They were stopped just by pinching out the growing tip to make the plant bush out.

Some varieties did this all by themselves and were known as natural breaks. All clever and interesting stuff. Show-time was long and hard. It started off by cutting the blooms and about thirty blooms were required of each variety. The ends of the stems were crushed and they were placed in deep flower buckets for a minimum of twelve hours. There were special boxes to pack them in for transit to the show. Canes were placed across the box each end in special holes in the sides of these huge boxes. The head of each bloom just rested on the cane, then another row just above and so on.

Jack Barton had quite a large van for transport and usually one or two others went with him, depending on the size of stand we were putting up and distance to travel. The timber stand was always ready on our arrival, all erected to Jack's instructions, i.e. so many tiers at what width and so on.

The first job was to cover all the timber with black material, then to put up the back row poles. These were wooden poles with hoops attached all the way down. Into each hoop a metal funnel was placed and filled with water. The blooms were then arranged into the funnels to form a display of about thirty blooms per pole. Jack did most of the arranging. I only had a go when he got so tired he didn't hardly know what he was about sometimes. We often worked right through the night, with very little to eat or drink, but managed to survive. We were not alone, either; the hall, wherever we were, would be seething with activity, but somehow it always seemed to take us longer than anyone else.

We went all over the country – Birmingham, Sheffield, Southampton, Bristol, Reading and always twice to Vincent Square in London for the Early Flowering National and the Late National. There was always great competition for medals awarded for excellence and Brownsland Nurseries were never far from the top; nearly always beating the local rivals, Woolmans of Shirley (Birmingham). They are still going strong but the nursery is over near Evesham nowadays.

We were paid an extra £3.00 per show and had to wait a long time to get it sometimes. On quite a number of occasions I went to the show on my motorbike, especially the early shows, so that when the show was up, or the work finished, I came home to water all the lates in pots on the nursery.

After the first season I was there, Stan Pope left and Bob Lamb came to take his place. We got on very well and he had a "goon-type" sense of humour. He was single and did his job very well, but would never do any overtime, except at show-time. Despite this, he was always the favourite. Somehow or other Jack seemed to treat me different to Bob. It did not matter to me, but I did notice this.

Jack put up another large greenhouse and he and I put all the heating pipes in. Heavy cast-iron 4" pipes, a flow and a return to and from the boiler all the way round the 'house, caulking all the joints with tarred rope and cement mortar. During the work he told me we were doing 5,000 boxes of bedding next year. After the current year that would be easy. The late chrysanths were all grown in eight inch clay pots. The lates were rooted first, they needed a longer growing period. The first cuttings were taken in January and there were the Japanese (Japs) varieties. The blooms of these are huge, eight, nine inches across, probably larger now. Again, all the Japs and lates were classified into their various groups according to the variety. There were also the singles, the blooms of which were up to five inches in diameter. When rooted they were potted into three inch pots and then about March into five inch and grown on slowly in the frames. The final potting was into eight inch pots during June. They were then all stood outside in rows and grown on until early October, when they were carefully carried into the greenhouses for flowering.

And so another year was coming to an end. We finished work early on Christmas Eve, a quiet time of the year. I had to make sure there was plenty of fuel placed handy to the stoke hole. Jack always stoked the boilers. I think he thought he was best at the job and he was probably right.

After work, and armed with a pay packet, I went into Coventry and met Bob (he went on the bus) at Waters Wine Lodge in High Street; wine and "shorts" only in there. Some of his mates were there as well. We did ourselves quite well and came out in a good mood. Bob decided to buy his girlfriend some nice undies, so we went with him to help him choose. Well, he had all sorts of advice from all quarters. I felt sorry for the charming shop assistant who could just be seen over the piles of various garments on the counter. The place was in uproar – all good-humoured. He eventually made his purchase and then we all parted company to do our own thing.

I always enjoyed a lone bit of a spend-up on Christmas Eve; just a few special goodies to enjoy. We only had two days off and nothing at New Year at the time.

We spent our time between Meriden Road and Glendower Avenue, having visited the other relatives previously. Naturally, the Matrix still played a part in our social life at Christmas and Saturday evenings.

1954 came in and followed the pattern set the previous year, although I did not get married again. At work I was able to start the plant programme earlier and so that went very well and the target of 5000 boxes of bedding plants was reached with very few hitches.

This was the year Uncle Harry and Aunt Marie of Australia came visiting. They stayed most of the time with my folks at Meriden Road and Aunt Ruth and family at Barford. Aunt Marie spent a lot of time looking up relatives of both sides of their family and I think one or two old friends that she had kept in touch with for almost thirty years. Uncle Harry had to keep himself occupied and for quite a long spell got a job and worked in the Estate yard with my father.

They both got on very well with Captain Wheatley-Hubbard, son-in-law of Mrs. Wheatley of Berkswell Hall. He more or less ran the estate and had a great knowledge of forestry.

We thought it was through David's visit the previous year that spurred them on to make the trip. Naturally they came by sea, one month en route in each direction. It was a dreadful summer weatherwise. I recall my mother saying "Fancy, there was not one evening when we could sit outside in the evening". Uncle Harry was surprised that we could ever sit outside after tea. He never came again and it was to be eight years before we had any more visitors from "down under".

By now we were enjoying two weeks' annual holiday, two days at Christmas, two at Easter, one at Whitsun – on Whit Monday – long before the Spring Bank Holiday was thought of and not necessarily at Whitsun which is seven weeks after Easter. We had the first Monday in August which was a Bank Holiday, then a long run up to Christmas. However, it was all with pay. I do recall a paid day's holiday for the Coronation on June 2nd 1953; Jack Barton was not happy.

During Uncle Harry and Aunt Marie's visit, the Australian cricketers were touring England and that provoked a bit of rivalry. My mother took quite an interest in the game for the first time and there was a lot of banter as the test matches ebbed and flowed. I seem to think we – England – did quite well that year.

My motorbike was now not all that reliable so I decided to sell it at an auction. It was not much good going to a dealer as I really could not afford another new one. However, it was sold and I bought an old 1935 B.S.A. off my Uncle Frank, husband of Dad's sister Elsie. What I was thinking of heaven only knows, an old banger in my incompetent hands. It cost £30.00 and Frank gave me £2.00 back for "luck money", an old custom one came across from time to time, but years ago luck money was I understand almost expected on some deals.

The bike was collected and performed alright, so we decided to go to Scotland for our holidays, on the bike naturally. The great Saturday came and after loading up, away we went. All went well till we got just beyond Ashbourne, having decided to go "the pretty way" up through the Pennines for the first time. No motorway for many years, the direct route via Lichfield, Stone, Stafford, Warrington and Wigan was, I thought, a bit dreary with so many towns to negotiate.

There is a big hill out of Ashbourne and a few miles after the top the bike seized up and we came to a stop. I was not too happy and Olive was having a good cry. "That's the end of our holiday. What are we going to do?" and so on. At that moment in time I hadn't got a clue, but did not say so. We had tea in a flask so we had that and something to eat sitting on the side of the road.

There was no traffic at all, as I recall, no-one stopped anyhow. After about three quarters of an hour, I cursed the bike and our "luck money" once again, sat astride the machine and depressed the kick-start. To my amazement the piston was free so I gave it a proper kick and the engine burst into some sort of life – hooray for luck money!

Now it was really time to think and plan. We decided first of all that it would be unwise to carry on, so after a big think, we decided to head towards home but not directly. Ray Wallis, my Army pal, lived at Bonsall not many miles away. We would try and get there first of all. This we did and found bed and breakfast at Cromford, near Matlock Bath.

That evening we spent walking around the area and would visit the Wallis family the next day. Mr. Wallis, Ray's father, was a rep for a grain merchant, buying and selling grain seed, poultry, pig and cattle foodstuff, etc. and he was on the 'phone. Yes, it was O.K. to call in the morning. They were a very nice family and it was always like going home. I had push-biked there a few times before I met Olive and went on the motorbike as well, often returning in the fog and icy cold evenings. Once we set off for home in a snowstorm, which fortunately petered out as we got closer to home.

Calling at the Wallis home in Bonsall on the Sunday morning, we were made welcome for lunch and lots of talking. I think Ray would have been courting, or walking out with Marcelene by then. They insisted we stay for tea which was always early at 4.00 p.m. on Sundays. Then onto the old B.S.A. and set off for home, at the caravan.

We came home very steadily, trying not to overheat the engine and after calling to report to my folks of the events, arrived home all safe and sound about 8.00 p.m.

We were supposed to be on holiday and I had a plan. We unpacked the pannier bags and borrowed a suitcase and re-packed that. Olive was ironing dresses and the like till quite late and eventually we were ready to set off once more. Up early on the Monday morning, caught the bus into Pool Meadow, Coventry, and into the office of the Royal Blue Coach Company who operated most of the regular coach routes in those days, together with The Black and White Coaches.

We managed to book a return trip to Ilfracombe and had to change coaches at Cheltenham. Coaches left Coventry for all parts at 8.00 a.m. and from Cheltenham at 10.00 a.m.

The weather was good to us and we stayed with Mr. and Mrs. Bishop by the Hillsborough, a welcoming retired couple who cared for us like family. During our stay we took the local bus to Newquay in Cornwall and stayed for a few days, returning to the Bishops to finish the holiday.

On one memorable day it was suggested we go to Heddons Mouth. Getting the local bus to Heddon Cross, walking about one and a half miles down to the pub (Hunters' Inn) where we took refreshment. Some-one at the hostelry suggested we walk on to Lynton via Woody Bay and the Valley of the Rocks. One should be able to walk there in X time, so we thought it would be O.K. and off we trotted.

The weather was hot and we really were not kitted out for serious walking. Also, we had nothing to eat or drink, apart from sweets, and no map which in the event was not required, although I would have had some indication of how far we had come, or more to the point, how far we still had to walk on our hike to Lynton.

It was a lovely walk up over moorland to begin with and then dropping down to a track at Woody Bay, with the blue, blue sea in view most of the time, following the track which was two narrow strips of tarmac with grass in the middle. It is now quite a good road with passing places from Lynton to Hunter's Inn and then on to Coombe Martin. It was, and perhaps still is, part of Woody Bay Estate. On we trekked and eventually out through a lodge and tollgate by Lee Abbey, which has been a place of religious retreat and learning for many years.

An uphill walk now to the Valley of the Rocks and we were getting weary and tired. Also, Olive had a blister on one foot. However, we had to catch a bus back to Ilfracombe and there was not a lot of time so onward and upward past the Lynton cricket ground and into the town to find the bus; sufficient to say we made it with less than five minutes to spare and at the time I could cheerfully have caused the bloke who suggested the hike serious bodily harm. It took us more than twice the time he suggested it should be. We did ache for a couple of days, and Olive did have a whopping great blister. So ended another of my famous walks. Since then we have been via Woody Bay many times and it is still as beautiful, also now one can have refreshments at the Toll Lodge and their strawberries and cream teas are superb. It is all well worth a visit.

One of the test matches was in progress whilst we were on holiday and eavesdropping on portable radios and enquiring about the score was quite important for me, if not perhaps for Olive. Anyhow, what started out seemingly disastrous ended up very well indeed, apart from blistered feet and aching limbs.

We returned home after a very good holiday made quite special by Mr. and Mrs. Bishop in their small terraced house at Chambercombe. At our first enquiry for B and B there were no vacancies and the landlady there recommended the Bishops to us.

We returned home to the schedule of work and looked forward to the weekends which still began for me at 12.30 p.m. on Saturdays.

I used the old B.S.A. for a while but did not have the problem investigated, thinking it was throwing good money after bad, as they say. The problem was either a faulty oil pump or a blocked oil pipe, probably not a major problem. With hindsight I should have kept the old "thrasher". It would be quite valuable today.

In the end I went out and bought a brand new 197 cc two-stroke Francis Barnett, a lovely little 'bike with a dual seat and I thought a "nice-looker". I could not afford a bigger model like a Norton or Triumph. My, or our, little modest performer was O.K. by me.

I also treated myself to a new long motorcycling coat and crash hat. It was only competition riders who wore motorcycling suits and enclosed helmets at that time.

As Christmas came closer I decided once again to make holly wreaths and apart from the usual orders from local people, I got a contract to supply a greengrocer's shop at the top of Hearsall Lane, just over the Common. Some of the work was done in the greenhouse at the weekends, at Meriden Road and at the caravan in the week. Conditions were rather cramped but the revenue would come in handy. Olive and I delivered wreaths to the shop in the evenings on the bus, quite a tricky operation I can say.

Talking of revenue, it was about this time that the Prudential Assurance Co. had another go at me. My mother was still paying my money to the agent, as it was convenient for both of us, on the fifteen year policies I had taken out at the age of fifteen and sixteen years. At the time house purchase was not really affordable on my wages. Also, although we were living within the City of Coventry boundary, we were on the Meriden Rural District Council Housing List for a Council house in the M.R.D. area. This was long before the administrative boundary changes when the West Midlands came into being.

The Prudential Insurance agent was John Burgess, about my age, and well-known and highly thought of in the area. He "worked" on my mother for a start and convinced her it was a good thing to do; then Mother "worked" on me and Olive, saying "John Burgess would not advise you wrongly". One always took notice of one's Ma. Well I did anyhow, and have always been glad I listened. With the result that I/we signed up for the endowment which could be converted to house purchase, a mortgage in effect.

So, 1954 came towards its end. By now, the caravan park was filling up but still no news of electricity. We made quite a few friends and Matty and Eileen Wilkinson who were on the other side of the circular drive were our closest friends. Some people thought that there should be better facilities and a Residents' Association was formed. Members met at the Hawthorn Tree pub on Broad Lane. We could see the pub from our caravan between the houses. One or two of the members must have been shop stewards at work and began shouting the odds. "We must fight the Farcroft Estate for our rights" they cried. I pointed out that I did not think we had any rights and thought the best method was requests and persuasion. The suggestion was disregarded and the Residents' Association achieved very little in all the time we were there.

1955 came in and Jack Barton, my boss, informed me that we were setting the bedding plant target at 6,000 boxes (60 plants in most boxes, 350,000 plants). We had another greenhouse being planned, but it would not be built and ready in time. Also, he was expanding the chrysanthemum side of the business as well, obtaining and growing all the worthwhile new varieties on offer from the breeders.

The new varieties were to be seen at the Royal Horticultural Halls at the early show in September and the show for the late and indoor flowering varieties in November. They would be inspected by a panel of experts from the "Chrysanthemum World" and given awards according to merit and each variety classified to its most suitable class, i.e. incurve, reflex, incurving and so on.

I went with Jack to Shoesmiths once, the major breeder of chrysanthemums at that time. Their nursery was near Guildford in Surrey. There were no motorways then and it was a long day out. Jack came away with a bundle of unrooted cuttings which he just got his finger and thumb round, worth a small fortune. He spent the next day preparing and inserting the cuttings into a rooting bed. I don't think soil warming equipment was available then. Some cuttings were cut into two and some made three. As long as they were trimmed below a leaf joint there was a good chance of obtaining a rooted cutting and eventually a flowering plant.

All the tip cuttings were labelled as these would provide the cuttings for the next year's crop. Tip cuttings were always considered to be the best and cuttings grew from the base of the old stool – the cut-down stem and root of the previous year's plant. Some varieties were very "shy" at throwing cuttings, very few appearing from the base. These varieties were treated differently. Each plant usually had three or four "branches" growing from the main stem. These were carefully prised off, and planted horizontally about half an inch deep in boxes about two foot six in length and with luck cuttings would appear from the stems where the leaf joints were. They did require a bit more warmth to get them going – one of the tricks of the trade.

The bedding programme was going well. I was kept very busy transporting topsoil in from the road where it had to be tipped by the delivery lorry, also peat and sharp sand. It all had to be passed through a half inch sieve (riddle) and mixed up with fertilizer and ground limestone to the John Innes formula developed by the John Innes Horticultural Research Station.

It took me half a day to keep the pricking-out team of ladies supplied with filled boxes of compost. Getting on into the season space for growing the plants began to fill up and the new greenhouse was not ready. We also had to install another bigger boiler to provide the heating. In the end, we had to stack the boxes of pricked-out seedlings on top of each other, one one way, one the other. I told Jack this would not work, but there was no choice in the matter.

That Spring was wet and cold, more than usual, resulting in a lot of seedlings "damping off" as predicted. We spent a lot of time filling up the gaps in the boxes. The boiler was eventually installed and Jack asked if I would work over the weekend to get the thing up and running. His brother Alan, an engineer, also was on hand to help. We had not finished by Sunday dinnertime and I returned to work in the afternoon. We were all – well I was – getting a bit fragile and fed up. Topping up the boiler in the open stoke-hole was Alan (often a bit on the bad-tempered side). I was carrying water in buckets to him when he snarled "Can't you get it to me any faster?" So, what do you do? I threw a full bucket of water over him and said "How's that?". I quickly got on my motorbike and went home.

Funnily enough nothing was said the next day or ever in fact. My overtime was paid in full and I was learning to stick up for myself. In my childhood days and right into life as a teenager, known I think as youth, I was never in the front of the queue, quite shy I suppose and lacking in confidence. The likely reason is probably my ten week spell in Northampton Hospital at the age of four and then the discovery of my poor vision (I was short sighted) when I started school at five and a half.

Subconsciously everything was alright, although I often thought I was not as good as the other lads, especially noticed in the cubs and scouts and at Balsall School. At Berkswell there was no football, cricket or rugby, only rounders now and again. At aged eleven at Balsall there were virtually no sports facilities and the War did not help. Therefore I had not had to join in any rough and tumble and disliked sport anyhow. I suffered from an inferiority complex. It was many years before it was shaken off completely. The A.T.C. and going to camp was a great help and I like to think my two years in the Army did me a lot of good in many ways.

Back to work and the bedding plants. We managed the 6,000 boxes alright, that is the pricking-out, but lost quite a lot owing to the poor weather and the fact that there was not enough space for growing on; also there really was not enough heat. Sufficient to say that although the target was met, we did not sell the entire crop.

It was one day at the end of the season that Jack Barton approached me and said he did not put any blame on me for the disappointing season, also that he was short of finances. Today it is known as cash flow problems. It was almost certain that the income from bedding plants was going to pay for the new large greenhouse, but he did not say that. He put a proposition to me and enquired as to whether I would find a temporary part-time job. He would pay my National Health stamp as usual and honour my holiday pay. Olive and I had planned to make another attempt to tour Scotland on our little Frances Barnett 197c.c. It was agreed I would try to find a part-time job, but it would have to be gardening of some sort.

Gardening jobs were really two-a-penny; some paid better than others. It must have been in the Coventry Telegraph that I saw an advertisement for a gardener, two days a week, so I made enquiries and found myself at a lovely house and garden on the Coventry/Kenilworth Road near to Cannon Hill Road.

Mrs. S was the employer and she escorted me all the way round her one acre garden. It had everything, kitchen garden, rose gardens, rockeries, two ponds, one formal and one informal, herbaceous border and shrubberies. The house was set back behind a spinney of mature trees and there was a Breedon gravel drive from the road to the big parking area at the front of the house.

The job was fine; the previous gardener was retiring and Mrs. S required someone who had some knowledge of gardening. All was well until she asked me what my charges would be and I replied four and sixpence per hour and fifty weeks per annum (22p). It had to be a year round job with no laying off in the winter. The going rate was about three and sixpence per hour (17p) if one was lucky. I do not think retiring Ted got anywhere near that. The lady blinked and stuttered a bit but as I was the only applicant – and she loved her garden – I got the job. When one has nothing to lose, one can be brave, or cheeky. It is called looking after number one and there were two of us and who knows what the future may provide. However, I assured the lady I would earn my keep and was quite willing to do anything within my capabilities during less busy times in the winter.

So it was agreed that I would work there on Mondays and Fridays from 8 a.m. till 4 p.m. with half an hour for dinner at one o'clock. Therefore you see my employer was quite crafty, my working day was cut short and no work on Bank holidays. It suited me and was to prove very useful later on.

This naturally was a new experience for me. Mrs. S was a keen and knowledgeable gardener and I did learn a lot in a very short time. We got on well as I was keen to earn my pay and to learn.

For the first week or two my orders were in the garden shed, all written out in order. First job on Monday morning was to put out the line for the washing and the last job at four o'clock was to take it in again. The house must have been run like a ship. There was a maid living in and I think she, Martha, was kept pretty well occupied. Martha was a contented little body anyhow. There were lots of situations similar in those days, the man in the house going off to business at say 8.30 a.m. and the "Missus" very much in charge of EVERYTHING else. Definitely not snobs, middle class I suppose, but we all knew our place and as long as we kept in it, all was well.

As I understand, Mr. S and his brother owned and ran M.H. Spencer Ltd. and their factory was in Priory Road, Coventry. The factory has been in Charter Avenue, Tile Hill, for many years now.

Mr. S was in my opinion a real gentleman. He always came to me in the garden and had a little chat. He was interested in my welfare and so on, then he would be off to business.

They were staunch churchgoers, belonging to Holy Trinity Church in Broadgate, Coventry, and Mrs. S did a lot of work for St. Faith's in Coventry, who among other things rescued and assisted deserted and needy children.

After a week or two I was left to my own devices. First job on Friday was to brush the drive, with a besom, all the way up to the house and including the parking area in front of the house. Everywhere had to be at its best for the weekend, then out came the fourteen inch Atco two-stroke lawn mower for the three hour task of lawn mowing. There was a large area for a small mower. Two-stroke engines were often a problem but this one was a little gem; it was always serviced at the end of the season and performed very well.

Then there was all the edging to do, plus the kitchen garden, so I was kept on the go all the while. At the stroke of ten a handbell would ring and a tray with a large jug of cocoa would be provided and again, dead on the dot of one o'clock, the same tray with a large pot of tea and a big bowl of pudding, Martha's special – lovely.

It was a nice introduction to jobbing gardening and Mrs. S was not a bad old stick. She always called me "Gardener".

Time was getting on towards our planned touring holiday to Scotland and, to tell the truth, I was not at all happy with this work setup (I had told Mrs. S of our holiday plans). Back at the nursery things seemed to be different in a way. I did not really enjoy the arrangements and I thought that they were putting on me a bit. Jack lived in an old double decker bus in the corner of a field on his uncle's farm at Exhall. He was growing chrysanths for the flower market there and I was asked to go and work there perhaps two days a week, and "old" Bob stayed at the nursery doing the best jobs. Perhaps Jack was worried about his finances or whatever, I don't know. Sufficient to say I was getting a bit fed up. Perhaps it was a sort of "no job satisfaction" on my part. I always liked to stand back and have a good look at the day's efforts.

We must have taken the Coventry Evening Telegraph at the caravan because just two days before our Saturday departure to Scotland, I spotted an advert in the situations vacant column, "Full-time gardener required", etc. I thought it sounded interesting but there was no 'phone number and no time to call round, or it might have been a box number. I wrote a letter stating that I would not be around till whatever date and that if the applicant wished, I would call on my return. My parents' address was enclosed and into the post it went.

Other exciting events were also happening in early July 1955. We were fairly sure – well Olive was anyhow – that there would be the patter of tiny feet at our caravan early in 1956. For the time being the good news we kept to ourselves, but times were busy and exciting.

We got away on holiday on the Saturday, on the road before eight o'clock and, as before, chugged northwards on our Pop Pop Pop Two-stroke Francis Barnett. The weather was not good, dull with drizzle, a bit yuk really. We made it as far as Kendal and thought how marvellous it was – it was considering all the towns we had to negotiate with no motorways or even a bye-pass or two. The plan was to have a look at the Lake District, which I had only heard about, if the weather was good. There was some improvement next day, but the cloud was low so we decided to carry on northwards. Up the A6 and a very steep hill from Kendal shrouded in fog (or cloud) to Shap Fell, a real wild and seemingly deserted area.

Carlisle was reached by lunchtime and fish and chips at a small cafe served us well. Then onward. By now it was raining. I decided to head northwest towards Dumfries, Dalrey and Ayr. One good thing, the rain cleared the fog away, but eventually we couldn't see anything for rain.

What a ride, never even saw a place to get a cup of tea. We made Ayr alright, if a bit wet and soggy. It was impossible to find a B and B so we had to enquire at a guest house (we were on quite a tight cash schedule). "Yes" she could fix us up "Come on in". This we did, including the two pannier bags, which were our "suitcases" and thankfully the contents were all O.K.

We were shown a very nice room and our host took our wet gear and suggested we had a hot bath. "When you are dry and changed supper will be ready downstairs" we were told, and so it was.

The table was full of eats – salad, cakes, you name it. I wondered what it was all going to cost and imagined us heading for home halfway through the holiday. But the thing to do was make the most of whatever presents itself, and we had had a miserable day weatherwise.

In the evening the rain had now stopped and it was lovely and bright so, after the supper, a walk along the prom on the Ayr seafront seemed a good idea, and so it was. The sunset was stunning, never before or since have I seen a sunset sky as superb. The sky was as if on fire from the north to south horizon, also overhead. The island of Ailsa Craig could be seen out in the bay. It looked like a big black boil sticking out of the sea silhouetted against the flaming sky – magnificent.

The guest house was very nice and comfortable and we woke next morning to find the sun streaming in through the windows. Most of the clouds had gone and a big breakfast was laid in the dining room downstairs. Our landlady brought in our clothes, including the motorbiking top clothes, all dry and neatly folded ready to put on and, in a way, it was like a fresh start to the holiday. Also, we had the bill, which was our most expensive stop, but very reasonable for the services rendered. I think we were taken pity on and must have looked bedraggled and perhaps a little bit despondent standing at her front door the previous teatime. We set off again up to the Clyde and crossing by the Gourock to Dunoon ferry. Our route from then on does not really matter but one evening we ended up at Pitlochry and I still had this little uneasy feeling about my job and Jack at the nursery.

We had our supper and evening walk as usual and on our return to the B and B lodgings there was a small table just inside the front door at the foot of the stairs. On the table there was writing paper and envelopes for the use of guests with the house address on all "poshlike". I helped myself to an envelope and notepaper, took it up to our room, and wrote out my notice to quit my job.

A week's notice by employee or employer was then the norm. I said a week's notice could be worked on my return. This I sent by recorded delivery the next day and the thought of work, or the lack of it, did not concern me for the remainder of the trip.

The weather got better and hotter by the day. Most of the time we were riding without our topcoats on to get all the breeze that was available. People in cars were sweltering in their mobile ovens, poor things.

We journeyed up the west coast and called at the famous garden at Inverewe, where palms and other tender plants manage to survive, due to the effect the Gulf Stream has on certain parts of the west coast of Scotland. The prevailing warm air from the south west keeps most of this area free of snow, ice and severe weather, but only close to the coastline.

We make the north coast at Durness and head east towards John O'Groats. Driving round Loch Eriboll we came across a man at the side of the road attending to an elderly motorbike; it was an ex W.D. (Army) despatch rider's bike. We stopped to see if help was required. It was no use asking me about repairs but we could have gone for assistance or whatever. In the event, there was no need, it was a Saturday afternoon and he was the local postman doing a little maintenance work. He lived in a cottage down a slope behind the roadside wall, hardly visible from the road – Ah yes, the road.

For a couple of days or more we had now been travelling on roads which consisted of two strips of tarmac and a grass strip in the middle with black grass in parts due to old oil dripping out from old cars. There were passing places to cater for cars when they met. They were few and far between, but EVERYBODY waved and slowed down to pass the time of day. People were and still are very friendly and pleased to see one.

We chatted quite a while with the postman and it turned out that his modest home was the nerve centre of the north west of Scotland.

Recently there had been a very cold snowy and severe winter in the north, roads were blocked with snow drifts and many farmers could not get to feed some of their flocks. The Royal Navy sent an aircraft carrier loaded with hay and feed and it was flown by helicopter to the most needy locations. Our new friend was the co-ordinator between ship and shore. It was quite an interesting interlude to visualise the snow and the carrier out in Loch Eriboll (sea loch) with aircraft coming and going. Quite an unusual operation for the crew as well I would imagine.

The journey is resumed and later on we decide to get B and B in the village of Tongue; there was nowhere else anyhow.

Our overnight stay was at the Smithy. They had two daughters in their early teens probably. The usual drill by now, shown a room, move in the gear, park the bike, wash and brush up, etc. and then tea, supper or what-ever one called it would be ready for us, all laid out in the front room. All very nice and cosy.

At this place it was a wee bit different, only inasmuch as there were a lot of callers at the front door. Why? What could be the reason? we thought. As we went out for our evening wander it was obvious WE were not causing the need for folk to come a-calling, although everyone we met – not many – were friendly towards us.

On our return curiosity got the better of me as people were still coming to the door. "It's Monty, the daughters' horse. He is not at all well and the whole village is concerned." And despite every care, poor old Monty died in the night and then everyone was back at the door again with their condolences. It really was quite moving. More concern could not have been shown had it been the horse's owner so tight must have been that village community.

The rest of the holiday went very well. The weather was perfect throughout. We saw the salmon leaping at Largs, then returned via

On tour in Scotland at Ullapool. Francis Barnett 2 stroke 197cc, 1955

Inverness and The Trossachs, re-crossing the border and coming down the A1 to Newark, Leicester and home. A super trip that is still memorable for many reasons, not least the financial expenditure which amounted to £36.00 inclusive of petrol and B and B, everything.

I think we were both earning £9.00 per week at that period. Olive was still at Banner Lane working 8.30 a.m. to 5.00 p.m. In the winter time I was in first and cooked the dinner and in the summer Olive was first home and she had the job. We always had fish and chips from the Broad Lane "chippy" on Fridays, then Olive did the weekly wash and, by now, we went across to one of Olive's workmate's who lived in one of the flats behind the Hawthorn Pub for a proper bath. Ours was O.K. but all the water had to be carried to and from, quite a fag after a day's work.

Yes, back to work after our holiday and I did wonder what sort of reception I would receive. In the event, all was well. Probably Jack was secretly pleased that his payroll commitment would be going down and also there would be no labour problems really till the next Spring. He also now knew how to produce bedding plants in quantity as I had introduced him to the John Innes formula for growing most sorts of plants, using more or less fertilizer for small or larger plants.

I did not get over home till the Monday evening and when I did arrive there was a letter waiting regarding the job I had written about before the holiday. There were two households living next door to each other on the Tamworth Road near Keresley, Coventry. They wished to share a full-time gardener.

There was a 'phone number and I hopped into a 'phone box and gave them a call to fix up an appointment to go and see the people and exactly what the job entailed.

One evening later in the week I presented myself at the house of the Lesters. They had been there only a short time and Bernhards of Rugby had been and done some work in the garden. Then we went next door to the brand new bungalow of Mr. and Mrs. Pearson. Again, the garden basics, lawns and paths, had been laid out by Bernhards. A quick assessment told me that the two gardens did not require anyone for a whole week. I was not prepared to leave Kenilworth Road anyhow. I told Mr. Lester that I had three and a half days available and was sure I could share my time between the two gardens and keep them both in good order. Again, I think mine was the only application, not surprising when people could assemble cars, motorbikes, and so on for more than double gardener's pay.

I was given the job and suggested working eighteen hours in both gardens per week, fifty weeks per annum with pay of five shillings per hour. There was not a bat of an eyelid from either man. We shook hands and that was that. On Tuesdays, Wednesdays and Thursdays my day was 7.30 a.m. till 6.30 p.m. with a half hour lunch break, and four and a half hours on Saturday mornings. They were three very long days but it gave me a weekly wage of £10.73p, which satisfied me.

Neither employer knew one end of a spade from the other and it was doubtful if they could name a plant. I had a free hand to do whatever I liked, but they both wanted colour in the garden. It was too late to put in bedding plants, so it was agreed to formulate a plan and do our best for the next Spring.

Mr.L, was a bookmaker; well, so was Mr.P. for that matter. Mr. Pearson was also a co-founder of the Longford Concrete Co., making paving slabs and all sorts of other concrete products, mainly for the building trade.

Mr. Pearson was a Bedworth man (Bed-earth), self-made with accent to match, and I am sure he married the girl next door. Everything was the very best, a Jaguar – the latest – in the huge garage; a short rotund man in a smart suit, a huge diamond tie-pin, and a trilby hat saw him off to business. He often got me to clean the car windows before he set off. "Dirty winders, dirty car" he would say.

Mr. Lester was younger, married with one son Rodney. Mr.L. knew all the sports personalities for miles around and in particular players and staff at Highfield Road, the home of Coventry City. And so I became self-employed, my own boss – a mistaken belief if ever I heard one, responsible for finding work, doing it and getting paid. Paying one's own National Insurance contributions, not being able to draw any unemployment benefit, no pay if away from work, sick or holidays or the odd day, half day or hour off. Being responsible for accounts and any Income Tax payable. No company pension or, latterly, no redundancy money. Yer on yer own mate!

CHAPTER 12

Going it Alone –
Self-Employed

None of these things really bothered me very much. I was aware of charging a little more per hour to pay for Bank holiday and annual holidays. No thought was given to Income Tax, not much was being stopped on my wages anyhow.

One person was indeed very pleased about it all – my mother – she was round the village telling one and all "John's gone on his own", etc. etc. Mother never faltered or failed to give me every encouragement and help possible.

I had not been at Tamworth Road long and Mr. Lester asked if it would be a good idea to have a greenhouse. I replied "Yes, if it could be properly looked after at weekends – Sundays". He said "Oh yes, just tell Mrs. Lester what needs to be done and she will do it". "Anyhow" says he, "a builder is coming to meet me this morning. I want some better paths laying. You tell him what you would like and we will go on from there".

Later on this fellow turned up and the two men had got their heads together. Then he came to me and said "Ernie has told me to build a greenhouse to your requirements. What would you like?". What an opportunity. I suggested a twenty-four foot long span house divided into three, the far end to be warm with some heat, the centre section the main heated part, and the entrance area cold. Ideally cold frames at each side, and water laid on.

All this was provided, hand-built, actually larger than I suggested and it was all heated. Together with new paths and pillars it must have cost a small fortune, but who was I to say anything. The builders were there for weeks but eventually all was finished.

Rider Betts was the main seed and fertilizer plus garden sundries store in Coventry. This is quite a time before garden centres came into being. Mr.L. opened an account there for me to spend as I wished. The manager was a very nice man and he allowed me to have anything for myself at a discount. I did so and was a customer for many years.

On the home front and away from work, other exciting news was about to be made known. It was confirmed that we were to become parents. A baby was expected next February, and so it was with joy we told our folks who were very pleased for us. My mother was horrified when she realised that our expected offspring had been bounced two thousand miles round Scotland. She thought we may have a despatch rider or a T.T. racer on our hands. Olive's mother took it all in her stride. She was already grandma to eight and probably the excitement had worn off, although she was very concerned for her daughter's welfare.

Four years previously, Olive's sister Lily and husband Alf adopted Delia. Lily always loved children and was over the moon when they had Delia as a tiny baby. We were most fortunate and not too proud to accept a pram and many other useful items of babyware.

I got into my new work pattern very well and all went smoothly. With the winter coming on it was impossible to work as many hours, therefore I laboured during daylight hours. Olive left work in early November and I carried on making Christmas wreaths as usual. We could divide the main part of the caravan into twoparts with a double bed in each, and this was handy and would prove very useful later on.

We kept up attending the dances as long as possible, also, later on Saturday evenings were spent at the "pictures". It was my philosophy that soon we would have to stay in, but to go out at any opportunity; this we did, although there was less and less space on the dual seat of the Francis Barnett.

1956 came in quite cold and it was a job to keep warm at work some of the time. All sorts of ideas evolved to create something energetic to do on arrival on cold winter's mornings.

On 9th February Olive was complaining of backache when I went off to work in the morning and on arrival home in the evening the place was deserted. All the arrangements had been made for Olive to go into the maternity ward at Gulson Road Hospital in Coventry. Our neighbour, Mrs. Palmer, came in to tell me she had 'phoned for an ambulance and Olive had been taken to the hospital.

In those days fathers and prospective fathers were treated like schoolchildren – to be seen but not heard. To be present at the birth may not have been unique, but it was uncommon and we were not wanted around. Also, I for one could not really afford time off, so I popped in to see Olive and came home and got ready to go to work the next day. Telephones were few and far between but they almost always worked, hardly any vandals about then.

Friday, 10th February, and it had snowed overnight. In fact it was still snowing as I set off for Kenilworth Road and the Spencers. On arrival I asked Mrs. Spencer if she would please 'phone the hospital. This she did, saying Olive was alright but there was no news then. The hospital would 'phone if and when there was anything to report.

It was snowing quite heavily and I was in the greenhouse having a Spring-clean and tidy up – well, the greenhouse was anyway, when Mrs. Spencer came out to inform me that I was a father. We had a baby daughter and all was well.

Very few fathers were present at the birth of a baby at that time – if any. As stated before, there was no pay for that sort of event. Olive was in good hands, therefore nothing to get concerned about. But at visiting time in the evening, guess who was in the front of the queue? There resplendent was Mrs. Webb with our daughter in a cot at the bedside; a mop of dark hair and that is all I saw of her for quite a while.

The weather was awful for motorcyclists, lots of snow and ice on the roads making driving difficult at times. Olive was at Gulson Road for over a week, then had some time at the Towers' home in Kenilworth. New mums were usually kept in for ten to fourteen days at the time.

Olive's Mum wanted to do what she could, and after leaving hospital, the three of us stayed at No. 2 Glendower Avenue for two weeks so that Olive could fully recover.

We naturally talked about names for our daughter and decided one name would be enough. I was not keen to name after a grandparent, or anyone else; also, we wanted a name that sounded alright if it got shortened, say at school for instance. Patricia was considered, but in the end we chose Valerie. Thankfully, she was a contented and I like to think happy baby – taking after who I wonder?

That two weeks at Glendower Avenue was a bit of a trial for me. Olive's mother was rather domineering. She was IN CHARGE of all under her roof; a hard-working and talented person in the house, with knitting-pins, sewing, dressmaking, everything. My mother-in-law would have done anything for me, and I for the two of them, except live there. Mrs. Holmes was a lady to admire, spending a lifetime working, she hardly knew how to relax.

Mr. and Mrs. Holmes brought up six children. Ernest would have made seven, but he died aged eighteen months. They bought their own house; how I do not know, as Mr. Holmes retired early through poor health.

I did pop out now and again in the evening, mainly to make sure the caravan was alright during the very cold spell. It was probably due to the weather that we stayed at No. 2 for a while. They might have worried whether or not the caravan would be heated sufficiently. No problems there. It was always nice and warm with our solid fuel fire and a paraffin heater; also, by now we had a Tilley lamp, which did give a very bright light indeed.

So it was that around the time of my twenty-seventh birthday we settled down to a completely new life – a new baby and recently self-employed – really everything in the garden was lovely.

Another thing, we had "our corns cut", in other words it was difficult to go out as a family and, as a result, we did not go very far as a threesome. I was very busy working anyhow, and I did hope to produce a lot of plants in the greenhouse at home. Not easy, but mother and my Father were quite good and happy to water when I was working my long days.

It was quite likely a longstanding desire to have a place of my/our own to develop a plant nursery or market garden, always to be dismissed as impossible owing to the lack of finances, and now there were more responsibilities to think about.

Some time previously I had been talking to Harold Hewitt, who owned Four Oaks Farm, and rented and lived at Blind Hall Farm adjoining. He was aware of my ambitions and invited me to go and talk to him one evening, which I did.

He put some thoughts and possible ideas to me, saying "I have the land, what about the field opposite your parents in Meriden Road. Move your caravan say into one corner. Mains water passes the field. There is plenty of farmyard manure available". Also, he had a lorry to transport goods and produce to and fro. Naturally I would pay a rental for the ground and services rendered.

I went away to think and talk about the idea for some time, in the end, thanking Mr. Hewitt and turning the offer down. I was doing quite well in my "field" that is, but thought I would be very dependant on one man, although he was most honest and a man of his word. Also, if the caravan was moved onto this area planning permission to build had to be applied for within a set period of time.

Another factor regarding market gardening was that the Berkswell area was always at least three weeks behind the Vale of Evesham producers. Therefore they always had produce available weeks before we could. Another idea bit the dust.

Next naturally there was the christening and of course it had to be at Westwood where we were married. Olive's sister, Lily, and husband Alf, together with my sister, Stella, were the Godparents. How we all got to the Church and back to our caravan I cannot recall, but we did have a celebration tea at 11 Farcroft Caravan Park afterwards. Thank goodness it was a nice sunny day when it was nice to sit out at the back. We would have been pushed for space inside had it been wet.

Everything went well, but Valerie started to cry quite a bit and nothing would pacify her. I suggested a spoonful of Woodward's Gripe Water, much to the vocal disapproval of Olive's Mum. However, the mixture was administered by some subtle ruse and there was not a sound from Val thereafter.

As Olive now had taken on the role of fulltime mother and caravan-wife, I started to pop home for my dinner. Valerie was almost always outside in the pram when I went up the drive towards the 'van. When she was able to sit up and take notice, the pram would rock from side to side at the

Olive with Valerie at Meriden
Road, 1956

approach of my motor-
bike.

As stated before, we
were very restricted
regarding going out, and
it was a real problem for us all to get to my folks at Berkswell. Mrs. Spencer
had given us a very nice cot for Valerie. How it was delivered I cannot
recall.

One nice Sunday afternoon, Olive and I decided to visit the Spencers. I
am sure prior arrangements had been made. We set off down Broad Lane
and along the Fletchampstead Highway, turning right at Kenilworth Road,
and trudging to No. 75. We were made very welcome and given tea and
cakes. After an hour or so we began the long walk home. It was a long way
and I was hardly, or begrudgingly, allowed to push the pram.

The Spencers did appreciate our visit. Mr. Spencer knew a little of my
ambitions and I think he was on the board of management of the Coventry
Building Society and was on the lookout for a property with a large garden.
The problem was my income was not really high enough to be allowed to
take on a mortgage. Also, a mortgage on an older property was even harder
to obtain.

To partly solve our transport problems, I/we decided to trade in my
beloved Francis Barnett and buy another motorbike with a side-car. We
had an Ariel 600 c.c. side valve job, not fast, but a good old puller. It would
slog on forever I was told. £110.00 second-hand, it went very well and we
both got on very well together.

One day, my mother was up at Balsall at the Gee's. Mr. Gee was the
Balsall Postmaster and owned the Post Office and quite a number of properties in and around Balsall. My mother and Mrs. Gee were keen W.I.
members and often got together to make jam and can fruit. The Women's
Institute purchased a canning machine for fruit, etc. and my mother helped
can many a quantity of fruit when in season.

Mr. Gee went in this one day and told my mother about this land for
sale just off Station Road in Balsall. "Tell him to go and see it" says he. So,
on the following Saturday afternoon, we load up on the bike, Valerie on
Olive's lap in the side-car, and off we go.

The land was up a narrow ash path, which goes off Station Road opposite Needler's End Lane. It is still there. At the end of the lane was a bungalow where we met a Mr. Wood. We were shown around the bungalow, which was of sound structure but did need a coat of paint. It was quite shabby both inside and outside.

It was a smallholding of eight acres with a huge pond in one of the fields, with water lilies and fish. The pond is now situated at the side of Kemps Green road, a haven for wildlife. We had a good look around, but Mr. Wood's asking price was £3,000, an absolute bargain for someone with cash to spend. Needless to say, it ruled us out as again no-one would grant a mortgage on that sort of property in 1956. Mr. Gee had told me to pull all the stops out to buy it as the land could possibly be building land in ten years' time.

It was not to be for us. The land was eventually built on in about the mid-seventies, twenty years on from the time we saw it.

There were more minor problems as 1956 progressed. By and large, all went well workwise. I split my hours equally between the two gardens on the Tamworth Road and they were beginning to look much better. We had loads of manure, which was dug in over the winter and so on. Mr. Lester told me to grow what plants I liked for the Pearsons next door. That was O.K. by Mr. Pearson, and it was agreed some of the greenhouse work would be undertaken in his time. Mrs. Pearson could not understand (or would not) this arrangement which was a very fair setup. She often accused me of not fulfilling my duties and so on, getting quite nasty sometimes. However, the problem resolved itself owing to the 1956 Suez Crisis. Petrol was scarce and I could not get enough to get me to Tamworth Road four times a week, so she was the obvious one to drop.

My working week was soon filled up. Dr. Meacock and his wife were great friends of the Spencers and they lived at Gibbet Hill. The other odd day was filled up with a day every other week for Mr. and Mrs. Page in Hob Lane. One day a month with Jim and Pam Thompson (I sat with Jim at Berkswell School). The remaining one day per month was spent at the home of Pam's parents in Station Road where for all three I did all the big jobs, digging and hedge-cutting, etc.

Since leaving Sunday school, Jim and I did not meet up very often. Now and again at a dance or social event, but it was always nice to meet up and his friendship, and now that of Pam (nee Overton) was, and still is, highly valued. Watch this space.

Incidentally, these employment moves were a good opportunity to increase one's wages and I always took advantage of that – not the clients you understand. They always ended up with value for money. Well, I never had the sack anyhow.

Holidays were out this year, although we did get up to Derbyshire to visit the Wallis family from time to time. By now, Ray was married to Marcelene, a very nice young lady who always made us very welcome. On more than one occasion I took Olive and Valerie to Ray and Marcelene's at

Steeple Grange, Wirksworth, their first home, where O. and V. stayed for a week, and I did a return trip the following weekend to bring them home. Marcelene even borrowed a pram on one occasion. There is a limit to what one can transport on a motorbike and side-car. Ours though had quite a large boot and proved to be very handy over the years, transporting a big variety of gardening tools, produce, importing quantities of holly, and delivering the made-up holly wreaths, crosses and chaplets. All in addition to family requirements.

During this time I was still very much involved with the Balsall and District Horticultural Society, being a committee member since joining. There was always the big annual show. The first year (1950) that I was involved with the show, it was held in a field in Station Road, Balsall, just about opposite where Docker's Close is situated. Mr. Jarrard, my boss at the time, was the President and he called upon Les Clarke, the head gardener, to put a bit of a show on at the entrance to the large marquee. Les had a two-cylinder Jowett van as a works vehicle, and so I was roped in to assist. We did a bit of a mock-up, first raiding the greenhouse and gardens for anything that was worth putting on show, and I like to think the end result was not too bad. The Society was pleased; also Mr. Jarrard gave his approval.

That "show field" got built on and we moved to a field on the Kenilworth Road, belonging to Mr. Gibbs, father of Ted (Dennis) and Donald. The field was opposite the entrances to Elmwood Close, also fields at that time. That again was eventually built on, so the next move was to another field near the corner of Kenilworth Road and Kelsey Lane and it was there that we, the Society, were stuck for someone to organise the refreshments.

Someone suggested my mother, but it definitely was not me. And so it was that David Crosswell, the local plumber, called on Mother. She was persuaded to take the job on. David guaranteed plenty of helpers and all went well. Naturally, all the ladies got on very well and it was at one of their meetings that Mary Holden spoke to my mother about a property for sale in Windmill Lane. Mrs. Holden lived in the lane, just a short distance from this property, and wondered if Olive and I would be interested.

There was no harm in having a look and one Saturday afternoon Olive and Valerie were loaded into the side-car. I put my spade in the boot and off we went to Windmill Lane.

There were in effect two plots for sale, one approximately fifty foot of frontage and a narrow plot of about twenty-two feet known as "The Bungalow" and "Rose View" respectively. The two plots covered just about one acre. "The Bungalow" stood forty yards or more back from the road, and "Rose View" a little further back, with a hedge dividing the two plots.

The whole place was in a sad state of neglect. The front gardens were non-existent, just weeds with a pathway down to the properties. My first desire was to find out what type of soil there was underneath the rubbish;

hence the spade. The first thing I did was to dig one or two sample holes. The discovery was a very light black soil which I thought would drain well and be easy to work. I was trying to avoid a heavy type of clay soil. Satisfied that there were possibilities for the place, then we had a look at the dwellings.

"Oh dear" – "The Bungalow" was built of shiplap wood with an asbestos tiled roof; a large living room with five doors off; on the right a roomy pantry, and next on round a door to another small room which could be a sitting-room or bedroom. The middle door opened to what could be used as a bedroom with another bedroom off that one. The final door was to what was called the "Junk Room". It had never been finished off. For instance, there was no ceiling, just rafters and tiles above.

There were electric lights in all the rooms, but only one two pin plug, which I understand was not too safe, not being earthed. The kitchen was brickbuilt with a bathroom at the far end, connected to the bungalow by a passage glazed on both sides. A bit of a jaunt from the living room to the kitchen.

There was an electric cooker in the kitchen, hired from the Electricity Board at twelve shillings (60p) a quarter. It was filthy dirty, covered in grease and dust. Water for washing and the bath was heated by an electric boiler, the same as we had at home. There was no mains water supply to "The Bungalow" but there was a mains tap by the gate of "Rose View".

In the kitchen of "The Bungalow" stood a pump for the water supply, over an old sink and draining board. The bucket lavatory was outside, backing onto the bathroom. "Rose View" had a free-standing (outside) washhouse cum scullery, or whatever one wished to call it, brickbuilt with asbestos roof, the lavatory just a small wooden shed. One entered into a lean-to kitchen and beyond was the main living room – a large wooden shed which I think was lined and insulated.

From the living room, one went along a narrow passage and up a few steps into the one and only bedroom. This started its life as a horse-drawn furniture removal van with two wooden wheels at the back and two smaller ones in the front. But, in common with next door, it was waterproof and dry and in dire need of some very hard work to get the place habitable.

The "garden" or ground went a long way back to a field at the far end. That whole area was literally a jungle, some old fruit trees here and there with fowl-pens and wooden pigsties thrown in for good measure. The hedges on both sides of "Rose View" almost met. It was quite difficult to find an easy way from one end to the other. Really something to think about.

The vendor was asking £1,500.00 for the lot, and he said that some time previously outline planning had been approved for a house "endways on" for the narrow plot and for a bungalow on the other plot.

Two big questions needed an answer (1) would Olive want to move to such a place with a nine month old baby? (2) Again, there was not a hope of obtaining a mortgage on such a property. For my part, I was quite keen to try and buy (somehow) this place. It had good potential, or so I thought. Olive was also willing to give it a go. She knew how keen I was.

So, it was then we got our heads together with the vendor, but there was no way we were going to pay £1,500.00. I seem to recall it took one or two meetings and the asking price gradually came down. In any case, we had only about £750.00 available anyhow, so the vendor said he would go to his solicitor to see what, if anything, could be done.

Eventually, he came back to us with a deal. First of all he agreed to sell for £1,175.00. His solicitors had drawn up a document called a Promissory Note, whereby we paid at least half the amount, the rest to be paid within ten years – wait for it – interest free. The vendor suggested we both used the one solicitor, making a further saving. Naturally I agreed to this, not realising that this was not good practice, for us anyhow. But, we all make mistakes and blunders. Fortunately, it did not prove too costly for us, although certain things were not pointed out to us that should have been.

We kept him waiting for a few days while making a final decision. Really, we could not go far wrong. The price was very good. He must have been desperate for a bit of the "ready". Also planning had been granted and it was our aim to build in the future. So, we paid somewhat in excess of half the amount and I told Les, the vendor, that if he needed any money to come and see me, and that if I could afford to pay anything off we would. We were living quite cheaply; the caravan was paid for, but we needed to sell it to pay towards the deposit on the land.

We had previously been to Gailey's Caravans at Meriden and they came round and agreed to purchase our 'van'. It never is as much as one hopes for, is it? So we accepted the offer. The problem was when I called to collect the payment I was met with something like "Oh sorry, did you not understand? We only pay out when the van is sold by us." We were not told this I know. However, we had an agreement to pay for the land and not enough money to meet the requirements. In the end, both our parents lent us £50.00, quite a bit then, and that solved the immediate problem.

CHAPTER 13

A New Beginning:
Windmill Lane

By now it was probably the end of October and my mother came once again to the rescue. We decided to move into "The Bungalow" in case someone wanted the caravan in a hurry. My mother set about "The Bungalow" during the day and I lent a hand evenings and at the weekend.

The kitchen was the worst to tackle. It was filthy dirty and very tatty, but after a good clean up and some paint on the walls and emulsion on the ceiling, it soon looked a lot better. We had a coal fire in there, cast iron off the floor job, with a hob on both sides. We managed to get the electric oven replaced. The one and only fifteen amp round-pin plug was on the cooker panel.

The main living room and one bedroom was painted and papered. And so it was, on a cold foggy Saturday, in the middle of November 1956, we moved in. It was a little bit traumatic saying goodbye to our caravan, warm and cosy, etc. I cannot recall the details, but remember borrowing Trevor Davies' tractor and trailer to transport most of our possessions, including coal from the shed and an old Singer treadle sewing machine from old lady Jarvis who died at Berkswell Almshouses in 1954.

Coal was still rationed eleven years after the War ended. It was badly needed for industry. Miners were in such short supply that young men had a choice of working in the mines or joining the forces for a time, known as the Bevin Boys.

I digress again. Something went wrong with the arrangements, which left Olive stranded at the caravan. In the end she asked if one of our neighbours could take her in the car. Thankfully he agreed. There were very few car owners on the caravan park.

I got the tractor and its contents to Windmill Lane alright. Everything unloaded and inside. There was not a great deal of stuff anyhow. We had bought some furniture from the vendors to see us through for the time being. There was also a request to keep and look after an old piano which we did, and cursed the thing many a time. It was *not* to be put in "the junk room".

By the time I unloaded and had a sandwich the fog was getting quite thick, also it was getting dark so it was decided to take the tractor back the next day. How we missed our caravan. It was a job to get the living-room warm.

Everything was very strange. We owed £100.00 and everything had to be carried to and from the kitchen. Had we done the right thing? We were spending Sunday sorting ourselves out and I went out the front to take the tractor back. Guess what? It would not start. I swung the starting handle for a long time, then I knew that Bob Jenkinson lived two doors away. In desperation his help was sought and eventually it coughed and spluttered into some sort of life. Most tractors then were started on petrol, then when the engine got hot the petrol was turned off and T.V.O. (Tractor Vaporising Oil) was turned on. Also, just before stopping the tractor engine for the day, the petrol was turned on again to fill the carburettor for the next starting.

Anyway, away it went, and it was then that Bob noticed a six inch wide gash in the tyre with quite a bit of inner tube bulging out. Oh dear. Anyhow, the thing had got to go back. Apart from anything else, I wanted my combo, which was down at Trevor's, Park Farm. Gently was the method and we, the tractor and I, arrived safely. Then I was worried about telling Trevor about the tyre. "Oh that" he says, "Been like it a long time. Should have said I suppose", all matter of factish. Typical Trevor Davies I suppose.

Back at "The Ranch", things really were a bit miserable; foggy cold weather; could not get the place warm. Coal was still on ration, also we did not wish to spend much. Owing money was not our scene. And work the next day. As it happened, it was Mrs. Spencer's so I was home in good time to set about painting out the bathroom. No mod. cons. in there – just a bath and two hooks on the back of the door. Hot water was heated in an electric boiler and cold water came from the pump over the sink. Still lots of folk did not bathe very often at the time. Once a week needed or not was the norm. I think.

It was the intention to make more holly wreaths this year and I was told about a fishmonger/greengrocer in Spon End. I called to see him one evening after work. He kept me waiting three quarters of an hour but I did come away with an order; he liked my sample. He also ordered berried holly – "I want a lot" says he. "O.K." says I.

That year I did a deal with a farmer down Cornets End. He had some super holly and I spent all one Sunday cutting it and transporting it to Meriden Road. The chap in Spon End was going to collect his holly from there, but when he told me he had bought holly in the market I was not pleased, so I told him no more wreaths. It was his turn to be hopping mad.

We were never to meet again. Also, I never cut any more holly to sell on ever again. It is slow growing and I always had regard for the trees when cutting holly.

So I did not make as many wreaths as I would have liked, but it did give me more time to myself and to do the many jobs that required doing. One thing, I did make the wreaths in relative comfort. A small room in the bungalow was turned into a "workshop" and with the fire going with old wood from the garden, all was well. The materials, holly, etc. went in through the window and the end product and rubbish out the same way.

In the meantime, sister Stella and Bill had moved from Meriden Road to a caravan in a field almost opposite Elmwood Close off Kenilworth Road at Balsall Common. It was an ex R.A.F. medical unit of some sort and made of steel; boiling hot in summer and bitterly cold in the winter. My mother pleaded with me to let them live in Rose View next door. No way was I opposed to the move and so, together with Peter and Gillian, they moved into Rose View described earlier.

At the time there were quite a few people in rural areas living in similar situations. Christmas Day 1956 saw us all at Meriden Road, sister Margaret was thirteen years old and attending the senior school at Balsall Street. The Heart of England School was being built.

We had a very nice Christmas. My mother always managed to pull out the stops one way or another. At least they had two offspring off their backs so perhaps finances were a little better. We put the kids to bed there and collected them the next day. Unfortunately Margaret had chicken-pox and Valerie caught it.

After Christmas I set about decorating the "little room" after nailing up the ceiling and various other jobs. It looked a treat when it was finished and we used it as a sitting-room.

Some time beforehand, "Auntie" Connie Mallard (one of our evacuees) died, "Uncle" Bert married again, as a matter of fact to his late wife's stepmother – work that one out if you can. However, they retired to Broughton Gifford in Wiltshire where Uncle Bert came from in the first place. He was footman to Lord Methuan from Corsham Court, I think.

When they moved we bought some surplus furniture, including a three-piece suite, a sideboard, two dining chairs, a three-quarter bed and mattress, and some floor covering. We had also acquired another three-piece suite from Olive's sister Lily and Alf. Due to the kindness of Captain Wheatley-Hubbard the furniture was stored at Berkswell Hall in a room in the stableyard, rent free.

Mother was pally with the cook and nanny at the Hall and would often go and help out at dinner parties and the like. My father would have done anything for "the old captain" as he called him, behind his back that is. Captain Wheatley-Hubbard was well liked. As Churchwarden he got involved with village life and would also lend a hand on the estate now and again. If they were working away from the estate yard he would load the men into his Land Rover and head for the pub at dinner-time. This suited my father down to the ground. I doubt if the men ever went to the pub on their own account – with the emphasis on account.

At the time, Captain and Anne Wheatley-Hubbard together with daughter Caroline and son Thomas occupied the south wing (or side) of the Hall and Mrs. Wheatley lived in the north wing.

Back home I was keen to get stuck into getting the place in some sort of order. It was a job to know where to start. There were only hand tools and an oldish wooden wheelbarrow which was a gift from my father-in-law, together with a spade which I still have and use often.

We dismantled the shed at the caravan and the greenhouse at Meriden Road and Harold Hewitt transported both to the bungalow on his motor lorry, not chancing Trevor's tractor again.

The shed and greenhouse were soon put up and I bought a big quantity of clay flowerpots in sizes from two inches to ten inches diameter from Mrs. Bolland on Broad Lane – she was the other evacuee during the war, "mother" of Bill, the alsatian.

I had an old copper, which I used for steam sterilising soil for bedding plants, etc. This was set up on bricks – there were plenty of them about – with space for a fire below. A metal disc was cut to fit two thirds of the way down the copper, kept in place with a half-brick underneath. About a gallon of water went in and was below the metal disc. Then sieved soil was loaded into the old copper. A fire underneath, steam rises from the water, an old sack over the full copper, and the soil is cooked when one cannot touch the sterilised soil for the heat. Hey presto, a slow job, but it worked.

The whole area was destined to be a real challenge. Where to make a start. In the end I chose the front garden. The bungalow being some sixty yards back from the road, progress was very slow. Stripping off the weeds and digging the cleared area, it was decided to grow vegetables for a start, at least there should be something "for the pot". The hedge down the right-hand side belonged to us and was completely out of control, about ten foot wide and ten feet tall, mostly hawthorn. It was keeping a lot of sunshine off our neighbours' garden at the back – a Mr. and Mrs. Harris who built their bungalow with second-hand materials, not sure when. They were delighted when I said that it was my intention to cut and lay the hedge, a job never undertaken before, but I did know more or less the technique of the job.

It was a bit slow and not up to the standard of my friend Don Gibbs, an expert. In the end it looked quite good and it lived and flourished, also a lot of firewood was available for the next winter. The neighbours were very pleased to have more sunshine in the garden.

It was not long before I came to the conclusion that some sort of mechanical aid would be a good thing, so a visit to the Carlton

Horticultural premises was made. This was attached to Cooper's Garage opposite the George in the Tree pub, now called The Shay House!!! Blimey, what a name!!!, where they sold horticultural machinery, mowers, cultivators and the like, nothing like the variety of machinery aids available today. Don Ford was the salesman; I knew him but not well. He was often at the Cameo Cinema in the days of my youth, a very good salesman and said to be able to sell fur coats on the equator.

They had a five H.P. Clifford rotavator, second-hand, and he brought it round for a demonstration. I had been used to using a Clifford at the nurseries in Kenilworth some five years ago, and trusted to rotavate in the greenhouses. It was a very reliable and manoeuvreable machine, also it did a very good job. The demo was very good, me being able to use it, and at fifty-five pounds a good buy – the equivalent of two weeks' wages, plus a bit.

The only way to clear the land and make a good job – as I saw it and was able – was to cut down all the growth above ground, dig out blackberry bushes, old soft fruit bushes and suckers of all description, then skim off all the growth and make a huge compost heap. This I did, a stack some twelve foot square, and it was soon four feet high and steaming like a mini volcano. It took just about all the year of 1957 to clear the land, which was then rotavated and some crops planted.

A log of hours worked and cash received was kept and the first year paid at the rate of two shillings per hour (10p). My pay for an hour's work during the week was at five shillings or 25p. However, I did enjoy the challenge and this was a big one.

The men from the Ministry came at my request and did a sample test of our soil, which did show a calcium deficiency. At the time farmers and market gardeners could buy subsidised lime very cheaply. I think it was two pounds (£2.00) per ton (20 cwt). I had two tons which was the quantity recommended and applied it later on during the next winter.

One way and another money was coming in. Bedding plants, salad crops, early potatoes, and later on sweet peas and runner beans did very well. The rotavator was paid for in one go and we also paid our debts fairly quickly. Also, Mr. S who we bought the property off was soon on the scene for money – if possible please. We were able to pay him a hundred pounds I think. Olive and I had agreed not to spend any money on the place unless it was vital, as long as the building was watertight and so on. We did watch the gutters drop off the veranda at the front, and that was unsafe, but it was not used anyhow; it was impossible to open the french doors that led outside anyway.

It was a big help with no rent to pay, also the rates were very low indeed and no water to pay for. By the summer we had invested in a few hens which were put in a shed (of a sort) down the garden. There was even enough wire netting to make a run for them as well.

Very soon quite a few locals were calling for our produce. I bought a set of scales with weights and a scoop. This was after a visit by the Customs and Excise (Weights and Measures) man, who must have been informed we were blissfully using kitchen scales. Nevertheless, no-one ever went away with short measure. He never came again.

So it was that with longer days and warmer weather, life was not so bad after all, mostly work and bed, as they say, and no holidays for me. We did manage a few trips out with the motorbike up to Bonsall to the Wallis's and a picnic or two in the Cotswold areas.

Another person I got to know was Ted Carr who had the nurseries at the end of Windmill Lane – Catchems Corner Nurseries. The place was owned by Les and Sally Beachall, who lived on the premises, the nursery being down the drive at the back. He grew bedding plants, pot plants and cut flowers. He, like me, also made holly wreaths at Christmas.

Ted had been offered a contract that he said he could not undertake and was I interested? "I'll say" says I. Contact was made with Mr. and Mrs. Bill Carpenter who had a florist business on the London Road, Coventry, quite close to where the large island is now at the junction of the Ring Road, London Road, and the top end of Gulson Road. He wanted as many as I could make, preferably a minimum of five hundred. Would I take in a sample of ten inch and twelve inch wreaths? This I did and came away with an order for one hundred and fifty twelve inch and threehundred and fifty ten inch, all to be at one price which was quite good.

The shop was called Elizabeth Anne, named after Mrs. Carpenter and their daughter Anne. I had got a job on my hands!! and only a motorbike and sidecar for transport, plus a full-time job.

The first task was to get up one morning before five a.m. for a trip to Francis Nicholls, wholesaler at Coventry Wholesale Market at Barras Heath. Bill Carpenter said to mention his name to the salesman. This I did and was treated like royalty. Apparently, he was one of their biggest and best customers for pot plants and cut flowers. The shop was on the London Road, right by a bus stop, and only a short walk to the huge Coventry Cemetery. People would get off the bus or stop their cars at the shop, make their purchases and then on the few yards to the cemetery. The premises were quite small but a little "gold-mine". They were only interested in top quality goods and a reliable service. One good thing. Mr. Carpenter was making arrangements to collect most of the wreaths. I would take the first batch for him to put on a show early in December and also the final few at the end, when I would be paid. They told me in the market that he was a good payer – on the dot.

I spent a lot of cash that morning buying well over six hundred frames, ten inch, twelve inch, crosses and chaplets. (Chaplets were heart-shaped without the vee top and made with laurel from the point upwards, to cover two thirds of the frame). Also needed were fourteen bundles of stub wire at seven pounds each, plus thirty reels of binding wire to bind moss onto the frames. I would still be undertaking any other orders that came along, retail that is.

Fortunately, I knew quite a few local farmers where holly could be obtained and I had permission to go into the old Mercote Hall premises. Mercote Hall had been a lovely place years before. The beautiful house was demolished in 1929, why I never knew, and the grounds just abandoned to go wild from then till now. In its hey day there was a large orchard where the coach-houses were, a kitchen garden, two tennis courts where I understand a lot of the, shall we say, "better off" or "in the know" played tennis. No sour grapes or whatever intended. There were also shrubberies and all sorts of other plantings, including hollies.

My arrangement with Captain Wheatley-Hubbard was to put any payment in the Church box.

Moss also grew there and many hours were spent over the years pulling moss. I gather it by raking now, why didn't I think of that method all those years ago.

How I managed to transport all the materials home I will never know, but I can recall coming up the Kenilworth Road and through Balsall with great bundles of holly tied onto the old combo.

Fortunately, I never saw a policeman who just might have stopped me. However, I could always see in front and behind and felt quite safe for myself, and other road users. Also, there was less traffic to bother about and no dual carriageway either.

This year the whole job was better organised. Wreath-making was to take place in the junk room, an area was cleared and a big worktable was made out of the greenhouse staging. The room faced the road and everything went in through the window and the finished wreaths and rubbish came out the same way.

Wreath-making is a labour intensive job so the frames were mossed up and stacked outside before the end of November. Next job was preparing and wiring the fresh berries. I found that it was best to cut the berried holly round about the twentieth of November and store it outside out of the reach of birds and mice, not altogether easy. Berries cut before that would start to wrinkle by mid December. The berries had to have the leaves cut off and then wired, all five thousand of them. The holly tips at the ends of the branches were saved, wired and made up, then the partly made wreath put outside and if an order was required quickly it did not take long to put in the variegated holly and berries.

Everything went very well that year. I did have a couple of days off to complete the order on Christmas Eve, taking the last few to the shop. They opened for four hours on Christmas Day morning and then went out to lunch. Not many folk did at that time. I was paid in full and we both downed a very large rum. Then it was home to help put our decorations up and trim the tree.

Since becoming self-employed, I was responsible for putting a stamp on my card each week. This was just a little less than when I was an employee, but there were no unemployment benefits. No work, no pay. This is why my clients agreed to engage me throughout the year.

It was not long before the Inland Revenue got on to me regarding Income Tax. I never did pay very much, but they wanted their dues, which was fair enough. How to work it all out was a problem for me – allowances for using the motorbike to get me to the job, how many miles per week for business, how much petrol used, what about repairs? and so on. There was an allowance for working clothes and money spent on materials at home, seeds, fertilizers, farmyard manure and so on. Letters went to and fro and, what do you know? I kept no copies – hardly knew what carbon paper was, the result being a right old mess that was beyond me to sort out. It must have been when I was talking to someone about it all that Jim Thompson's name was mentioned. He will sort you out, I was told. This was mentioned to Pam on my next visit. "Oh yes" says she, "he attends to no end of accounts in his spare time". Eventually a meeting was arranged with Jim and he undertook the job of looking after my accounts, an arrangement, which went on for about twenty-five years.

The lad, Jim, I shared a desk with at Berkswell School went on to Leamington College for further education. On leaving school he was articled to a firm of accountants in Birmingham until he finally passed all his examinations and became a chartered accountant. Just a few weeks after he was called up to do National Service with the R.A.F. On demob he became the company accountant for a large bakery in Coventry and it was at this time he took my accounting problems under his wing, as I said, with lots of other small acounts in the area.

He provided me with a small accounts book and the first entry is dated 13th April 1957. Earnings for the week £9.15.9d (9.79). Other entries – receipt 18th May 1957 Bedding plants £20.30; 1st June Sweet Peas 19.50 (they were very early); 8th June, Peas and Early Potatoes £8.50; 28th June, Lettuce 87p. Additional items up till August were Cut Dahlias, Asters, Chrysanthemums, also Tomatoes and Runner Beans, Wallflower and Cabbage plants.

Selling the produce was always a bit of a problem. Quite a few local people came to the door, often at mealtimes, but always welcome. A local greengrocer (Maiseys) had most of the vegetables, but the tomatoes had to be graded. They only wanted more or less a cetain size – eight to the pound size in fact.

Occasionally, I would go down to Berkswell Village and meet my father for a couple of pints, still the old style pub managed by Mr. and Mrs. Jeffcote. She was a very nice person and on one occasion I enquired if I could take my flowers to The Bear and sell them to their clients. "Certainly" she says. So that is how I moved the sweet peas. Olive and I made them up into bunches of about thirty and arranged them in a wicker basket and off I went on the old combo. Usually about eight-thirty on a Saturday evening I would stand just outside the back door where everyone came out to go to their cars. There was a price card on the flowers and I never had to "hawk" anyone. They got to be known as "peace offerings" and so on. Most folks were in a good mood when they came out and often I was sold out in half an hour, but not before Mrs. Jeffcote had received her special bunch – Crawler did someone say? It was a very useful exercise, which carried on for a few years. Another bonus was that they had all my spare large tomatoes for the restaurant. I also sold asters, dahlias and chrysanths.

1957 was a hard working year, well they all were really. It took me the whole of the year to clear the ground, and then some. In addition to the growth to compost was the amount of scrap iron of all descriptions with a lot of old and useless sheets of corrugated iron. The scrap iron dealers were everlasting at the door after it. We told them that it was all going in one lot when I had it all together. There was one guy who seemed more genuine than the others, and he was the one chosen to have it. In the end he arrived with a big lorry. The deal was for him to take it all, every scrap. This he did and went away with a huge lorry load. It took two blokes all day to carry it up the garden, and they paid me £1.50; we were just happy to see it go.

In those days the dustmen came on a Monday and in addition to scrap iron, a lot of old bottles, glass, and tins were dug up. I filled two dustbins full over the weekend and wheeled them up to the gate and for about eight months the binmen took away the rubbish. They were very good and in fact always have been.

It must have been towards the end of 1957 that I had thoughts about another greenhouse and discovered that I could purchase a Prattens' fourteen foot by twenty foot assemble yourself job very cheap, no record of the actual cost. I decided to go ahead and after paying the deposit a plan of the requirements arrived. It meant building a base wall three feet tall, leaving a space for the door. I had dug up enough bricks (700) for the job, therefore only required to buy sand, gravel and cement.

My knowledge of bricklaying was not too good but I got it upright and square. The only thing I did not do as I went along was to point up the brickwork. It always looked a mess but it did the job.

The existing greenhouse was heated with a coke boiler heating four inch cast-iron pipes, so it was only a matter of obtaining more pipes, joining up to the existing and lagging the short length between the two houses and we were in business. But first of all, the thing had to be put up and it was winter time. I decided to do it after tea with an electric light extension from the bungalow with the bulb hanging over the convenient clothes line which eventually I had to find another tree to relocate it. Most of the work was done in the dark.

Arrival at Windmill Lane. Olive with Robert, Valerie and 'Fluffy' the cat

When the time came to fix the timber parts onto the brick base our neighbour, Norman Hazel from "Lynwood", came round and gave me a hand. I was so grateful and he would not accept any reward. The ends of the greenhouse came assembled and glazed so it wasnot too difficult to erect, but it was nice to get it completed and be able to spend the evenings in front of the fire again.

It was always a little difficult to decide exactly what to grow now that the area was cleared. I would have liked to work full-time at home and specialise in something or other, but lack of capital was always a problem, if I was going in for herbaceous or alpine and rockery plants for instance. So I carried on with the jobbing gardening and "sort of" catch crops at home not being brave enough to give up the day job. I could not afford to anyhow.

There were a few changes of venue for work. I left the other job on the Tamworth Road at Keresley and started gardening for Doctor and Mrs. Meacock at Gibbet Hill Road next to where the University of Warwick is now. The Meacocks were great friends of the Spencers. He was a dental surgeon and had a surgery close to Coventry railway station. He was a member of the Henry Doubleday Soil Association. This was many years before the Association set up their shop at Ryton near Coventry. As a matter of fact, we visited Ryton Gardens in 1997 and I was not impressed at all. The quality of the vegetable side of things was in my opinion rather poor, with yellowing foliage and not a lot of vigour. The flower borders and fruit trees all looked good. Dr. Meacock did not believe or allow any digging. The soil at Gibbet Hill was a heavy red clay. One could have made bricks with it. A lot of compost was made; everything went on the compost heap. The area was well organised. I called it "the factory". There was an old farm chaff cutter for cutting up sprout stems, etc., an ancient forerunner to a shredder. Chaff cutters were used on farms for cutting up swedes and mangolds for cattle. A big handle fixed to a wheel turned the cutters and the swedes, etc. dropped down from a hopper above. It was quite hard work. I helped Shep. Squires with this job when we went round the sheep with him on a Sunday afternoon when Stella and I were of school age.

Back to Gibbet Hill. Quite surprisingly, the vegetable garden did very well indeed; super brassicas and potatoes, although there were quite a lot of those little black slugs around. Not surprisingly, the root vegetables like carrots and parsnips were almost a failure. They could not penetrate the hard ground. The flower garden did quite well, but was always short of compost – the veg. came first.

About the same time, I started helping out Mr. Gibberd. He was a gents' outfitter, an old established family business trading in Earl Street almost opposite the Council House in Coventry. The shop was a single storey pre-fabricated job, one of many put up in Coventry to provide temporary premises to replace bombed property and there was a lot of that about in Coventry. Thursday was my day there. The Gibberd's lived on the Kenilworth Road almost opposite the Spencers and it must have been through them that I got the job.

Most Thursdays Mr. Gibberd managed to get the whole day away from the shop. In those days all shops closed for a half day once a week and it was Thursday in Coventry; Wednesday in Balsall when all shops closed at 1 pm. Michael Chattaway is the only shop to have a half day closing on Wednesdays nowadays. I digress – again.

We used to work together in the garden and it was a real pleasure for both of us. I never knew what would be going on in the garden on arrival. Mr. Gibberd's "passion" was alterations, to flower beds, shrubs dug up and moved, and so on. Sometimes the regular maintenance work would only get done when he had to go in on Thursdays.

We often had a beer during the morning. It was all rather relaxed. One year, he took me and others to Shrewsbury Flower Show and we had a superb dinner on the way home. He had a very nice sleek Riley "Pathfinder" car – that was a good day out.

There were "highs" and "lows" in 1958. One evening in mid-September I arrived home as usual and sat down to my cooked dinner. I was halfway through when Mr. Maclaren from next door came round. They had a telephone and he had received an urgent message for me. My mother had met with an accident at Four Oaks, Berkswell, and had been taken with sister Margaret, aged fifteen, to the Coventry and Warwickshire Hospital. Would I collect my father and take him in as a signature was required because an operation was to be undertaken.

So, I dropped everything, jumped on the old combo and set off for Meriden Road. Father was a bit surprised at the request saying "She's only had a bit of a bump". However, away we went, all in our old working clothes, and soon arrived at the hospital to be told Mother had a fractured skull. They could not wait for a signature and had gone ahead with an operation. By now it was about seven o'clock, the beginning of probably the longest four hours of my life. After some time we sent Margaret home, or rather to sister Stella's who by now had been housed by the Meriden Rural District Council in Needlers End Lane, Balsall Common. Father and I waited and waited. No news, but I recall anxious and probably sympathetic looks from hospital personnel going to and from the recovery room where Mother was.

Eventually we were asked would we like to see her, being warned that her head had been shaved, also she was not conscious. We went in and the scene has been with me ever since. Sufficient to say I wish I had declined the offer and been able to remember my Mother as she was. My father never ever said a word about what must have been a dreadful ordeal for him. From then on the signs were not good and at about eleven-thirty we were told that my mother had died.

For some things we were thankful. She, we were told, never regained consciousness after the accident. It was a nice way for my mother to go. With a fractured skull any sort of recovery might have had problems for her and being an active person she would not have liked to be an invalid of any sort, so we did try and console ourselves a little with these thoughts.

Father and I then came back on the 'bike to Stella and Bills' at Needlers End and told them the news. Sister Margaret was there. And then we came home to Windmill Lane and Father stayed with us overnight.

Next morning I took Father down home about nine o'clock and standing on the front doorstep with a big bunch of flowers stood Mrs. Huggins (Mother of Jeremy Brett, the late actor) of Berkswell Grange. How she got to know was and still is a mystery. Mrs. Huggins was a very kind and thoughtful lady.

The funeral took place some days afterwards and I cannot recall any memories of the service. There was a gathering back at the house in Meriden Road afterwards. I do recall getting back and Father getting out of the car and almost running to the bottom end of our long garden. Some folk wanted to go after him but I said "No, leave him be; he will be back soon". And so it was. He was composed and alright from then on. Someone asked him "What are you going to do now Albert?" and his reply was "Well, plenty of others have the same problem, and we (he and Margaret) will do the same as them, get on with it". He was then sixty-six and had already decided to carry on working. Mother was fifty-eight.

So, this is what Margaret and my father did, shared out the chores and helped each other – and, got on with it. Whatever else, they always listened to "The Archers" before washing-up.

Margaret was doing well at the new Heart of England School at Gypsy Lane, Balsall Common. The staff were very keen to make a name or gain a good reputation for the new school. They gently pushed or persuaded the students to their limits, quite right too. Towards the end of Margaret's time at H. of E., one member of staff told Margaret that he thought she was capable of gaining a pass in Physics. He offered to tutor her after hours, but she said that she went home on the school bus. "No problem", says he, "Take Physics, have a go, and I will run you home afterwards". Could that happen today? I think not. However, she agreed and gained another "O"

Level to leave school with.

Earlier in 1958 I had invested in another greenhouse which I wanted to site halfway down the garden. I thought it was a neighbourly act to speak to our neighbours at "Shrubland". "Fine, go ahead. Best of luck" were the answers, so I went ahead and ordered the greenhouse. It was to be fifty feet long and twenty-one feet wide, glass to the ground of the "Dutch" light type, i.e. each pane of glass approximately five feet by two foot six inches, each pane in its own wooden frame and all fixed onto a metal superstructure. The whole house was built on a rail track with the ends of the house hinged to allow it to be folded up so that the house could be pushed along the extended permanent track and cover another crop. It was possible to grow three crops a year with the one house starting off with early lettuce, followed by tomatoes, then the house would be pushed over a growing crop of chrysanthemums at the end of September, and then back to the lettuce again where the chrysanths had been growing.

This worked quite well, the only problem and a major one at that, was selling the produce. As I have said before, a shop in the village, say, could not cope with the quantity and there was not enough for the wholesale market.

Christmas 1958 was more hectic than anything before. There were the usual holly wreaths, plus a lot of chrysanths to sell, all in addition to my gardening jobs, which after all was the main earner. The other projects were really sidelines, although I suppose I was feeling my way, not at all certain which road to go down.

The wreath-making that year was done where Stella and Bill had lived next door. Their living-room was turned into a florist shop cum workshop. There was a fireplace in there so I could keep warm. I hardly saw anything of Olive and Valerie for about three weeks, working away all day, getting in holly at weekends and working till 2 a.m. and sometimes even later.

Two days before Christmas there was still quite a lot to be done so I did take two days off my normal work. On the night before Christmas Eve I worked all night, well, until about three-thirty when my eyes just would not stay open, so I put on my old motorbike coat, got down on the floor in amongst the holly leaves and prunings and went to sleep for an hour or so. When I woke up the fire was out and it was pretty cold.

I did not want to go and make a drink and wake Olive up, so I re-lit the fire and got stuck in again. The rest of the order for the shop was completed about four o'clock on Christmas Eve, then I had to deliver them to London Road, Coventry, get paid, and have the usual large glass of rum with Bill Carpenter, then come home through the rush-hour traffic, no Ring Road, and so on then.

There were still some private orders to do and it was about ten o'clock when I made my last call at Freddie and "Dibbs" Fields at Four Oaks. I said that I had hoped to make The Bear at Berkswell for a pint with my father but it was too late. "Dibbs" said "Sit yer down and have a drink here", which I did. Then it was home and to putting up the Christmas tree and decorations. Olive was expecting our second baby within the next month or so, and she had instructions from me not to climb on chairs and things.

I think it was again about two-thirty when I fell into bed for an eight hour kip, the first one of that length for some time.

Fortunately we were going to Stella and Bills' for Christmas Dinner, together with Father and Margaret, and they all came here on Boxing Day. This was a routine, which we kept up for some years, alternating the venue. And then it was back to work the day after Boxing Day and no New Year's Day Holiday at all.

It did take a little time to recover from wreath-making. It was all standing work and my ankles were all swollen. I was tired out for days and declared that it would be different next year, but the opportunity of extra earnings was the driving force – to get the place paid for and who knows what in the future. I was thinking on the lines of a pair of semi-detached houses, but without the cash there was not a lot of point thinking anyhow.

It was only a few weeks after Christmas when our next baby was due. Olive was under the care of a midwife from Balsall and Doctor Gaston. It was very early on the morning of January 24th that things began to happen. It was to be a home confinement and the little bedroom was to be the place. It was nicely decorated and quite cosy, by standards of the day.

The midwife was sent for and I was put in charge of supplying hot water, etc., and very little else. Again, husbands were definitely not wanted at the birth, so I paced about in the adjoining living-room. It was a real thrill to eventually hear the crying of our son whose name was to be Robert. He really had got a good set of lungs, even at that early age.

I had given myself two weeks off and once the midwife had gone really enjoyed myself cooking the meals and doing some of the housework. I did pop out into the garden in the afternoons. It was seed sowing (bedding) time in the greenhouse and there was always plenty to do.

If I recall correctly, Robert was well behaved, very few problems at night, and Valerie was another "little mother" to him. And so Olive and I settled down once again to a busy life, me outside and she looking after two youngsters – and me, a job she took on and did – and still does – with a good heart whatever it takes.

The facilities in our old wooden bungalow were really tough going. Olive had been used to a far better way of life at home and also in the caravan. Probably washing the clothes was as grim as anything, with only a basic electric boiler for heating the water. Getting clothes dry was a problem and I did buy a Creda Debonair spin drier, which was a great help and lasted for years.

It was also a problem with the kitchen away from the living-room, down three steps and along a passage, keeping an eye on the youngsters in one place and working in another. Also, there was only an open fire for warmth, but naturally we did have a fireguard. For all that, it was still very nice and rewarding to come home in the evening and warm up in front of a nice fire.

At this time one or two folk asked if I could rotavate their gardens in the Spring in preparation for Spring planting. A lot of people at the time still had large back gardens and grew their own vegetables. There was the problem of getting my Clifford rotavator around so I found and bought a small trailer, which I towed behind the combo, which was not a fast machine, but a good old slogger. It was a rare sight around the place but it worked very well. The trailer and machine probably weighed about five hundredweight in total. What's that in kilos?

Also at this time Don Ford (who sold me the rotavator) set up as a landscape gardener. He lived in Elmwood Close close to the centre of Balsall Common. We met in the village occasionally and one day he asked me to go and work for him, but for the first time or two I declined with thanks. Then one day I asked Don what sort of money he paid and the upshot was about a third more than I was getting then, so I said I would think about it. In the end the offer was too good to ignore so some of my clients were given the option to match Don's offer or I would be on my way.

No-one did match the offer, so a start was made working for Don, two or three times a week. At the time there was a transport cafe where Arden Close is now – Nutt's Cafe. Charlie Nutt was a big pal of Mr. (Pop) Seeley, Headmaster of Balsall Street School. It is almost certain they were the prime movers in starting the Balsall and District Horticultural Society which I joined in 1949 and have been a member ever since, with probably a few lapses from time to time.

However, the D.L. Ford workforce assembled at the cafe at 8 a.m. for the day's orders. There were about four chaps then, and then me for three days per week. It was my intention to stay self-employed and this arrangement suited Don, i.e. no work, no pay for me.

For a start most of my work was on garden maintenance, clearing borders, cutting hedges and generally keeping properties tidy. Don also took on mowing and he would drop a mower off for me and I would get around on the old combo. Don was no gardener, he hadn't a clue what was involved with keeping a garden tidy. I would often get on the site and find the lawns six inches high and naturally it took twice as long to get them back down. The clients were not always very happy either.

The other blokes were engaged in laying lawns, fencing and slab-laying for terraces – they are called patios now.

Don then went into the turf business, buying a suitable field of grass, mowing it off and weed-treating it ready for sale. "Old Doug" was the turf cutter. It was mostly cut by hand in 1960; "Old Doug" was a grafter of the highest order. He was never beaten on a job. He would find a way round any problem but it was not always the right way to do it.

By now Don possessed a small lorry, a five tonner I think, to deliver turf with and collect materials for all the jobs.

At the time houses were springing up everywhere, the demand for turf was great, and all of us had to help out at the weekends. No builders laid any turf then. There was no problem to sell houses so why should they go to extra expense.

"Old Doug" worked like a slave but was paid piece work and was on a good thing – very hard work though. First of all, the turf had to be "raced out", a special tool cut the turf vertically into pieces one foot by three foot. This he did after a trip to the pub at lunchtime. Racing out enough turf for the next day's requirements, then back to the pub till closing time, then a walk back to the field for a kip under a hedge till first light, then the cutting would begin again. This routine was quite common, say, for two or three days towards the weekend when the customers had time to lay it. Turf was one and nine pence and two shillings per square yard (i.e. 9p and 10p). The ten pence was supposed to be of better quality, but it was almost always the same.

We arrived at someone's door one day to deliver some one and ninepenny turf and the lady came out and said that they had changed their minds and would like the two shilling turf. "No problem" said the driver, "It's on the other side of the lorry. I will go up the road and turn the lorry round". We all had a good laugh on the way to the next drop.

Don really sort of "muddled along", promising customers a start date which he knew he could not keep, and then Ron Hurford and Michael Grealy came on the scene. Mick, an Irishman, was the lorry driver and Ron was to be foreman. Ron was a good organiser and the running of the business and the quality of the work improved.

Ron had been a lifetime gardener working under his father at The Moat and later on the Coventry Parks Department which was responsible for all the horticultural work in Coventry. There was a nursery at Canley and it was all run efficiently by Mr. Bill Shirran. The parks, open spaces and city flower beds were immaculate and there was no vandalism. Ron was in the R.A.F. during the latter part of the War, a navigator on bombers. After the War he worked with or for (I never knew which) Jack Smith of Tile Hill.

The only thing that I did not like was that we all went to the pub at lunchtime. It was impossible to work the same after only one pint, but it was usually more. However, we survived.

Eventually, Don bought a big rotavator, a Howard "Gem", probably about seven hundredweight. I think that is about 400 kilos. Not many (no-one in fact) liked using this machine which had three forward gears and a reverse. I got on with it very well with its powerful diesel engine making the machine do the work and not mauling my guts out. So guess who had the rotavating jobs, rotavating kitchen gardens and preparing areas for turf laying and so on?

Around about this time the Royal Agricultural Show came to Stoneleigh on a permanent basis and Don soon had his feet under the table. There was a lot of work to be had and he was in the thick of it, laying turf and paving slabs to the various hirers of stands. Often materials like slabs were only hired and were re-claimed and sold on after the Show.

One day in the previous winter Don 'phoned me. I was at home because there was snow on the ground and outside work came to a halt. He had had an enquiry from the National Bee Keepers Association requesting a design and quote to construct a bee garden. He had not a clue. Would I go and see him? So off I went and in a couple of hours we had put a drawing of sorts on paper, to include paths, a rockery, and plantings of trees, shrubs and perennials, etc. that were attractive to bees. Much to our surprise the job came in and I was instructed to do the rockery and planting. We went to Hornton Quarries at Edge Hill for the stone, pieces up to half a ton. The job turned out very well – I like to think. Don got paid anyhow.

Don also took on floral decoration work, without a clue as to who was going to do the work. In the end no-one else was forthcoming so again, yours truly took it on and I had but very little idea how to proceed. In fact I had a wander round the Show watching others and copied them. Don did provide the pot plants from somewhere.

The first year of the Show at Stoneleigh was very wet and there were very few permanent roads constructed, just grass avenues between the stands. My last job before the Show opened was to put in a pond and rockery, also floral for the A.T.V. Television stand next to the Grand Ring. This order came in very late. I was working till 9.30 p.m. most days and still was not finished by 10.00 p.m. the night before the Show opened, so I was back there at 5.30 a.m. the following day and completed the work at 9.00 a.m., one hour after the official opening of the Show. All was well there, but chaos reigned. All the "roads" were deep in mud, vehicles stuck all over the place. I was in my working clothes and decided to have a look at the Show F.O.C., a small reward.

There were lots of front gardens to turf and it only needed one job on a site and all the others came out enquiring about quotes. Don was an extrovert type of chap and he would discuss the jobs with Ron at Nutt's Cafe before we all set off for our various tasks. Don would say "We've got four bob a yard to do that front (20p)" or "We are getting so and so for that fencing or paving".

All the information went down in the back of my notebook for future reference.

Old Doug was full of tricks. The front gardens were often littered with builders' refuse, old cement, half bricks, bands off the packs of bricks and so on. As I was rotavating I made a pile or two of this rubbish to go away, but Doug had other ideas. He dug a big hole and buried it. Naturally some time after that it would sink, leaving a big depression in the lawn.

The classic one was down Station Road, a new bungalow, and a very nice couple. The job was to turf the whole of the back garden, which was two foot tall with grass. This was pre-rotavator days. Undaunted, Doug set about skimming off the grass, then he dug a trench along one side and bundled the grass in. Then another trench some six feet further over, using this soil to top up the first trench, and so it went on all over the site. It looked fine when it was finished, but six months later the lawn had "waves" in it; all the trenches had sunk.

One morning Don said to Doug "What did you get up to yesterday?" They were putting up a six foot fence in Leamington. "Why?" says Doug, "The ground was so hard for digging holes, we cut some off the top of the posts." That all altered when Ron arrived. He was a very good landscaper, in particular with hard landscaping, paving and stonework. I did learn a lot from Ron, mainly by watching and instruction.

CHAPTER 14

Gaining My Wheels

Things by now were going very well for us, Olive and I, and I thought it was time I learned to drive; another string to my bow, and I probably would be more use to Don, never thinking that I would possess a vehicle, a four wheeler that is.

An instructor was recommended from Kenilworth, so I signed up at seventy-five pence an hour. I think I had sixteen lessons, took a test and passed first go – as I did with my first motorbike. But before that not having a vehicle to practice in put me at some disadvantage. However, Don Ford and his drivers were very good and from time to time let me drive to and from the jobs.

One time we were working out at Sutton Coldfield and Ron suggested I drove the lorry home. Mick was not happy but we all got in the cab and had an uneventful journey but as we got out of the cab Mick was still not a happy man. I took my lunch to work in an old shopping bag, together with a ten foot tape, etc. and my "L" plates.

Another chap working for Don Ford at the time was Lionel Holtom who lived with his mother and brother Roger down by the station. His father was killed in an accident at Berkswell station some years previously and Lionel also worked there in the signal box, helping Don in his spare time. Although he was a few years younger than me, I had known him for many years.

Lionel by this time had started to visit Freda in Bromsgrove Hospital. Lionel's folks took the Sunday Mercury newspaper and one Sunday an article appeared about Freda, together with a photograph. It stated that Freda had entered a beauty competition and was not able to be at the judging event as she was in hospital for treatment for a T.B. hip. Lionel wrote to this "Brummagem beauty" and was soon making a regular trip to

Bromsgrove in his small Austin A30 – I think it was. However, one day he asked me if I would like to go with him for some driving practice. This I accepted with thanks and while Lionel went to see Freda I sat and waited in the car – until – one night, there was a "Royal Command" to visit this lovely creature and, was not disappointed. Freda sat up in bed like the Queen of the May, and from that day to this she has been the lively and bubbly person we all love and respect, despite the fact she has had a lot of aches and pains to put up with, including further operations and so on.

Naturally they were soon married and came to live in Kelsey Lane, just round the corner from us. Thus began a friendship that has gone on ever since, sharing joys and sorrows along the way.

Having passed my driving test I was anxious to get behind my own steering wheel. The old Ariel combo was more or less on its last "tyres", very shabby and not at all suitable to take Olive, Valerie and Robert anywhere. It was used very much as a work horse and had more than earned its keep.

One Sunday before Robert was born (autumn 1958) we went up to Derbyshire on the combo to visit Ray Wallis and his family. Coming home the heavens opened up and the carburettor or whatever took in water and the bike came to a shuddering stop. Thankfully the sidecar was waterproof and I was well protected from the elements. The rain soon abated and stopped altogether, but we were stranded somewhere the other side of Tamworth. A motorist came along on his way to London and offered to give us a lift. Today one would not even think of accepting, but Olive and Valerie needed to be getting home.

They loaded up into the car and sped off into the evening, leaving me with a "duff" bike and I hadn't got a clue what to do.

As I said, today one would not dream of taking such action, but the young man looked straight and honest and duly delivered Olive and Valerie to the Pool Meadow bus station where they caught a bus to Broad Lane. And there I was stuck on the side of the road and thought I would have a go at starting the bike. Much to my surprise and delight and relief, the engine burst into life. I can only guess the water wherever it was had dried out by the heat of the engine, and so I was on my way and more or less followed Olive into the caravan. Once again, all's well that ends well, and I had no further problems afterwards with the 'bike.

Looking round for a vehicle, not sure how much to spend or commit myself for was a bit of a problem. In the end it was decided a van would be the most useful form of transport. O.K. for work and carrying tools, etc. I was getting more and more turfing and paving jobs, also Don could send me off on my own.

In the end I bought a two-year old Bedford van from C. and E. Motors on the Fletchampstead Highway where the Homebase store is now. £350.00, and I required a loan of £100.00 over eighteen months from the bank. We only had one bank in Balsall then, the National Provincial, later to become the National Westminster. An account had been opened early in 1958 and I was well known to the Manager, Mr. Bill Garlick, not because I was always in debt or running to see him, I hasten to say.

Getting this loan was like asking for the Town Hall clock – a questioning and grilling session. However, the bid was successful and the van was duly purchased. It was rather interesting to note that the loan was spread over two Christmas's and on both Mr. Garlick paid me a visit, clutching gifts of port and sherry. Not requiring a loan since that date there have been no further gifts of any sort. Does it pay to borrow?

Having this new toy meant that we could all go out again. I bought, or begged, a coach seat, which was put alongside the driver's seat and it worked well, although it was not fastened down in any way. Fancy doing that these days.

One of our first trips was to the Wallis's near Matlock. They had probably moved to Whatstandwell by now. Ray had married Marcelene and lived at Steeple Grange just outside Wirksworth.

Another Sunday we took father and Margaret to Llandudno for the day. There was no holding us now.

The van, a 15 cwt or three quarter of a tonne carrying capacity, made a big difference to my life really. Apart from being able to transport the four of us around, I was more use to Don Ford. I kept and used my own tools most of the time and was given the job of carrying out all the rotavating with his big diesel engined Howard "Gem". It had three forward gears and a reverse. Most of the other blokes hated the sight of it, but by making the engine do the work, I found it easy to handle.

They fixed me up with two lengths of scaffold planking to load and unload and away we went. Don or Ron gave me a list of addresses and instructions, "This is to be a lawn, veg. garden, or whatever", and I would rotavate to suit. It all worked very well. In addition, I could lock my tools up, there was a shelter from bad weather, and a place to have my dinner.

I was in clover. Nevertheless, it was hard going using that machine all day. That was the first time that my legs and knees ached a bit.

Now there was a motorbike and sidecar for sale, a bit like a flying scrapyard in reality. The sidecar hood more or less had to be tied on – this was long before the M.O.T. test was thought of – and it's probable that the Ministry of Road Transport saw me knocking about, probably towing a trailer with a 7 cwt rotavator on the back, and decided it was time to take some sort of action. If that was the case it took them many years to devise the M.O.T. scheme which did in fact clear the roads of a lot of unroadworthy vehicles.

Don Ford bought one very old lorry and sent me and a lad out with it delivering turf. I drove it all the way to Allesley Park and could not get higher than second gear, but, just like an old donkey or mule, the thing behaved perfectly on the way home.

Ah, the old bike. At the time a young fellow called Gill Chick lived by Don in Elmwood Close, known now to some of us as "Slum Alley". He also worked for Don and set his heart on owning my old Ariel. I wanted £15.00 for it (big deal) and trusted the bloke to pay up as he departed with my "scrap iron". Another lesson learned, I never saw him or my money again. I must learn not to be so soft.

Time was moving on. I was getting more and more jobs of my own, although I never pinched any work off Don. If an enquiry was made whilst I was working for him, it was referred to Don or Ron. Don paid me a mileage allowance for the van and never ever queried my figures.

Towards the end of 1960 we had paid off the loan on the property. The old bungalow was ours, together with about one acre of land with a seventy foot frontage. "Rose View" where sister Stella and Bill lived for a while was demolished

In those days there were two corner shops, just down the road at Catchems Corner. Mr. and Mrs. Mason had a grocery store, also two petrol pumps right on the road junction. Although we got on well with them, most of our weekly shop was done at Woolley's on the other corner. Anyone more helpful and obliging than the Woolleys would have been very hard to find. They would deliver an order, however large or small, and as well as one could imagine, all the news could be had, although it was never a "gossip shop". They also sold fruit and vegetables, Mr. Woolley getting up early and going to the Barras Heath Wholesale Market three or four times a week.

Mr Woolley was an electrician by trade having been employed by East Midlands Electricity Board in Coventry at one time. He helped us out once or twice with new 'rings' for the cooker at one time.

One day at the shop the conversation must have got round to houses and building, etc., and Mr Woolley told Olive that when we were ready to build Mr Pyle was the man to talk to. He lived in Meeting House Lane, and his father lived next door, so we thought about it, and decided that talking about houses, etc. would *do* no harm. I called Mr Pyle – we had no phone, put him briefly 'in the picture', and made an appointment to see him and talk it over

CHAPTER 15

Bricks and Mortar

John Pyle worked for an estate agent in Kenilworth and had built a house for himself and another next door for his parents in Meeting House Lane, a bungalow for his brother in Balsall Street East and I understand another one somewhere. We were made welcome on our visit and he said that really we ought to be talking to his architect father. However he said we could talk and take down some details and he would come back to us in a couple of weeks or so. I think that I have stated that we had paid off the loan for the land by this time. We put all our cards on the table, telling him of the state of our finances, which only amounted to a few hundred pounds and we also said what we would like, not daring to think we could afford to go ahead with a project at this time.

However, eventually we went back to see John Pyle and all the drawings were spread out over their dining-room table. "Have a look at these" says he, and there lay the plans for a detached house, three good size bedrooms, bathroom and a garage plus the luxury of solid fuel central heating. My first reaction – and I said so – was that we could not afford anything like that. John Pyle's reply was "If what you have told me was true, then you can afford to go ahead". The scheme was to sell half the frontage, about thirty-six feet to him. The plot went back about fifty yards from the front to the back. The sale of the plot gave us a very good deposit for the building of the house. We were quite excited at the prospect and the first thing to do was to obtain a mortgage. Around about 1955 we had taken out an endowment policy with the Prudential Assurance Co. The object of this policy was to convert it to house purchase when required. This was for £1,500 and seemed a lot of money to me.

It was decided to go ahead with the scheme as the offer for next door plot was I thought fair. The specification for the house was drawn up and included decorating and just about everything that one could think of. The builder was supplying and erecting the fence all round his plot and all the outside work like paving, etc. At the time builders were just beginning to turf over the front gardens of new houses. This turfing was a clever move because it was a good way of getting the fronts tidied up and helped the sale of the properties. Don Ford took on some of these contracts with the big building firms and old "Doug" came into his own again. He would dig a big hole on the site and all the refuse went into it, lumps of concrete, brick-ends and everything else that was in the way, glossing over the top with soil, and no-one was ever the wiser – well the customer never was anyhow, until he came to plant a tree or shrubs – too late by then.

During the legal search it was discovered there was a covenant on the land relating to the hedge dividing the two plots. One may recall that one plot was about twenty-two feet wide and the other about forty-nine feet. This was the first we knew about the covenant, as no-one had said anything about it to us. One of the reasons why we would never use the same solicitor for both parties, a lesson learnt and taken on board. As one can imagine, it took some time to sort out all the paper work and legals.

In the end we had to pay for two indemnity policies to safeguard the owners of both new properties should the covenant (or the breaking of it) ever be contested. We were very fortunate to get the mortgage from the Prudential when we required it. At the time there was a sort of credit squeeze in the finance market. We were told we were the only successful applicants in the Midland area during that particular month. The fact that Olive and I had a good track record with the company did help – so we were informed. John Pyle was the builder and clerk of works and he recommended Thomkins & Co. as solicitors to act for us, and Henry (Mick) Biggerstaff who had lived in Gypsy Lane, Balsall Common, who was a solicitor as we were led to believe.

However, all went well and one Sunday morning early in April a gang of four Irishmen turned up to dig out the foundations. I had bumped into these lads from time to time on my jobs around new building sites. They were considered the best gang in the area. They went off for a pint or three at lunchtime and at 4 pm they had finished. Footings out, two and a half feet deep and levelling pegs in ready for the concrete. They were back a day or two later after the buildings inspector had been. Arriving about 4 pm together with the ready-mix concrete lorries, the footings were in and the gang had gone by 6 pm. That was the way the whole project proceeded. The bricks were on site and Frank Webster and his mate Ken were the bricklayers and they sometimes had a carrier (I think). They finished the building in a month and during that time there was no rain to hinder their progress. The carpenter/joiner worked on his own from just lengths of timber, no preformed trusses for him. He must have had some help from someone setting up the gable ends and the ridge piece, but I was not around.

Into the month of May and we were expecting our number three in the middle of the month. Again it was to be a home birth but there were problems. The midwife (Nurse Villenueva), a real smasher, was sent for and she in turn sent for an ambulance. It was quite a scramble getting Olive over all the building materials into the waiting ambulance and away. They went with me in pursuit to bring the midwife back. Valerie and Robert had a little holiday with their aunties. Olive was back home the next day with Jenifer. A way had been cleared through the building materials in the meantime. Valerie had started school in the previous January and my sister Margaret was working at the school as an assistant to Mr. Booen, the headmaster, prior to going to a Teacher Training College in Liverpool for three years.

It was a very busy time for Olive and myself as one can imagine, but the prospects of the new house and having three lovely children spurred us on. Youngsters I think are the best as tiny tots. They do not answer back. However the house was coming along very well as the various materials were required so they arrived on site followed by some of the best tradesmen around, plumber, electricians, plasterers, etc. The house was completed at the end of July but we did not move in until August Bank Holiday Monday which in those days was the first Monday in August. We had the choice of wallpaper or emulsion to decorate the rooms and as the walls dried out quickly we chose wallpaper downstairs plus stairs and landing and emulsion paint in the bedrooms and bathroom. The decorator was an exceptional tradesman doing a lot of rubbing down before the final gloss finish. The whole job was rounded off by a lady who came in to clean. The floors were scrubbed and all the paint splashes removed from the windows. The place was like a new pin. We could not move in as the Prudential had not made the final payment and we had to wait until four weeks later.

In due course Mr. Gauge of the Meriden Rural District Planning Office called round to instruct me that the old bungalow must be demolished forthwith. They were afraid squatters might move in. I managed to persuade him to let us keep the old brick-built kitchen and he agreed. It has been a real good tool shed ever since. "Just make it all uninhabitable quickly" says he "and all will be well". It took a long time and a lot of hard work to demolish the place. To get rid of the refuse, etc. I had doors at both ends of the garage enabling me to drive straight through. The bricks from the three chimney stacks went into a farmer's muddy gateway and the very useful timber boards went all over the Parish. Sheds were built. One man put a floor in the roof space of his bungalow and so on. The back garden was a tip, nonexistent in fact, so Valerie and Robert had a free hand as a play area. We did make a flower border down the left-hand side of the garden but it was to be some time before we had a proper lawn. I did make the patio fairly soon after we moved in, but making time for a proper garden had to wait.

Soon after moving in we had a visit from the men from the "Pru", something to do with house insurance. I had to take out a policy to safeguard against not being able to pay, should I die for instance. In the event the policy would pay for the house, Olive would become the owner, and the insurance company would get their money. As the two men were leaving and halfway out of the door I just mentioned that a pension scheme would have to be my next objective. With that they were both back in the house like a pair of hounds on the scent of a fox. "Don't get excited" said I, "We must sort ourselves out paying for the house and so on". "Can we come and talk to you?" they asked. "Yes" said I "but no deal until we sort ourselves out". A date was fixed and three agents arrived and sat down. My first words were that no deal would be done that night. An interesting proposal was put to me, which sounded quite good and we talked for over two hours. They would not go home. In the end the Superintendent got quite shirty, got to his feet and said "We might as well go, we will be doing no business here tonight", to which I replied "I told you that when you came in". In the event my pension policy was taken out and the first payment made on June 8th 1962 and carried on for thirty-two years until I retired at sixty-five.

For some years I had not had a proper holiday, hardly a day off in fact. If there was any shopping to be done for clothes or something for the house, it was usually undertaken on a wet day when it was impossible to work outside. I always had a day off to go Christmas shopping, well someone has got to do the paying. Funnily enough, it always seemed to clear up by the time we got to town, hence the old saying "rain before seven, fine for eleven". The first attempt at a holiday was a trip to South Wales. We borrowed a tent and loaded up the van and away the five of us went. Jenifer was very young so we had to take lots of baby clothes, napkins, etc.; no disposable jobs then. I cannot recall where we were but it was raining when we stopped at a camp site and struggled to put up the tent. We did survive obviously but it was blinkin' awful. However, with true grit and determination onwards we went thinking it would be better when we were in one place for the duration of our holiday. The sun came out and put a different complexion on things and we soon found ourselves near Saundersfoot and I spotted a sign in a hedge "Caravans to let £1-00 per night". We were in, no messing about, and spent the rest of the week in comparative luxury. That was the end of our one and only attempt at camping. We enjoyed

View of our rear garden and bungalow from the bottom end, 1959

our stay and, as they say "all's well that ends well".

The next year we thought it would be nice to go to that area again and Don Ford recommended a bungalow in Saundersfoot. As usual I was very busy and could not get away until early October but we managed to book this bungalow. However the workload was such that on the Saturday morning I was up before five and heading for Hagley Road, Birmingham, between Halesowen and Hagley. I had promised to rotovate a large area for a landscape gardener from Bournville whom I had got to know, a Mr. Wardle. Arriving soon after six I was pleased to see there were no properties too close so I would not disturb anyone. It was a huge area of ground – about half an acre, but the going was good, the ground worked well and the job was done by about noon. Then I had to return home, top up with petrol. And OK, there were no motorways or fast routes and I had never been that way before. After cleaning out the van it was time to start on myself and, guess what, it was raining hard. However, I think it was well after 4 pm when we finally set off complete with pram and cot in the back of the van. The pram was tied front and back so that it would not move and could not tip over and Jenifer spent most of the journey in it. On all our travels our youngsters were always patient and good which was a great help. Most of the trip to Saundersfoot was in the dark and the teeming rain.

Fortunately, we found the place easily and the key, let ourselves in to be met by the most glorious open fire; it was so welcome especially as I had been out and about for over sixteen hours.

The holiday was nice, the weather not too bad for Wales that is, we got round quite a lot, bought a mantel clock for the lounge in Tenby (which is still going). Being October there were not a lot of people about and no problems with parking. We found a nice cafe in Saundersfoot by a car park and left poor old Jenifer in the pram in the van whilst we used the cafe. It was a lovely area to explore, Pembrokeshire (known as little England beyond Wales). There was Amroth, Stepaside, Manorbier and a very nice coastline all around. Broadhaven and Solva, there was virtually nothing there.

Then it was back to the old routine of work and bed. Getting organised once again for the annual holly bashing, as we knew it, still undertaking the 500 for Mr. C in Coventry. By now the factory was in the garage, very handy to the house to answer the 'phone, etc. Although it was an awful lot of work it went like a well-oiled machine more or less.

Oh yes, the telephone. This came soon after the house was built and our new neighbours moved in next door. He needed a 'phone for the business, he was working with finance. At the time there was a shortage of lines into the local telephone exchange (before calls were connected automatically). A lot of people shared one line, which could only be used by one person at a time, known as a party line. Sometimes one had to wait one's turn. By this time I was keeping in touch with my clients via the public telephone at High Cross and often spent half an hour there in the evenings.

The big 'mobile' greenhouse at the end of the garden, 1959

Sid, our neighbour, and I decided to apply for a party line and were successful because of our business needs. In fact it was known as a business number and calls were cheaper than a private line. This carried on for many years and ours was the last one to go onto a single line. I digress back to the holly wreaths.

Soon I developed another idea which was to cut up the holly in the garage and I was allowed to wire up in the house. Spreading a sheet on the floor and others on the settee I was able to wire in the comfort of a nice warm room, be with Olive more and also save on some heating outside. It was very cold in the garage sometimes but I literally stood over the electric fire and did manage to keep warm. I could not work with cold hands anyway. Although I could not wire up as quickly indoors it was nice to get inside. David Thompson had been helping me on Saturdays when it was convenient to both of us and it was a natural progression that he came to work for me in the new year of 1963.

Unfortunately for me, the end of 1962 and the first ten weeks of 1963 was one of the worst winters I can recall. My actual earnings for ten weeks was just £17 and I had David to pay as well. On top of that the Bedford Van was showing severe signs of old age and there was more red rust than black paint showing, and the rear doors were ready to fall off.

We had quite a lot of snow in January followed by freezing cold weather, therefore when the snow thawed a little in the daytime, it turned into ice at night. Travelling was difficult. I really was at a loose end. Work at home was impossible and it was in February 1963 that Aunt Marie and cousin Esther arrived from Australia. They came by sea, taking a month, and left home in a heat-wave. They stayed with us for quite a while and it was fortunate that we had a warm, centrally-heated house. The cold weather did not seem to bother Aunt Marie and she and Esther were taken out and about as much as possible. A staunch churchgoer, Aunt Marie wanted to attend church, preferably one with a good organ. She played the piano and loved to have a go on an organ. We went to the Methodist Hall in Coventry a few times and the organist played before and after the service. Esther and Aunt Marie eventually went to a flat in Leamington and undertook various employment to subsidise their finances.

CHAPTER 16

The First Car

It was some months previous to this visit when we acquired our first car, about June 1962 in fact. One evening we had arrived back at Don Ford's shop in Station Road after work and a fellow turned up in a car and asked for Don. I went and found him and it transpired that he was going to give Don a demonstration run in this car. Don said "Jump in and come for a ride". What do I know about cars? Anyway, I was in no particular hurry that evening so off we went and I must say I was very impressed with this Austin Westminster, cream in colour with a blue speed flash down the side. It shone, paint work and chrome, 6 cylinders of power under the bonnet, with overdrive, very sleek. When we got back Don was wanted on the 'phone and then I said to the salesman "If Don doesn't have the car could I have first refusal?". "Sure" says he and about a week later he called in at home; we were not yet on the 'phone. Would I call and see him at his house in Duggins Lane? "We may be able to do a deal" says he. I duly called and it transpires that he (Dennis Cooper) wanted a lawn laying; would I give him a quote, which I did. The outcome was that I laid this lawn, paid £100, and took possession of the car which lasted a lot longer than the Ford Zephyr that Don bought.

That year we went to Rhyl in North Wales for our holidays. We shared a bungalow with Bob and Margaret Thompson and their two girls for two weeks. Their Sarah and our Jenifer were only babies and it was ideal; and we had the car. I thought Rhyl was awful and the weather was bad as well. We only went on the beach once during our stay. Still, it was a nice cheap break away from the daily grind.

Somewhere around this time Don Ford had bought a property in Station Road where the Midland Bank now stands, a small double-fronted

Our bungalow from the front.
New house being built in
front, 1961

cottage with the front
door in the centre. Mrs.
Turney had a small gro-
cery shop in the front
room. Don gutted the
place and the plan was to
open a shop selling garden machinery, etc. and have a repair workshop at
the back; he did know a bit about that sort of business. The windows and
the doors came out, the stairs were done away with and there was one great
big mess. One lousy wet and cold afternoon two or three of us were getting
the floor ready for concreting in the front area. Old Doug was there as well
when a bloke came along the path in his pinstripe suit, bowler hat, an
umbrella in one hand and a briefcase in the other. Up to the gap where the
window was he put his head in and said "I say, is there a Mr. Douglas or
Mr. Smith about please?". Old Doug was at the back and heard the question. He was off down the back garden path, over the six foot fence at the
end and away, not to be seen again that day. It seems that Mr. Douglas or
Mr. Smith (never knew his proper name), Old Doug, had never put a stamp
on his card (National Insurance contributions) or paid any Income Tax,
until then anyhow. Ever after he was in the net like the rest of us.

Don was really branching out, the shop was duly opened selling horticultural machinery and other sundries to do with the trade. There was also
a workshop at the rear for repairs, etc.

It was during the winter of 1963, about February I think, that I saw an
advert, probably in the Coventry Evening Telegraph, for a caravan for sale.
This was a Willerby four-berth van suitable to site at the seaside for
instance. I went off through the snow and ice to Allesley to have a look at it
and thought it would provide cheap holidays for the five of us. Where to
put it was the problem but Don had offered to have it behind the shop, outside the workshop. So we went ahead and bought it. Due to the fact that it
was a bit elderly it came cheap. Well made, clean but not posh, it was alright.
The one big problem was there was no bed in the end bedroom but I
acquired a very good sprung double bed frame which I set on blocks and
with the mattress made the bed about a foot off the floor – fine for the kids.
There was a solid fuel fire in the main part and plenty of storage space.

Next came the task of where to site it. We were not too fussy which
was just as well because I was soon to learn that most sites are owned or

controlled by the caravan sales companies. However, good fortune smiled on us once again and we found a site at Clarach Bay not far north of Aberystwyth. I have no idea how we found the site but all was well, the rent was reasonable, but there was no service on the site between any lettings. Next thing was getting it down there, but no problem as Vic Hicks, who was farming in Hob Lane, offered to tow it there with his Land Rover.

It was after Whitsun when we finally got all fixed up. Olive and I went to the Whitsun Crock Fair on Hearsall Common and bought crockery and cutlery, etc. to equip the van. One Sunday morning at 5.30 Vic and I set off for Aberystwyth wondering how it would tow. Would the tyres, springs, etc. be O.K.? In the event everything was fine, it took a long time but we arrived safe and sound. Vic is a very good mechanic so I was in good hands. We soon had the van sited and jacked up level. We spent some time having a look round and finally set off for home. Vic had been up and about some time before we left home and coming home he got very tired, in fact I'm sure he was almost asleep at the wheel but he declined my offer to help with the driving. However, we arrived home in one piece, a job well done, but really clapped out.

The van served us well for about four years. Often I would take Olive and the youngsters down on a Friday evening. I thought nothing of setting out in the Westminster at 9.30 pm. We filled the footwell in the rear of the car with luggage. Then we placed a mattress over the seat, etc., a couple of blankets and pillows, and the kids piled in and were usually asleep before we had gone far. Our route was to Alcester and Worcester and then the A44 all the way to Aberystwyth. On arrival we would open up, transfer the youngsters, have a cup of tea and be in bed soon after 1 am. Then we had two full days to relax. At school holiday times I would leave them there for a week, setting off for home at about 4 am and arriving at 7 ready for work and another two days off the next weekend.

We let the van out from time to time, charging a very modest fee, and always explaining about the one bed and so on. All went well until one time almost at the end of the season a man called on a huge motorbike and sidecar to ask if he could book the van for a week. I agreed, he paid up and went on his way. On the Sunday morning after this family moved out on the Saturday I had a 'phone call from the Site Manager to say that the new tenant was not satisfied. He said the van was not clean, a lot of children's washing was left behind, etc. He would not stay there. It was fortunate that the Manager could find him an alternative van. The outcome was I reimbursed the client in full, the Site Manager accommodated our next and final client, and that was the end of any more letting. We decided to dispose of the van. We were ready for a change of scenery anyhow.

All in all we had broken even on the van but how to get rid of it was going to be a problem. I think there was a caravan graveyard close by but before enquiring I had another 'phone call from the Site Manager to ask if we wanted to sell it. He knew of someone who was going to build a house for his own use and a caravan would be ideal to live in while the work went on. I agreed and without any haggle I suggested he pay us £25 and anything he made over and above this was his. Deal done and apart from collecting the contents that was the end of that little enterprise.

As just mentioned I was ready for new horizons and places to visit. Even now it is very rare that we visit the same place twice. The world's a big place and I would like to see as many of the best bits as possible. With the above in mind, and some months before disposing of our caravan, we decided on a week in North Devon and managed to book a caravan at Kentisbury Grange, near Coombe Martin. It was all very nice and we were shown the van by the Site owner, Peter Warmington. Also on the site there was a small shop and a licenced club open in the evening. The club occupied two rooms in the big house (The Grange). Part of the house was converted to holiday flats, the whole place was nice, well kept and welcoming.

Our pattern for the day was usually getting up late (I'm still very good at that), having breakfast and often preparing a picnic, trying to be out by 10.30; there was never a rush as we were on holiday. In the evening we would often end up in Ilfracombe about twelve miles away where we would find a nice restaurant or cafe for a good evening meal. Our offspring were always well behaved (although I says so) in spite of having to wait a long time to be served. Then it was back to the van and while Olive got the kids ready for bed I went to the Club for a pint or three. Anyhow, had I stopped to help I would not have done it properly. There was a super atmosphere in the Club. Everyone there was on holiday and intent on having a good time.

Towards the end of the week I discovered Peter was selling four vans at the end of the season, including the one we were in. As it happened I had a few spare quid at the time and we decided to purchase the one we stayed in. So began a ten year relationship with the North Devon area, a place we never tire of. I think the coastline from say Minehead round to Hartland Point takes a bit of beating with high cliffs, Woody Bay, Woolacombe and Saunton Sands, Barnstaple, Clovelly and many more. Inland there is Exmoor. The weather is not as good as Cornwall but one cannot always have everything. More on caravans and the area later on.

During the early sixties there was so much development going on and a lot of work about. Houses were going up like mushrooms, as a matter of interest the M1 Motorway was up and open. Providing one did a good job of work one could not go wrong, in my experience anyhow. I never had a big problem getting paid for services rendered, having my own code of practice (sort of). It was seldom that I undertook any job without first giving the client an estimate or a quote. If I was not sure I would estimate between two sums say not more than £120 or less than £100 and this worked very well, especially with folks I knew. Sometimes I had to wait a while for payment or even call round now and again, but over the years I estimate only failing to recover £300 or so. Everybody was charged the same rate for a job whether they had a Rolls Royce or a push-bike but there were times when a bit of cunning had to be applied. One day I called at a property to look at a job, and on leaving, the gardener (whom I knew very well) said "You will be lucky to be paid by him, I have a long wait for my pay". So, having worked out the quote I added 10% and got the job. On completion I sent the bill with terms on the bottom "Please deduct 5% for payment within 28 days". It worked, being paid after five weeks. I never felt guilty about getting a bit extra from those sort of people. One slow payer had not coughed up after six months so a visit was paid one wet morning. Knock, knock and the door opens and this chap says "Hello John and what can I do for you?" I gave him a polite reminder, I was invited in and after a coffee and a chat came away with five cheques, all post-dated, with the largest amount on the final cheque. However, they all went through and the debt was cleared after ten months. That was not quite the end because shortly afterwards this same guy was on the 'phone again wanting more work doing. I declined with thanks.

One non-payer never to be forgotten. This chap lived in a big house and called me in. He was selling the house and wanting a big tidying job undertaking; mow the orchard, rotavate a big kitchen garden area, weed the long Breedon gravel drive and so on – tomorrow! "Sorry, no way" says I, but in the end I promised to go for about four days and do the most important work. When the bill was submitted he refused to pay anything because all the work was not completed. I only promised to do what I could.

When it comes to giving quotes and estimates one can often not be sure how creditworthy people were, no modern computer files then. My aunt at the time was an agent for Whiteman Fuels, the coal merchant in Kenilworth. My uncle and aunt had the business until they retired and knew a lot about a lot of people, a sort of computer if you like. So I often popped into the office in Balsall village if I thought any useful information was forthcoming and it often was. "Oh they are O.K., but be careful with old so and so". A very handy grapevine. My aunt was very blunt and straight to the point and sometimes with colourful language to boot. However, we always got on well but a lot of what she said was best forgotten. We had many hilarious interludes in that office. There was never a lot of money about but usually a fair amount of fun to be had.

By this time, the mid-sixties, the youngsters were growing up. In 1964 Valerie was eight and getting on very well at Balsall Street School. She always had to work at her schoolwork to keep up with the others. That particular age group and class were all bright and able, also very nice young people to know. Robert was five and on the bottom rung of the ladder, more than a bit lazy in many ways, not just at school. His sisters waited on him quite a bit which probably did not help. However, he was a bright and cheerful youngster who loved the 'telly to bits. Jenifer was three and a very

Our first car – Austin 'Westminster'. Cost in 1962 one lawn and £100

busy young lady, flitting about like a butterfly but not concentrating on anything for long, perhaps taking after me.

I am not sure when we first had a TV but it would have been about this time. Valerie and Robert were coming home from school and asking if and when we were having a 'telly. My mind went back about twenty-five years to when I pestered my father for a radio, and then I decided that something ought to be done about it. Once again good fortune was on my side and I discovered a chap in Kelsey Lane who had one to sell. Don Ford knew him and was the contact so it was that for the sum of £15 we became the owners of a small (I think 12") 'telly. It was a very good picture and kept us amused for many years, although I did not watch a lot of TV, only in the winter months. Only now am I catching up on the early "Dad's Army", "Only Fools and Horses" and so on.

With reference to "Dad's Army", it is very interesting. I was only ten when the War began and we had a Home Guard platoon in the area but I could match up local characters to those taking part in "Dad's Army" from Captain Mainwaring to Private Pike. I was not aware of any goings-on as per Sergeant Wilson and Mrs. Pike, being far too young and innocent.

Jenifer was only three or four when we first went to a Butlin's Holiday Camp. We were looking for something which involved a complete holiday in the true sense of the word. No self-catering and washing-up to bother about and so on and so forth. The thinking was that Butlin's was not expensive and there would be plenty to do, or nothing at all if one so wished. We booked up to go to Filey in Yorkshire, full board, all in, the idea being that if we did not like it there would be lots of places to visit in the area. Came the day and we got ready the night before and were ready and on the road about 4.30 am at the Whitsun break and it was Whitsun then. We arrived on the car park at Filey about 8.30 and had our breakfast of cereals and a flask of tea and then went exploring, to find that we could not have our chalet until some time later on. However, we were soon installed, the youngsters in one chalet and Olive and I next door. Very comfy on a full board basis and second sitting at mealtimes, which meant we could all have a lie-in in the morning, and in the evening the nightly show began soon after dinner. There was a full orchestra of sixteen or seventeen musicians playing for dancing in the Viennese Ballroom. Everything much to our liking with plenty of entertainment for all ages. The youngsters would not stay on their own though but they were not all that old. Val would be no more than nine, Robert six and Jenifer just four. We took a short cut through the ballroom to the dining-room and often a record for dancing would be playing and one or two keen types practising their fancy twirls. Jenny said, with some authority "Mam and Dad don't do that" and was quite taken aback later to discover that Mam and Dad did do that, probably not as many fancy movements as some but we always enjoyed a dance. We all enjoyed Butlin's at Filey so much that I never saw the car again till our departure on the next Saturday. This was the start of many Butlin's holidays usually during the Spring half-term at the end of May. Over the years we sampled Bognor Regis, Barry Island, Pwlleli and Minehead which I think was our favourite and best one.

Very soon there were three at school, all making good progress. There were one or two "Must try harder" and "Could do better" in the reports. They were escorted to school by various kind folk and met afterwards by Olive. At this time we seldom went to Church, being rather busy with work and family. Often I had to see someone on a Sunday morning as it was the only convenient time. However, we had a new Rector, the Right Reverend Bishop John McKie. He was the assistant bishop of Coventry, the bishop being the Right Reverend Cuthbert Bardsley, a big big man in more ways than one, with a big booming voice to match. There was no dozing off during his sermons. Although most of Bishop McKie's work was in Coventry or the diocese an atmosphere of change took place. He was an Australian with three daughters, Jennifer, Jane and Janet. The fourth daughter, Kristin, was born at the Rectory not all that long after their arrival at Berkswell. John McKie was very popular. He would often pop into "The Bear" for a beer and he had quite a few at home as well. Soon after his arrival the Parochial Church Council (P.C.C.) held a campaign, I suppose a mission really. In those days Ted Gibbs, Miss Ida Midgley, Frank and Margaret Hayward and Kenneth Hope, to name a few, were the stalwarts of Berkswell Church and the local families were targeted regarding Church and in particular getting the children to Sunday School. On the second Sunday of the month the morning service was a family affair and we trotted along with our three and they attended Sunday School from then on. Elsie Thompson was Superintendent of the Seniors and Ida Midgley in charge of Juniors and Infants. It is probably fair to say that Ted Gibbs was very much involved on the admin side. Just as an aside, I think that it is right to say that in 1999 there was no-one living who has done more for Berkswell Church than Dennis Edward (Ted) Gibbs. It is a great pity I think that he is no longer a regular attender at Berkswell. The reasons are Ted's and I will say no more.

So we started going to Church again and I soon found myself as a sidesman and it was after Bishop McKie retired that I was elected to the P.C.C.

Bishop McKie was a well educated man and a great theologian. His sermons were good, so the learned would say, but lots of the time they were over my head. One Sunday morning after the service he was met by his charming and younger wife, Mary, who addressed him by saying "What the hell were you on about this morning John?". His spinster sister, Miss McKie and his mother-in-law, Mrs. Goodwin, also lived in the area. It was a sad

The new house in 1962 (note the Bedford 15cwt van)

The trio in the back garden, 1962

time when the McKies took up the living at Packington and went to live in Little Packington Rectory. The combined job of assistant bishop and Rector of Berkswell was too much for one person. A working party went to Packington Rectory one Saturday to have a garden tidy, a mammoth task and I recall their dog pinched my lunchtime sandwiches. I was soon fixed up with something to eat. On retirement they went back to Victoria, Australia, apart from one daughter. The Reverend Geoffrey Dingle became the new Rector and he was to stay for over twenty years.

Probably my next good fortune was our second car. The old Austin Westminster was getting the worse for wear, the body was anyhow. Once on the way to Coombe Martin where our caravan was sited we were well loaded and had a puncture near to Cirencester. I had just about found the tools and spare wheel when along came an AA Man who stopped and very kindly did the job for me. As a matter of fact he was on his way to assist a member who had broken down. It was very noble of him to help in these circumstances, especially as we were not members of the AA, but he did suggest we think about joining and at the time I did think it might be a good idea, but sorry Mr. AA Man, I did not. My policy through life has always been to pay when it is necessary and to pay promptly and cheerfully. We must have saved hundreds of pounds not joining extended warranty schemes and the like. The term used nowadays is "peace of mind"; for everything I have peace of mind without joining in. However, in other circumstances and with certain people, women on their own for instance, it could be a good thing. Anyhow, my next bit of good fortune. After our trip to Devon it was decided to change the car and I made up my mind that a Rover would be nice. There was a Rover 95, 100 and 110 among others but these were the big sit up and beg type, very comfortable and plenty of space for five of us. Watching the adverts in the newspaper a Rover 100 was advertised at £450. This was ignored as too expensive. However, the following week the asking price was down to £400 and soon again down to £350. It was then I 'phoned my friend, Bernard (Bunny) Poole. He was the owner of a Rover and worked for the firm in the Development Department. He was willing to go with me to see the car and after putting some spare cash in my pocket we set off for Coventry. We arrived at the address and were taken to the garage at the rear. A chap opened up the garage doors to reveal this big shiny monster. I could not hear the engine as he drove it out, spotlights and chrome overall. The three of us went for a spin with Bunny in the front to try and detect any odd noises; there were none. On our return we were left to debate for ten minutes and Bunny said "You will not find a better deal anywhere". When the fellow came back I extracted the notes from my pocket and enquired whether he would take three hundred pounds for the car. Much to my surprise he agreed and the deal was settled there and then. It was in fact a superb motorcar and gave us very good service. I only parted with it when Olive decided to learn to drive. A Rover 100 was not a good car to learn in, one thing it was very heavy on steering but very solid and safe.

It was about this time when my younger sister Margaret completed her three-year teaching training course at St. Catherine's College in Liverpool. She had done very well there and her specialised subject was, and still is, mathematics. She acquired a job at Bidford-on-Avon High School which has long since gone. She found digs in Stratford, just off the main road at the bottom of Bordon Hill (off Evesham Road), commuting to school on the bus. Soon we heard that a Mr. Cooper was taking her to and from school in his mini-van. I/we all thought – I think – that Mr. Cooper might be an older member of staff but he eventually turned out to be about twelve months Margaret's senior. We all took to and liked Peter Cooper who was now "keeping company" or "walking out" with Margaret. He was a teacher of the sciences, keen sportsman, rugby and cricket in particular, a very good actor and real nice guy.

My father had been a widower since 1958 and he worshipped the very ground Margaret walked on. He did not appear to interfere with Margaret's life, but he was probably a bit concerned for her wellbeing. Fortunately, it is my opinion my sister grew up quickly after our mother's death, she being the youngest by some twelve years plus. She was used to adult company and that must have been a great asset. My father moved from Meriden Road down into Berkswell Village I think about 1965. He went to live in one of the bungalows in Lavender Hall Lane, opposite the almshouses or flats (I wish they would choose another name for these dwellings, like "the houses on the green" or something). The bungalows were built to replace four elderly cottages for retired Berkswell farm and estate workers. It was ideal, not too much to keep clean. My sister Stella used to go once a week and "do" for them, but I think Margaret's bedroom was mainly ignored – nuff said on that one.

And so it came to pass that the handsome Pete popped the question and was accepted, and before long a wedding was being planned. Saturday, 25th March 1967, was the date at Berkswell Church, with the reception at "The Bear Inn" just up the road, keeping up some sort of tradition "out of the church into the pub". We had the Cromwell Room upstairs which was a very nice setting and my/our Rover came in for the bridal car. The only disappointment, as far as I know, was that Margaret wanted champagne but only got sparkling wine, just like other folks at that time. Peter had a mini-van at the time which was not very well hidden opposite "The Bear". The "vandals" found it and really went to town, lipstick, balloons, pebbles in the hubcaps and so on. Then someone drove it into "The Bear" carpark all ready for their departure, to where we knew not. However, Margaret and Pete had the last laugh because just at the last minute they made a dash for Pete's father's Vauxhall Viva and were away in a flash. Pete's Mum, Iris, was not aware that she had to return home to Rugby in the much-decorated mini-van and, yes, they were stopped by the "boys in blue", but all was well and I think all but Iris had a good laugh.

I am pretty sure that we had not met the Cooper family before the wedding, in fact we had not seen a lot of Peter. We were invited back to 123 Lower Hillmorton Road which was the beginning of a friendship that was to last for the rest of their days.

Margaret and Pete set up their home in Meadow Drive, Alcester, and guess who had the job of laying out their garden? The soil in the back garden was the hardest that I had experienced, my big 7 hp Howard diesel "Gem" would only get in about three inches so we laid the turf on that, and it never did make a good lawn. The old Roman Ickneld Street ran in that area and I reckon it was well padded down by legions of Romans. Anyhow they had a patio, borders and a lawn of sorts, and were happy with the results.

Olive and I and sometimes others had many visits to Alcester and district, we never saw Pete play rugby but I understand he was a useful number fifteen and a cricketer playing for Temple Grafton. The club square was on the property of Grafton Country Club and their annual dinner, presentation of cups, etc. and dance was held there. We had the pleasure for some years to be invited to what was a very good dinner and dance. Club members joined in later on, or was it the other way round? They also had a gaming room, blackjack and roulette, sixpence per bet with halfcrown stakes (2$°$p and 12$°$p respectively). I could not really afford to gamble but did so on this occasion and came away about £9 to the good. Then I told Olive.

Life was probably very much of a routine at this time, with plenty of work about, laying lawns and patios, sometimes a complete garden, fencing, rockeries and ponds. By now we could leave the three youngsters with babysitters and enjoy an evening out now and again.

Dinner dances were quite the fashion and a lot of the local organisations held annual dinner dances, probably as fund raisers, and sometimes as in the case of Grafton Cricket Club an occasion to award the prizes and trophies won and earned in the previous season. The local schools had their do's, and the local National Farmers' Union (now just a dinner). The Barston and also Meriden Young Farmers' Club, the Conservative Members, had a gathering. My first was at Forest Hall in Meriden. This was quite a while before I met Olive, probably soon after coming home from doing my National Service. The headquarters of the Woodmen of Arden Archery Club, claimed by some to be the oldest archery club in the country, had their own bowmaker. The last one that I knew of was a Mr. Warmingham, the family had been (and maybe still is) resident in Meriden for many years. The Forest Hall was a nice setting for a dinner dance with a high ceiling and oval shaped (if my memory serves me correctly as I no doubt had my eyes on other things). In another room there were long lockers on one wall with a badge or coat of arms on each door. I presume each member had one in which the longbows and arrows were kept. The

Woodmen wore a uniform or dress, which included a tunic which must have been very smart. To the best of my knowledge the Woodmen of Arden are still in existence, certainly archery still takes place on the archery ground.

Back to the dance. Mrs. Joan Hope who ran the dancing classes in the Reading Room called on my mother with a ticket for this dance for me if I wished to go. Perhaps someone was ill, I know not. "Would it be too posh for me?" says I. My mother encouraged me to go and, as I almost always did as I was told, I decided to go. Mrs. Hope said my lounge suit would be fine as it was "dress optional", so with an extra polish to my shoes, off I went. This, by the way, was about 1950 and some time before Olive came on the scene. Although I was a little bit self-conscious on arrival and during the quite lavish dinner, i.e. which set of "irons" do I use now? sort of thing. All went well. As soon as the band struck up for dancing I was quite at home. With reference to "eating irons", Stella and I had been well brought up, but not used to eating out at all. Very few country folk ate out at all, mainly for two good reasons. The first was that there was no such thing as "pub grub" or "bar snacks" and restaurants were only found in towns and hotels. The second reason was that not many could afford it anyhow. The dance was something to do with the Packington Estate, as my Aunt Gladys and cousin Jean were there, much to my surprise. The main hall had a huge fireplace. The fire was fed with four foot lengths of firewood with sparks flying as the logs were dropped on. The shelf or mantelpiece was very wide and held a large array of pot plants in flower. It was a splendid event and it was there I met Betty as I have said some time before Olive came on the scene. Betty was the daughter of the gamekeeper at Packington and she was some four years older than me. She loved dancing and was always prepared to cycle a good distance to a dance. We "kept company" for quite a while, cycling to various dances and also the cinema or "the pictures" as we knew it.

Margaret's husband, Peter, and his father, Ces (never did know for sure whether he was Cyril, Cecil or who) were members of a Freemasons' Lodge in Rugby. Olive and I were invited quite a few times as paying guests to the "Ladies Night" this was the Freemasons way of thanking their wives for turning them out all smart for their meetings, it was quite an honour to be asked to attend. Dress was, and still is, dinner jackets and black bow ties for the men and at the time long dresses for the ladies, a real posh affair and most enjoyable, although we had never experienced anything so grand before.

Reception was at 5.30 pm and as we went in we were announced to the Grand Master and his lady by the M.C. complete with white gloves and ceremonial staff. We shook hands, had a brief chat and went into the reception area to receive a glass of sherry. Then we were all shown to a place at the tables by one of three stewards and awaited the arrival of the Grand Master and his entourage to occupy the top table. They were clapped into the very nice Masonic Hall. Then followed at least a five course dinner with a variety of wine served by a table steward. Mostly the stewards would be junior members of the Lodge. From time to time the Head Steward would bang the table with his gavel, followed by two others. It frightened me to death the first time. The M.C., on his feet, would then announce that the Grand Master wished to take wine with whoever – the ladies, his family, guests and his stewards; a signal for those mentioned to rise and take wine. Then naturally came the speeches which usually were very good and entertaining, the ladies all received a gift from the Grand Master and his lady. The dinner naturally ended with coffee and then the Grand Master, his entourage, and the ladies and some of the brethren retired to the Temple for an organ recital.

No male non brethren were permitted in the Temple, and it was suggested that I might like to lend a hand moving the furniture around ready for the dancing to commence. I ignored the suggestion and adjourned to the bar. The dance was always very nice with a band playing our sort of music and we were made very welcome by everyone. Ces always requested The Merry Widow waltz, he got an old-time waltz but never The Merry Widow, to the best of my knowledge. Another always was The Dashing White Sergeant" – a dance performed in sets of six, a man in between two ladies facing another trio in an energetic form of square dance, probably of Scottish origin.

During this period of the Sixties dinner jackets and long dresses were in fashion again and it was a treat to see all the ladies in their finery. By now our three youngsters were growing up and we were able to leave them with babysitters, or perhaps I ought to say childminders. In this respect we were very fortunate as Freda and Lionel Holtom were living just round the corner in Kelsey Lane and they often sat in before Andrea came on the scene. My father was happy to help out but we tried not to be too late when he held the fort. Mr. and Mrs. Burton, a couple sort of getting on in years, were also great "sitters-in". Ernie Burton I knew from way back, he was the attendant in the cycle shed at the Cameo Cinema in Balsall. We paid tuppence (less than 1p), to park our bikes under cover at the picture house. When we came out Ernie had long since gone and it was a bit of a stampede to retrieve one's cycle. Anyhow, Ernie and his wife often brought something with them to amuse our youngsters. They even brought "The Mousetrap Game" and I think they were all amused with that. Ernie was also a great storyteller, some of it was true, some embroidered a bit, others embroidered a lot. Our youngsters were quite often on the edge of their seats with mouths open at some of these tales. Mrs. Burton just sat there nonplussed, perhaps a little amazed at the goings-on herself. We kept count once of the lengths of time he was working for various people. We got him to be about 110 once, a romancer or thundering liar – take your pick, but harmless and we were indebted to them both.

Another sitter was David Adderley from "Cariad" next door. He was studying for his final examination for accountancy at the time and I am pleased to say he passed.

Time now to backtrack a few years to developments at our house. It was about 1964 that work in the garden took a bit of a nosedive, being so busy with landscape work. There was little or no time for doing very much at home. I still carried on growing bedding plants and tomatoes, chrysanths, and lettuce, etc., but never knew what to do first. A decision eventually had to be made and as landscape work paid the best so the garden got neglected. It just grew weeds but fortunately I possessed a large 7 hp rotavator, a Howard diesel "Gem". This was put over the offending area from time to time but the weeds persisted and when the bullfinches were feeding on the seeds of the docks it was time for drastic action. I am not sure where the idea came from but growing Christmas trees (Norway Spruce) was mentioned in conversation somewhere. This seemed a good idea so a real effort was made to cultivate the ground for planting in the Spring. The whole of the rear garden from where the double width starts was planted with trees about 20 inches apart in rows and about 3 feet between the rows. Two mistakes were made. Firstly the trees were too close together and secondly far too many were planted at the same time which meant that a whole lot of trees were for sale at the same time. They got going quite well and now and then I would run the rotavator along the rows to keep the weeds at bay, but the rate of growth was not what I thought it ought to be. That summer the tomatoes did not get planted in the greenhouse at the bottom end of the garden.

It was decided to try and sell this greenhouse as it looked as if no time could be found to work it. Also it was a problem selling the produce as there was never enough to warrant a journey to the Wholesale Market and probably too much for a shop to cope with. Again good fortune was on my side because soon after there was an advertisement in my trade magazine, The Horticultural Trade Journal. A nurseryman from Market Harborough way required exactly what I had. I 'phoned him, he came over, we did a deal and soon afterwards he arrived with men and a lorry and it was all done and dusted by teatime. It was in very good condition with all the nuts and screws coming away easily which made the job go well. The new owner of the greenhouse was interested in our Christmas trees. We had to carry the greenhouse in bits all the way up the garden between the rows of trees which had not grown very much. He suggested I discontinued using the rotavator in between the rows and allow grass to grow instead, and to keep the grass short by mowing now and then. It made all the difference and a "Hayter" 5 hp rotary mower did the job a treat.

The money received from the greenhouse was spent on a holiday in Scotland. We borrowed a touring caravan from my friends John and Pearl Kirby. The five of us set off rather late in the day, which was quite usual for me, trying to squeeze one more job in before setting off up the M6. We got as far as the Wigan area before deciding to seek a parking place for the night. Naturally we had not booked anything and caravan sites were few and far between at the time. In the end, probably in desperation, I found a police station and was directed to a slip-road cul-de-sac close to the motor-way. No facilities whatsoever but then the gypsies never had any either and we could have a wash O.K. and managed. Up to a point the whole holiday continued in a similar way but we had a good time nevertheless. One night was spent on a site near Oban where it was raining just like it can in Scotland. There was no space to put up the awning, Val slept in the car and we never did find the place for washing. Another night was spent at the Visitor Centre at Glen Finnan on the way to Malaig. They were very kind to us there, often we almost got devoured by those Scottish midges before getting the awning assembled; all good fun you understand but things are much better nowadays thank goodness.

Just over a year after sister Margaret and Pete were married we had another very sad occasion in the family. It was on May 1st 1968 that my father died. A Wednesday and Olive as usual on that day had gone to see her mother at home in Glendower Avenue off Broad Lane. The youngsters were all at school and I called in home to have my packed lunch rather late at about 2.30 as I was finishing a job off somewhere. The local Berkswell policeman, John Peake, came to the door and after coming in he told me the sad news. My father had "sat in" for us the previous evening and was fine when I took him home at around 10.30. Wednesday was the day to col-lect his little pension from the Estate Office at Home Farm, or Chapel Hill, as father called it, at 12 noon. We later learned that he had not been all that well for some time, although he had to take daily tablets for a heart problem. On this particular day he must have felt fairly well because he got out his bike to go out; he had not used it for some time. He got as far as the Rectory gate in Meriden Road and was seen to fall off the trusty old steed. Arthur James was travelling the road and saw it all but by the time he got to him my father was unconscious. Andrew Davies from Park Farm also witnessed the scene from further away. Father was taken to Warwick Hospital and then the heat was on to get hold of me. P.C. John Peake came and collected me later on and we drove to Warwick for identification. He was a very nice and caring policeman. It was with gratitude that I saw my father looking serene and at peace. He had told a neighbour a few weeks previously that he would not be a bother to his kids much longer. My father was never a bother to anyone. Latterly he would go to Sister Stella and Bill's on a Saturday and I would collect him from "The Bear" on Sunday lunchtime after enjoying a couple of pints and a game of dominoes which we both enjoyed with Lou Dawson, Ron Fletcher, Jack Underhill and oth-ers. We were often late back and the roast was all ready for carving. Olive was a bit put out and had every right to be, but after a pint or two father was very chatty and all was soon forgiven.

The funeral took place at Berkswell soon afterwards. The usual sincere service was conducted by the Reverend Geoffrey Dingle. I am sure this was the last occasion when a person was carried on his last journey by his workmates and friends, almost a ritual once upon a time but not often nowadays. In days gone by it eliminated the cost of hiring bearers and it was regarded as an honour to be called upon to act as a bearer. My father was called upon many times, perhaps the greatest honour being to assist seven others, farm and estate workers, to bear their employer, the late Charles Joshua Hurst Wheatley, to his final resting place in 1943.

We often wonder if father hung on to see Margaret happily married and settled into her new life. We were often invited over to Alcester where she set up home with Peter. Father also assisted me with laying out their first garden. In fact, all of us got involved going over for the whole day and ending the day with a super dinner put on by the ladies. Afterwards Friday night was still domino night at "The Bear" although it was seldom that I ventured out at Sunday lunchtime after father died. Instead Horace Taylor would call in at our home just about coffee time. No, he would not partake of coffee but I very soon discovered a large whisky was most acceptable. Horace was a remarkable man, his doctor told him so some years later when he went for a medical for an insurance certificate at aged 70. He was not on any doctor's list, had never been ill, drank like a fish and was a heavy smoker, preferring cigarettes with "spats" (filter tips). Horace and his wife Doris lived at the rear of Berkswell Hall. A gardener all his life, he was the gardener for Mrs. Wheatley at The Hall, working just two and a half days a week where once there had been at least six men. I can just remember that last real head gardener, a Mr. Westbury, who wore an apron and arranged all the flowers and plants in The Hall. Also he would go to Coventry and order his requirements for the garden from Whitcombs, the seedsmen, and Mattersons for tools, etc. All the head gardeners had their own secret recipes for potting compost. I am fairly certain peat had not arrived on the scene.

My first encounter with peat was about 1946 when the first bale I saw was called "Sorbex" from Russia I believe. The old gardeners used old mortar rubble, leaf mould, and dried sieved manures, and there were probably far fewer plant diseases and pests about, certainly very little whitefly to worry about. They go up like a flock of pigeons in my greenhouse sometimes despite regular spraying. Back in the forties and fifties there was "Auto Shreds" for pest control in the greenhouse, which killed all and sundry, even the person using it if care was not taken. "Auto Shreds" consisted of shredded paper or the like impregnated with nicotine. The correct amount was calculated according to the house cubic capacity and then small heaps of the shreds were placed at intervals, starting at the end away from the door. The material was set on fire and allowed to smoulder. This was repeated all along the house and then the door closed and locked. It was banned and taken off the market, to preserve the mother-in-law no doubt, or even the Mrs., who knows? A joke.

The head gardeners of yesteryear were encouraged by their employers to produce super produce, be it fruit, flowers, pot plants or vegetables. Mr. Westbury's speciality was chrysanthemums which he grew to perfection and showed off at various flower shows, no doubt at the old Bingley Hall at Birmingham and the Drill Hall in Coventry at the Chrysanthemum Society Shows. I understand he was most successful and gave Colonel Wheatley something to boast about when they entertained the "guns" for luncheon during the shooting and hunting season. The North Warwickshire Hunt, which was based in Rouncil Lane, Kenilworth, until it was disbanded (probably about 1985), met in Berkswell on occasions before the War, sometimes at The Hall or by the Lodge gate in Meriden Road. I saw them meet only once. The hunt never came on the Berkswell side of the railway line after 1939. In those days a lot of people would walk many miles in a day following the hunt.

Now back to Horace or "H" as he was known to some folk. He told Rector Dingle one day, after I had introduced him, "plain H" he said "Easy to remember – two poles and a cross". "H" was really a mate of my father and he became a good pal to me. He had a Morris Traveller, an estate type vehicle with woodwork to hold the window glass and he was probably as fond of his "Bella" as he was of Doris, his wife. It was always nice and clean and well oiled and the doors just needed a little push to close them with a nice click. Woe betide anyone who slammed his car doors; I did it only once. When it came time for the m.o.t. "H" would wait while it was done, pacing up and down, smoking one fag after another like a first-time father outside "Maternity". Previous to his eighteen or so years' gardening for Mrs. Wheatley "H" had been Chauffeur/Gardener to the owner of a large roofing company, living in a small dwelling above the garages. "H" could not read or write but this was not a great handicap to him or it never seemed to be anyhow. He would drive his employer all over the country with his black dinner suit and tie, etc. stowed in the car boot and while all the other chauffeurs were washing cars "H" would be dining with the boss. This arrangement meant that "H" had to be up early in the mornings sometimes to clean the car ready for the day. His boss would often be talking big business in the car or at dinner with his associates who would query "H"'s presence only to be assured that anything could be said in complete confidence. He was so loyal to his employers and his friends and expected, and often demanded, the same in return.

He had many sayings or quotations like "If you can't speak the truth keep your mouth shut". Taking it easy was "Graze awhile" or "Grazing". A parting remark to his male friends was "Keep 'em open this muggy weather, cold weather, or whatever it was"; he was of course referring to one's bowels, an expression still used by one or two now and again. "H" had nicknames for lots of people, males, apart from his wife Doris who was just as well known as "Murphy" or just "Murf".

Captain Wheatley Hubbard, married to Mrs. Wheatley's daughter Ann, was known as "Rockerfeller", Bert Wagstaff, the chauffeur, was "Ben Cartwright", someone else was "Father Christmas". Arthur Powell was a sergeant in the Special Police; he was "The Gestapo" and I was "The Brigadier", from The Archers I think, all good fun and no-one knew who we were talking about.

Harry Worrod, known to some as "Rock-M-Daddy", I have not the slightest idea why, was the verger at the church and also kept the church-yard tidy. He had a motor mower, a scythe, and two strong arms. It was acknowledged that he was the best man with the scythe for miles around. The grass was shaved off to leave a lawn-like finish. The fifteen flower beds were always bedded out twice a year by him as well. These beds were along the side of the drive up to the church and each one contained a standard rose tree. It got to the time when Harry could no longer undertake all the work in the churchyard and he asked Horace if he would look after the flower beds. He said he would if John Webb would also help out. I agreed and this led to me doing the work for well over twenty-five years, first of all with "H" and, when he retired, on my own. I also provided the home-grown plants twice a year. On more than one occasion I did a "special" to coincide with the Flower Festival, a bi-annual festival begun in the sixties, 1966 I think; the church year in flowers starting with purple flowers for Advent, Christmas and Easter being white, Whitsun red and so on. One bed was blue and white for the fifty-third Berkswell Scout Troop, and gold and blue for the Girl Guides, gold for Harvest, etc.

The rose beds have now gone, a pity really but the soil was "rose sick" and the bushes did not bloom very well, being grown in the same soil for many years. On more than one occasion "H" and I clipped back the yew trees surrounding the War Memorial. The Memorial stands on unconse-crated ground in order that any denomination or otherwise could pay their respects to the departed. Even up to the end of the 1940s other religions would not enter a Church of England. When Mrs. Ann Wheatley was mar-ried to Captain Raymond Hubbard in 1948 and was known thereafter as Wheatley Hubbard the church at Berkswell was full. The head cowman was a Roman Catholic and was invited to the wedding. He accepted and attended but apparently he and his wife found themselves in all sorts of trouble with the R.C. Church Authorities.

Up till about 1988 the Annual Church Meeting to elect the churchwar-dens was held on Easter Monday morning at 10 a.m. after a short service of Holy Communion. The meeting was held in the vestry and entry was via the flight of steps outside the church. This was to allow any member of the Parish to attend the meeting and vote for the churchwarden of his or her choice. This could be achieved without going into church. Not many peo-ple attended the vestry meeting unless there was anything exciting likely to happen, like an election for a new warden or perhaps something controversial. Once upon a time at Berkswell there was a Rector's warden chosen by the Rector and the parishioners chose the people's warden.

Many years ago the Rector and churchwardens were very important people in the Parish, overseeing all sorts of duties, including distribution of alms to the needy and so on. Today these people are still important but mainly involved with duties appertaining to the church. I understand that churchwardens still have powers to arrest wrongdoers. They are the Bishop's representatives in the Parish and are responsible for their Parish Church, the fabric and contents thereof. The Rector has "The say" as to what takes place in the Church and churchyard. For quite a number of years I was engaged to mow various parts of the churchyard, a paid contract, the area around the War Memorial and on the right of the driveway, the cremation plot and so on. Often I would meet some very interesting people during the visits, people whose parents had lived in the Parish or they probably had themselves. Occasionally it would be someone I knew in the past. One day a big tall man came striding along, I spoke to him and he said he thought he knew me and said he used to be the Rector. "Oh" says I "you must be the Reverend Bursell" then, "Mr. Bursell" he corrected and that was not pursued further. "Well" said I "Had I been a regular churchgoer I would have known you" – he made a nice reply and said how he loved "this place" and hoped to be buried in the churchyard one day. A grave space was reserved for him but not used upon his death.

One evening Olive and I were tending the flower beds and a lady came along and spoke to Olive. "Is that John Webb over there?" "Yes" said Olive. "Oh, I think he is a distant cousin of mine". Sure enough it was Brenda Minton (nee Vaughan), the daughter of Bert Vaughan who was under-chauffeur to Colonel Wheatley before the War. We had not met for probably thirty-five years but since then we have kept in touch a bit more, meeting up on special occasions and so on.

Towards the mid-sixties I seemed to become more and more involved in Parish and village activities and organisations. One of these was the Scouts, I always had a soft spot for the Berkswell Troop who at the time were meeting at the old private school situated behind the village post office and stores. The old scout house was no longer safe and the late Miss Downes' old corrugated iron school not much better; it was common for people to fall through the rotten floorboards. Funds were very low so it was decided to set up a tote at a shilling (5p) a go. Each participant chose three numbers (or was it two?) between 0 and 30, and winning numbers were drawn on a Monday evening.

George Teague was Group Scout Master then and worked at Massey Ferguson. He roped in quite a lot of punters. Others did the same and it became a nice little earner run by a most dedicated band of people, Frank Bull, Phil Vines, Frank Hayward who was Treasurer. Helen and Bill Wilkinson hosted the draw night for a long time.

Plans were drawn up by Robin Fryer, an ex-scout, if there is such a being, now training to be an architect. This building was to be a two-storey grand affair, store room and office upstairs and meeting rooms on the ground floor. A gantry and pulley were to be used for getting equipment up and down, all very good and nice on paper, but going to cost a lot of money. It was difficult to persuade George that really it was beyond our reach and that by the time sufficient funds had been raised to cover the estimated cost inflation would have pushed up the cost even further.

One Sunday afternoon the five of us Webbs were out in the car looking at a job at Fenny Compton, if my memory serves me well. We passed Compton Buildings and their display area of sectional buildings. I called in and enquired about buildings suitable for a Scout H.Q. "Oh yes" says they, they always do anyhow. We came away with loads of brochures and price lists and sure enough there were buildings that I thought quite suitable for our needs and, more important, at a price the funds could cope with more or less. Convincing George Teague was not easy but he finally agreed to go ahead, there was really little alternative in fact. Guess who got the job as Clerk of Works? First priority was to seek permission from Berkswell Estate whose land it was and still is. I wrote to Captain Wheatley Hubbard in Wiltshire and he was in full agreement as to our wishes and requirements. The building would be on a lease, the Scouts paying a peppercorn rent. Next job was to submit plans to Meriden Rural District Council as it was before we became West Midlands and under the umbrella of Solihull District Council.

We chose a two-bay building which was to be divided into various areas, i.e. store room, kitchen, ladies and gents' toilets, a Scouters' room for Seniors, office and the main Meeting Room. I did not totally agree with the interior layout and after a lengthy and quite heated discussion, that was a battle I lost, but taking on the Teague family in their house, what chance did I have? One thing we all respected each other's opinions and never fell out. There were all sorts of things to undertake, water and electricity supplies, access to the main sewer, etc.

Eventually a start was made one Sunday morning dismantling the old schoolroom. As it was "knocking down time" we had an army of helpers of all ages. Then it was clearing the site and preparing for the concrete base. All the concrete was mixed on site with the help of Ron Hurford's mixer. It was noticeable – very – that as the work got harder so the numbers of helpers dwindled down to a few stalwarts. It took getting on for twelve months to prepare the site and in due course the building arrived and was erected. By this time we really had had enough and contractors were engaged to put in the sewer connection and some other jobs. The new scout house was duly opened with quite a ceremony on Saturday, April 25th 1970. Ceremonies began with a parade led by a scout band to the Church for a service, also the dedication of new scout colours (by Reverend G.

Dingle), which was given by Berkswell Mothers' Union. "Skip", Mr. George Teague, welcomed one and all back at the new headquarters and the official opening ceremony was undertaken by Mrs. C.M. Wheatley, J.P., of Berkswell Hall. Mrs. Wheatley was President of the Coventry Scout Group and always called the Berkswell Troop "Her boys". She was assisted by Mr. S. Bracewell, County Commissioner, and Mr. R. Skitt, District Commissioner. The Troop has always been an open one allowing any denomination to join. There were displays by the scout band (5th Coventry), also the scouts and cubs. The usual refreshments in the Reading Room for adults, and a "bun struggle" for the lads. Finally the presentation of awards. I was one of many to receive a scout's "thanks badge" which I still wear and treasure.

One evening in 1970 at a meeting of the P.C.C., it was stated that the Management Committee of the Reading Room was depleted and needed new blood. The idea was to recruit two people from all the village organisations to form a new Committee. I got the job, together I'm sure with Robin Hope. The Committee was composed of very busy people, as most Committees are, and George Teague was Chairman. The meetings were always interesting and it was amazing how much was involved in the running of a village hall. Berkswell has been, and still is, most fortunate to have such a place to meet and hold events.

Once upon a time there was a caretaker, Harry and Mrs. Worrod, who lived next door and really looked after the place. Harry would drop in and check up after every function, being paid extra by the hirer for late night dances. Afterwards the Committee could only hire cleaners and some were better than others. Having said that, keeping the Reading Room clean and tidy was a thankless task, the premises being abused by some of the hirers. But as I have said, we in Berkswell are most fortunate to have such facilities. To the best of my knowledge the Lant Trustees (the Lant Trust) purchased the premises from the Wheatleys or Berkswell Estate in 1945 and since then the Trust has paid for most of the major repairs. In the 1970s the lettings never produced enough income to be self-sufficient. However, it must be stated that the Committee were always most sympathetic to most Parish organisations when it came to letting charges. There were always representatives of the Lant Trust sitting in at meetings.

At the end of my first year they must have been desperate as I became Secretary. Blimey, what have I let myself in for? All went fairly well until the next A.G.M. when George Teague resigned from the Chair and Evelyn, his wife, also resigned from the Committee. Well, I got rid of being Secretary but I found myself as Chairman. And do not refer to me as "Chair", they get sat upon. Come to think of it, so do Chairmen. That was a job I had for seven years until 1983 when things really got out of hand and there was little time to call my own. It was an interesting and quite enjoyable time really with one or two interesting incidents, easy to recall.

During that time there were quite a few discos held at the Room, some run by young amateur D.J.s. Often there was little or no supervision, the Committee could not provide any and although the hirer was held responsible, this was largely ignored. Damage to the room often resulted and clients were noisy on departing and en route to and from "The Bear". After some time the residents of Meriden Road requested a meeting with the R.R. Committee to put their complaints to us. One resident had an ornate gateway with a carved wooden globe on each gatepost and they had disappeared.

They duly attended a meeting and put forward their various complaints and this one chap chirped up saying "And yes, someone pinched my balls!". No comment. Afterwards they all sat there awaiting the deliberations by the Committee. I thanked them all and they were informed that it would be fully discussed and they would be fully informed of the outcome. Not what was hoped for or expected and away they all trooped, probably to hunt for wooden balls. In due course it was decided not to allow any more discos as we could seldom recoup money to pay for the damage. Also, we had our neighbours to consider and the reputation of the Reading Room.

On another occasion the Lant Trustees invited the Committee to consider what structural improvements would enhance the premises, we being more in touch with the hirers. We had a special meeting and talked about alterations at great length. It was decided that both the Ladies and Gents' cloakrooms and toilets were in dire need of attention and the kitchen needed to be enlarged and improved. New curtains and interior decorations were also on the list. The Trustees engaged an architect whom I and others met at the Room, and he went away with our requirements. His plans were drawn up and on our inspection he had drawn up his own ideas of what we should have rather than our suggestions. We never saw him again and I often wonder if he was paid. A local man was then instructed (better not name him). Blow me if he did not do the same. Myself and two others met him in the Room and he put his point of view. This was rejected as not being what we wanted and not using the facilities to their best purposes. We were not very popular with this fellow and in the end I told him that if we could not have what we wanted we would have nothing. We got what we wanted.

A spate of fund-raising activities got under way. We had a "curtain-raiser" dance, there were cheese and wine parties, very popular at the time. The Womens' Institute presented a clock which I was pleased to accept on behalf of the R.R. Committee. Oh yes, I can sing "Jerusalem" along with the best of them.

The Shrove Tuesday parties in those days were fantastic affairs, the Sunday School staff always put the event on, in aid of Sunday School funds. Perhaps rather stupidly I would not go until our youngsters started Sunday School, perhaps apprehensive of what some folk might say. In any case it was impossible for Olive to get three children to bed and be at the Reading Room for 7.15. When we went first of all it was always Fancy Dress to start.

Mrs. Elsie Thompson was the Sunday School Superintendent, together with Miss Ida Midgley for the Junior School. The stalwart behind the scenes was Ted Gibbs, famous indeed for his trifles made in washstand washing bowls, getting on for three foot in diameter. Probably our first time at the Shrove Tuesday Supper I dressed up like the late Arthur Haines, as a tramp; it might have been a Tramps' Supper. Anyhow, as it was difficult with the youngsters and childminders and so on, we were late. Judging had taken place and two other things did not help. First of all I was told "had I been on time I would have had a prize" and also, after the judging, all the other participants had changed back into party frocks or trousers and sports coats, and there was me strutting around all evening in boots and socks with the toes out and an old mac tied up with binder twine, milk bottle tops for medals and a battered old trilby hat.

Another year the Fancy Dress theme was a Shipwreck Party. One was supposed to grab what one could as the ship went down. Some time earlier we had been out and bought a new coal scuttle, a sort of copper effect with the name of the make being "Waterloo", printed in large letters on the box. This gave me an idea. I imagined I was in my orange shorts when the alarm sounded, I put on odd socks, one short, one long, a pair of sandals and my orange shorts. The aforementioned box had the bottom kicked open, and a length of string at the top from corner to corner. I stepped in the box, pulled it up, put the string over one shoulder, nothing above the waist apart from a gaudy necktie and a boy's cap. Hey presto! I had to get changed at the Room and we were early this time. Poor Miss Midgley came in just as I was changing, screamed and beat a hasty retreat. However, I was rewarded with first prize and yes I did change after the parade.

Mrs. Elsie Thompson, of Rock Farm, Back Lane, was the enrolling member, otherwise in charge. The seating capacity for the Room was supposed to be 120. On that occasion about 170 sat down to supper. We had to sit at a table on the stage with perhaps 35 others. However, everyone was served with a lovely supper. There was organised pandemonium when the tables were dismantled and stored away ready for the entertainment. This was always put on by local talent. Mrs. Kay Fensom lived in the village at "The Priory" in Spencers Lane and later at Blind Hall Cottage, a small house at the top of Blind Hall Lane, way off the road, a lovely spot just about all to oneself. Kay loved to sunbathe and when the farmer was carrying loads of corn sheaves the workers would stay on the load and got a good look over the hedge into the garden, the sunbathing area. The old privy was up the garden and Rex Fensom would take his mug of tea and newspaper for an extended stay, or a long sitting. And why not? With the door wide open and a superb view towards the village.

Again I side-track. Kay Fensom had stage experiences, an actress perhaps, and she would whip her volunteers into some sort of form for the entertainment. We had all sorts, song and dance, one year the scouts put on a Campfire Sing Song. There was no shortage of comedy, all laughing at each other. Two men, one big, one small, put on "The Dying Swan" from "Swan Lake". The blinking thing refused to die. Eventually yours truly got enrolled. I do not think it was any talent, just that I was daft enough to say "yes", and that is easy when one's arm is halfway up one's back, being twisted. Parts included a Barber's Shop Quartet, a Wilson, Keppel and Betty Sand Dance with Freda Holtom and Ron Jackson. Probably the best was a Strong Man act with four or five others. We performed all sorts of tricks, party pieces and so on, shinning up ropes, etc., all dressed in pink long johns, striped tee-shirts and leopard skin leotards. The finale was me holding up the rest in a pyramid with bags of "Oohs" and "Ahs", contorted faces and so on. This was panned out a bit but when all was assembled I just walked away, the others being suspended on various props, and took a bow. All great fun to be involved in, and I think the audience enjoyed it too. In fact it was so popular that it was put on again later on as a fundraiser in aid of the Reading Room Funds.

I think I can honestly claim to have had more fun in the Reading Room than anyone else alive today, from the age of about two till now. I was taken to the Welfare Clinic, run by the midwife/district nurse; the Girls' Club Bulb Shows, parties, socials, dances, etc.

Back now to 1970 and our family are really growing up, Val 14, Robert 11, and Jenifer 9 (Yes, there is only one "n" in our Jenny's name). I went to register her at Meriden, the Registrar lived and had an office in a lane behind the Queen's Head pub and I presented myself there. He was an abrupt and bad-tempered man, or had he had a bad day? Asking me all the details regarding Jenifer, "One 'n' or 'two' " he barks out. "One" says I, thinking it would be easier for Jenny to spell. It has haunted her ever since.

Valerie and Robert attend school at Kenilworth Grammar School by passing their ll-plus Examination. They catch a bus just down the road at Catchem's Corner. They are getting on there alright but struggle somewhat at times. Jenifer joins them there in 1972 so they are all under one roof, so to speak, and it does simplify matters for us only having one school to support.

Some years previously the P.T.A. at Balsall Street Junior and Infants decided that a swimming pool would be a good idea, and so it was. All parents were requested to donate sixpence (2°p) per child per week. We naturally were all in favour and it took some years to get going. Jenny was the only one of ours to learn to swim.

Kenilworth Grammar School was a very different kettle of fish. A very formal atmosphere. Mr. Mitchell, the headmaster, was one of the old-fashioned sort who set a fine example with his manner and immaculate dress; short hair and highly polished shoes. I often felt most uncomfortable when visiting the school. There was a Parents' Evening before the Autumn Term began, very formal and probably a bit frosty. We were all invited to donate towards the Library and so on. However, the P.T.A. did an excellent job, I thought, and organised some first-class evenings. We missed the high-brow do's but came into our own at the Christmas Dance. It was always a superb evening and we did get to know other parents and formed friendships that lasted long after the youngsters left school.

This led us to other dances and dinner dances in Kenilworth, Leamington and Coventry, and naturally they sometimes came over to our events. At the time there were lots of dinner dances and all the ladies wore long dresses and most of the gents climbed into dinner jackets, bow ties and so on. It was nice for me anyhow to get out of my working togs and have a nice evening out. I organised one or two at the Royal Court at Keresley in aid of Berkswell Church. It was easy then to sell the tickets, probably not so many other attractions and also most people could dance proper like. In 1961 the Royal Court Hotel was part of the hospital, only maternity I think. Jenifer was born there in May 1961. Blow, I've given her age away.

CHAPTER 17

Flower Festivals
and Life in the Parish

Dodging about a little now, it was September 1966 that the first Flower Festival was held at Berkswell Church. At the time it was a very new idea as a fundraiser and I think the idea came from Mrs Wheatley or Mrs Margaret Hayward, both stalwarts of our church at the time. As an aside, Frank and Margaret Hayward served on the P.C.C. for a total of over 90 years. Modern day Church Laws allow a maximum of three years and re-election after a break of one year. This rule would have left them heartbroken so much did they devote their lives to Berkswell Church. For the Flower Festival it was decided to seek the assistance of no less than eight flower clubs from the locality. There was no theme, religious or otherwise, but the Church was beautifully decorated. There were organ recitals – a Willis which is held in high esteem by those organists and people that know about such things. It always sounds very nice to me. Morning coffees and afternoon teas were served. There was also a produce stall near the well. The Rector at that time was Bishop McKie, Assistant Bishop of Coventry. We had Reverend W.K. Neville as our part-time Curate whom we shared with Claverdon. We also had to share Bishop McKie with the rest of the Diocese, a man and family that were very well liked and respected. Mr. Kenneth Hope and Mr. Frank Hayward were Churchwardens. Mr. Hope was the local builder and ran the business from "Meadow Bank" opposite "The Bear Inn" on Coventry Road. Three dwellings occupy the site of the old builder's yard. The paint shop and carpenter's shop being converted. The Hopes were also undertakers, Mr. Leeson being the very able carpenter. They lived on the corner of Meriden Road and Coventry Road.

A lot of us teenagers at the time always gathered on the crossroads by "The Bear" on Saturday night, or rather it was Sunday a.m. by the time we got there. A bit of an inquest here and there on what had gone on during the evening or otherwise. We never made a noise under that huge tree that leaned out over the road (I think it was an elm). It obviously grew out into the daylight from the shadow of the trees in the spinney. Anyhow, Mrs. Leeson always put her head out of the window and enquired as to whether we had any homes to go to. Well, it did cause a giggle or two.

The Flower Festival was a great success both spiritually and financially. I am sure it was the first year that we also had an exhibition of Berkswell memorabilia. Mr. Kenneth Hope and Mr. Bob McLaren were the organisers. All sorts of things were produced and put on show and I wonder if this is where the seeds of the idea for a Berkswell Museum were sown.

I know that it was an ambition of Mr. Hope's as he was a great hoarder as I understand it, and as one who was involved in just about every Parish organisation, he had access to all sorts of paperwork. People that hoard often get talked about by others, mostly those that are tidy and do not "save things because they may come in handy one day". However, if no-one saved things there would be very few museums and we would have less idea as to how things were in the past.

I referred to Mr. Kenneth Hope as "Mr. Berkswell". He walked around the village, was observant and spotted anything that required attention, Church, Reading Room and so on. "Mrs. Berkswell" was, of course, Mrs. Wheatley, a real lady who took an interest in just about everything; a County Councillor, District (Meriden Rural before Solihull and West Midlands was dreamed up) and Parish Councillor, a JP, President of Coventry Scouts, Vice-Chairman of Berkswell Church Council (the Rector is always Chairman). She was also a school governor at more than one school, and the list goes on. Never one to take "no" for an answer, she never backed down. Mrs. Wheatley was only called Christobel once to my knowledge, in public that is; a remarkable lady in my opinion, she was married to Colonel Charles Joshua Hurst Wheatley and living in luxury at Berkswell Hall with at least eight staff and two chauffeurs to look after them. There was a butler (Mr. Fletcher) and a cook (Mrs. Dempster). There was a staff of six gardeners with Mr. Westbury as Head Gardener. As a young lad I often thought I would like a job like his.

The War came in 1939 and there were great changes at the Hall. Then the Colonel died in 1943. Mrs. Wheatley threw herself into War work, working on all sorts of committees. She adapted her life to suit and became more involved with folks in the community, in fact became one of us. The alternative would have been a rather secluded lifestyle. Bert Wagstaff continued to chauffeur plus a few other tasks thrown in; drawing the curtains night and morning seven days a week. He did not mind in the least, and a more trustworthy and loyal man did not exist.

Bob McLaren lived in Windmill Lane and was Clerk to the Parish Council and Berkswell Charities, and he well knew the workings and needs of the Parish.

Further to opening our brand new scout house in April 1970, The Chief Scout, Sir Charles Maclean, came to Coventry to visit the City of Coventry Scout County on the weekend of June 20th to 21st 1970 – the two events had no connection. On the Saturday evening a group of us from Berkswell attended a dinner and dance at the Leofric Hotel, Broadgate, Coventry, held in his honour. It was a grand affair with a menu in French. Why is this I ask? What is the matter with good old English? Answers in sealed envelopes please. There were Toasts, two proposed by Mrs. Wheatley and one very amusing response from the Reverend Canon Laurence Jackson, Vicar of Holy Trinity, a man that could and did get his message across. Various awards were made by the Chief, then it was dancing for all. Next day, Sunday, there was a special Scout Service at Rough Close, located off Tanners Lane, Tile Hill.

Rough Close was a forty-two acre woodland area purchased from Berkswell Estate in about 1948. It was opened in the summer of 1949. During the Second World War, my father and his mate, Teddy Barrs, felled all the useable timber on the site for the War effort, and left behind a lot of bushes, birch, willow and nut, to name a few. This was the ideal site for the Coventry Scouts. Each district had its own area and there was a huge area for the camp fire and also the open-air Church.

The service was conducted by a Scout Chaplain. The hymns were real rousers, "Praise to the Lord the Almighty", "Guide me oh thou great Jehovah" and "Who would true valour see". The address was by the Bishop of Coventry, a big, big man in every way; no napping with him around. Phil Vines and I went along to that and memories of that weekend are with me still.

Meanwhile, other happenings went on as normal, the domino gang met at "The Bear" on Friday evenings; "Chip out" or "Penny Knock" was the version we played. Horace Taylor was an ever present and one evening enquired as to whether I would like to be his guest at "The Felons" Dinner. The existence of "The Felons" was known to me from way back in time. Mr. Seeley, the Headmaster at Balsall Street School was a member, also Charlie Nutt from the transport cafe where Arden Close is now. I accepted with thanks and on the third Wednesday in May we all congregated at the Reading Room. It was and still is an all male organisation with the correct title of "The Berkswell Association for the Prosecution of Felons". The one and only meeting of the Association is held at 6.30 pm prior to the dinner, apart from Committee Meetings.

The bar was open about 7 pm and there I met people that I had not seen for many a day. After a couple of pints we all settled down for dinner of soup followed by boiled ham, broad beans, peas, carrots and potatoes, not forgetting the thick parsley sauce. The pudding was apple pie and cream, followed by cheese, biscuits and coffee, which rounded it all off very nicely. The Rector is always invited and he says "Grace". Toasts and replies followed, "The Queen" naturally, but she has never attended to reply

The Syd Lawrence Orchestra. A dinner dance at Chesford Grange near Kenilworth

so far. We toast the Association and local Government Officers and guests. The Chairman of Meriden R.D.C. (nowadays the newly installed Mayor of Solihull), and perhaps the local policeman would reply, also a guest would reply to that toast. By this time it was a comfort stop before the entertainment began, much needed.

For me the evening was a real treat, a superb atmosphere, at the time there were fewer members than today. There was a family butchers in Coventry owned by Palmer's, and two of the family were members and supplied the ham, all piping hot. They wore white coats and straw boater hats and carved at a side table, really nice. I was so impressed that I enquired about becoming a member. Horace must have put my name forward because before the next Dinner I was in. Lionel Holtom was my first guest; each member is allowed one guest. That was way back in 1971. In 1996 I became a life member. The original and first records are sadly missing but the Association was formed well over two hundred and fifty years ago. It was begun by local landowners before the days of a police force in an attempt to protect their properties and interests. The membership was and still is five shillings (25p). Life members do not pay any membership fees. The Association has always had its own solicitor. Mr. Sidney Snape was in that office when I joined. Mr. John Penn is now the solicitor. The Association pays rewards for the apprehension of felons. A new reward was introduced some years ago, a reward for the conviction of anyone causing or dropping litter. It is thirty years since I became a member and there have been a few changes. There is now a best-kept village or parish competition held every year between Berkswell, Barston, Hampton-in-Arden, and Meriden. Judging takes place in April

CHAPTER 18

Holidays Abroad

It was at a dominoes gathering one Friday evening that I mentioned holidays abroad. 1972 in fact. Louis Dawson from Four Oaks used to go to Spain, often twice a year and always came home very tanned and having had a good time. I was a bit apprehensive going on our own for the first time, one night Lou said "let me know when you want to go and why not make up a foursome". He and his wife Hilda were quite a bit older than Olive and I, but they were very much "young at heart" and always ready for a bit of fun. So after a while of mulling things over we agreed to give it a try. One of the Dawson sons knew a travel agent in town and Lou came one Friday to dominoes and announced that he had booked a holiday for us to Arenal, some eight or nine miles east of Palma, the capital of Majorca, in mid November. He did assure me it would still be quite warm and there was plenty of evening entertainment in the resort. We departed in mid November for a week full board at the Hotel Reina Isobela, for the sum of about £90-00. Quite an experience checking in at Birmingham airport, also the flight and transfer to the hotel. Olive's sister Lily and husband Alf came to our house and looked after the youngsters whilst we were away, Jenifer was 11 and a half and just getting settled in a Kenilworth Grammer School. We all had a super holiday, the sun shone, we lazed on the beach, strolled round the shops. Coffee mid morning, and in the afternoon – often with a brandy. It was quite usual for youngsters of about 14 years to frequent cafes for coffee and brandy on their way home from school.

There was dancing in the hotel on some evenings, one evening we joined another foursome, who were already "armed" with a bacardi and coke – the "in drink" at the time. The other two couples informed us they were on a pre Christmas "booze up". To obtain a glass they had a drink from the bar then produced bottles of whisky bought on the aeroplane coming over which were hidden under the cushions of the sofas we sat on. What a night we had, cutting all sorts of capers on the dance floor – and so on. At the end of the evening two were very much helping the other two, we four were O.K. – honest. I remarked, on retiring, that they would probably have a late breakfast, but not a bit of it because when we came down they were all finished breakfast and just going out. One of the women (cannot recall their names) was just about "out" the night before and I got her a little bit worried when I said, "Please be careful tonight, I am not putting you to bed again tonight". All in all in was a very nice holiday, a new experience, one that I thought I could sort of get used to.

It was a bit of a rude awakening on returning home with Christmas only a few weeks away and the holly wreath season about to begin. However, all was well and all the orders were done on time. For some time I had tried to persuade Olive to learn to drive, without any success – until one day, I think it was Jenifer came home from school with a note, Robert had probably lost his. They were in need of "dinner ladies" at Balsall Primary School, to my surprise Olive was interested, saying that the earnings would pay for driving lessons. She applied and got a job, supervising the youngsters at lunch-time, in the dining room and in the playground during the lunch break. All the ladies were entitled to a lunch when duties were finished.

All holidays were supposed to be taken during school holidays and Olive got into all sorts of trouble for "swanning off to Majorca during term time. She was sacked by Mr Booen the Headmaster, but immediately reinstated, but that was the end of holidays during term time for the next eighteen years.

Olive was known to some I understand, as a bit of a "dragon", the youngsters were made to eat all of their lunch, also she would not tolerate any "tricks" they got up to in the playground.

There were at least 3 other major happenings in Berkswell during the end of the sixties and early seventies. In no particular order they were

1. the restoration of Berkswell Church
2. the Festival of Berkswell and
3. the lake in the park went dry.

Number 3 first and I think it was in 1970 that the lake "sprung a leak". The lake is fed by two streams at the south end, one stream from the well in the village and the other rises in the Carol Green/Benton Green area. At the north end there is an embankment or dam with two outlets one at each end of the dam/bank. On the far end of the bank nearest the Hall there was a boat house and in the wood a hydraulic ram to pump water to the Hall. When I was a kid the footbridge over the outlet would be the source of a leak. Water would start to trickle from a point where brickwork was joined to the bank. My father and some of his work colleagues would have to go to the old "clay workings" at the rear of Lavender Hall in order to do a repair job. I suppose they would "puddle" the clay and force it into the offending cavity. Lavender Hall was undoubtedly the area of the old brick-yard connected to "The Brickmaker's Arms" pub in Station Road.

Prior to the 1970s this problem was known to the gamekeepers and ear-lier still Col. Wheatley would have spotted any problems, but on this occa-sion the contents of the lake went off down the stream with one big rush I was told, water, fish, the lot. I am not sure of the fish that were there but certainly pike and roach. It was just left for two years with the original steam running through the centre. Then in the summer of 1972 the restoration work on the lake began. Two huge steam driven traction engines arrived and set up one on each side of the mud pan which once was the lake, a large two sided "bucket" was attached to two wire cables, one from each engine. The "bucket" was hauled from one side of the lake to the other taking with it all the mud and debris and dragging it up on each side of the lake, this, as one can imagine, took some weeks and the whole area looked and was one huge mess. Eventually the banks were repaired and the lake allowed to refill, the mud on either side eventually dried out and I suppose was re-seeded down to grass. There was, I understand, a problem with algae, this was sprayed. As the balance of plant life and oxygenating plants and so on began to grow, so the water became clear and able to sustain fish. As I understand it angling clubs were contacted and the successful club had to re-stock with fish and maintain the lake as a fishery. The lake has been a private fishing location ever since. Way back, local folk were permitted to walk around the far side of the lake as far as the island and the first outlet and dam. But people took advantage of this privilege, letting dogs run free in amongst sheep and cat-tle and all sorts of other abuses. Eventually it was fenced off with large "Keep Out" notices and that was the end of another village perk.

I am sure that when we were kids the lake froze over more than it does today. It was always a bit of a challenge or a dare to see who would cross the ice first, one year John Kirby and Eddie Horsley were bragging, "they had been over the ice first today, this morning. I told Jim Squires – the estate shepherd – who told me HE crossed the ice the night before.

One winter when I was about 6 or 7 it was very cold and one weekend "the world and his wife" were on the lake, skating and, for those without skates, sliding. Taking a run and sliding as far as possible, coming off the end and repeating the process to get back to the starting point once again, all good fun doing "squats" and "one leg", etc. A section of ice at the boat house end was roped off for the use of invited guests at the Hall. My father had the job of putting up the ropes and retrieving them when the thaw set in. One time he came home with a pike, how it was caught I know not. Pike has rather an "earthy" taste but we lapped it up.

No 2 – In the mid sixties it was decided by the Rector (Bishop John

David McKie) the Churchwardens (Mr Kenneth Hope and Mr Frank Hayward) together with the Church Council (P.C.C.) to restore the stonework of the Church. I am sure – but it is only an assumption – that it was the idea of Mr Hope, he was getting towards his retiring age, his staff consisted of just two men. He loved the Church and I firmly believe he wanted to leave this life with the Church in a good state of repair.

An appeal for £5000-00 pounds was launched and there was a very good response, our first flower festival in 1966 was probably to launch the appeal.

Eventually work got underway, George Hammond was the stonemason and Ivor Mould was his assistant. With the exception of the porch and vestry above, also the tower, all the remaining parts of the Church were painstakingly restored. Most of the work was on the exterior but the crypt received a lot of attention. During this part of the works a cavity was discovered roughly between the two parts of the crypt. No one seems to know for certain exactly what was there years ago although quite a few theories have been suggested. Until about 1860, as I am told, the western end of the crypt was unknown. Apparently a stone mason was working on a wall at the west end of the known crypt under the chancel in fact – when his hammer had a hollow ring sound as he worked on the wall. He decided to investigate and soon made a hole through into the east end area. Hitherto the only way into the crypt was via two narrow flights of stone stairs, one behind today's lectern and the other from behind the pulpit. Replaced then by another entrance from the north aisle.

The restoration was duly completed at a cost in excess of £8,000-00 including architects fees. As I wrote before I am sure Mr Hope saw this job as a final contribution to the Church in Berkswell. That is only MY assumption knowing how much time was spent on the project.

The porch and vestry above was restored by John Redfern of Balsall, an expert at restoring and converting old properties. His work in my opinion, (and many others) was "second to none". Work on the tower was deferred, probably through lack of cash or that the tower was not in a bad state of repair anyhow. But a section of wall was knocked out and replaced with bricks, the architects idea was, I was informed, "To get them used to it". His idea was to eventually clad the tower with bricks, I didn't go on him much after that. The bricks were taken out and replaced by stone in about 1995. The tower is still awaiting its restoration, there are a few cracks here and there which an eye is being kept upon, but nothing major is in the offing at the moment. (The present day is now 2001).

By now 1973, our 3 youngsters are growing up, Valerie is 17, Robert 14 and Jenifer 12. Val has been "feeling her feet" for sometime now. Discos began to feature, also meeting up with school friends, etc. She had been confirmed at Church some time previously. Val was the same age as the Rectors son Richard, therefore, there were quite a number confirmed at

Berkswell at the same time. There were some adults including David and Ellen Watkins from "Watkins Roses" nurseries and garden centre on the A452 between Balsall Common and Hampton in Arden – nowadays Blooms. I had been a member of the Parochial Church Council for some 5 years and a sides-person for longer.

The confirmation, Ah, yes, the Rector Geoffrey Dingle suggested we had a party in the Reading Room for the confirmation candidates – he had quite a few guests at the rectory and he probably thought it was an easy way of giving them supper. Guess who got the job of organising it all – yours truly no less. We decided parents would pay enough to cover overheads – hire of room, etc. The supper was known as an "American" supper, i.e. all bring something plated to be pooled. Or, in the case of a Church "do" "A Faith Supper", hoping they all brought enough. In the event everything went well – almost. It was at a time of problems in industry, short time working and so on, two and three day weeks were the norm for some. For the party, relatives were invited – Olives' sister Lily was a Godmother to Valerie. Ida, another sister, came with her son Brian who is not a Churchgoer, however, I introduced Brian to the rector. Brian stuck out his hand and said "Hi Ya Vicar, how is the one day a week going then?" Geoffrey was not at all used to this sort of talk, and for a moment it did show, but he laughed it off and all was well. I did feel a little uncomfortable for some time afterwards and have never forgotten it.

The social life of our youngsters became a bit of a problem, all – or most – of their friends were in Kenilworth. I always offered to take them where-ever they wished, but Val in particular did not seem to like asking, proba-bly Dad did not do it quite right. Taking Val to a party or disco I would naturally drop them off outside the hall and pick them up the same way, I learned much later on that this is not the way to do it. Apparently young-sters should be transported and collected from a point away from the venue, in order that they can arrive and depart independently – and Val was and still is very independent. Also I should have remembered from the past that probably one of the highlights of an evening was after the event was over. However, one lives and one learns, often too late though.

Time marches on, and we get to February 1974. Val was 18 years old on the 10th and by half term, end of February, she was studying for "A" levels, the exams coming later on in the year. There were lots of discos at the Lanchester Polytechnic in Coventry where she liked going. We always wanted to know who was getting her there – and back home again, and what time she would be in. We seldom had an answer in full. Whether it was because she was now 18, or just wanted to be independent or simply stroppy I do not know, however, during the week of half-term she was returning home later and later. We "tackled" her one night and without going into detail Olive and I were informed that she was considering leav-ing home "to live with Jim".

It was two weeks of utter misery and perhaps disbelief for Olive and I before Val departed. What had we done to deserve this, etc. Jim did have the decency to come and see us and talk. There were no raised voices and no falling out, we were just so upset and disappointed, she was not turned out of home, it was her decision to leave. From then on I did not want to know, got on with my work, and "play" as usual.

Ten months later our grandson Adam came on the scene and we did go and see him, followed by rare visits to the flat they were living in, together with Jim's Alsatian dog "Tania". I never looked forward to going for more than one reason, although we got on O.K. The soft old dog was a big help. More later.

My work features again, and a lady from Blossomfield Road, Solihull called me in. Very fond of perennials there was a long herbaceous border all down one side of the garden, somewhere in the region of a 175 yards in length and about 8 feet wide. There was a gravel path and along the back of the border then a tall hedge. The brief was to lay a random paved path at the front, irregular width, sort of a long zig-zag. Mrs Alice Fryer who had a small nurseries on Waste Lane, right opposite the end of Windmill Lane recommended me. I was engaged to do the work, a job I enjoyed, something a little bit different. One day Mrs S asked if I knew a landscape architect? my reply was that I may be able to help but I was not a landscape architect. A very polite "no thank you" was forthcoming. These friends wanted to redevelop the majority of their rear garden in Solihull. I recommended Mrs Hazel Fryer – Alice's daughter-in-law. I was thanked and Mrs S said she knew Hazel and why did she not think of her.

I forgot all about it until one day Hazel phoned to enquire "was I interested in quoting for some work". "Yes thanks" says I, and very soon I was on my way to Solihull to see this job – a Saturday morning – with plans and a load of papers under my arm. It was quite a big job, shrubberies and a big fish pond featured. All the paths were to be York stone crazy paving. There were two or three visits to make before I had got it sorted in my mind – and also on paper. The quote went in and it was quite a while later that I was notified that my quote had been accepted. I was told that two or three others were invited to quote but I think they all declined because there was no access for a tractor or JCB. It was always my belief that I was better off without big machines, they do make an awful lot of mess especially if it is wet. So in the late spring of 1975 it was sleeves rolled up and oil the wheel-barrow and away we go. Although it was jolly hard work I really did enjoy the work. I met Mr A when I went to measure up and only saw him about twice during the time it took to do the job, over 3 months in fact. No one "bothered me at all, I think Hazel popped over there in the evening now and again.

By the time it came to plant the shrubs we were into a hot dry summer, and I had to replace any casualties. However, Mrs A did a great job on watering, she must have taken pity on me I think, I was more than grateful

The first crop of Christmas trees, 1970s

for the help, by now a lot of other jobs were piling up and clients getting vocal and anxious. This job was the start of a friendship that has gone on to this day. Soon afterwards I was called back to Blossomfield Road, the home of Mr & Mrs S, to dig up the herbaceous border, divide and re-plant all the perennials, that "kept me out of mischief" for a while.

At the May half term, after Valeries departure, all the four of us went to Llorret de Mar on the Costa Brava in Spain, It was a cheap deal, staying at the Rosamar Park Hotel which was a bit basic but it had a disco, which I thought Robert and Jenifer would like, in the event they never went near the place. Coaches turned up very late for the revellers and left engines running, the service in the restaurant was very slow and the food O.K., but not a lot and not all that special, despite all that we did have a nice holiday, also it was a new experience. One thing it taught me to read the brochures very carefully thereafter. If it ain't in you don't get it.

The next year Olive and I went to Benidorm around Easter time. We really enjoyed that, staying at the Avinida. Right in the old town, evening dancing, suitable for our age group, although I was only 46. We had one big night out on the town, an organised excursion first to see Spanish gypsy dancing, baubles, bangles and beads, I was captivated by the Flamenco rhythm and dancing, clicking heels and gestures of all the dancers. We were then taken to another venue for more Flamenco, this time a sort of "stage come professional show", nothing gypsy about this, but the same or similar interpretation of rhythm, for me absolute magic, loving any music that can be danced to. Although I have never been to the ballet. Oh, Benidorm was O.K. out of SEASON! It was not the only thing that I was "captivated" about, and Olive had nothing to do with it.

Our brother-in-law Alf Garlick, was married to Olive's sister Lily. They worshipped at the then Radford Congregational Church in Radford Road, Coventry. Some of the members were quite talented and used to put on shows for their Church members and would "tour" now and again, they came to Berkswell Reading Room two or three times, I had little talent but got "roped in" now and again nevertheless.

One day Alf rang to see if Olive and I would like to join the concert party (The Good Companions) for a trip to a Birmingham cinema to see this film, The Sound of Music. It was going to be a fairly expensive night out for us, but after some thought we decided to join in. At the time cinemas and films did not feature with me, and The Sound of Music was completely unknown to us. However, a few days later Alf phoned to say that they could not book in Birmingham, it would have to be Leicester. I was very apprehensive when we left home quite early on the Saturday afternoon to go to Radford to join the coach. It was a very nice picture house, nothing like the Cameo in Balsall. I settled down, the curtains opened to reveal a screen the likes of which I had never seen before – wall to wall. The lights went out and the title music began to play, there were speakers all round the auditorium and a few more besides. When the film was shown initially the building was wired up for stereophonic sound. I think that is what it is called anyhow. From then on I was in paradise, for me The Sound of Music had everything. Super story, acting and presentation. I came out of the cinema in some sort of a whirl, I do not remember anything till we arrived back at Lily and Alf's house. Wonderful. When later on we acquired a radio-gram The sound track of the S of M was the first L.P. I ever bought, and we still have it. It is a bit sad really I never make time to play records or listen to much radio – except sometimes at meal times.

It was a few years later on and I was finishing a job in Mantilla Drive in Styvechale (pronounced Stychill). When one day I went next door for something, and at the far end of the garage stood this rather nice radiogram which I discovered was for sale, they were having a more modern audio set for Christmas. £15-00 was the asking price and I did not argue, and at lunchtime on Christmas Eve brought it home in my van or pick up. I always wanted a gramophone.

1976 was the year of the big drought. I for one do not wish to see that sort of weather again, never seeing everywhere so burnt up, anything that should have been green went brown, leaves came off trees early. Fortunately I had work that I could do, but planting and new lawns was a non-starter. Looking around today there are lots of trees with dead wood sticking out of the tops, a direct result of the drought of '76 in my opinion. One day, in the summer of that year, we went on a coach trip to Skegness, and there it was impossible to tell where sand gave way to lawns and gardens, it was all the same. Olive and I went to the Lake District for a few days but that was still nice and green everywhere. Earlier in the year we went to Diano Marina, northern Italy which again was nice, then, the next year, 1977, saw us on The Sorrento peninsula, staying at a little village on the famous Amalfi Drive, called Minori, the scenery here was absolutely superb with the villages on a sort of shelf. The road high above the water and "snaking" round the coast for miles, that I think is when I came to the conclusion "no more Spain" for us – lovers of outstanding natural beauty.

1977 was the year of the Queens Silver Jubilee, and so, the usual celebrations were organised. One of the major events was to be a barn dance at Home Farm, the home of, and with kind permission of Mr & Mrs Briscoe. This was to the sixth barn dance Olive and I were involved with, all fund raisers. The first one was organised by The Mothers Union, as their effort for the Festival of Berkswell in 1972, the Archers of radio fame later copied our idea. To go on the air. As a husband I got involved, we had to wait for the Briscoe herd of milking cows to leave their winter quarters, then the big clean up began. There was a pig roast with "Sos" Warmingham the butcher, organising the roast and supper, he was the best delegater I have ever known, probably the best butcher as well. The two porkers were cooked in the bakery oven next to his shop in Station Road and he had me there at half past midnight to turn them over. We had a super evening, about the only good weather for a Festival of Berkswell event. The only "complaint" we had regarded the pong, which was quite noticeable, but fortunately not where the eats were served.

In future years the Reading Room committee took over the running of the barn dance, for very much needed funds. The room was rather shabby at the time. Mr Briscoe had a new barn built, this one with a nice smooth concrete floor, used I believe as a "maternity ward" at lambing time and later as a grain store. So we had to hop in between these two happenings. This new building was perfect, an adjoining building for the supper and bar. The field car park very close. The band and callers were installed on a farm wagon.

By far the best barn dance was part of the Queens Silver Jubilee celebrations, Olive and I sold 500 tickets, there was also a long waiting list. All the tickets had gone and were all paid for a week before the dance. There were flags, bunting and an atmosphere I had never experienced before, one could "cut it with a knife". The band was called "Barrys Best" and we always had Joe Hodgson to call the dances, he was a teacher by profession and was first class.

These dances went on for quite a few years until people seemed to loose interest, and today (2001) it would be very hard work indeed to sell 100 tickets. Times do change and with it interests, hobbies and leisure time pursuits. But I do think today's people miss out on a lot of fun activities that our age group enjoyed so much – I did anyhow.

Early 1977 saw me back working for Mr & Mrs A in Solihull, there was an extra job on the patio that, for whatever reason, was not done. On the first morning Mrs A brought out a coffee almost before I took my jacket off, also mentioning that they had bought a house in Sedburgh, some 6 miles to the east of the M6 and 12 miles east of Kendal in Cumbria. I was told that their two sons were boarders at the famous boy's school in the town. There was a small garden to be laid out but they knew no one there who they could engage to do this work. Another hour passed and still she was "nattering on " about their house, which once was part of the old workhouse, now re-developed into houses and flats. This went on all morning, I was full of coffee so I said if the garden was a problem to them I would consider going up there and do the work. Just what she wanted to hear, so in the end I said I would go if I could take Olive with me and stay in their house. No problem, they are very nice folk and the boys had always time to talk, yes, to the gardener. We are often, even now in the 21st century, considered as one of the lowest forms of human life. Happily to say not by any of our friends, just a few of my clients of the past and the odd present day snob.

I didn't want to go all the way there to measure up, so suggested that they took a few photos and supplied me with measurements. This they did and we talked over a couple of whiskies. They wanted a maintenance free garden, and a free standing (viewed from both sides) wall to the roadside of the garden, which was way above the road, but Mrs A was a "sun worshipper" and wanted a little privacy. This was worrying me somewhat, I knew how to build it, but was not too confident of going to Yorkshire and building a York stone wall. I came home to do my sums and I phoned Crossleys. The firm I always had my York stone from, a very nice family, who it was always a pleasure to do business with. Did they know anyone that would go to Sedburgh and build a wall? Yes they did, problems solved, they later gave me a quote for the wall and all the other stone I was proposing to use. Formalities over, we arranged a date to go, Mrs A would be there to explain the workings of the house, and we would all arrive at mid-day. We arrived a few minutes early, just as the last pieces of stone were being unloaded.

The wallers were two young men, and one of them had an aunt in Lancaster, probably some twenty miles away, we or rather Olive, looked after them during the day. Olive received the workings of the house, mainly the boiler and emergency phone numbers, also the milkman. By one o'clock we were on our own, the two lads had a small wall to take down. While they were doing that I went in search of sand, gravel, etc. I was told John Dawson was the man to see, coal-man and building materials. I presented myself at his premises, which was the old railway station and goods yard. A happy sort of man, I told him I was doing this job at Loftus Manor, and I would need sand, gravel chippings and cement. He said "its all over there and the cement is in the shed, help yourself I have got to go out".

"What about paying?" says I. "Oh, come and square up when you have finished, that will do me". I have found out since that that is the way of life in those parts. I also discovered later on that he was a lay preacher with the Methodist Church, and journeyed many miles on a Sunday to minister to perhaps only very few people. We started the job on Wednesday and the wall was completed by Saturday lunchtime.

The garden was quite small and one had to walk round the house to get there, no back door, only one at the front. I was laying a quantity of second hand York random paving, different sizes and different levels but a generous area on one level for sitting out – and sunbathing. One or two locals began to take an interest, one old fellow from up the road came every morning, I called him the clerk of works. One thing they could not understand was the weather, it was perfect, warm and sunny, and raining at home. Robert and Jenny stayed at home, discreetly watched over by friends.

The first week I was up and at work early and soon had the "back broken" of the job. Thereafter I would work on some days until lunch-time, then spruce up a bit and go out in the truck. I had a Volkswagon 1 ton – pick-up, the second I had had – second hand. Marvellous vehicles.

The house was at our disposal for 3 weeks and when the job was completed, we had a day or two off – touring round the area. An area I never tire of. On our return I was invited to visit the "A's" and bring the bill. I was paid and a couple of scotches, and said how much we had enjoyed the whole thing. At the end of the evening I enquired as to whether it was their plan to hire the house out for holidays, his reply was "Well not really, it is mainly for friends and relations — but if Mr & Mrs Webb would like to go again I do not see any problems". I thanked him and thought what could be nicer than that. And since then we have been back quite a few times, sometimes pleasure only and at other times mixing business with pleasure. In other words – to tidy up – the garden and prune back the shrubs and so on. When Mrs & Mrs A go there they are kept very busy visiting their friends in the area, also Mr A is now a governor of the school, a very high honour indeed.

April the 4th 1978 was our silver wedding anniversary, is it really that long? was the thought then. I decided to push the boat out a little bit further and booked a two week holiday in Sorrento. We departed in March and came back on our anniversary. Again, for me, it was all so different, scenery, Italian food and fairly reliable public transport, etc. We went up to the top of Vesuvius, it was very quiet, only whisps or stinking steam – I don't think it was smoke – emitting from various crevices. Pompeii was incredible, and even more so Herculanium, which was buried under 20 ft of solid lava. I understand a lot of Herculamium is still buried and built above, the only way that excavations can carry on is by purchase of properties when they become available.

Our holiday to Sorrento began at Luton Airport and we were sitting in the departure lounge when a couple walked towards where we sat, and I said, "that looks like Kathleen and Robert". It was, they were going on exactly the same holiday as us, although, Kathleen was "on a mission". She had been married twice before, her first husband was killed in action close to Salerno where the big invasion of Italy took place. We went with them on the SITA bus – to Salerno and went on down the coast to see the old ruins of Paestum, there are huge remains of buildings, minus a roof of course, awe inspiring. How did they build such places all those years ago. Anyhow, on our return Kathleen was overwhelmed, with difficulty they had found the grave, not in a military cemetery, but I seem to recall it was in a local Churchyard – Kathleen and Robert were Catholics, so they would have something in common with most of the local people – they told us the grave was immaculate, even adorned with fresh flowers. On making enquiries they were told that local people take on the responsibility of looking after these isolated graves, taking responsibility from the War Graves Commission. At the end of the 1970s our Robert was still in Kenilworth with his rather menial work, but he was soon to get another job, assembling metal garage doors in Warwick – he seemed to be happy and contented with his lot and it was pointless to interfere.

Jenifer did not do awfully well at school, but on leaving wanted to go into catering. Being in the Solihull Metropolitan Borough they could offer nothing. Birmingham College of Food had a full compliment, as had Henley College in Coventry. I think the Grammer School in Kenilworth (Careers dept.) were helpful, they eventually persuaded Solihull MBC to pay for Jenny to attend South Warwickshire College in Stratford Upon Avon. They also provided most of the transport costs. I took her in the mornings to catch the bus in Kenilworth, and one of us picked her up in the evening. Jenifer studied there for three years and I am sure really enjoyed it all, having a good rapport with the tutors, a fairly lively lot, I think. It was there she met Alan Maslen, he was a year in advance of Jenny. A very nice lad who lived at Alderminster. We went to one or two special evenings put on to show off their newly acquired skills. A French evening, where naturally everything was French style, I clicked for les escargots, it was more like lumps of rubber – something had gone wrong. It was a fun and wine night, and I think Jenny drove home, I did not.

Another time a medieval banquet, serving wenches, the lot, mead, ale and wine – oh dear. Again I did not drive home. As time went on one of her best pals was Carolyn and she did some spare time work – evenings, etc. – at The Charlecote Pheasant Hotel and Restaurant. Owned by Mr & Mrs Heuterstein – a German couple – who "knew their stuff". Jenny was taken on as well and they all got on very well, towards the end of the course at the college Carolyn and Jenny were offered jobs as under-managers, which they accepted and lived in.

Sometime previous we sold our caravan near Coombe Martin in North

Devon. The two youngsters now growing up no longer took great pleasure in going there, for my part something always required attention when I went there for a holiday. There was not a lot of house/caravan work to do although we had a major blitz before coming away. Also I was a bit better off, but the final crunch came when the local authority decided that caravans were to be rated. One other thing, the property owner was not as hospitable as he once was. We were probably not spending enough money with him, I do not know. We placed an advertisement in the local paper with all the details and also that we would be there from 9 'till one on this Saturday morning. Two lots of people came, but it was not what they were looking for, however, at a few minutes to one an old VW Beetle came screeching to a halt and "this thing" got out, sorry mate! Just thongs on his feet, long rough hair all round his face, and wearing what looked like a night-shirt. But a prospective customers, or anyone else should not be judged on attire, he came in and spoke with a very cultural voice. He said our van was just what he wanted, but could not pay a lot, I said "what about £75-00 and its yours from here on. He agreed and we included all sorts of things that we would have no need for, like blankets, etc. He told us where he lived, and his plans. He had bought a property in Patch-Hole a small hamlet we would often pass through on the way to Ilfracombe. That Saturday was the last night of the season, and when we got up on the Sunday morning all the toilets and showers were blocked up with dustbins, water turned off, so for the time being the bushes had to suffice. Anyhow, we soon loaded up the Morris Traveller and were on our way to Patch-Hole without a backward glance, delivered the goods to Mr Yoga. He had done the house up very nice with one big room with a maple floor to teach yoga. He planned to live in the van, which was to be sited in the back yard and hidden with a tall fence. How he proposed getting it in I do not know, the entrance was very steep and narrow, it was not my problem. The only other item regarding the caravan was that the local authority wanted to know who we had sold it too, and I could not answer that one. It was nice to be "shot of it" but we had some good times there and thereabouts, still one of our special areas. Financially we more than broke even and our visits did not cost any rent.

Trusting it is not too boring – a phrase often heard today, I have NEVER been bored in my whole life, never had the time – but any readers will soon realise that I enjoy my holidays and am "sort of" feeling my feet in that direction. In 1979 we tried something new to us – a European tour by coach, organised by Thomsons and titled European Highlights. We met up in London and were transported to Dover. Crossing the Channel by ferry as foot passengers, meeting our coach and driver also Nigel, our "mother hen". Our route took us to Brussels, Trier, Munich, Saltzberg, Vienna. Then back via Saltzburg, Innsbruck – a trip over the Brenner Pass into Italy, Lucerne via Lichtenstein and finally Paris for two nights. It was fairly hard going, but we were so well looked after. Six different currencies

Valerie with our grandson Adam aged 2

to cope with for starters, but Nigel guided us all smoothly through any problems we might have. The idea was that we may see somewhere or some part of a country that we would re visit. That was certainly the case, we fell in love with Austria hook line and sinker, or we were hooked. I really refer to the Tirol in the west of the country, with its high snow capped mountains, rushing rivers and streams, green meadows and wild flowers galore. Good food, beer and wine – not to mention an ice cream, and a big slice of gateau in the afternoon. All served up by friendly people, most of the time anyhow. They have to be reasonably nice, a very large part of the Austrian economy depends on tourism. The one thing we cannot be sure of is the weather, it can rain at any time, we often refer to the 4 o'clock shower. A small white cloud will appear on the horizon, probably in a gap between the mountains, it grows quite quickly bigger and darker. That is usually notification to get back to the hotel or better still a nice little place for beer or tea or whatever one might fancy. We are usually prepared for inclement weather, a rucksack with water proofs extra jumper, drink and chocolate bar, especially if we are in the sticks or out of town, which was usually the case.

In 1980 Jim Thompson, who was one of the Churchwardens, was planning a holiday experience to the famous Passion Play at Oberammergeau with a week in Austria. The planning started some time previous to 1980 and Olive and I put our names down as interested, went to an eventual meeting and discovered it was for more than I wished to pay – they were flying from Birmingham. I still wanted to go so went to Carrick Travel in Kenilworth to make enquiries. Yes Cosmos were doing a trip by coach, via

Victoria and Dover. We booked and Olive's sister Ida and our niece Sylvia came as well. We had to be at Victoria Station early so we booked an overnight stay and a taxi to get us to the station. It didn't turn up, so we had to walk with all our luggage, Olive and I had done a recky the night before, and in fact it was not too far for us, but a long way for Ida in her high heels, she never wore anything else. We made it, me going back to lend a hand, and then Sylvia was scared on the escalators, so I am nipping up and down like a yo-yo helping bodies and carrying cases. It seemed and was "Cosmos Day" a special train to Dover, over the channel as foot passengers. A special luggage trolley labelled for each destination on the other side. It seemed like chaos to me, somebody said "where are you going?" I told him, OK on the train then, and that was it. We all disembarked on the other side in Calais and the whole seething mass were ushered to waiting coaches, far too many to count. We kept walking till we found ours, seemed ages since disembarking. It was not till then that we were checked, paperwork, etc. They soon had the luggage stowed away and as the coaches got all their clientele on board they departed. I did not like the system, but fortunately it was fine and the girls didn't moan.

All went very well, we stayed in Mosern, a small village about 3 miles from Seefeld, and the sun shone lovely for us, we were limited to walking, Ida and Sylvia never did any. During our stay we were taken to Oberammageau, staying 2 nights and then returning to Mosern to finish off our holiday. We came home captivated by the scenery and really everything about the place, it had just about every thing – but no guaranteed sunshine. We also enjoyed the passion play and Oberammergau.

Sometime in the latter part of 1980 Jim Thompson announced that he would almost certainly be leaving Berkswell. I had sat with him in Berkswell School, he was a clever chap and good at "sums" so it was not at all surprising that years later he became a chartered accountant. He became a partner in the firm in Birmingham where he was first articled, during his time he acquired an account for the firm. This firm grew and expanded to an extent that they invited Jim to be their chartered accountant in North Wales. This caused Jim a lot of soul searching agony. Never did a man love his parish and Church more than Jim. He was the caring son of two elderly parents not in good health. They however insisted he must go. The offer, I understand, was one not to be refused, what a decision to have to come to. They decided to go in the end, and this would leave many vacant "jobs" in the parish. Jim was a member of the Parish Council, Churchwarden and Church Council member. On the committee of the Association for the Prosecution of Felons, Berkswell Charities trustee, the Lant Trust and a governor at Berkswell C of E school. It was decided to have a farewell party for Jim and Pam, and I enquired as to whether I could arrange the entertainment. Yes that was OK and it was to be "This is your life". No one knew what was going to happen only it was unusual for the entertainment to come first. An "American Supper" made the feast easy, there was no room for a bar. I set about the surprise list, writing to the ex midwife that brought us into this world, a school pal a very good friend with whom Jim (and sometimes me) played at Rock Farm. Folks from village organisation, their bridesmaids. The widow of his best man. Reps from Meriden Young Farmers and so on and so on, the Chief Clerk from the office, it goes on. Organising it all became a mini nightmare, it was like driving an express train and could not stop it.

On the Saturday afternoon of the party Jim called in as I was putting the last few things in place, papers disappeared in all directions and all was well. He knew about the party but NOT the surprise. The room was packed, lots of his family and there were a lot of Thompsons, and people from all his connections and so on. The surprise guests were requested to go directly into the Lant Room, quickly quietly all hush hush. I had no means of knowing if they were all there when Jim and Pam arrived, and I think they had a surprise at the reception they received. All was ready on the stage when I produced the obligatory red book. Poor old Jim he just went to bits and said it had taken all his courage to get there, so much was the emotion that had welled up within him. We sat Jim down and gave him time to compose himself, all the time he was saying he could not do it. Most of the people still did not know what was planned. Pam was telling him what a lot of work had gone into it. In the end he perked up and said "OK I suppose this is what you were up to earlier this afternoon you bounder". Pam went up on the stage with him, and we were up and running. My job from there on in was to link each item and let Jim's surprises do the talking. Jim was fine after that. And after over 20 years I am still taking the blame – serves you right they cry. "They" turned the tables on me once, but you will have to keep reading to find out.

As I said before, Jim's departure left many gaps to be filled. I was already Chairman of the Reading Room Committee, and fortunately was not invited onto the Lant Trust or the parish Council.

Certain pressure was applied to try and persuade me to stand as Churchwarden (Jim was still living in Berkswell). Oh by the way one definition of a committee is as follows:

A committee is: a collection of the unfit
                    chosen from amongst the unwilling
                    by the incompetent
                    to do the unnecessary (Phil Mason)

I was told more than once that the best committee is a committee of one.

Prior to 1980 the Annual Meeting of Parishioners met in the ancient Tudor vestry at the Church. Everyone entered via the flight of steps outside the Church to elect the two Churchwardens for the next 12 months. It was traditional in Berkswell anyhow for the Rector to nominate his warden and those assembled to elect a peoples warden, this as I understand it, and proved to be not truly lawful.

In the event, Olive and I were going to Sedburgh for Easter to Mr & Mrs A's house, so I would not be around to be elected as Churchwarden. Jenifer had become engaged to Alan and his little 600cc bubble car was often outside our house. We had met Alan's parents Barbara and Roy, also his brother Robert, they had a very nice bungalow at Alderminster, a few miles outside Stratford on the Oxford road. They were coming with us to Sedburgh, Barbara then was quite badly disabled with arthritis in just about every part of her body, but she was like so many others with "problems" – a fighter and no give in type, always cheerful and wanting to live life to the full. We had a wonderful weekend, and the sun shone for us, we toured round in Roy's car, he had been to a few company gatherings in the area and one afternoon had tea on the lawn at "The Bellsfield" at Bowness, all waiter service with a magnificent view along Lake Windermere. And the cost was not much more than Joes Café, lunches out and an evening meal at "The Dalesman" in Sedburgh, a pub where service and quantity and quality of food – and beer – has not altered in over 20 years. Nice "local atmosphere" as well.

On the Sunday morning Barbara enquired would we like to go to Church, and I replied yes. But where? We were C of E, they came from Swansea and one was Baptist and one Chapel of some sort. So after a bit of thought I suggested the Methodist Church in Sedburgh. Fine. We received a very warm welcome – as one always does from the Methodist people. We were seated in the middle of the Church, Holy Communion was explained so we all felt quite at home.

We all returned home on the Tuesday afternoon and in the evening I rang Jim Thompson to hear about the meeting and more to the point, who were the new Churchwardens.

Usually the Rector would nominate the warden of his choice and the people would elect theirs. However, I was told that the meeting became very heated, one of the past wardens had said that the Rector should not choose a warden, both to be chosen by the parishoners, the methods of the past were not legal and never had been. These statements really put the "cat amongst the pigeons", so much as that the other Churchwarden resigned, I do not know quite why or when. So two new wardens were required. In the end it was decided to postpone the meeting till the following Sunday evening – to follow evensong. Often there were very few people attending the meeting of parishoners on Easter Monday, and if there was anything controversial it was put off till the next Sunday, when more people would be present to "have their say" and vote. Jim told me there were four nominations and my name was on the list, naturally I did not have to stand, I did do a lot of hard thinking during what was left of that week.

Probably a little praying as well. My decision to stand for election was finally made at the end of evensong, my thoughts – or some of them – were that if the congregation did not want me I would not be elected anyhow. In the end I was duly elected together with my friend David Watkins who owned Watkins Rose and Garden Centre at Bradnocks Marsh. David had not even been on the P.C.C., so it was a whole new ball game to him and more than a bit daunting for me.

Each year Churchwardens are required by Church law to be INSTALLED as wardens regardless of past wardenship. The Archdeacon visits one Church in the Deanery (we are part of Kenilworth). All the wardens are hosted by their supporters and introduced to the Archdeacon... All wardens back in the pews declare an oath of responsibility, etc. The Archdeacon then delivers his address – each new warden has a copy – often about church finance, maintenance and the "nuts and bolts" of keeping a Church going. No punches are pulled. Then we all have a cup of tea and go home but, we do not forget the Archdeacon's address. I can still see him now. On the evening appointed David could not go so we had a "private session"." I think it was in Kenilworth. We were given a copy of the address and took the oath. As David knew little of the workings of the church I decided we would go together. The Churchwardens are the Bishops representatives in the parish, they are responsible for the Church building, repair of, etc. They must notify any wrong doings by the Rector, or any one else in connection with the Church. They still have powers to arrest in fact.

I knew by becoming a Churchwarden that I would automatically become an Ex. Offico trustee on Berkswell Charities together with my fellow warden and the Rector. In the distant past the Churchwardens were parish overseers, allocating grants to the poor and so on. I believe there were quite a few needy people around in years gone by. The title of the Charity was and is Berkswell Church, School, and Poor Lands Charity.

The Charity is responsible for looking after 16 Almshouse properties in the parish, and is also involved with the Parish Church and the C.ofE. school, the village shop, a farm, 4 houses, 2 parcels of woodland and various areas of land around the parish. There are four other trustees elected by the existing trustees, they have to be approved by the Parish Council. A clerk "does all the work". Mr Bob McLaren was clerk to the trustees at the time. Within a few months he wished to resign and take life easier. It was decided that he should exchange places with Mr Arthur James who duly became the new clerk to the trustees. The trustees had an annual dinner known as The Founders Day Dinner, when the trustees took it in turn to host the evening and pay, there being two hosts every year in turn. The dinner was held at the home of Mr and Mrs Arthur Powell in Meriden Road until they finally retired. Thereafter the dinner was transferred to various venues including " "The Bear Inn" Haigs restaurant and latterly "The Bulls Head" at Barston. I found being a trustee interesting, enlightening and very worthwhile.

After the Vestry meeting to elect churchwardens for the ensuing year, 1982. Left to right: Frank Hayward, past warden; Dennis E. Gibbs (Ted elected 1983); John Webb, churchwarden; David Watkins, churchwarden; Rev. G.P.W. Dingle, Rector; John Stokes, past warden; John and Una Clements Vergers; and Arthur James, past warden

It is traditional at Berkswell Church that a Churchwarden is on duty at every Sunday service and I did not really look forward to being at Church soon after 7.30 a.m. on a Sunday morning, midmorning and evensong were where my interests were. In the event it was no trouble at all and I did enjoy the service and a time of complete peace and quiet. Duties usually meant 2 services one Sunday and one the next, also tying in with David's duties at the garden centre. I did feel "out of my depth" from time to time, mainly with trying to express my thoughts and feelings into words. But most people understood. Also I was expected to read a lesson now and again, at special services, I hated that, finding it difficult to read even after practice. Whilst I was warden The Church clock was "playing up" and refused to function. It was decided to ask Bob Thompson who was an engineer at Jaguar Cars and Ken Woolley, the village blacksmith and engineer, to investigate. They discovered one of the problems was a badly worn bush which Ken took back to the forge. One day a client was there and enquired as to what it was. Ken told him it was part of the Church clock and he was repairing it. Off went the client and some time later something went wrong belonging to his employer, that is no problem says he, I will take it to the blacksmith, "he is working on the Church clock at Berkswell" to which the employer replied "Oh I hope there is a faculty for this work to be undertaken. She was the wife of an important person of the diocese and he "had a word" with the Archdeacon. The result was that the Rev. Geoffrey Dingle, David and I were summoned to his study – I think in Baginton – to be read "the riot act". We, as fairly new wardens did not realise that any works, additions alterations, etc. to the Church needed a faculty, which had to be paid for. The Rector should have known this. We were accused of allowing people to "tinker" with the Church clock, we assured the Archdeacon that Ken and Bob knew what they were doing. I said surely he did not really think we would allow any Tom Dick or Harry to tinker with our clock. He softened a little and agreed that all Churches were not as well looked after as Berkswell. He really made his point, but we ended up with coffee and biscuits. However, Ken did write to the lady who "split" on us. He really told her off in a sort of nice way, I have never read a letter like it before or since, cussed her into a heap without swearing, if you follow me.

The Church then was always short of funds, what Church is not, they cry. Various campaigns had been tried and they were partially successful, it was decided to do more either by a stewardship campaign or by trying to increase the congregation i.e more souls, more money.

A stewardship campaign was ruled out and we decided to have a mission and called in The Church Army. A Captain Charles Harris came and addressed the P.C.C. and his parting words were "if this is in any way a fund raising exercise it will not work". Everything went very quiet. It was decided to go ahead and there was a lot of work involved, I for one probably should have done more but I really had no spare time, and others were in a similar situation. The mission went ahead and some said it was quite successful, in my opinion, it was a complete waste of time, and some money as well. The whole event was half hearted from start to finish and Charles Harris was right.

Being Churchwarden for me, was an honour, and I felt privileged to be in that position, the first "blue collar" worker to hold that office following in the footsteps of the likes of Col. Wheatley of Berkswell Hall and many other celebrities. Just after David and I were elected Mr & Mrs Hayward put on a buffet luncheon in our honour at their home at Cherry Tree Cottage, Truggist Lane. Anyone that was anyone was there, and a finer lunch I have yet to experience, it was all there and beautifully set out. David and I were highly honoured indeed. I do not think anyone devoted more love and time on Berkswell Church than Mr & Mrs Hayward, I did address Mr as Frank, but never Mrs Hayward as Margaret.

I completed two years as Churchwarden, and what with that job as well as being chairman of the Reading Room committee, also Berkswell Charities, nothing was getting done at home, so I did not stand for a third term. At the first meeting I attended of the Charity Trustees we were informed that someone had to become a governor at the school, they all looked at me, and I looked away, my thoughts were again that it was quite an honour to be asked, but I did not think that job was for me. In the end a person was chosen to represent the trustees and this arrangement worked very well – although not the ideal.

Holidays again now, and one place that I always wanted to visit was the Keukenhof Gardens in Holland, the Dutch bulb-fields. I had read about this place, 72 acres of gardens, a showplace to show off their displays of spring flowering bulbs. All the tour operators allowed about 4 hours there – it you were lucky. I wanted a whole day there and there was only one way as far as I could see D.I.Y. This I set about to do, a trip into Kenilworth to see if Carrick Travel would be prepared to organise accommodation in Holland, also a coach and driver. I had worked for a Dutchman in the village, a very formal gentleman and decided to seek his help regarding places to visit, etc. I was amazed and delighted when he agreed to work out an itinerary and came along with his wife, and be our courier. All went very well and we managed to fill a coach. Carrick Travel engaged Arnold Shaw Coaches from Warwick and we stayed in Scheveningen at a very nice hotel. The only brief that I gave Jan (our courier) was that we would spend the whole of one day at Kaukenhof. It was a super holiday, everything was organised for us, a day at the bulb fields, another in Amsterdam with a cruise on the canal system, also visiting Marken, a village on what was the Zeider Zee. Zaanse Schans, an open air museum of windmills and all sorts of trades including a clock maker and clog maker. Peter Thomas, our driver, knew his way around, which made life easy and he was included as "one of the party". It was Peter's big ambition to find a Rum Toft, a jug for preserving fruit in rum – or other liqueur – Jan managed to find one which was duly presented on the way home, which reduced a 6'2" 16 stone rugby player to tears, he was so overcome. So much did Olive and I enjoy Holland that we paid a return visit later on to go to the Floriade. This is a Dutch horticultural "shop window" which takes place every ten years. A large area of land is reclaimed from the sea on which the show is held, a huge project, and after the summer long show the land is put to some good use. We stayed in Amsterdam and enjoyed it all very much.

CHAPTER 19

At Home in the Garden

1982 is now upon us and May 22nd was fixed for Jenny's wedding to Alan. Alan did not want a big occasion at all, but his mother did, in the end there were about 60 guests. The wedding was at Berkswell Church and the reception at the Charlecote Pheasant, where Jenny was an under manager. It was her wish to go there so that her work colleagues could see her and pop in for a drink. A lot of the local ladies rallied round and helped decorate the Church, lots of wild flowers were used especially on the pew ends. Jenny had been a member of the choir and they gave their services. As I was a Churchwarden Church fees were waived. We did arrange a sherry "reception" for the choir and bell ringers, etc. after our departure. Under prior instruction from Alice Fryer, who was a florist I made Jenny's bouquet, also flowers for the bridesmaids, the ladies sprays and gents "button holes".

It was a lovely day weather-wise and every arrangement went well, we had one of Jenny's ex tutors from the college to act as M.C. and toast master, he also assisted the hotel staff waiting on the top-table, Jack (Jacko) O'Connel was quite a character. There was no noisy disco in the evening, both sets of parents deciding to do their own thing once Jenny and Alan had departed on their honeymoon. We had a gathering at home, the whole day was one of the most wonderful of my life. Everyone was so happy.

With Jenny working at Charlcote Pheasant we went there now and again, it was a carvery and quite reasonably priced and the food "on the plate" was very good. The Huttersteins ran the place very efficiently, which meant the staff had to work very hard. The owners were also very much involved, and set a good example to their staff – and, hard work never did anyone any harm, so they say. Now and again there would be a special evening, such as a Bavarian Evening with the "Heidel-burgers" and their oompah band, drinking songs and German type dances, waltzs, polkas and so on, all very good fun with a superb meal to boot.

Alan and Jenny began married life in a flat off the Alcester Road in (or near) Stratford and soon had it very nice. Alan did not make the grade at catering and started work at Samuels the jewellers in Stratford. He was "into" pop music and had six or seven guitars in his possession, he and three others formed a group known as "3 and a bit" – the "bit" was Lynn, wife of one of the other members. We went along to one or two of their gigs and they were not too bad I suppose, but the only "modern dance" tempo they knew was a waltz, not one of the four could dance "our sort of stuff" therefore it was almost all "jungle music". I know that I am old fashioned and my theory is that dance "music" has turned full circle – it all started in a small clearing in the Jungle (Rainforest nowadays). It is also said that usually ones favourite music is what we all liked in our teenage, as far as I am concerned that is absolutely true. Although the big band era was probably at its best between say 1938 and 1950 (I was 21 in 1950) I have to this day been a big band fan. The Glenn Miller orchestra being my favourite also Tommy Dorsey, Jimmy Dorsey, Artie Shaw, Benny Goodman of the American and Ted Heath. Joe Loss, Geraldo, Oscar Rabin to name a few on this side of the pond. I also enjoy trad jazz and Dixieland. Anything one can dance to I like. The Spanish Flamenco and Italian Tarrentella. I have never been to the ballet and never fancied myself as a ballet dancer – Hooray they cry.

There was still lots of work around, despite a lot of unemployment and "credit squeezes" I always had a full order book, by now, the early eighties. I had been a "one man band" for some years. I enjoyed my own company and working alone, it did give me complete freedom to start and stop as I wished, although I hardly ever took a day off, perhaps essential shopping – Christmas, etc. – always on a rainy day. The very worst was when it was raining when I got up in the morning, and it would often be fine at twelve midday – hence the saying, "Rain before seven, fine for eleven". Having then to go out and start work was hard going, nevertheless as soon as I arrived and made a good start all was well. I mostly bought my materials from local supplies, Don Ford, till he went bankrupt, it was quite common then for accounts to go on for three months or more, in the case of Don, I had quite a lot of materials from him and also worked for him. But I always had a "settling up" when I owed him more than he owed me. The last "squaring up" was just days before he was declared bankrupt, he swore he had no idea what was to happen and I did believe him, I was most fortunate it could have cost me dearly. Deeleys were the same, but they eventually brought in a monthly account system, and really it was much better for all concerned. Often I required materials from sources where I was not so well known, York Stone from near Halifax. Marshalls walling blocks and paving again from Yorkshire. Breedon footpath and drive gravel from

Derbyshire and so on, this was paid for C.O.D. it often carried a discount and if one was ever offered I took advantage of it. After all it was sometimes two or three months before I saw my money back. I always traded "in the black". Again I was fortunate that my clients hardly ever kept me waiting to be paid, I did try and treat them all fairly – as I would have wanted to be treated myself. Naturally there were a few that were "awkward", sometimes I had to work harder to get paid than doing the job, then the offender sometimes had the cheek to ask if I would do another "little job for them", I was always far too busy – thank you. But I was fortunate in over 40 years of self employment I only "lost" about £350-00. This is very good by anybody's standards.

CHRISTMAS TREES AT 'MERIGLEN' Some parts of our garden carried three crops of Christmas trees (Norway Spruce). I bought in young plants about a foot in height and planted them in rows three feet apart and eighteen inches between each plant. This planting is in fact a bit too close together, however, it was a means of utilising the ground which for some time had only produced weeds. The trees grew at about ten inches per annum, and therefore it took about six years for trees to become saleable, there is not a lot of money to be made only producing a relatively small amount each year – they did not all grow at the same rate.

The income received, together with the sale of holly wreaths was welcome at that time of the year, a little bit of "insurance" against any real bad weather between Christmas and Easter. They were sold wholesale and retail with some clients coming early to choose their tree – talk about fussy, tape measures came out and so on, I would go down the garden with people to try and help, but in the end gave them a label to fix on. People like their trees dug up and fair enough the needles did stay on a bit longer.

As time went on no more planting was carried out, I did not want to be digging out too many trees at over 60 years of age. Eventually as the trees went gaps and clearings started to emerge. Helped on its way by an unfortunate occurrence. We were away somewhere on holiday in the summer one year when our neighbour had a bonfire in his garden some distance from his hedge between the two gardens. Apparently he went in the house at lunchtime and the fire crept through dead grass and fanned by the breeze, everywhere was quite dry and very soon there was quite a blaze which had spread through the hedge and was consuming our Christmas trees. The fire brigade attended and soon had the fire under control but not before quite a number of trees were black instead of a nice green colour. Mr & Mrs McLaren our neighbours were concerned and came to see us on our return, saying that he was fully insured for that sort of thing, and that I must make a claim, I was not too happy about that, however he did convince me and I did submit a claim. Some time after the insurance assessor came round and wanted to know on what the claim was based and how had I arrived at the claim figure? A very good question. My answer was that Christmas trees are sold at so much per foot in height, and that I had counted the damaged trees and calculated the various lengths at the going rate per foot. He went away a little amused, but satisfied, and my sale of Christmas trees was a little previous that year. The dead trees were dug out at the end of the year and that did create quite an area of ground, and together with other trees sold did make available ground in addition. It was decided to make a vegetable garden with part of it, there is nothing to compare with fresh veg straight from the garden and onto the plate, some things do need cooking first.

Early in the next year at least three of my clients wanted a new herbaceous border preparing and planting. So I thinks "why not us as well"? Yes please, I thought back, and we began collecting plants, my clients by and large were my friends and as soon as people knew plants arrived from all directions. A start was made on Good Friday, digging and clearing an area where the trees were and by the end of the Easter holiday the border was prepared and most of the plants were in the ground.

From the road and past the house, and for perhaps fifty yards further back the garden is about 38' wide. The area immediately behind the house was laid out in 1963, two years after the house was completed. There was the two bungalows to demolish and dispose of, mostly timber, a lot of it was burnt on an open fire in the lounge. We were allowed to keep the old kitchen and bathroom, it has been known as "The old kitchen" ever since and it has been very useful as a tool shed, also seed trays, spare wire netting, garden canes and all. The other odds and ends that "may come in useful one day." Like almost everybody else a good old clear out is undertaken now and again. I do know one or two that never have a clear out – nuff said. Beyond the old kitchen is the old lavatory – it never was a W.C., now used as a coal house. Then comes the greenhouse, this "Robinson" is a 10' × 13' cedar wood house which replaces the other two I had, they have both done yeoman service. It is heated in the winter by a specialist greenhouse electric heater, three elements plus a fan controlled by a thermostat. Very efficient and I think cheap to run. At the time (early 1980s) I only had it set at 40° F. just to keep "Jack Frost" out, there was really only geraniums plus a few odds and ends in there. But it was always full of plants – no half larks.

From the greenhouse the garden doubled to some 72 feet in width as we retained the back land when the building plot was sold in 1960. This double width went back for a further 250 feet to the field at the end, it was on this area that the Christmas trees were grown. It became a mini forest, and there were times when a trip to the bottom end was very infrequent, so thick were the trees, it became a bit like a jungle, although I did keep the grass cut short between the trees with a Hayter rotary mower. The new border and kitchen garden was very successful, although all the pests came "out of the woodwork", pigeons, bathering birds, club root and cabbage root fly, carrot fly, black and green fly to name a few. I persevered, making a few adjustments here and there – I gave up growing carrots. As time went on more areas were cleared of trees, the ground cultivated and perennials and shrubs planted, we had a "secret garden" in one place.

One summer we decided to open the garden one Sunday afternoon, and dared our visitors to try and get to the bottom end, there was only one way there and the same way back, it all caused quite a bit of fun and visitors did enjoy it all, we put a collecting box out for a charity, and it was all well worth while, I have always enjoyed meeting and talking to people so really a good time was had by all. This was the start of more ambitious openings later on.

CHAPTER **20**

Accountants and Clients

During all this time Jim Thompson had been my accountant, firstly I was one of many clients he looked after from home. Mostly I would pop down Hob Lane to his home nearly always about 9.30 p.m., after he had had his supper and wound down from the days toils, my "few pence" would be no problem to a man of Jim's calibre. Eventually the accounts were absorbed into his firms files. Jim departed to North Wales and I stayed loyal to the firm of accountants, well I did not know any other. On a wet day I would take all my books to the offices at Five Ways Birmingham, often 3 years behind with the accounts – not my fault, and Inland Revenue did not seem concerned in those days. In complete contrast I was forced to "join another club" in 1975. Jim discovered my receipts turnover meant that I had to register for VAT. It was regulated according to turnover during 3 months, six months or per annum, and I exceeded the amount allowed some 2 quarters ago. We are dealing now with Customs and Excise and THEY wanted "their" money. When I enquired how to obtain money from clients who had already paid their bills I was told to send another account for the VAT – as they had. There was no way I would do this, so, it cost me quite a sum. However, I was a member of "the ways and means society" and that came in very handy.

After some six years the government of the day raised the ceiling of the amount of turnover before VAT was payable so it was one "organisation" from which I resigned. Try as I did I could not get my accounts up to date and I did not enjoy being three years behind. One wet day I phoned the firm to ask if my books had been examined for that year, I wanted to get on with the next twelve months. The chief clerk said, "Yes all done", so I jumped into the car and went to Edgbaston to collect them. When I arrived home it was fine so the bundle was put away and away I went to work. It was some weeks later – another wet day – when the package was opened and I had a horrible feeling the books had not been examined. There were no red ticks or green squiggles, nothing. I got on the phone to their office to check and sure enough nothing had been done, no apologies "You will have to bring them back" Right" says I "but there is one other thing – in amongst my books there are books belonging to another Mr Webb from Sutton Coldfield" Silence, then, "Ok, bring them back at the same time OK" "Thinks me" I will have to ponder on that one.

I was working close to home and two other fellows who I knew well were working in the house, I joined them for the usual mid morning break, and told them of my experiences with the accountants knowing they were with the same firm "Oh" says Tony "we gave them up some time ago, couldn't get anywhere". They told me that they were very satisfied with their man in Kenilworth. With that I asked and was given his name and location. When I went home at dinner time I phoned the office and spoke to a secretary, told her my approximate annual turnover and could I please have an estimate of their fees – the accountant was away at lunch. I went back to work in the afternoon and on returning home in the evening Olive said "you had better tidy up a bit, the accountant is calling at six o'clock. He did, almost like an whirlwind. Lets see your books, returns the lot, I said I wanted an idea of cost. "Who are you with now?" he says, I told him and the reply was that his charges would be less whatever they were. Then I produced the other mans books to which Mr D said I will return them if you wish and the Birmingham firm will send all relevant documents, etc. to me. I think they are bound by law to do this. He then went away with my books and papers and within fifteen months or so I was up to date with the tax man, the first time ever. I did have three lots of tax to pay in a relatively short period of time, and a fair old bill from Mr D, however, it was far less than the previous accountants costs and a bigger saving on income tax. I have always found the Inland Revenue very fair and very understanding. On quite a number of occasions I have had tax repaid, etc. and the payments have arrived promptly, due I am sure, to the way my accountant operates. The VAT man is different, I was a few days late with a quarterly return once, and the Customs and Excise came down on me "like a ton of bricks", a very nasty letter indeed. What sort of letters do there persistent offenders receive I wonder?

As well as lots of small jobs like repairs to fences after gales, re-laying paving paths and patios, now and again bigger and more interesting jobs came along. A new doctors surgery in Kenilworth was built and I had the job of landscaping the gardens, it was due to be opened at the end of June and the lawn areas were to be sown with grass seed, the period was hot and dry, the areas to be seeded a bit like the Sahara, I told the clerk of works the seed would not germinate, and to keep it all watered would be time consuming and therefore costly – they chose seeding to save money. My instructions were to carry on which I did but it was September when the grass began to grow. A bit later on the Practice Manager asked if I would suggest a plan for planting trees and shrubs in the autumn, this I did and was given the job. It was all planted up by mid December and the following day it snowed and froze for a month or more, however, only one plant was lost and I had the contract to look after the outside area till I retired, about fifteen years later. In all that time I hardly got to know any doctors or staff, they were all very busy people, most importantly – for me – my cheque always came back very promptly. They were all very nice. Another client phoned from Barnt Green one day, an appointment was made and I went over one Saturday morning. They were friends of existing clients in Solihull. A big brand new house sitting on a very large plot. They required a bit of everything, a big big patio, kitchen garden, shrub borders and a dry-stone retaining wall. A lot of work and something to really "get ones teeth into". All other areas were to be seeded. The biggest problem was the quantity of stones to get rid of, literally tons of them. I landed the job and although at 27 miles each way and long days it was most enjoyable, especially building the dry-stone wall with lovely brown coloured Hornton Stone. The stones were a problem as I was raking out for the lawned areas, there was a tip close by, but it was expensive and I was scared of getting punctures and getting stuck. I had the use of a private tip close to home, so brought a load away each visit. I have returned since and most things got away and grew very well. Whilst I was there, the people in another new house next door sought my help and later on began another marathon job, a more extrovert pair, he had a job with a large construction company and went all over the world, his wife often hardly knew where he was. One day he had three breakfasts. Breakfast at home before going to Birmingham Airport for the shuttle to Heathrow, the 2nd breakfast on Concord en route to New York and no. 3 on his arrival. He worked all day and returned by the normal schedule flight in time for a BBQ at lunch time the following day. At coffee time and for tea in the afternoon I always had to go into the kitchen, helping myself when Mrs S was out. The door to the hall was always open affording a view of the front drive. One afternoon there was the roar of a car and a grey coloured mini fairly tore up the drive, Mr S got out and came in and tossed the keys to his wife "A little present for you he says " A limited edition Mini. We cannot afford it she says "Too late "says he. But we can't afford it says Mrs S "Don't worry" says he. But it was ME that went home a bit concerned, but I was reassured my cheque was OK and so it was. That couple lived there lives to the full. A few years later I was called in by a Circuit Judge living in Harborne, after measuring up the job we all sat in the conservatory enjoying a coffee, – I have been around a bit one will gather – when I enquired as to where they had acquired my name from, "Oh our builder" was the reply Mr so and so (I've forgotten the name) "I do not know this person" says I He built houses in Barnt

Green they informed me. Well, I had seen this person go on and off the site when I was working there and often put my hand up to him, but never met. And he recommended me some years after. Very nice I thought. It is interesting that all those jobs and many more were the results of undertaking a very small job in Solihull.

It was fortunate, I suppose, that jobs were put my way in and around Berkswell village, in 1976 it was decided that there was a need to extend the Churchyard, burial space was running out. The Church owned a small plec or field of probably $1^{1/2}$ to 2 acres next to the existing Churchyard – on the other side of a wall. I was a member of the P.C.C. (Parochial Church Council) and it was decided to ask a landscape architect to submit a drawing or plan. She was a trainee at the time I think. The plan duly arrived and was presented to the P.C.C. at a meeting, as well as a plan for the graves. There were to be borders of shrubs, etc., hedges – all sorts, more like a garden. But, not practical, I enquired as to who would cut the hedges and weed and prune the shrubs – deadly silence – well we were on about the graveyard. The plan was left "on the table" and the Churchwarden (Frank Hayward) came to me afterwards and said "You've put the cat amongst the pigeons have you not". I repeated my question to him to which he replied "You devise a plan then". "OK I will" said I.

At the next meeting, plan in my hand – not on posh paper as before – my ideas were presented and accepted by all. In my experience, many committee members would follow any leader – without thinking, up any blind alley. However, my plan was drawn up by a friend and sent in for approval – or otherwise. It turned out to be otherwise, the Church architect disapproved and duly sent HIS idea of what we should have, graves going in all directions, chevron fashion, some east to west others north to south plus again a hedge and borders. And again the P.C.C. thought how nice it was – until I pointed out that all graves must go from east to west, and the deceased face the rising sun. More "Ohs" and "errs", so back went the plans to the architect. The plans came back more or less as my drawing. But still with the hedge and borders which it was decided to ignore for the time being. I was given the job to lay out the new burial ground, it was designed to cater for the next 50 years. The area was wild with docks and thistles abounding – up to four foot tall, the whole area was ploughed up. There was an old stable and brick sheds up in the far corner. The area was used by the rectors of yester-year to stable their horses which pulled their traps, etc. for visiting people of the congregation and so on. A J.C.B. was hired to do a certain amount of levelling, and to dig out the footpaths and demolish the shedding. There were some very nice old bricks but they all were used as hardcore under the footpaths, which were finished off with very fine gravel. Then it was the major job of raking out ready for seeding and it took quite a while, one section was completed and seed sown during a showery spell of weather, then out came the sun and the weather was boiling hot. I was working away there in June/July 1977 and had my little radio for company when Virginia Wade won the ladies singles at Wimbledon. It was so dry and it was a hard decision as to whether to put the seed on or not, there was well over £325-00 worth of the stuff, also at one end where a start was made the weeds had already started to push through again. The seed went on, I did not want to have to cultivate and rake out again. As the seed was raked in amid a cloud of dust I began to wonder if the right decision had been made. The Rector, Churchwardens or anyone in fact had not bothered to pop in and have a look – nor did they. A month went by before any rain fell and there was no sign of grass, only an awful lot of weeds, including lots of docks. A week after the rain a visit was made and the grass was just coming through – salvation. It was left a week and then I took my rotary mower down, we had had more rain, by now the weeds were six inches tall and the grass just above an inch. When I had finished I rather hoped no one did call in and have a look, it was an awful mess, nothing like a lawn at all. Anyhow, another mow after a few days dispersed the cut grass a bit more, and after about five cuts it was looking quite good – apart from "millions" of docks. I sought the advice of a farmer friend and he gave me some special spray, which worked. I had to allow the weeds and grass to grow to six inches tall again, and mowing was hard work with my push job. However, in the end it was the best result I had ever had growing a lawn from seed. That was one job where I really earned my "corn", but it is quite nice to go there and think to myself "I did that". And finally when I was Churchwarden, some four years later, the Church architect came on his quinquinenial visit to inspect the Church and premises, I escorted him round and he said he would like to see the new Churchyard. He looked around and eventually asked about the hedges and borders, I told him the Church could not afford it, an answer he accepted. I hoped my sin would be forgiven, we never did have hedges or borders just a few ornamental trees. Who needs borders anyhow in such a lovely peaceful setting? I was contracted to do the mowing in the Churchyard for quite a number of years, that is the areas where the grass was kept short. Round the war memorial, along the side of the drive, the cremation area and so on.

The Flower Festivals continued every other year, and were and still are very popular, people come from miles around to our festivals. By now we always had a theme to work to, in 1983 it was hymn titles. Some themes, in my opinion, were a bit obscure, over the top or only understood by people who really knew religion and their Bible and lots of visitors including me sometimes found it difficult to understand "the message" that was being put over. However, it was a time enjoyed by all, opening with a short service on Friday morning and continuing till evensong on the Sunday. Morning coffees, plough-mans lunches and teas were available also a produce stall, which usually sold out very quickly. It was also decided to persuade people to open their gardens, and that was by and large my job, we did have as many as seventeen gardens open more than once, in the village and further afield. A map was provided to help our visitors.

Olive and I were occupied at the Festival stewarding and helping with teas, etc. therefore, our garden could not be opened. We did open from time to time at other times of the year. The star attraction was always The Forge, home of the Woolley family. Jack was the gardener and always provided a superb show. I think he took a week of his holidays to make sure all was well. He also had a collection of artefacts, all laid out in his shed, together with marquetry work, he even worked out the plan of what the picture was to be and went on from there. Ken's interest was aviation, he did become head of the Royal Observer Corps after his RAF service. There was a large nissen hut at the top end of the garden and another museum of all sorts of aviation artefacts. He did start to restore a 1st World War fighter plane. It was a haven, mainly for boys and their dads. It was, I am sure, in 1980 that John and Una Clements came to Berkswell,, they were our new Vergers at Church, both vergers in their own right, but it was Una that was officially the Verger. They belonged to the Guild of Vergers and John was Chairman of Vergers in the Midlands for quite a few years. John followed his own profession during the week. Una's duties outside was to look after the Churchyard, there were just no tools or mowers any good, I had my say in the matter and said that good equipment should be provided. Despite the fact that money was in short supply I got the PCC to agree to purchase two mowers and essential hand-tools. After a while I was relieved of my mowing job and very soon Una had the place nice and ship shape. She won the Best Kept Churchyard for the whole of the Coventry Diocese once and tried very hard to repeat the process. I swear in the end the grass was too scared to grow.

Everything inside the Church had to be just so, and it was. Rector Geoffrey Dingle was "easy going" and quite happy for them to get on with it. He was more or less waited on hand and foot. The communion was all prepared for him at the alter, hymn numbers on the boards, the Rectors book In position and open at the right page, also the bible on the Lecturn ready for the reader – who ever it might be. John Clements later became a Lay Reader and could take most services, but not Holy Communion or weddings. A Lay Preacher can in fact take Holy Communion with a special permission from the Bishop, the bread and wine to be consecrated at a previous service by a fully ordained clergyman, and now at the end of the nineties by an ordained lady. John and Una lived in Grove Cottage next to the school and was rented from Berkswell Estate by the Church PCC. One job that was undertaken whilst I was Churchwarden was the pollarding of the three large lime trees at the side of the footpath beyond the Church in the Churchyard, the trees only have short trunks about 12 feet high. Huge branches were cut from the top of the trunks probably five or six, each one the size of a tree in itself.

One day one fell or blew off, crashing over the path and pushing some grave headstones over. A tree surgeon was consulted and it was decided that they should be pollarded as they were unsafe. At the same time a monster beech tree was found to be diseased with a fungus and unfortunately that had to go as well, with the proviso that other trees were planted to replace it. We tried 3 times to get one going and failed every time – beech trees and hedges are known to be difficult to establish sometimes. It was a big job and expensive and I did miss that superb beech tree, a magnificent specimen.

I think it was 1982 that the first Garden Festival was held. Probably copying festivals held in Holland, known as the Floriade. The first U.K. festival was at Stoke on Trent and covered a large area, previously used for coal mining or something similar, anyhow, it was reclaimed land. Everything connected to horticulture was represented there, the trade, leisure, sport and so on. We had a day there and it really was most impressive, so much to see and do – and buy. There were laid out gardens, water features of all sizes, waterfalls, rockeries, etc.

Two years later another garden festival took place right on the banks of the river Mersey at Liverpool, unfortunately this was not as good, not enough time had been allowed for trees and shrubs to put much growth on, also the weather prior to opening was so bad. Olive and I did go and there was still plenty to interest us and we did have a nice day.

Number 3 was held in Glasgow and we gave that a miss, however, the final one – as it turned out – was a disused mining area near Ebbw Vale in Wales. I thought this one was probably the best, perhaps some teething problems had been ironed out by then. To the best of my knowledge they all made a financial loss so we have had no more.

CHAPTER 21

More Holidays

The desire to go on holiday is never far away and in 1983 I decided to organise another holiday, a few people had shown an interest in Germany and The Rhine Valley in particular. So off I toddled once again to Carrick Travel in Kenilworth for them to help out with the hire of a coach and driver and hotel accommodation. There were not as many "takers" as the Dutch trip, but with over 30 people it was on.

Arnold Shaw coaches once again provided the service with Arnold himself driving, we stayed at The Germania Hotel at Aulhausen, which is a village about a mile from the Rhine near Assmannshausen. A wine growing area where the locals talk, think, dream and drink little else than their wine. We were made very welcome at the hotel and dinner was just about ready when we arrived, we were delayed somewhat due to the Rhine being in flood, some thirty feet above normal, and that is a lot of water. There was quite a long detour to arrive at Aulhausen on the "other side" of the river. Normally there are lots of barges, holiday cruise ships and all sorts of other craft on the Rhine, but owing to the high water nothing was going anywhere. The river was very quiet, it is most interesting – to some – to see the variety of boats on the river. Further downstream near to the Lorreli Rock the river narrows and the current can be very swift and some barges need the assistance of a tug, they are still operating at Assmannshausen. There was just time for a quick wash and down to dinner, the far end of the dining room was the bar area and as we had our meal one or two local people came in and invited us to join them, although there were cases to unpack and so on one or two of us joined the group. The usual problem arose – none of us spoke any German and their English was very limited. In amongst their group was a lad called Oliver and I told them we had an Olive and that sort of got things moving, it is amazing how one copes with trying hard and a bit of effort. About six of our party were there and after a while a man enquired as to whether we would like to visit his farm one evening, the invitation was accepted with thanks and the only evening available – don't know why – was the following evening. That's fine, straight after dinner tomorrow. The boss at the hotel was the frau – usually is isn't it? Husband Tilo will take you, show Arnold where to go in the coach. So after dinner we all loaded up and journeyed about 4 miles back into the wine growing country areas. On arrival we were met by Paul, pronounced Powell there, he escorted us round the farmyard and implement barns. Machines and buildings were immaculate, no mud or dirt on the tractor tyres or anywhere else. It was far to wet underfoot to venture onto the farm or into the vineyards so we were all 30 of us, invited inside, into the keller in fact, downstairs into this big room with a bar at one end and invited to take a seat at one of the two huge highly polished oval tables. A couple of ladies placed little mats for wine glasses in front of everybody and out came the wine, I made a discreet enquiry and discovered we were guests of Paul and it was "all on the house". This information I kept to myself. Once again there was a problem with language but as I said before "when push come to shove" it is amazing what can be accomplished. During the evening Paul beckoned a few of our party out of the room, I was a bit curious but took no notice. After a while there was the sound of banging, thump, thump, bang bang, so an investigation had to be made, only to discover a full size automatic bowling alley and there our party were, having great fun. A few of us stayed close to the bar, and Paul, and he brought out a special wine, Auslasa. Just about the finest available, this was not offered to all, but the unfortunate ones never knew. We were highly honoured indeed. Eventually, we took our leave with our thanks and on the way back I suggested we ought to try and return the hospitality, but how? It was decided to think about it and decide on what to do at breakfast next day.

Prior to all this we had enquired about the possibility of some music for dancing one evening and our hostess said they had a record player and records, which we said would be fine. Someone offered a bottle of whisky for Paul but in the end a party was decided upon. We asked our host and hostess if they would invite Paul along and anyone else around that would like to meet us. AND we would foot the bill. The party went very well, Paul was so touched – his wife was away somewhere – we could not have done better. Two other guests were Herr and Frau Mengel, he was the manager of the State vineyard, just down the road, on the way to Assmannshausen, they joined us at the table and Freda and Lionel Holtom were also with us. Herr Mengel spoke quite good English and was OK as long as we spoke slowly. Freda and Herr Mengel hit if off straight away, Freda was a bit disabled and Herr Mengel had arthritis. We were all soon on christian name terms, which is probably unusual for the sometimes formal Germans, they were Walter and Irene – they pronounced her name

ERAINA. The wine flowed and we all had a very happy evening, Freda enquired of Walter as to whether he had ever been to England, "No" he said – "but we intend to go one day". In her hospitable and welcoming way Freda enquired "When you come will you stay with us?" Walter thought and said "I will think about it." Walter then invited us all to a wine tasting where they lived, and worked at the vineyard down the road on the way to Assmannshausen and the river Rhine.

The only time available was next morning at 10.00 am, O.K. it was "on", we wanted a wine tasting session anyhow. 10.00 am was a little early in the day perhaps but what the heck – "go for it". We did – Walter told us a lot about vines, his particular job, experimenting with new and different varieties of vines, cultivation methods, pest control and so on. Then on into the wine making department, fermenting to bottling. Then on to the tasting, Eirene and the staff served samples of 5 or 6 different wines and we could order if we wished. We did – and the orders were boxed and delivered to the hotel where we collected the money in payment that evening.

We went out in the coach most days. Arnold Shaw, the coach owner had to have a rest day so we all went to Rudesheim, which is a small town a mile or two upstream from Assmannshausen. Everybody goes there, the "great wine centre of that area" – my opinion. Commercialised, but nice with a hive of activity in the Drosselgasse a street of restaurants, wine cellars and souvenir shops. There is also a musical instrument museum in the town, which is also the home for the distilling of Asbach brandy A cable car takes one up to the Niederwald and the statue of "Germania" which commemorates the unification of Germany many years ago. We had a tour round the area, the Rheingau vine growing area, millions of them, acres and acres, rows and rows, everywhere pristine, no rubbish weeds, just immaculate. Heidelberg and the Necker valley another day. During our stay the water level on the river went down a lot, Bingen Ferry was the first movement soon followed by barges. Towards the end of our holiday we were able to have and enjoy a cruise on the river, it was a memorable holiday, some of us have been back since but more on that later.

CHAPTER **22**

Ernest

It was in the early 1970s that Olive and I were chatting about relatives and started talking about her sister Violet. Vi was the eldest "child" of the family and was grown up and married before Olive was born. She was wed to Charles Jarvis a Berkswell man whose parents lived at Shirley Farm in Back Lane. Charles and Vi never had any children and moved around somewhat. Brook Farm, Pickford Eastern Green, a farm at Wolston and I believe a job at Dumbleton near Evesham. From there they moved to Turley Holes Farm at Cragg, some 6 or 7 miles north of Halifax Yorks around 1944. During our conversation Olive mentioned that an "Ernest" was living with Vi and Charles, she remembered him on her visits to them when they lived locally to Coventry. To cut a long tale short Ernest turned out to be the same Ernie that I knew as a kid in Berkswell. I wrote about him earlier as, a "rough and ready" lad that used to sort of run wild around the village. As I said before he just "disappeared" from Berkswell and "turned up" in Yorkshire. I had never met Vi and I think that the last time Olive saw Vi was around about 1945 on a visit to Cragg with another sister Lily. "Why don't we go up in the car and visit" says I. The reply was that Olive was not sure as to what sort of reception we would receive from Vi. After asking the same question once or twice more the suggestion was made to go one Sunday and if we were not welcomed we could always return home. So it was that Olive and I together with another sister Ida and son Brian we set off on a very nice Sunday morning heading for Cragg. We took a scenic route in order to get something out of our trip and came over the moors and started to descend a hill into Cragg, stopping in a lay by and hopping out to admire the view. Looking down and over a valley we sort of decided that the scattered dwellings and small farms must be Cragg. One dwelling "caught my eye", it looked partly like a heap of stone, the house had a whisp of blue smoke coming from the chimney –

Ernest on his tractor at Turley Holes Farm, Yorks

despite it being a lovely warm day. Back in the car we made our way into the somewhat scattered village, down another hill and past the church of St John's in the Wilderness and on over a bridge to the Hinchcliff Arms pub where I made enquiries. We had arrived – almost. "Go up that little driveway opposite and it's the place at the top" I was told. Away we go up this very rough track loose stones rattling round the underside of the car, very steep in bottom gear, Ida hanging on for dear life. Arriving at the top facing a closed 5 barred gate and on a notice in big letters PRIVATE KEEP OUT "Thinks"!! I have come this far, etc: On and yes it was the place I had seen from the top road. I got out of the car and the dog was barking himself silly, and as I walked towards the gate the door of the house opened and out came this figure, white hair flowing in the breeze and a hessian sack apron, lovely and clean. I thought it was Old mother Riley. Young folks – ask your mum or dad. She was shouting and saying it was private and we had no business there. I said are you Mrs Jarvis, reluctantly she said "yes". Then I told her who I was and that Ida Brian and Olive were in the car. Poor lady she was overwhelmed somewhat, eventually she shut the dog up and invited us in. Apologies were made for not writing, none of us had a phone. Anyhow, in a few minutes all was well. The whole place put me in mind of what it must have been like in the days of Dickens. I don't think Charles had got out of his easy-ish chair by the fire – it was the only one to be seen. The house was stone built, probably would survive an atom bomb, there were narrow mullion windows letting in very little day light. The floor was huge York stone slabs, or, they call them flags, perhaps a bit uneven here and there. A large scrubbed kitchen table with old dining or kitchen chairs around, we did all find somewhere to sit. Ernie was missing then, he did arrive after a while. He had been round the sheep, I think, I thought there was wool behind his ears, he kept his cap on but in the end I decided it was hair. Poor old Ernie, he was more "wild" than when I knew him as a kid of about 12/13 in Berkswell, but he never needed a shave in those days. To put the record straight it must be said that the house was clean despite the fact there was no water on the tap, no gas or

Ernest on his visit to
Berkswell, 2000

electricity telephone or TV. A
small portable radio did provide some sort of a link with
the outside world. In their
early days there Charles had a
small T.T. tested herd of cows
and a milk round, and whilst
he was out ran the errands
and did the shopping. Ernest,
as he was known in Cragg
worked most of the time for
the local council, it must have
been quite a handicap
because he could neither read
or write and never did learn
the skills that we all really
take for granted.

There was so much to
talk about, never stopped in
fact. Charles and Ernest were most interested in what was going on in
Berkswell, Ernest 's memory was incredible – perhaps because his head was
not too full of other knowledge – he could recall names and places jogging
my memory. Thinks !! I wonder if my head is the same as Ernest, up to now
my memory regarding my writings have all come from my head – "Oh well
so what?"

Ernest has never lost his Warwickshire accent regardless of living in
Yorkshire for well over 50 years. It was, all too soon, time to journey back
home, – please come again they said, let us know if you can. On the way
home there was a lot to talk about and I'm afraid we had a laugh or two at
their expense, and that has gone on ever since. Having "broken the ice" we
did visit them on a few occasions, it was rather a long day out and time
could not be spared to stay. On one visit we discovered Charles had more
or less retired. The impression was guessed that he was not very energetic
anyhow. They very badly wanted to return to Berkswell, I am sure I was a
Berkswell Charities Trustee by then and the almshouses were mentioned.
It was a job to know what to say, Berkswell people have first chance when a
property becomes vacant and anyhow the properties are only for couples

and Ernest made three. So I promised to ask questions, but the answers were already known. Charles died soon after and left Vi as the tenant. They only had a few sheep and Ernest I think, was made redundant and did the outside work. The property was owned by the Yorkshire Water Board and let to the Forestry Commission – or the other way round. It was then sub-let to Charles at the princely sum of I think, £2.00 per week, house and some 40 acres. It must be said that there was not one square metre of level land anywhere, one was either going uphill or downhill with every step – unless one followed a contour that is. It could have been a lovely place with the right occupants, lovely views, woodland, etc. All the water came from a spring further up a hill, and piped down to at least two properties, nice fresh spring water, as cold as ice. Olive and I took her sisters up to Cragg for the funeral and stayed B and B with Mrs Nelson on the top road. The first of quite a few stays in their big and comfortable bungalow. The surrounding area is very nice if one likes open moorland, stone built villages, hillsides dotted with properties, some wooded areas, etc. Hebden Bridge is just down the road, well worth a visit, it must be said however, that it is all a bit dreary in wet weather.

After Charles' death it was Ernest job to do the shopping, he had a fairly ancient tractor and went on that and was well known for miles around, really his only pleasure was the pub and his pipe and although he often fell out with folks he always seemed contented with his lot. Despite falling out with people now and again, there always seemed to be one or two that would stand up for him, repair his old tractor from time to time, take him to another pub now and again. Above all Vi did her best for him as we will find out later on.

CHAPTER **23**

More Fetes and Holidays

1983 followed the pattern of most years, after our holiday to the Rhine came the Church Fete in June opened this year by Jim and Pam Thompson who made the trip down from Colwyn Bay especially. It has been said of him that he "left a foot behind in the parish, either that or, when the car is going south it will not pass Berkswell". Whatever, it is always good to see them both. The fete was held at Berkswell Hall in those days, that and the Christmas Bazaar was run by a very small committee and everything just seemed to happen – fall into place like a jigsaw puzzle. One day years previous I was in the Churchyard and the huge old wooden wheelbarrow had been put out by the bonfire, it looked in fair nick and I asked Frank Hayward (previous Churchwarden) if I could have it, thinking it would be nice full of plants in our garden.. He said "take it away, it is only going to be burnt". So it was that this big old barrow was acquired, it needed a few nails here and there – it probably should have been screws – and a couple of coats of paint in green and yellow. From a distance it looked like new. Then I had a brain wave – I think that was what it was! Why not raffle the barrow at the fete? Yes they thought this was a good idea and left me to it. The barrow was lined with polythene sheeting and filled with compost and planted up with summer flowering plants and was well established by fete day, then a further idea was "hatched". Raffle it off to be won for the summer only – then – having the barrow back and re-filled with plants and bulbs for the spring i.e. another raffle at the November Bazaar. The ticket buyers were all aware of the "rules", I would deliver and collect with my pick-up truck The idea took off very well indeed, with a bit of "leg-pull" about having it back. Over the years it must have made over £1000-00 for the Church funds, in the end it all became very fragile, one leg came off. It was pensioned off to a permanent place in our garden, with a few bricks to

prop it up. Therefore, we also had a lot of pleasure from that old wheelbarrow.

Three big lime trees were also pollarded in the Churchyard that year,
and a huge beech tree that was deceased had to be felled as well.

A flower festival in September this year with the theme using hymn
titles, or first lines. Our biannual festival is always very popular, most of
the arrangements undertaken by parishioners and local ladies. Every flower
festival so far has made more profit than the previous one; but just as
important it is a way to "preach", shall we say.. To make people aware of
what THE CHURCH is all about.

John Clements our verger took part and completed the Coventry
Marathon in 1983, which in its early days part of the route took in
Cathchems Corner and Windmill Lane and then Hob Lane. He declined a
cup of tea, and went on to complete the marathon.

That same year we had another holiday in Austria. Harry Shaw ran an
overnight coach to Oberndorf between Kitzbuhl and St. Johann and we
decided to give it a try. In those days overnight travel was OK. We were
younger and more to the point it was better value than flying, in other words
longer breaks for less money. The journey took twenty-two hours from
Coventry to Oberndorf, arriving at 7.45 am. The luggage was locked in a
room on arrival because our rooms were not available till lunch time. People
to return home were still in the rooms and departed on the same bus during
the morning. We bought some breakfast and were out walking before 9.30
and guess what? it was raining hard by eleven. The holiday was very nice and
we departed the village in a heat-wave, at the end of the holiday.

At the close of 1983 life at home went on more or less as per normal.
Olive was still a "dinner lady" at Balsall Street Primary School. Work for
me went on as usual, never a problem for me I always enjoyed my work and
managed to please my clients, also get paid.

Valerie had been left home now for almost ten years, living now with
Jim Griffin and son Adam at Wolston, and would be eight in December.
Olive and I were very very disappointed when Val decided to leave home to
live with Jim for two years I did not want to know. Naturally we were here if
needed for anything, but we were never called upon. Valerie was and is a
most independent person, and must be admired for that. It was Val that
really made the effort to "break the ice" and as the years have gone on
"things" have blossomed. The sad part is we did not see much of Adam as a
youngster and probably it is my fault. Robert was working in Warwick making Up and Over garage doors in the main. He enjoys a pint or three and
very fond of the pub atmosphere – as I did. I think – well I know girls did
feature now and again, but as far as I am aware nothing serious. He more or
less kept his own council and deeply resented any enquiries, he had various
motorbikes and eventually a car and was very much "a non mechanical animal" like his old man. Like a lot of others he got into a few scrapes and had

to sort out his own problems, never involving "Daddy" or "Mummy". Although occasionally he would take notice of advice. Robert for a time did keep company with some unsavoury guys, but thankfully, it did not last all that long. I like to think common sense prevailed. He was a clever and intelligent, well read lad and could have done better for himself. However, he appeared to be happy and contented and there is something to be said for that.

Jenifer was married to Alan and their first home was a flat just outside Stratford upon Avon, which they shared with Bonzo the cat. The flat was above some shops where young folk gathered in the evenings making rather a lot of noise and nuisance. Jenny and Alan protested to these people which only made matters worse. Eventually they moved into a very small older property in Wellesbourne. Tiny but just right for a couple out at work all day.

With that situation all was well with the five – or seven of us. In addition to the above, being resigned from being churchwarden I then decided to retire from the office of chairman of the Reading Room committee (Village Hall). This gave me more time to catch up on a few jobs at home like interior decorating and work in the garden, the extra freedom was very nice. I did remain a member of the Church Council (P.C.C.) for many years.

Holidays once again featured in 1984. The February half term saw us in Albufiera on the Portuguese Algarve where we did enjoy a week in an hotel on B and B. We both had "one day off" with a tummy upset though. It was all very nice, but not quite "our scene" so in August we had another group holiday to Austria. This was our scene – and still is – Again we travelled overnight to Seefeld with Kathleen and Michael, Freda and Lionel, Bob and Margaret, Geoff and Innes, Vi and Alan. Staying at the Hohe Mundi hotel right in the centre of the town, all very nice except the beds were hard and the Spanish waiter in the bar was a crook.

We did a lot of walking during our two weeks and never ran out of subjects to talk about. The gateaux ice creams and warm apple strudle were all sampled and found to be up to the usual standard. On the ground floor of the hotel there are shop premises and the main one is a café and it is there that the very best goodies are available, making the choice is the difficult part of it. In the afternoon an organist entertains and he can play anything, probably even the 1812 overture, although I have never requested it or heard it. In the evening there is the usual Tyrolean evening, folk dances all performed in national costume, it really goes with a swing and I love it. Various hotels had dancing in the evening an organist, duo or trio playing all sorts of music from waltzes and polkas to the Beatles. Our favourite was "Fritz and his swinging zither" at the Lamm hotel just down the road.

During the day time there was/is walking in superb countryside, lots of huts for refreshments, etc. The beer and wine is good, the locals are

A well earned rest, rambling in Austria

friendly. The only thing not "under guarantee" is the weather, it can be dull and it can be dull and wet – with lots of sunny warm days as well. It was very seldom we were kept indoors by the weather for long. For Olive and I MECCA.

1984 holidays were completed in September by another overnight holiday to Austria. Harris's of Bromsgrove advertised a "cheap and cheerful" – my definition – to Walchsea. This is a small village just yards from the border with Germany (Bavaria). Six coaches from various parts of the country descended on this village and although at times we had to "go with the herd" it was very nicely done, we stayed with six others in a small pension on B and B and had vouchers for an evening meal, it worked very well, we were able to sample Austrian fare if we wished. Lots of entertainment in the evenings made for a most memorable holiday.

This sort of set the pattern regarding holidays for the next year or two. Zellam Ziller two years in succession. The Zeller-hof was I think the best hotel we ever stayed in. Managed and probably owned by Annie with husband Franz as head chef. She was a "cracker", very good looking lady, always so smart in the national costume. On our first visit we went with Geoff and Innes Brett, travelling overnight in one of Nielsons double deckers. We travelled in the lower deck in what was known as "the lounge", just eight of us, four facing four with lots of space for my long legs; this is important to me in coaches and aircraft.

On our visit the following year a group of twelve again descended on Zellam Ziller, this is where and when I became famous (or otherwise) for my flat walks – no hills. On the first morning we set off up through the trees to a café or hutte with a chapel close by that we could see from the village. Two hours later we were still climbing upwards. Occasionally, perhaps at weekends, the hotel organised outdoor jollification's, out would come folding tables or trestles also wooden benches. Food, wine and beer would follow. Music was provided by a duo or trio, playing all the waltzes polkas and folk songs, one guy – all in lederhose national costume – would "tell the tale". I think some of the jokes were a bit resique judging by the raucous laughter, all good fun I suppose, all fine as long as one had a drink in front of them.

A visit to Keukenhof in Holland with Jenifer

CHAPTER 24

At Home and Abroad

One evening back home I sat reading the evening newspaper and spotted an advertisement in the entertainment column for "An evening with Blaster Bates. " I had heard of this bloke, a demolition expert that would blow anything up, for a fee naturally. He had the reputation of being a speaker of some note (a raconteur?) relating tales of his explosive exploits and people he had worked for. I thought this would be a good fund raiser for Berkswell, one big mistake I made was hiring him and profits to go to church funds. I phoned the phone number in the newspaper and obtained Blaster's phone number, and the fellow on the other end said "You will have a long wait, and it is not easy to get hold of him". Undaunted I phoned and spoke – I presume – to Mrs Bates. Mr Bates never answers the phone I learned later on. A date was booked for some fifteen months in the future, no deposit required, it will be £55.00. Please send full details how to find the venue. Word got around and all those that had heard of this guy wanted to be there.

I booked St Peter's hall in Balsall, arranged a firm to supply a licensed bar and a local caterer – Angela Jones to supply the plated refreshments. Now stand back. All sorts of "dismal johnies" cheered me up, saying "he won't come" – "you'll be lucky" and so on. There was nothing in writing. Apparently he had a reputation for not turning up – probably the fault of the organiser. However, folks were clamouring for tickets including one or two church members, no idea what they were letting themselves in for. As a precaution I got a friend to supply and fix up a microphone, also with a record played attached. Blaster Bates had made six long playing records of his exploits, I knew someone who had the full set and gave him free tickets to provide the records – just in case. About ten days before the "do" I phoned and spoke to Mrs Bates just to confirm, etc, saying all tickets were sold, etc. "Hang on a mo" says she "I can't see anything written down here. Hang on" After what seemed like an eternity she came back to the phone "I've found it everything is OK but please send details of how to get there and time, etc: I did not make any comment, so as not to "rock the boat". I did send another lot of details, location times, etc.

Comes the night, doors open 7.30 for 8.00 "kick off". We arrive at St Peter's hall before seven and there are quite a few cars in the car park and a queue at the door. No sign of the "bar", food – or records. The tables and chairs were already set out and the people supplying the bar soon arrived and as soon as they were ready we let in the hordes. If folk have a drink or two it makes most of them happy somehow. 7.30 Room full – still no sign of the food, the records or Blaster Bates.

Angela is perhaps a bit like me – only much better looking – sometimes on the last minute and in fact turned up in plenty of time. The "customers" all had to lift up their glasses as the paper table cloths were laid. "Has he come yet?" "Is he here". Crumbs it was like looking out for Father Christmas. Lionel Holtom was waiting for B.B. in the car park where we had saved a parking spot – and – he did arrive at about ten minutes to eight. By this time the bar had run out of beer, a problem soon solved I learned later.

I met the big man, big cheerful looking guy, an old army rucksack over his shoulder containing the "gubbins", his props, a bomb detonating cord and so on, I did wonder if the roof would still be on when we left, then I thought, well he has got a neck as well, and no missing limbs. He had a pint looked around, jumped on the stage and was very soon in full flow, no introduction needed or wanted.

Derek Blaster Bates recounts his very humorous experiences in down to earth agricultural and colourful language. I think it is called "Old English". No offence intended to the agricultural industry, they are the salt of the earth. All of them. First half and "eats" then away we go again, one or two of our church members had long gone. Some you win...Blaster finally finished at around 11.40 instead of 10.30. As he was driving he had a final half and chatted about everything except money. In the end I did get a word in and said, "can I pay you and how much?" "What did the missus say" says he. " Fifty five pounds " I replied but that was a long time ago. "Have you had a good night" he enquired. "Give me what you think". So I had a think and gave him seventy pounds. He never counted it, spit on it, put it in his top pocket, we shook hands all round, and he was soon on his way back to the "Salt Mines of Cheshire" – his words. What a night, what an atmosphere what a man – and the records never did turn up. Also nothing was ever said by the few that walked out, but I would be careful who I booked for a church fund raiser in the future.

On the domestic front life was about the same really, lots of work which I did enjoy.

Valerie and Jim were living in Wolston and son Adam was eleven years of age in 1984, we visited now and again, perhaps not as often as I/we ought. We did miss out on seeing our grandson growing up – and – one cannot put the clock back. Robert was making metal up and over doors in Warwick, we did not see a lot of him really, which is perhaps the norm for parents and offspring today. My father and I were good mates, I would do anything to be in his company. In the garden, playing cards in younger days, walks on a Sunday evening, haymaking and harvest – helping local farmers. John Davies, later, son Trevor, also Jack (John) Dawson. And later on down to the The Bear Inn at Berkswell for a pint or two, mild ale was the working mans drink then, one only had bitter beer if one was in the smoke room with perhaps ones better off friends, no darts or dominoes in the "smoke" either.

Jenifer married to Alan and living by now in a tiny little house in Wellesbourne, just right for two plus their cat "Bonzo", with a name like that is it surprising that their pussy cat was a bit anti-social.

Olive still a "dinner lady" at Balsall Street School, and me as busy as ever. One or two interesting jobs coming my way. The residents of Elmwood Close required 4 trees digging out – roots and all. Two cherries and two weeping willows. They were well over 25 years old and I set about them with an axe and a shovel, plus a mattock and saw. The first three were no problem falling as planned, the last one a biggish willow was presenting small problems, I always left all the branches on as this weight helped the tree to fall often breaking the last few roots. With this one a rope was fixed up the tree and tied to my V.W. truck, and the strain was taken up, but this tree refused to fall – rocking about very well, but? The end property quite close by, had an entry next to the tree which had a hard perspex roof, eventually the tree fell – not quite where intended. As it fell the many thin whispy branches "rattled" along that corrugated roof, no damage was done, but the lady of the house wondered what the din was and I was not a very popular "Johnnie".

Later on a lady, living in Knowle, called me in, and I duly called round, the lady lived alone and was very business like and straight to the point, so much so that I was given the work and set about it with a will and we got on very well. She was a keen and knowledgeable gardener, and made me aware that she was in charge and would not be intimidated, not that I wanted to take over or do other than what she wanted. All went well and towards the end of the job Mrs S came to me and said "John, you may think I am completely mad, but I am looking for another house to live in, if I am successful would you be interested in laying out the garden". My reply was "Yes of course, providing estimates are acceptable and so on".

Some eighteen months or more went by and one day there was a very excited lady on the phone "I've found it, I've found it, my house, will you come and have a look". No name or anything but I did recognise the voice.

An appointment was made and I toddled off to Solihull, we viewed the garden from all angles, even upstairs. I think my client had been waiting for the previous owner to leave – or die, I think she died. The garden had not been touched for over seven years, it might have made Alan Tichmarsh, Tommy Walsh and Charlie Dimmock of the T.V. programme "Ground Force" scratch their heads a little. A plan was put into operation, the job would be undertaken in stages, which would suit me fine, not being tied to one job for too long. An area was cleared to begin with to make a holding area for plants from the garden in Knowle. A block drive and side borders at the front was the first major job. Paver blocks were just becoming popular at the time, and it did cause a lot of interest for the neighbours and locals. The rear garden was to my clients design, I think a long standing ambition was being fulfilled in this project. I did have a little input here and there and I really did enjoy this job, although some of it was quite a challenge, not least digging out a large laurel bush which covered a big area of garden, some of the branches were nine inches think. There was/is a border all the way round the garden, and the planting represents the rainbow starting with dark colours on the left and working round in a clockwise direction. Not long before the garden was completed, my client came down the garden and said "John I have been thinking, it is time you called me Elisabeth, not Bet or Betty – Elisabeth". It was very difficult for me at first, but soon got used to the idea. Some time later on Olive and I were privileged to receive an invitation to lunch, a house warming for all her friends. We were pleased to attend, it was very interesting to wander round the garden glass in hand and hear the comments about the garden. Also it is very nice that we have all remained good friends ever since.

Another job in Kenilworth, was to replace a boundary fence, I could write a book about boundaries fences and neighbours, but there were no problems here. The man backing on knew all about the work and was quite happy, I made a start and this fellow came along and passed the time of day, he was reassured that any mess would be cleared up "OK mate" he said. It did cross my mind that this man looked familiar to me, but dismissed the thought and got on with the job. In the afternoon I was enjoying a cup of tea when this fellow returned home from collecting his newspaper. He stopped and spoke asking if I was from Kenilworth "no" said I, "I'm from Berkswell". "Blow me" says he "I was born in Berkswell or rather just up the road out of the village". Then I "twigged it" and said "Yes mate I was born in the same house as you", "Blimey, how do you make that out?" "Well" says I, "You are Bill Webb? Correct"? "Well yes" was the reply. Well I am John Webb, Alberts son". There followed quite a chat, Bill got me that job on Meriden Golf Coarse in 1947 getting on for forty years ago. Bill it seemed had a little problem with angina, which he said " was under control". I met his wife Jean, a charming little Welsh lady, who made a fuss of me. Come on in and tell me something about the Webb family. "Thinks hey up, watch it John – boyo", Bills life had been full of happenings is perhaps the best description. I do not think the family knew the full story, after all it was none of their/my business. He came from "under the gooseberry bush" – or probably the blankets, son of one of my spinster aunts. We always knew him as Uncle Bill and did not like it many many years later when some of his cousins addressed him as "cousin Bill". He was brought up by his granny – my father's mother who I never knew. Around about 1933 or 4 he married and shared a cottage with an elderly gentleman at Four Oaks Berkswell, his wife was a very attractive and nice person. Bill had a B.S.A. motorbike and side-car – his pride and joy, sometimes on a Sunday morning my father, sister, Stella and I would call on Bill and would take us for a short spin. That was really something to brag about next day at school. Bill I am sure (almost) was in the Warwickshire Yeomanry before the war and was called up immediately war broke out and soon found himself in France, at the time of Dunkirk he must have looked after "No. 1" – my own assumption. He got back to England I understand, some other way, not via Dunkirk. A little man in stature, but I imagine well able to "look after himself, and I would think relish a bit of a scrap against "Jerry" (The Germans). Wriggling in and out of scrapes. He volunteered and re-mustered in the Airborne Division, a glider pilot I was told —but not by him. He went back to France "by air" this time at the time of Arnhem, not sure where. He survived the war, but his marriage fell apart, then he either lived with or married a person from Meriden, that was when he got me the job on the golf course in 1947. Then I left to do my national service and saw very little of him from there on.

We would all meet up at family funerals, which he always attended. Promising all and sundry that we must meet up now and again, but we never did. Probably in common with lots of other families. It was years before I heard of Bill again. About 1985 I decided to go for swimming lessons, to Warwick University, where they had a pool at the students residences between Westwood Heath Road and Charter Avenue – it was once the teachers training college years before for young lady students. There being no facilities for swimming in Berkswell even now. The baths in Coventry were both bombed, the nearest place was the river Blythe at Temple Balsall or at Bradnocks Marsh. Even as a teenager I was busy with jobs, "pictures" and dances anyhow – my excuse. However, a chap joined the swimming group and on hearing my name said that he knew a Webb, Bill Webb. And so it turned out to be "our Bill". He worked in a seed shop in Coventry owned by his wife, my swimming mates aunt, I think. He told me Bill lived in Kenilworth but I never followed it up and paid them a visit. Bill died about 1998 and I did go to his funeral at Canley Crematorium and there was only one other Webb there. But, although I understand Bill was not a member of the Royal British Legion or any Old Comrades Association, there were more than 25 members of the R.B.L. present and six standards were carried in memory of him. Gone but not forgotten.

Nine years to retiring age and my trusty old VW one ton pick up was "giving notice to quit" – retiring age. It was impossible to find another, every body hangs on to them. It must have been Ken, my neighbour and good friend who suggested looking at a new F.S.O. Based on the Italian Fiat, and the LADA in particular. I saw a new one in the showroom at Sparkhill Birmingham and decided this 12 cwt pick up would do me fine. It would not carry quite as much as the VW, but one cannot have everything. Let them bring the materials to me thinks I. Cost in 1985 was just £2650-00, on the road. It was a great little worker for me, nice to drive – just enough room for my long legs. It lasted almost until I retired, the body was worn out, it was quite a sad day when I drove it to the scrap yard, the engine was perfect with less than 45,000 miles on the clock.

Yes, and the swimming I really enjoyed, I did get a bronze award but never really mastered the sport, could not co-ordinate my breathing.

All the time travel and holidays are never far from my thoughts, travel brochures and maps hold an attraction for me and it was in 1987 we were all booked up to go to the Marbella area of Spain, then within about 10 days of departure we were told there was a double booking – ours, would we care to choose another hotel. I wanted a hotel with a heated indoor pool, to improve my swimming, they could not supply so we had all our money back, but no holiday. Some days later I walked in from work and said to Olive I fancied another holiday in the Rhineland area of Germany. She was reading the *Evening Telegraph* and said "What about this then?" It was an advert for a boat cruise on the Rhine and Moselle rivers, one week all found for £200-00. The same amount we would have paid to go to Spain. We booked a basic cabin as the supplement for en-suite was a lot more money, travelling by coach we joined the Dutch owned and operated boat at Koinigswinter near Bonn and discovered we had a nice cabin with all mod cons. The boat had been refurbished since the brochure was printed. It was superb trip visiting Winningen, Cockem, Boppard, Rudesheim, Koblenz where the Moselle flows into the Rhine – Andernach and the Ahr valley by coach to Ahrweiler, a wine growing area producing red wine in particular, and then on to our final destination, Cologne, with a day to spend at the cathedral and in the city. The Dutch crew were superb and were all so obliging and welcoming, we did arrive at the ship very late, owing to lack of transport at Calais, but that did not make any difference, dinner was served as usual. Would that happen here? I wonder. It was a lovely holiday made all the more enjoyable as we were taken out for the day by Walter and Irene from Assmannshausen while the ship spent the day at Rudesheim. We toured round various vineyards and wine cellars with Walter, he, meeting up with his friends and always there was wine to taste. Walter being a wine master, eats drinks and sleeps wine, it always seems to be the subject for discussion. We arrived back at Walter's vineyard and home and Irene had prepared a superb meal during which I am sorry to say I passed out, I soon came round again apparently. It scared them quite a bit and Olive as well, and I felt awful about what had happened. As I say all was soon well, and all too soon Walter was taking us back to the ship, I asked him if he had ever been on board any of these cruise ships, and he said he never had. He had lived over 60 years by the side of the Rhine and had only been on the ferries. Before disembarking I had enquired about bringing our friends on board and the purser said "Of course". So Walter came on board and found the bar where it was drinks all round "on the boat" as they say. That did round off a very memorable day for more reasons than one. Never did find out the cause of my faint, everybody blames the wine – except me.

Back on the domestic side of life we were to discover events were not so good with Jenifer and Alan, a marriage that I would have backed to last for ever. Their marriage had been rocky for over six months before we were aware of anything wrong, yes – Jenny would come home alone and make excuses for Alan, I knew he never did like coming here anyhow, he had 8 or 9 guitars and although he did not read music was "mad on" the pop scene. He was part of a band called "3 and a bit", i.e. three instruments and Lyn – "the bit" singing, we did go to one or two of the gigs they were playing and I thought noisy but not bad. Some of the "tunes" were just B....awful. But who's judging who? However, it is a long long story and they finally split up, in my opinion Alan had been "spoilt", he only had to ask or probably whinge for something and he was given whatever he wanted. It is only fair to say we never did hear his side of the story, so cannot lay all the blame at his feet. He was a bit immature perhaps, also somewhat irresponsible, although his parents – who we were very fond of and got on well with – from the word go were very generous to Jenifer and Alan when they married providing all sorts of things for their new home, even her car when she had a re-placement. At their parting, they were in debt, Alan had credit cards for all sorts of things and spent money very freely. In the end he said to Jenny that if she took on the debts, he only wanted his personal things. That is when Jenny told us what had happened. She accepted the ultimatum and Alan kept his word on the matter. I think his parents laid the law down on that one. Alan's mother Barbara (Babs) suffered terribly with arthritis, it was everywhere in her body, she had problems walking, sitting and sleeping, but a very determined lady indeed. Roy had a good job and they had help in their lovely bungalow at Alderminster near Stratford, where we were invited from time to time, they also came to visit us occasionally. We never called in unannounced, always phoning first. Babs and Roy never took sides after the split and tried to help Jenny if they could, but she would accept no help from us or anyone, I was allowed to do a few jobs for her though. Although she was working full time she took an evening and/or weekend job. At a pub in Wellesbourne that had been completely refurbished and they were looking for staff, Jenny applied and was taken on and fitted in very well. Being fully qualified in all departments of catering she could and did anything called upon to do, even training new staff. How she managed I am not sure, the house was very small, and there was nothing to worry about, also I would imagine it was good therapy, taking her thoughts off the events – and she did enjoy the work and company. Eventually her finances were on an even keel thanks to her bank manager and building society.

It was not long afterwards that Babs health went from bad to worse, cancer was diagnosed which she fought with courage and great determination. She was given a life expectancy, which in the end was very accurate, she wanted to, and did stay at home for her last days —after a short time in hospital. We were due to go on holiday to Kirchberg in Austria and went to see her at home, I have never witnessed anything quite like that visit before or since. She had a device fitted for self injection when the pain became unbearable – morphine I assume. We were shown into her room by Roy and there sat up in bed was Babs, looking like "a million dollars", she was a nice looking lady, I thought so anyhow. Time was spent chatting, Joking and so on, tea and cakes just like a tea party – well it was. Jenifer was wonderful to her mother-in-law, Babs wanted Jenifer to sort out all her possessions, which she did, a brave act by the pair of them, and also for "poor old Roy" who could only stand by doing all he could to help. Babs died soon after just a few days before we were due to go on holiday, we did wonder what to do but Roy insisted on us going away, there was nothing we could do anyhow. We were told that Jenifer was "a tower of strength" at Bab's funeral, she was the only one Roy wanted to be with. At the time of the funeral Olive and I were way up a mountain and were able to spend a few minutes in peace and quiet, remembering a very brave lady indeed. Roy retired from his work about this time and naturally was very much "at a loose end", he took holidays to all sorts of places, this is what they had planned before Babs died. The following year Jenny, Olive and I went with Roy to Holland, and in particular the bulb fields at Keukenhof. Our fellow passengers (coach) could not fathom us out, one young lady and three more senior – I was some way off being an O.A.P. There was also two Webbs and two Maslens. We had one courier that we had met before in Germany, mad as a hatter, in a nice way of course. We had a dance in the hotel one night and Jenny was quite popular and this guy asked her who she was sleeping with that night. We "strung them all along" for quite a while, till someone asked point blank who was who. Roy was with us on my birthday in March and was planning a holiday to the south of France with his sister-in-law and brother-in-law and said he may have a problem as one of them may not get time off work. Rather rashly I said "Never mind, if they cannot make it we will come instead" This is what happened, Roy knew someone with an apartment at Frejus in France between San Tropez and Cannes and he made all the arrangements. We set off in his big 3.5 Rover automatic to catch the overnight ferry to Le Havre all O.K. except it was packed with fans going to the Le Mans 24 hour road race. We came off the ferry soon after six a.m. and were soon eating up the miles, or kilometres. Cutting this tale short we arrived at Frejus at about 8.30 p.m. after doing well over 600 miles, a bit tired, but a lay in next morning put that right. We had a superb holiday, Roy knew how the French "did it" which made things easy for Olive and me. We had a week in the apartment, which was very tiny, but adequate – just. We then set off for the Savoy area taking in Monte Carlo where it poured with rain all day. To Grasse and by passing Grenoble to Gap and Annecy then a more or less direct route back to Le Harve. Another experience and great trip.

Since those days sadly Roy's memory has gone almost completely and he has moved away so we hear nothing of him nowadays. Another holiday to Austria in September concluded our holiday activities for 1988. Eleven of us went to Mayrhofen this time a holiday resort at the end of the Ziller valley, it is impossible to go further south except on foot, which we did. A magical place with hikes for all abilities. Four narrow roads go on just like fingers on ones hand, all dead ends, ending high in the mountains. The left hand road goes off to Brandberg and on some miles to a reservoir. The Ziller river accompanies one all the way rising in the mountains beyond. We never did make that reservoir. The next road goes up to the Stillup valley and the Speicher reservoir. The third "finger" took us to the Schlegies reservoir and if one wished a hike through the mountain to the Italian border about 5 miles away. I have done that one twice the second time it was snowing hard but, strangely, not cold. Just over the border there is a big stone built mountain hut where one can stay the night or get fortified on soup, hot meals – and beer, I chose the soup and beer. Perhaps not all that wise as there were no bushes on the way back, the odd big rock did solve a problem for some of us – more than once.

There were lots of marvellous walks in that valley, another one took us to the Berlinner Hut. Built like a fortress before the 2nd World War, all the usual facilities for hikers and no one is ever turned away regardless as to how many people are already there. A hard slog to get there. Olive made it once, never again she said afterwards. All the reservoirs are to make power for the country, a good percentage is sold to the Czech Republic I was told. That is how the roads came to be constructed in the first place. The final route takes one to Hintertux where one can ski all the year round, we have not tried that yet – skiing I mean. Just beyond Mayrhofen, is the mountain village of Finkenberg where tourism first began in that area. A man named Hards I think from Solihull visited the area and started tours to the area. Sadly Mr Hards must have had "hard" times as the business closed. A lovely place everything guaranteed – except the weather, anything can happen and sometimes it does, but it will not put me off going again!

My good friend and neighbour Ken Allen managed to take early retirement about this time, he lives just "two doors" away and over the years he has been a great help to me, a first class engineer he can make anything and repair anything. We could visit each other down the garden by using the end of the garden in between us, with permission from the householder naturally. I would often be working away and he would creep up behind and make me almost jump out of my skin, a trick we still play on one another, given the chance. His sense of humour fits in with mine and we have had many a laugh. Ken likes to be kept busy, and always is, and on retirement found plenty of jobs to do around house and home, then one day I think he enquired as to whether I needed any help with my work, he being quite a keen gardener. I thought another pair of hands now and again would come in handy, so a "deal" was struck. Ken would turn out and help to suit us both. If I did not want help he stayed away and if he wished to go out for the day, so be it O.K. It all worked very well indeed and those arrangements carried on until I "called it a day" five or six years later. It was much better for me because I had always worked late in the afternoon, the idea was that wherever I was working I would be home for six p.m. Ken had only worked till five p.m. and so we "knocked off" at five, quite a luxury for me, a habit I kept up thereafter. We both enjoyed working together, it was poles apart from what he had been used to, no white coats and staff canteen on my job. It was no doubt a bit of an eye opener for Ken especially when we were working shall we say on the bigger properties to find that people in big houses were just as friendly as his work mates were. I was so fortunate to work for so many kind and considerate clients, quite a few remain good friends till now. Even now Ken still helps me and my ex clients from time to time. Occasionally we three go out for a pub lunch. A retired gentleman's luncheon, it is most enjoyable indeed.

One January Ken and I were having our "picnic" sandwich lunch and he produced two rather large pieces of Christmas cake, his sister Pam always makes him a cake for Christmas because he is the only one in his family that likes it. Pam is a superb cook and this cake and quite a few other pieces went down very well from time to time. Some time much later on Olive and I were at a party of another of Ken's sisters – there were five girls in the family, four at the party, and we all sat out on the lawn and the conversation turned to cakes, me with the big mouth started on about Pam's Christmas cakes, where I had sampled it, how good it was, rambling on non stop. I did not hear but Pam was wishing that Johnny Webb would shut up. It appears that the other sisters did not get a cake at all and two of them in particular were a little bit peeved. More about those cakes to come in the future.

CHAPTER 25

More About Ernest

Olive and I still went up to Yorkshire now and again to Cragg where her sister lived, they dearly wanted to come back to Berkswell for their last days, but it was just impossible. Charles died first and Ernest, who lived with them since he was about fourteen, looked after the holding as best he could. There were only a few sheep anyhow, and I think a neighbour had a part as grazing land. Ernest had an old tractor which he did a few odd jobs with – when it was running that is. A mechanic down the track would do a few repairs now and again, lots of people were very good to Vi (Olive's sister) and Ernest although no one in the village had ever spoken or seen her (Vi). He did the shopping on the tractor and sometimes in the winter it was the only way he could get down the track and on to the road, three quarters of a mile away through the snow. A few years after Charles' death Vi became ill and was taken to hospital in Halifax, this was the first time Vi had been off the premises for twenty one years, in the meanwhile electricity had been installed and mains water laid on, even a bath put in. On one visit Olive's sister Ida went with us and told Ernest he would be alright for a bath now. His reply was that he didn't think he would be "getting in there very often", still is his broad Warwickshire (county) accent, at least it was not full of coal.

When Vi died we were on holiday at our friends house in Sedburgh, Cumbria, the news came to us via a neighbour there. Next day we went down to Cragg having arranged to meet Ida from the train later on. We saw the undertaker who made all the arrangements for the funeral. There was a little café down the road and we had visited quite a few times on our visits, getting to know Doris the proprietor quite well. Usually Ernest was with us. When he was not with us around the village no direct questions were ever asked but people we spoke to were always keen to find out about

Celebrating with our good friends Freda and Lionel Holtom

Ernest. Where did he come from? etc. also any information about Vi who no one had met or even seen. We did not know the answer regarding Ernest but no one seemed to believe we were not even related – to the best of our knowledge he certainly was not Vi's son. But whose? It was none of our business anyhow. It was quite surprising how many people attended the funeral service, were they being nosey? Forgive me for saying that and I am sure the answer is NO Doris provided refreshments for everyone and flatly refused any payment for her work. The people we met in Cragg were, on the whole friendly to us and kind to Ernest. Although he could not read or write he stayed at Turley Holes Farm. Vi was very wise in more ways than one, all three of them had lived a very spartan life, not having what we call "proper" meals, and managing with no mod cons. Vi did have a little radio set, her only contact – seemingly – with the outside world. She knew what was going on and in some ways quite "with it". Sometime before her death Vi had had the tenancy of the property transferred into Ernest's name, he was the sitting tenant. She also changed his birth certificate which Ernest did show us, presumably to save him any embarrassment in the future. Ernest had always "fallen out" with folks at the pub but often it was soon all over and he "fell in" again. People accepted him for what he was. Certainly NOT the village idiot, but perhaps a rough and ready character more to be pitied than blamed, always willing to accept a pint at the pub – and totally honest.

He did get cheated a few times, the drive up to the farm was fearful, steep with loose pebbles, etc. all the way. The stones would rattle round the wings above the car wheels making an awful clatter even driving slowly. One day Ernest had the "tarmac boys" in, he had no money so they agreed to do a small area of drive at the entrance to the farm yard in exchange for some sheep. They went off with their lambs and left Ernest with two strips of unrolled tarmac, he was powerless. A few years later the owners decided to sell. An inquisitive person explored the possibilities regarding purchase of the property. However, a man came to Ernest – the tenant – with a proposition i.e. "let me buy the place FOR you Ernest, then I will do the house up to live in, and you will have an adjoining self contained place for yourself." Ernest had known this guy for sometime and had done a few jobs for him, with his tractor, haymaking, etc. This fellow – lets call him Bill – that was his name anyhow, contacted us to say that Ernest was in full agreement, also he would like Olive and I to go to witness the signing of the documents. Eventually this we did, and all seemed above board, although we did not read any small print. We were not related to Ernest or even his next of kin, so really we did not feel like checking out the pros and cons. As it turned out basically everything was above board. Fairly soon Bill moved two caravans onto the farm, one for him and one for Ernest, he was quite cosy in fact, but we did wonder how he would fare in the winter, I bet it is a bit bleak there. It could be made into a lovely place with moor land and woods all around. Work began on the house and Bill moved in, Ernest then occupied Bills more spacious and better equipped van. No sign of anything being done for Ernest. In fact he was the one destined to be "done". Quite a while later on, one November day, Ernest received notice to quit from Bill, and was naturally worried stiff. He made one or two enquiries, the D.S.S., etc. and was getting no joy then he phoned us. I made a couple of calls and the Citizens Advice Bureau was mentioned and I was given the CAB phone number at Hebden Bridge. We made contact with Ernest and told him to visit the CAB office next, this he promised to do. I phoned their office next day and he had already been. We thought it best to go and try and help, which we did, they took the steam out of events and told him to try not to worry. The CAB were wonderful. Conveniently – for some – no one could find copies of the agreement, Ernest never had a copy, and no one could recall the name of the solicitor in Rochdale. Was I negligent? A question I have asked myself more than once. However, Ernest was scared of Bill and the sensible thing to do was leave the farm. He was re-housed in a suitable flat in Todmordon, some miles from Cragg. We did go and see him there and he was clean and shaven, some furniture had been provided and he had a television set. He really was "in clover", a new man, he must have had some tuition from someone. He kept his place clean, was taught how to shop for essentials, even a little basic cooking, he was also better dressed, hardly knew him in fact. But, he did miss the folks of Cragg and he was minus his dog. He had also been advised and encouraged to quit the pub, more to the point the beer. He had a stomach ulcer I think, not surprising – perhaps considering the eating habits and diet of the past

Ernest also suffered with arthritis, one leg and one knee. He did miss his pals and kept badgering the authorities regarding a move back to the Cragg Vale area, he was more than a bit aggressive from time to time I was told, but eventually he moved back to Mytholmroyd (Royd for short) A small one bedroom flat in a complex for people that had no other place to go, it is a very nice little pad, warden controlled. The residents are checked every morning, I think they have to be up and dressed by 9 a.m. Thank fully he is very happy there, all his needs have been supplied. Bus fares for seniors are only 10p I think and he can go to Halifax market or more or less where his fancy takes him.

The CAB were quite willing to take on Bill in the courts, in the meantime Ernest had recalled the solicitors name, but in the end, with the exception of Ernest, who was not consulted, it was decided not to proceed. The main points being Ernest was happy and being well looked after, also if a court case was won (paid for by the state I presume) it would cause more hassle in the future for Ernest. So Bill got away with it, but as far as Ernest is concerned, all is well. At the time of writing, he is still there in residence. He came down to Berkswell and stayed with us for a few days in 2000 fulfilling a burning desire to visit Berkswell again. It was incredible, he left here around about 1942/3 and as I took him around he knew who lived in every house at that time, also the shopkeeper, post office proprietor, landlord at The Bear Inn, etc., although he was only 12 or 13 years old. It was hard work having him, I had a job to read the newspaper or watch the news without an interruption from time to time. I must be thankful though – and I am. For there but for the grace of God there go I.

Berkswell Hall and Estate was purchased by Mr Joshua Hirst Wheatley in 1888. The estate, at the time, comprised of most of Berkswell parish.

Mr and Mrs Wheatleys son Charles Joshua Hirst took over the hall and estate in 1925 until his death in 1943. There after the estate was managed by trustees with agents overseeing the business of the estate. Mrs Wheatley continued to live at the hall until she became unwell. Her last days were spent in a nursing home in Wiltshire. Mrs Wheatley took a great interest in the parish and in particular the church. Her daughter Ann was patron of the living and lived in Wiltshire.

There were a lot of concerned people about. What would happen to the parish, the village and so on. Thank fully little has changed in the appearance of the area, but in common with everywhere else the whole way of life has changed – no need to dwell on that one. We are very fortunate that the village is a conservation area, we still have our church and peaceful churchyard, the stroll to the lake or Hampton in Arden, for those with the energy. The village green, stocks, wishing well, Reading Room (village hall) and the Bear Inn are all still very much intact and there for everyone to enjoy.

Before the hall was sold for conversion into flats or apartments there was a two day sale of the contents of the house and gardens, etc. It caused quite a stir in the area, and further afield. Southerbys I think, conducted the two day sale with security guards present some time before the sale. Lots of items came out of cupboards that had not seen the light of day since the early days of the war, when lavish entertaining came to an end – at Berkswell anyhow. It was, I understand, a very good sale – from the sellers point of view, it would have been nice to go to the preview but like lots of other occasions work had to come first.

The conversion I think was done very well, I had the opportunity to quote for landscaping there, but I could not complete the work by the builders deadline, so I had to opt out. Over a period of time the whole of the hall and stables, garages and other out-buildings were all converted into dwellings. The old stables, now the mews, looks very nice and would be my choice if we decided to live there, but we are not going anyhow. Mrs Wheatley had a housekeeper to "do" for her and probably some one to assist with cleaning. The lady in question really did look after Mrs Wheatley and lived with her now retired husband in the old laundry, which is situated way behind the hall all on its own – through the spinney and over a brook. A delightful bungalow with the old laundry attached. Mrs Wheatley arranged for this couple to have the right to live there for their remaining years. The old laundry itself is still as it was when the last washing was done there, the coppers, drying racks, special high sash windows, flat irons the lot. I did have the pleasure of a visit when a man who lived there visited Berkswell for a scouts reunion in 1991.

Mrs Wheatley's housekeeper has now died, but her widower still lives there with the pheasants and all sorts of other wildlife., the only problem is they do not mix with keen gardeners. I do wonder what will happen to the laundry when the occupier passes away or decides to leave. Hopefully Mrs Wheatley sorted that out as well, she was a very business like and well organised person. The Wheatley family had their own burial plot in the churchyard at Berkswell – she was the last "Wheatley" to be interred there, and she arranged for the Woolley family to have the use of the remaining burial plots, a very nice gesture to one that had looked after her so well over many years.

CHAPTER 26

The Games People Play

Olive and I do not go out a great deal, quite a few occasions it is out to supper to members of our holiday group, from time to time, we have a "return match" here at home. We try the local "pub grub" now and again, always happy to sus-out a new venue.

Then someone mentioned the Pudding Club. Well we must look into and investigate this one. Somebody knew someone that had been, held at the "Three Ways Hotel" Mickleton, between Stratford and Evesham – roughly. We got a party together, booked and went along. There is a reception with wine, elderflower when we went, then we all sat down to a basic – not too big – first course, a roast, probably 80 to 100 people. Then they parade the puddings – chefs and other staff, eight or nine old fashioned puds are brought in with great ceremony. People – guests are served, spotted dick, roly-poly pudding, sticky toffee and so on, table by table. Then they go round a second time. After that is if "free for all", all the sauces and custard is available as one wishes. Our hostess for the evening advised us all to drink lots of water – the very thought, rughh -. The advice was taken as water is supposed to alleviate any "full up" feeling and flatulence. I sampled all of the puddings and the good advice worked – for me anyhow. We thought we might do that again sometime – never made it so far, must try harder. Lionel once tried to book, but could not make it, and it was a long time afterwards when he phoned and said he could book The Pudding Club on the 12th March, the day of my 60th birthday. A crowd of us were going out to Sunday lunch next day, but I thought why not, left it to Lionel, who I could trust with my very life. He would book and pick us up and take us, an arrangement often made. 7.30 p.m. 12th March. We were to pick up Innes from Four Oaks was well.

Nearer the time I thought about it – 7.30 ? Spoke to Lionel and queried as to whether we would get to Mickleton in time, he assured me we would be alright and it was left at that. Lionel is NEVER late anyhow. Comes the day comes 7.30. No Lionel, Olive and I sat waiting and just said "I wonder if there is any jiggery pokery going on", as it was my birthday, and in the next breath had forgotten it, well, anything COULD have happened.

It was 7.40 when they arrived, no comments at all. We set off to collect Innes, going through the village there were a lot of cars parked, oh good, thought I, there was a music concert in church and what a good crowd, thought I. Then the Reading Room came into view and the Bablake Wine Lodge van was parked outside. Thinks me, someone is having a "do" at the Reading Room and I did not know about it, where upon Lionel drove into the Reading Room and said "No pudding club tonight John we are going here instead," before one could say or have time to think, we were inside the room and only the stage was lit up. I was being pulled and shoved up onto the stage. My sister Margaret was up there, but it was not until I heard the strains of the "This is your life" signature tune that it tumbled to me what was going on. They had really pulled the stops out for "little me". Innes was representing our phantom destination, the pudding club, with two cushions inside her dress. Ray, my army pal and his wife, Marcelene came, also Jim and Pam Thompson from Colwyn Bay. Others said nice things about me – all true naturally and perhaps I should have been more modest, but lapped it up. There was no time to think about what to say or anything in fact – and – I had no idea who was sitting out there in the darkness. All was well and it was an evening where even now, 12 years on, everything about it is still crystal clear. I never did find out all the details about who did what. The initial idea came I am sure, from sister Margaret, backed up by Freda and Lionel and A.N. Other.

One night previous to the party the phone rang and it was Lionel "Oh" he said, "can I order half a yard of gravel". I was surprised knowing his garden and enquired "what for". He was going to make a path, I did call in and have a look at the idea and could not quite make out his intentions, however, I forgot all about it and his gravel never did turn up. It transpired he wanted to talk to Olive about the party and I "put my foot in it" by answering the phone. The gravel was the first thing that Lionel thought of, I wonder what he would have done had I tipped it on his drive one day. The garden seat which I was told to sit on – with Olive at my side, was a collective gift from quite a few friends, it is still being put to good use in the garden.

I had organised and run a "This is your life" for Jim Thompson when he and Pam departed Berkswell for Colwyn Bay in 1981, so mine was probably a bit of cum-uppance.

Holidays in 1989 took us to Seefeld in Austria and later on in the autumn to Fort William in Scotland.

It was another group holiday to Austria by overnight coach, Edwards a firm from the London area. We joined at Dover and were taken there by

The holiday gang in Seefeld Austria. Back left to right: John, Andy, Lionel, Vi, Michael, Arthur, Bill, Alan and Martin. Front: Innes, Olive, Freda, Kathleen, Marjorie and Rita

mini-bus, the thing rattled and bumped its way there, we were glad to get out and wave it on its way. The holiday was good and during the two weeks we walked miles. Seefeld is one of our favourite locations, but there are plenty more to try out in the future, our favourite cake and pastry shop was on the ground floor of the hotel, we were always spoilt for choice, but never disappointed.

I am sure we have walked all the paths from Seefeld that one can explore from our base in a day, north east, south and west, we often used the Postbus, taking us or bringing us back from further afield. At Seefeld there is a funicular railway taking one high into the mountains, used by the skiers in the winter. From there we walked out on a narrow path gently rising, Michael and I were the first of our group to get to the top of Reitherspitz mountains. One day, we got a to a point where there was a sort of cross over area between two mountains, and the next part of the route was up a wide and long ladder, fortunately it was fixed to the face of the mountain, so it was not too difficult for me, we had haversacks on and I do not like heights, all was well, but the route to the top from then on was hard to follow and tough. In the end Michael made a straight bee-line for the top and although I did not approve of the idea really had no choice, but to follow. There were a few hairy moments for me when I ran out of rocks to get hold of – turfy peat tends to come away in ones hands. "opps a daisy." Having made the summit we could see our lunch stop, a mountain hut perhaps three-quarters of a mile away in the direction of "down", another session of scrambling to get there.

It was fairly cold up there, as we walked in to the hut where there were a good number of "mountain walkers". These folks – including women – climb into the mountains and spend the whole time walking/hiking from hut to hut including overnight accommodation. Michael walked in wearing shorts, which I am sure caused a buzz of conversation in German or what-ever. They were all wearing big jumpers, lederhosen, thick socks and big boots. A friendly lot and I know why, they had obviously eaten as there was no room on the rough and rustic tables with benches to match – no chairs. The tables were full of empty beer bottles and a good time being had by all. The menu is basic, lots of soup, usually pea, goulash with big hard dumplings and the like, they are probably ex army cooks in those huts. However, we did not want a lot, it had all got to be carried back to Seefeld and we were walking all the way back. It was definitely a shorter walk the next day. We caught the post-bus more than once and went to a district called Leutash and walked to lots of mountain huts from there. One day we had trout and new potatoes for lunch all "swimming" in hot melted but-ter, the trout had been grilled by the way. One day Olive and I came upon a pond close the side of the road – full of trout, they were swimming. Lovely clear and clean water fed by a small stream, how long I wonder would they survive in these parts, sad is it not? A great temptation, there I would imag-ine for some. When in Seefeld we always go back to the Habhof Hotel at Mosern for lunch or perhaps tea and cake in the afternoon, although we know no one there. The usual standard is still the same. Ref: Our first stay in Austria in 1980.

Innsbruck is only about fifteen miles or so away in the direction of down, probably a descent of over 3000 ft. Public transport to Innsbruck is by train, a lovely little journey in and out of tunnels with sheer cliffs on one side and a sheer drop on the other side. An interesting city – the capi-tal of the Tyrol with its royal palace and gardens, green water of the river Inn. The Golden Roof in the old part of "town", also the famous Olympic ski jump which one can walk around. It is interesting that at the point the ski jumpers take to the air is a super view of the cemetery straight in front of them. Seefeld one of our favourites.

A late holiday at the end of October to Fort William was another trip that year. Harry Shaw of Coventry supplied the holiday, we provided the money, not a lot as it was, I think a half term "cheapy". Superb value stay-ing at the Alexandra Hotel right in town. A trip out every day and as the weather was not very good it was a blessing. We travelled miles and miles, Inverness in the east Malaig via "The road to the isles" in the west.

The best for me was on our drivers rest day, there was an excursion offered by Colin, a Yorkshire man, and his battered old Mercedes coach – as we discovered later on. A half day trip £3.00 (1989). He picked us up from the hotel at 10.00 and off we went up the north side of the Caledonian Canal along narrow roads with hedges and bushes flicking the sides of the coach as we went along. I should say we had quite a surprise when Colin and his coach arrived, just a little scratched and a few minor dents here and there. Colin was resplendent in full Scottish dress, kilt, jacket and a dirk in his natty socks. The interior of the coach was spotless and very comfortable indeed, it transpires that Colin was a great asset to the town and was highly thought of and respected.

We journeyed quite a distance although it was slow going on the narrow and twisting road ending up at Achnacarry where a laird resided in a grand grey fortress looking place, close by was a small but interesting museum to one of the Scottish regiments. (I think the Seaforth Highlanders) miles from anywhere, I would like to go back. It was the area where the Commandoes did a lot of their World War II training way out in the wilds, I bet some of those guys wondered what they had let themselves in for. Colin was very informative and humorous with it. We arrived back in Fort William and were deposited at a huge shopping complex and, thought I, is this it? Do we have to walk the rest of the way, has the bus had enough. No way, Colin said be back on the coach at whatever time, we are off to Glen Nevis later on.

We were glad to be able to get something to eat and drink, our first since breakfast. We were not on the point of starvation, perhaps a drink was more important. The meals at the hotel were super, breakfast was hot and cold help yourself, there was no excuse for not having enough to eat. The evening dinner was just the same ample helpings and a choice.

CHAPTER 27

More Work, Clients
and Problems

Work wise I was always very busy, thank goodness, I like to think my clients were well looked after and with just a few exceptions they looked after me.

Holly wreaths still featured at Christmas time, outside work came to a halt early in December, no longer was the midnight oil being burnt, but I was often at work at 5 a.m. in the mornings. The garage was my workshop and it was cold in there. From time to time, it was possible for me to keep warm with an electric fire immediately at my rear, where I stood or sat, it was all down to a "fine art" now, although work was a little slower sitting on a bar stool, and with the bench at exactly the right height it was much easier and less tiring. However, I was always glad to finish off the last one, sometimes cutting the delivery time a bit close, probably having to get ready to go to the Christingle service if it was Christmas eve and it often was.

One of my most "difficult" clients was Miss J, a spinster the same age as me, we would often meet up years ago at Mrs Hope's dancing classes, when we were sixteen and "fancy free". Miss J lived on the main road in a tiny cottage – with her mother – near to The White Horse pub and opposite the Heart of England School. They were both very deaf which did not help very much, it was not too difficult as all I did was to cut their hedge and get rid of the hedge cuttings. The old lady died and J retired from her job in Birmingham. As time went on she became totally deaf and more "difficult". Asking Olive, who she met in the village "when is he coming to do my hedge, I always did it in August, trimmed then it only needed one cut per annum. Being deaf she almost shouted when speaking, the whole village knew what she was on about, and the whole village knew Miss J. She sometimes gave me a "torrid time", but always gave me tea and cake twice a day. Everyone including me felt sorry for her, but more than once declared that I would never go there again, especially as one day when, again Olive bumped into J in the village "Huh" she said "I suppose you are spending MY money". And another day I was working in a garden for two other customers and along comes Miss J saying "why had she not had her receipt, you are quick enough to send the bill to me". In actual fact Miss J always insisted on paying me when the work was finished – I never had to send her a bill at all. Everyone felt sorry for Miss J and probably her lonely life, a T.V. and radio not being much help and I did carry on cutting her hedge until she died.

One year I had cut the hedge and had no means of disposing of the clippings. It was all quite dry and I decided to burn the rubbish on a grass area just outside the property. Arriving there on the Saturday morning quite early, I got a bonfire going, the smoke going parallel with the road, no house very close, so all was well – until the wind changed, just as the bonfire really got going, straight across the main road, just like a curtain hanging over the road, to make sure the fire went O.K. I used a "garden firelighter", an old tyre off a mini car. The cars did not even seem to slow down, there is a pedestrian crossing very close, the tyre had got going well and there was no way to put out the bonfire. I did not know what to do, perhaps it was only a few minutes till the smoke thinned out, it seemed like hours. Somebody must have been looking after me as all was well and the remaining rubbish was burnt a bit at a time. Another time, way back when I was helping Don out, he sent me off one Monday morning to roto-vate someone's back garden in Radford, Coventry. It was a very dry time and the sight that greeted me was a really rough garden, wooden panel fence all round and dead weeds four foot tall, and I had to rotovate it all prior to turfing. A bright idea came to me – burn it off. Knocking all the weeds down away from the fences and arming myself with a wet sack just in case I needed a flail fire extinguisher – put a match to it. It went very well and I was well on the way to getting it all burnt, being kept quite busy with my flail – when I was aware of voices quite close, looking up I saw about eight or nine ladies sleeve rolled up and wearing their "pinnies" "Crumbs" – Monday – washing day. They were not happy mummies, how-ever, I got on my knees (almost) and apologised, said I was only a mere man and the smoke would cease forthwith – if not sooner. That part of the job was just about done anyhow. One of the closest encounters with "injury at work" ever.

Over the years I suppose I have been fortunate in being able to dispose of rubbish incurred in my work as a landscape gardener. Hardcore was always in demand by farmers for making good muddy gateways, but some-times getting to the muddy gateway over fields was impossible. When I first started landscaping, in about the early sixties, I had a lot of material from Deeleys, they were builders and stocked sand, gravel, cement, etc. It was easy to drive in load up and be away, they had their own tip, just off

The centre of England: Meriden Green stone cross. Michael, Kathleen, Olive and John with visitors from Australia

the road to Knowle and they gave me permission to tip there, there was seldom a vast amount. It was a bit of a "fag" getting the key to the gate and taking it back again, but I was very grateful – and it was free of charge. When it was beginning to fill up Jim requested that I look for somewhere else to tip.

A visit to the landfill site this side of Coleshill was successful, shall we say there was an agreement between me and the site foreman which worked very well for a long time – until one day I turned up and my mate was on holiday, that was the final visit there. However, the tip closed at 5 p.m. but householders were allowed to tip out of hours outside the gate. This rubbish was taken inside and dumped every morning. "All and sundry" were soon joining in and I did the same, until that eventually came to an end.

I was then given permission to tip on a private estate on condition all the rubbish went into the tip and not on the top. No trouble, any hardcore was used to make a solid track to the edge of the hole and in went the rubbish. All was well until one Christmas Eve – a tarmac contractor was doing a drive for me and started work on the morning of Christmas Eve, he phoned up and said he had my rubbish on the back of his lorry, all the tips were closed, could I help. I was "up to my knees" in holly, and daughter Jenny went with him to show him where the tip was – at least a mile off the road. All was well – I thought, until the farmer told me not to go there again, enquiring why, he told me there was a whole load of rubbish, including over a ton of tarmac deposited on the top of the tip. The offer was made to remove it straight away, I was told it had been done, albeit with great difficulty by one of his men with a tractor. Middle of winter I did not go and check up. Another tipping facility gone, and not my fault. The farmer – who is a good friend spoke his piece, I apologised and explained and we have been the best of friends ever since.

My next tipping site was in Fen End, a bloke I knew had a hole that required filling in. It was not easy to get in, straight off a very narrow road, up a steep bank and a sharp turn to get to the hole. The only way in was in reverse, and sort of a short sharp charge, which was more difficult in wet weather on this site we stacked all the burnable rubbish to one side – Ken was helping me by now. Then when it was dry an hour or two would be spent there with a big bonfire and, show me a bloke that does not enjoy a bonfire. From an early age I could always get a bonfire to burn, easy with a "garden firelighter, it was OK there, no houses at all for some distance. Sometimes the heap would be twenty yards long and 6 feet high and would all be gone in a couple of hours, lighting the fire so that the wind would blow the flames straight through the heap. I tipped there for quite a number of years – again until we were working in Kenilworth clearing a site cutting hedges and so on, getting a site ready for the builders. No fires were allowed and skips would have been expensive, there was a lot of burnable rubbish to dispose of. I had my tip so that was the answer. It was the end of July, very dry everywhere and hot. Ken was ferrying the rubbish and a fair old pile was accumulating, so on one trip he set fire to it and came back for more, not telling me he had fired it – he loves a fire as well. The owner of the hole (my tip) went "bananas" no damage WAS done, but if the fire, unattended, had spread anything could have happened. Another facility gone, and more apologies from me. I had to agree with the reasoning but again, we are still speaking.

About this time a new regulation came into force, one needed a permit to carry trade waste – rubbish, etc. – on the public highway, not to tip. A call at the refuse transfer station – the tip – in Kenilworth to enquire was fruitless, I rang the council house in Warwick, they could not help – try Coventry. Same story, try Solihull, which being in the Borough of did make sense. They had not heard of this new regulation, we will ring back, anyhow, after a while they sent a hand full of forms, fill them in and send us £95.00, then I would be OK for five years.

Back to Kenilworth tip and they said sorry you cannot tip here, but we will make sure, the outcome was that I was given permission to tip on payment of a fee. No problem, it would have to go on my clients account anyhow. That arrangement carried on almost until I retired when all trade rubbish could not be disposed of at Kenilworth, you will have to go to Princes Drive in Leamington. My little F.S.O. truck decided to retire before me and for the last twelve months or so I managed with a trailer behind the car, trailers were allowed, but I took big loads in and got a few "dirty looks" from Paul the site manager, who by now I had got to know quite well. As I have written before, over the years good fortune has been on my side in many many ways, and I will be forever grateful for that. Vic Hicks, who farms just round the corner in Hob Lane, has been a great help to me, he allowed me to store surplus materials in a small area of about 3 yards by 12 yards. Broken slabs for crazy paving, bricks, slabs, stone, sand and gravel, he would never have a penny piece and I am "in his debt" for ever. He did however, have a lot of hardcore over the years. Another amusing little episode. Another paving job in Balsall for our dear friends Freda and Lionel Holtom, again very hot weather, I was working in their back garden and had taken to wearing shorts – not a pretty sight they cry! At the end of the day I decided to put on my trousers over the shorts to go home, just as I did so Lionel came through the back gate, home from his work. "What's this m'lad?" he said. I have never been allowed to forget that one.

CHAPTER 28

Christingle

For quite a few years now Olive and I had been parish secretaries for The Children's Society, a charity that looks after deprived children. Orphans and teenagers, including those on drugs. People around the area have collecting boxes for money and we empty them once a year. In the past we organised sponsored marrow growing, also sunflowers. The charity was originally "The waifs and stray society" under the wing of The Church of England. Another major fundraiser is the Christingle service held at Berkswell at five p.m. on Christmas Eve.

There are two major services in Coventry, one at Holy Trinity church to which Olive would attend, with people from Berkswell C of E School. They took and presented a "purse" of money – as did many more schools.

It was in the late seventies that our rector The Rev. G P W Dingle said he would like to have a Christingle service at Berkswell, at the time we had a crib service at 5 p.m. on Christmas Eve. The idea being that mums could bring their youngsters to a short simple service, then go home and put their little darlings to bed. That idea was probably dreamed up by some old bachelor. However, the first ever service, held in the children's corner – I think that sounds better than the South Aisle – as it is called today, it proved very popular and soon had to be held in the main body of the church.

It was decided to go ahead with a Christingle at the same time on Christmas Eve, guess who had all the work to do. Obtaining oranges, dried fruit, cocktail sticks and red tape. Yes real red tape, also candles, plus putting them together.

The Christingle service originated in eastern Europe from the Moravian church, a Protestant sect. An orange represents the world, the orange is cut at the top and a small candle inserted, this lit is the light of the world – Jesus Christ. A band of red tape – the blood of Christ – is fixed

The Christingle 'factory' at Meriglen. Left to right: Peter Flynn, Bob Thompson, Olive, Mary Goode, Margaret Thompson and Freda with Lionel seated

round the orange (we use red butchers tape from a reel). Four cocktail sticks are stuck into the orange representing the "four corners" of the earth, north, east, south and west. Onto the sticks fruit, nuts or, we use dolly mixture sweets, are pushed, these are the fruits of the earth. All copied by the then Church of England Children's Society as an act of worship and much needed fund raiser.

Our Christingle really took off, and now writing in 2001 – the service is the best attended of the year, one year we had 530 in attendance, that included babes in arms – the lot – all counted by a fellow with a calculator. As a matter of fact, as one responsible, it was quite frightening, what if there was an accident, or whatever? In the event, we were well looked after, my opinion anyhow. Another time we had real problems during a period of flu and bad colds, etc. We had no rector to take the service, he was "missing" throughout the Christmas season, David Clowes, one of our lay readers, stepped into the breach. There were no vergers present, no churchwardens and at three thirty pm we were informed that the organist was not available, no one had notified him regarding the service.

One member of the congregation was Richard Hare, a very talented chap aged about fourteen, he became our very nervous and rather worried organist, very "musical". I suggested he practised hard on the first two lines of all the popular carols to be sung, every one would know the tunes backwards. It is pleasing to record that we had a bumper turn out – despite the flu and it all went very well.

Olive and I have a good team of willing and capable helpers, without them we would have struggled many times. The year that there were 530+ attending the Christingle service there could have been a serious disaster, a lot of people at that service went upstairs into the gallery, at the end of the service we could not open the one and only exit and entry door. The sheer weight of bodies had pushed the ceiling timbers down on to the door, by moving people away from the area above the door it did open.

The gallery was closed forthwith, it was later discovered that the ends of the joists were rotten and it was a major job of work to get it put right. John Redfern, a builder from Balsall Common was given the job. A first

'Her and him' having fun

class man, especially in restorative work and working with ancient timbers.

The opportunity was taken to make the gallery into a meeting room, removing the pews and carpeting the new floor. Curtains were hung to screen off the main body of the church, also a separate heating system. The result was a first class job, being called The Upper Room thereafter.

CHAPTER 29

Australia

For a long time really, I had been thinking about visiting Australia, my elderly aunt of about 90 years was there, cousins Betty, David, Alan and Esther, as well as friends were there as well. There was no response from Olive when I occasionally mentioned the idea, it was after all quite an undertaking, when, how long for, could we afford it, perhaps at the top of the list. Initial enquiries were made, we paid a visit to Carrick Travel In Kenilworth and we came away with a lot of literature – and more to the point no objections or otherwise from Olive. I have always suggested our holiday plans where to go, etc. But nothing so "adventuresome" or foolhardy had been undertaken before, another question that was asked of myself was, do we go now or wait until retiring age in 5 years time. The more I studied the brochures the more convinced I became to go AS SOON AS POSSIBLE.

Olive does not like the weather too hot or too cold so that had to be considered along with many other things, I wrote letters to my cousins with our intentions, not I will add with any intentions to impose or scrounging. Our friend Sydney, the daughter of our one-time midwife and district nurse, lived with her husband Rowan and her mother, who had gone to live with them in Melbourne. Sydney emigrated to Australia in the 1950s with her first husband Harry, we had known them both as they lived locally, but were never really close friends. We would all be at the local dances together, Harry worked in the gardens at "The Moat" after I left, we did go to tea on a Sunday a couple of times and they visited us in our caravan.

It was very sad to learn that Harry died in Australia, not all that long after their arrival, leaving Sydney with 3 young children to look after and "bring up". She could not afford to come home – but "made of the right stuff" persevered and with help from one or two people made a go of it.

So a start was made on planning the trip, various operators offer package deals with various stop-overs and the one decided on was Singapore, Melbourne, Perth, Hong-Kong and home. Jenny phoned one evening to say that Carrick Travel were having an Australian promotion evening at their shop/office in Stratford. We went along and got talking to Mike Carrick and he enquired "did we realise that for another £100.00 per person we could have up to five stop-overs "No", we did not but we went home with yet more literature and more calculating of finances. By now we were receiving replies to letters and discovering more about my cousins and Australia. Sydney invited us to stay with them, her mother and second husband Rowan. Come and stay as long as you like were the instructions, they lived in Greensborough, half an hour on the train north of Melbourne city. Cousin Betty lived some 200 miles south of Melbourne near Mirboo North, almost as far south as one can go in Australia. Her daughter Barbara, lived in south Melbourne and Locksley, at Williamstown, again south of the city right on the edge of Port Phillip Bay. Casandra and her partner Max were in north New South Wales "in the sticks" at Nimbin. I did not know anything at all about any of them really, only snippets gained from David and Esther when they were in England.

Alan, I discovered, had retired early from the police force. He had done very well, leaving school at fourteen he finished his career in the top ten of personnel in The Western Australian Police. He had two grown up offspring, but his wife had died sometime before, suffering from cancer. We were invited to stay with Alan and his lady friend Dorothy for a couple of weeks. They lived in Busselton, some 150 miles south of Perth, not too far from Nannup where they were all brought up as youngsters. David lived in Dianella, a suburb to the north of Perth some 20 minutes on the bus. He had been married twice and parted from his second wife about the time we left home for Australia. Cousin Esther remained a spinster and had a small house (they are mostly bungalows) near where my Aunt Marie lived in another suburb, not far from the city centre. Esther had retired and invited us to stay, but at the time of our visit she had "conveniently" pushed off on holiday. My uncle Harry had died long ago and Aunt Marie was living in Swan Cottages, sheltered accommodation for the elderly. So, with offers of help with accommodation we – or I, decided to go for it. With places to stay in Melbourne and Western Australia it was to ease the financial burden, Esther and David and Aunt Marie had stayed with us a few times in the past, so I did not really feel that we were sponging on anyone. Being quite happy to pay our way. It took me over a year to plan our route, we took up the deal with Carrick Travel which allowed us to stay in any stop-over as long or short as we wished, as long as everything was booked. It would not be a problem to write a whole book on our trip, but here I will just outline our itinerary and a few experiences.

We set off for a three months trip on the 18th August 1990. Our first stop was in Singapore, taken, to our hotel at a fare "rate of knots" by a local driver in a taxi – all in. We stayed there for five busy days of sightseeing, Raffles Hotel was closed for a refurbishment so we never had a gin sling.

On to Cairns, Queensland Australia for a week, where we were to meet cousin David who planned to take us with his wife all the way south to Sydney. David was touring all round Australia in a V.W. camper van, and I could write half a book on that alone. He was there but no wife, we learned much later on that she could not stand him or his camper van anymore and they parted company on the side of the track in the middle of a desert near Broome. W.A. More to the point, we were to stay with David towards the end of the trip.

We saw the Great Barrier reef – or a tiny bit of it. Left me a little bit disappointed, very little colour as one sees on TV. A trip on the Kurunda railway and the Atherton Table Lands also Daintree and Cape Tribulation, where Captain James Cooke was ship-wrecked – and got going again. We made excuses to David and flew on to Brisbane where all that was arranged was a hire car. Our fellow passengers seemed to vanish into thin air and there was no one to meet us, and no car. Enquiries were made and we were soon on our way south towards our friend Barbara and Surfers Paradise. Met up with Barbara, had a nice day in her company, then set off for Nimbin to meet cousin Betty's daughter Cassie and her mate Max. They lived about 10 miles down the track from Nimbin, in the rainforest with their two young daughters, sharing the rainforest – it was "jungle" when I went to school – with lots of snakes, including pythons and plenty of other nasties. Their self-built house was some six feet off the floor on nine poles (3 x 3 in a square). The entrance was up a very rickety gang-plank. Not bad inside, but they said it got very musty and damp in the long rainy season. We were staying in a motel some distance away, very nice and comfortable B and B, but cold at night and miles and miles from anywhere. After a very interesting and entertaining week, it was back to Brisbane, hand back the car and a flight on to Sydney for an eight day stay. Again, plenty to see and do. The city, a coffee cruise, and the Bridge and Rocks area, also the Opera House. Another hired car took us out and about including The Blue Mountains.

Then a four day coach tour to Melbourne via Canberra – Australia's capital city – the Snowy Mountains, Arlbury and Beechworth. Some two hours out from Melbourne the coach broke down and we were rather late arriving but "our Sydney" was there to take us to their home. There we were able to rest up – but not a lot – get the washing up to date, and my diary journal written up. We stayed two weeks and they insisted we stay there again before moving on.

We met up with cousin Betty and her daughter Barbara, and a very interesting day with son Locksley, I found all my Australian relatives a little bit unusual – and – they probably thought the same about us – I don't suppose I will ever know. And unless they read this ....!

The package deal we were on with Carrick Travel allowed us a certain number of kilometres we could fly, so after Melbourne we hired a one way car and drove to Adelaide via the Great Ocean Road, taking it leisurely for 3 days, there was then three full days of sightseeing in and around the lovely Adelaide. The Barrosa Valley wine tasting, Harndorf where German people settled and the city itself.

Next a long flight to Perth to be met by cousin Alan, he is six foot four and although we had never met I recognised him straight away. We stayed with him and his lady friend Dorothy for about two weeks and were taken every where one could get to, there and back in a day, including the village of Nannup where they all lived as children and, until leaving home. That was one of the highlights for me, standing and looking out over the 90 acres my dear old uncle had tamed from virtual jungle – "The bush". A mixture of trees, scrub and undergrowth, which we saw plenty of. They called their property "Hillcrest" to where I used to exchange letters with Betty all those years ago. There was a big big lump in my nostalgic old throat. I was and still am very fond of Alan, he is not a very good correspondent, we only have a line or two at Christmas.

At the end of our stay Alan took us the fifty miles or so to Bunbury – the end of the railway line south – to go to David's in Perth. We were met by David who had arrived back about three days previous from his three month trip round Australia. David lived in a very nice area at a spacious bungalow type dwelling, and it was obvious all the dusters were "in the wash", and the vac was "up the creek". Our bedroom was not too bad, but I recalled reference from the funeral service "ashes to ashes, dust to dust". It is a teaching that man (Adam) was created from dust and that we go to dust after death – well – there was definitely someone coming or going under our bed. Again I could finish the other half of the book on cousin David Hough, some of it is in my journal which I took out with me while we stayed there.

Perth is another lovely city on the Swan River, some ten to twelve miles from the coast and estuary at Freemantle. We were out most of the time except for sleeping, even for breakfast, after discovering David's shopping and eating habits, buying and keeping foodstuffs months beyond the recommended date for consumption. We were there mid November and he was using milk with a use by day of March. I wanted to get out but Olive said no. Oh dear.

Perth city is not very big, but I thought it was very nice with Kings Park and the river. Rotnest Island and Freemantle visits were enjoyed, and a four day trip to Coolgardie, Boulder and Kalgourlie gold fields was quite an experience and interesting. Gold is still being mined in the area by very advanced methods.

We saw my Aunt Marie a couple of times who I liked despite the fact she was a very "straight laced" person, being over 90 years of age and some thirty years older than me. She had been through very hard times indeed, leaving her small but cosy little home in Stratford-upon-Avon at aged twenty six or so, and having worked in a drapers shop.

Engaged, I assume to Harry, boarded a ship, and spent a month at least sailing to Freemantle, W.A., and really a new way of life probably undreamed of. Harry met her off the ship, they were married and after a day or two in the Perth Hills it was to Nannup they journeyed, by what means I know not, it might have been by rail even in 1926 or so. Harry had been working in the timber industry and there were old railways in the timber area of W.A. Alan took us around some of the places his father worked. Donnybrook comes to mind, also Jarrahwood. There was and still is a large timber mill in Nannup.

Harry had first of all lived in a "Humpy" an oblong or ridge tent, a wooden framework with a tarpaulin stretched over the top, on their marriage he had built a wooden dwelling himself, which was improved as time went by also to cope with the four offspring. In over fifty years I understand Marie never really got to grips with the Australian way of life completely, and faced with dire financial problems in times of depression, etc, also the fact she was not all that domesticated in the kitchen, probably had an effect and influence on their youngsters – who knows. However, it was very nice being able to meet them all, and in particular saying a last goodbye to Aunt Marie at a bus stop on November 11th 1990 in Perth, over 90 years she flatly refused to take a taxi home. We had spent an hour or two with Esther who had just returned from one of her "jaunts". David was too mean or could not be bothered to come and take his mother home, or pick us up. He lived about 25 minutes drive away – but – his mother had done his washing that morning.

One thing I will never forget is our simple lunch at Marie's little place, we joined hands while she said a prayer for us all followed by grace, another lump in my throat – and even now writing about it all.

That was the end of our trip to Australia. WORTH EVERY PENNY, but I never added exactly how much the trip actually cost, there was money left over, so why worry!!

We had three full days in Hong Kong seeing some of the sights, sounds and food and then the worst flight ever (with British Airways) cooped up with little room for my knees and the smell of curry most of the way. "They" do say though that Brussels Sprouts odour also upsets some people. A superb trip and almost straight into holly wreath making and digging up Christmas trees.

On Friday/Saturday December 9/10 we had a major snowfall, I was up at 5 a.m. pitch dark outside, and it was snowing heavens hard, wiring holly facing our large outside window. Snow was settling on a cotoneaster shrub under the window and I looked out from time to time as the settled snow crept further and further up the window. I wondered whether to carry on or not, I certainly could not deliver to the shop, further more, people would not be buying either. It was early in the winter to experience such a heavy fall of snow, when it stopped at about 11 a.m. we had snow some twenty inches deep. Often, if the weather turns cold at that time it can remain the same for weeks on end, 1940 and 1947 were the last really deep snowfalls, but 1963 was probably the longest time when it was impossible to work outside, I was unable to do any gardening work for eleven weeks. However, our 1990 downfall was all gone by the following Wednesday evening, which for everyone was a blessing with Christmas just days away. The snowfall in fact, was quite local, very little snow some 20 miles away at Rugby, but people south of Warwick were without power and light for days. The weight of snow pulled trees over, one property in Kelsey Lane, just round the corner from us – had five conifer trees down over the drive, no one could get in, or out. On the Sunday morning I waded round with my chain saw and made a way through. There were one or two folk out in their 4 x 4 four wheel drive vehicles, most of them did not know how to handle them and got stuck. It was more than chaotic for a while, but all was soon back to normal.

CHAPTER 30

The Boy Scouts

I have always had a "soft spot" for the Berkswell scout group, in fact a start has been made – by me – to record the troop's history. I have a lot of taped interviews with some "old boys", one or two of the original members. I think all of them have now gone to the great jamboree in the sky, nothing, or very little in writing, so far. I plan to cover the period from the start until 1946. That is the next project after this lot of scribblings.

The original scouts started to meet about 1928 and as I understand it the warrant authorising a troop came into being in 1931. The 53rd Coventry, and although we are in the county of Warwickshire, the troop decided to remain attached to Coventry and the Earlsdon area in particular. I may have suggested a sixtieth reunion, in any case some one did. The very efficient troop committee took it in hand and invited me to assist, I did have my uses knowing people that others did not – contacts and so on. We advertised the fact and wrote to all we knew and decided to make a weekend of it, the same weekend in June as parish Sunday (St. John Baptist, 24 June). A reunion on the Saturday afternoon with escorted tours to the parish museum and the church, tea provided. A B.B.Q. in the evening, which our scouts organised. The troop organise a big B.B.Q. every year – in September, with entertainment – the works – as a major fund raiser.

On the Sunday the whole troop, cubs, scouts, ventures and veterans paraded to church, together with the Royal British Legion, Brownies, Guides and other village organisations. There was the usual scout band (5th Coventry) to lead. A special request was made of the R.B. Legion who were pleased to let the troop parade their union flag (Union Jack) instead of their own. Only one union flag is permitted in any one procession. After the service we had another gathering over coffee and departed at lunch time, a most successful and happy weekend.

CHAPTER 31

Home and Away

At home most things went along as normal, normal for us anyhow. By now Olive had been retired sometime from her "dinner lady" job, but I dare not say – to become a lady of leisure, it would not be true at all.

Val, Jim and Adam at Wolston, Adam at 15 years soon to leave school, they all seemed to be happy and contented. It was suggested to Robert, aged 31, that he left home, this was before we visited Australia, he did in fact do so. Quite a while back he was informed that a super market chain were recruiting potential managers and management personnel, he applied and was taken on and taught the business, how to manage a shop. Within ten weeks he had "his own shop", fairly small and not too profitable we understood. Prove yourself there and move on kind of thing. He was still at home during that period, he did move on once or twice. The working hours were, I thought dreadful even for a single person, he had to be there at 7.00 a.m. six days a week till 6 p.m. Monday and Tuesday, his "half day" was Wednesday, when he was lucky to leave before 2 p.m. Thursday, Friday and Saturday, they were open till 8 p.m. In the end he gave up and left, the pay was fairly poor as well, he said. Afterwards he landed a job as barman at The Tipperary Inn – just up the road at Meer End. He was in "his element" there, really enjoyed it all, and the locals thought a lot of him. He later moved on to other licensed premises in the same ownership, found his niche in the pub/restaurant trade.

Jenifer, to the best of our knowledge was back on an even keel, she never would ask for, or accept any help from us in fact Valerie and Robert were the same. She had since left her job at the civil engineers and building firm she worked for. "The Encore" pub and restaurant at the bottom end of Bridge Street in Stratford were seeking someone to manage their bar meals and come up with completely new menus especially for lunch time.

Jenny got the job and made a big success of it and was very popular with all and sundry, well she is wherever she goes and whatever she does.

Jenifer had only been at "The Encore" for a few months when a position was advertised to work in the office of a tool hire company with two depots, the money and potential sounded good and Jenny applied for it, feeling a bit guilty having been in her current job for a short time. She landed the job, a small company were looking to train a person to the position of company secretary. The person she was to be trained by was suffering from cancer, a director of the firm who wished to retire. Jenny started work at their office and went from "strength to strength" so to speak, and, as a biased dad, am sure she has been and still is a great asset to the company and her boss who incidentally is a wee bit younger than Jenny and a very nice man. In the meantime Jenny had met Steve, who worked in the next office back at the builders firm, he, we were told later on, was very kind to her, without going into detail they eventually were married and moved house to a very nice place overlooking green fields in Wellesbourne. Steve, a very quiet fellow, but Jenny has "brought him out of his shell" quite a bit. A grand chap, we could not wish for a better son-in-law. Jenifer is now the company secretary of three depots and is kept very busy.

At home the garden takes up a lot of my spare time – well just about all of it really, as Christmas trees are sold, so areas are cleared, I try to clear one area every year, the ones that do not make the grade are dug out, the resulting poles usually end up somewhere as rustic fencing or arches so all is not lost. As each area is cleared a thick layer of compost, three inches deep, is cultivated in and the area made into ornamental garden, we have a kitchen garden as well and are more or less self sufficient in vegetables. I grow mostly perennials and shrubs, the plants cuttings, etc. given by my clients and friends, I even buy some now and again. In the summer we often visit gardens open to the public under the National Gardens Scheme. A good chance to buy good plants quite reasonable in price and often rare specimens are available on the plant stalls.

First we had one path to the bottom end of the garden, through the trees, down by the boundary hedge, then one on the other side to match with access to our "secret garden" in the fir trees. After a while there was quite a sizeable garden at the bottom end, a real surprise for first time visitors. We ended up with a block of Christmas trees left in the middle of the garden, far too big for the average home, but I sold about a dozen or so every year to churches, schools, and a factory in Coventry always had five, in the end I sort of got into trouble because the trees were too big – to see my little pick-up truck almost buried by trees was a funny sight, it turned a few heads in Coventry as well.

Eventually another pathway was made through the centre of the trees, that had a nice effect on one and all – even Olive and I. Looking back I often wonder how I managed it all, Olive did help from time to time, by her own admission a "fair weather gardener", but whatever she did it was a bit less for me. I really enjoyed our open days, usually with a plant stall at which I was always kept very busy all afternoon.

Some year or two later on we did – and still do – open under the National Gardens Scheme together with others in the area. Known as Balsall Common Gardens, there is usually eight gardens to visit and all the gate takings go to the scheme and takings for teas, and plants, etc. are donated to The Helen Ley Home near Kenilworth, a home for sufferers of Multiple Sclerosis where they also provide respite care. We think a very worthy charity to support.

On the first occasion we opened over 640 visitors came through our gate in under five hours, fortunately they did not all arrive together. There was no mess or litter left behind, the lawn took a battering here and there, but very soon recovered, also I could not see any signs of cuttings being nicked, this is a habit I strongly disapprove of, pinching cuttings and seeds. Ask and it shall be given, most of the time, as I have found out, there have been times when I have thought "I would like one of those/a bit of that" and often an enquiry produces favourable results.

Collectively we have made over £3,000.00 on a Sunday afternoon, a satisfying feeling, meeting people and friends, also having a lot of fun – well I do anyhow.

After our "big spend" going to Australia, we drew our horns in just a bit in 1991, taking our holidays closer to home. Sometimes though, staying in England CAN be more expensive than travelling further afield. We have always been most fortunate with some holidays, one of my clients had a cottage in Helford village, just yards from the small quay on the south west side of the Helford river in Cornwall, this cottage was offered to us free of charge so about this time we tried it out for two weeks. On the whole we have never been lovers of self catering, preferring, when on holiday to leave all housework to someone else, that is my definition of a holiday. In Cornwall as elsewhere really it was no trouble to have our breakfast and eat out for the rest of the day, sometimes taking a picnic, another event I am not too keen on. At work I picnic five days a week and do enjoy a change. Moaning over – promise, we really did enjoy Cornwall with its natural beauty and "olde worlde" villages by the seaside. Fish and chips always seem to taste better at the seaside too. Crossing the river by rowing boat ferry one day to visit Glen Durgan and Trebah gardens that run right down to the side of the river estuary. Walking round Frenchman's Creek and to St Anthony was superb.

We also had a week in Yorkshire, Skipton, Grassington, Pately Bridge, Kettlewell and Malam Cove to name a few of the "ports of call". Wild and rugged countryside, sometimes well off the beaten track. We always found nice places to stay and were always made very welcome. With B and B it was usually possible to find out what was happening locally, best pubs for an evening meal and the best route for the following day, not necessarily the shortest or the quickest but the most scenic. "Oh and do stop and look at this or that".

We never tire or get fed up when visiting our friends house in Sedburgh, 10 miles from Kendal in the Yorkshire Dales, we often discover new places to visit with the Lake District just to the west and the dales locally, lots of little side roads to get lost in, small- town markets and the like.

In January 1992 we are off again to a completely new destination – Maderia the garden island. Even at that time there were lots of plants in bloom. Fascinating place we stayed near the airport and Machico on the east coast, our intention was to do some walking, which we duly did. The island is not very big but mountains rise to over 6000 feet above sea level with lots of rain falling on them. Very little rain falls on the lower areas, so many years ago a system called Levadas was constructed. These are a series of small canals, varying in width and depth from about 1 metre down to about thirty centimetres (1 foot) the canals collect water at altitude and drain down to the lower levels, on a gradual fall along the contours of the hillsides, often going miles to actually travel a very short distance. The water irrigates properties lower down, property owners have a certain time – day or night – to divert water from a levada. Being on almost level ground with a footpath at the side of most levadas makes ideal walking in lovely surroundings, once one has arrived at a starting pint, often by bus. Sometimes these canals are hewn out from the cliff, like sides of a mountain with a narrow path and a "long drop". I am not into that, about 15 feet drop is enough for me. I will not go far up a ladder, the bedroom window is quite far enough, trees I can cope with a bit better, but ladders and heights are not my cup of tea.

Lots to do and see on Maderia, both in the mountains and in the small villages and Funchal the capital, I hope to return one day – perhaps in April, which is said to be the best time for flowers and things horticultural. A themed holiday, there featuring gardens would be ideal for us, we sampled bananas purchased at the side of the footpath, which took us through a banana plantation. Another item on the menu was Espada. A fish to be found – so they tell me – in very deep sea water, very nice on a plate with roast banana. The botanical gardens overlooking Funchal was very good with lots of plants showing early flowers, we did not go for tea at Reids on this occasion, again probably next time.

Just to fill the year in holiday-wise Austria was once again "on the menu", still in the Tyrol – but a wee bit different Lermoos our destination in 1992, we did go quite early in June and saw an abundance of wild flowers. Lermoos, Biebervier and Erwald form a triangle perhaps about three miles from each other. The moos is a flat area in the centre between all three, nowadays it is drained and fast flowing steams flow through with trout, and all sorts of water weed grow at the waterside. The farmers were just beginning to cut the grass for the first time, no herbicides here, a mixture of grasses and wildflowers of all sorts. Some folk would say weeds, whatever it does make superb cream for the cakes pastries and strudle. The walking was very nice with mountains surrounding the moos with the tallest mountain in Germany – the Zugspitz – just beyond Erwald. One lasting memory of this holiday was the evening of June 21st, the longest day. Local people had walked up into the mountains and lit flares all round the rim of the mountains, there were also designs in flares, a church steeple, a crown and an anchor. The flares, we discovered later, were pots with wicks and filled with oil. It did make a wonderful sight as we watched the torch bearers return back down the mountain tracks. We did stay in a very nice hotel there "guarded" by a big St. Bernard dog, the proprietor had in the past been an Olympic skier, and another one lived across the road. A holiday we all enjoyed with a lot of easy walking and plenty to keep the keen hiker happy. Our holiday friends went back there the next year, even booking the same rooms in the same hotel. Olive and I opted out because I do not like repetition of that sort especially so soon.

In the garden I have always had a passion for – wait for it – propagation, not being able to throw any cuttings away, trying to root them instead, geraniums in particular, but also shrub prunings and anything along the way that I thought would be nice, often asking my clients for "a bit of this or that". All the seeds in a packet would be sown, ending up with lots of bedding plants and seedlings from friends and special offers in gardening magazines. They must not be thrown away!!! Some were sold here and there, the church fete, open gardens and so on, but there was still all sorts left and they all had to be watered. Only the dead and dying were got rid of. I am sure it was our good friend Alice Fryer who suggested to me that I could and should take any surplus plants and produce to the Women's Institute market. I gave this some thought and made enquiries.

Anyone, male or female can join the WI market as a producer, cost just five pence. At Balsall the market is on a Saturday morning between 10 and 11 o'clock. All produce must be top quality and labelled with ones name, membership number, description of item for sale – name of plant, etc. – and the price. Every item had to be invoiced in triplicate and booked in to the market before 9.30 and any unsold items booked out again by a market supervisor. Rather a rigmarole in fact but I decided to give it a try.

There was also baking products for sale sweet and savoury, bread, jam and pickles. Another stall sells beautifully made handicrafts, baby clothes, cushions, soft toys, you name it, also notelets and the like, all at very reasonable prices for quality goods. Altogether it was time consuming, Friday evenings and Saturday mornings were taken up with "marketeering" as I called it. Spring and autumn were the best times for me and plants, no one wanted my produce in the summer or winter, holly wreaths were produced in December, but not the slightest demand in January. The whole event

Plant stall at the Church fete

was, for me most enjoyable, my fellow marketeers were/are a nice crowd of people. The monies, although not great, was always useful and I did learn a tremendous amount about plants – especially perennials from Alice Fryer at this time nearer ninety years than eighty, she had been involved in professional horticulture all her life, together with her late husband Bill. For quite a number of years they ran a small nursery at Catchems Corner, just at the end of Windmill Lane below our house.

Writing now, in 2001, I have retired from marketeering, but still drop in now and again to see them all, and it is nice to receive a nice warm welcome and sometimes a cup of coffee, this, another little "earner", tea, coffee and biscuits are served and quite a few ladies make a pleasant little outing at the market on Saturdays, long may it continue.

It was in 1993 that cousin Alan in Australia informed Olive and I that he and Dorothy (his lady friend) were coming to England in May. Letters went back and forth, as they were staying some of the time with us, Alan was to hire a car for the whole period of their stay and they wished to visit Ireland and requested we went with them. You make the arrangement, ferries, accommodation, etc. was my brief, and we will fall in with your arrangement. With only about a year to go to my retirement age I decided to take a three month "sabbatical" holiday, apart from my small mowing contracts and probably a few jobs here and there, my order book was not too full of booked jobs so there was no problems in that direction.

Olive and I journeyed to Heathrow to pick up Dorothy and Alan, who were quite a while emerging from the flight – Alan was minus his luggage. He was assured it was O.K. and would be delivered to our address later that day. On the way home we talked about all sorts of topics including our millions in the small country of England, driving along the M25 and M40 and via the Warwick bypass to our house we passed no built up area and they wondered and asked where everybody lived.

The weather was chilly and dull when they arrived and Dorothy wanted an anorak, she had set her mind on a particular one, so we set off for Coventry and later to Solihull shopping. This set the pattern for their visit, anything fancied had to be sought. Dorothy was keen on crafts and in particular art, she did some painting at home. No craft or art shop was driven past there after, we often had to turn round and go back – if possible. The day dawned early for our departure to Ireland, it was an early start for the long drive in Alan's hire car to Pembroke Docks. We made the ferry alright and it was a long crossing to Rosslare. Our first night was booked at a farmhouse, some twenty miles away, we phoned from Rosslare and ordered an evening meal to save going out to find somewhere. We found the place eventually and we all took an instant dislike to the place, Dorothy most of all, truth to say it was not too clean, certainly not posh. Dorothy was "playing her face" at Olive and I, moving furniture round in their bedroom, what for I know not. We were miles from anywhere, "out in the sticks" and I said we must make the best of it and hope for better things to come. The dinner was not bad, but the place did nothing for ones appetite. Our departure next morning was just a bit strained and driving down the drive Dorothy sounded off again, Olive answered back in no uncertain terms – I was amazed – and she was in tears, a very very rare occurrence indeed. It was a very quiet morning, I was dreading the next stop and the accommodation which was pre-booked. Some nights we had to find our own, that I decided would be a job for Dorothy. "Herself" simmered down after being "spoken to" by Olive, even Alan said "bravo" later on. The holiday itself was very nice, we journeyed to Bantry in the west and toured round The Ring of Kerry and The Dingle Peninsular heading north and back across the centre of the country for a day or two in the Wicklow Mountains. We met some very nice people, without exception all most hospitable and friendly, no reason not to be in fact. We returned from Dublin to Holyhead and motored down to Colwyn Bay to stay overnight with Pam and Jim Thompson, who had invited us to stay when they heard of our plans.

Another excursion took us to Chartres in France for a short stay with our friends there, where we were entertained and saw some of the sights of Paris, some forty or so miles away, also some of the Chateaux of the Loire valley. Alan, doing a good job of driving in Paris, and on the right of the road. We saw the house and garden of Monet which suited Dorothy "down to the ground", but she thought his paintings should have been there not in galleries all over the place. Alan did most of the driving, it was supposed to be shared, me being accused of being an aggressive driver, amongst other things, she could have been right of course, but no one else has said so, probably too polite. In Australia there is so little traffic on the roads, except in the major cities, they struggled to get used to it. Their visit disappointed me in a way, they arrived without a plan of "things to see and do" with the exception of craft and art studios and shops – any shops. BUT it was their holiday and they were paying and that was that, they I felt, were the losers. However, although Dorothy upset us both in many many ways they did really look after us when we were with them in Australia. In fact the only praise I got was for my lettuce. Dorothy had not tasted anything like it before, I told her that the only difference was that my lettuce was growing one minute, cut, and on the table five minutes later. That really applies to any garden produce. When I was jobbing gardening working for Dr. M who was a member of the Soil Association H.D.R.A. he told me that vegetables lose a third of their nutritional value within twenty four hours of being harvested. Alan and Dorothy were not staying with us all the time, but at "going home time" Dorothy had accumulated a lot of mementoes, etc. I managed to find her an old suitcase to pack it all in and I think she went away happy. She did say what a really tough time they/she had had in her childhood and young days, much tougher than my uncle and aunt apparently. It was not long after their return home we learned that Dorothy and Alan had parted – but remain good friends, should we say "all's well.........?" Oh, is that not nice?

We must go back a little bit in time now. Our good friend Innes came to Berkswell as a newly qualified teacher, Miss J.I. Mulligan, taught at Berkswell C of E School and was, and still is very popular with one and all. It was many years later that we became closer friends, Innes and her late husband Geoff came on holiday with Olive and myself to Zell am Ziller in Austria and together with other members of "the gang" we all enjoyed holidays together for quite a few years. One day Innes told us of her pen friend, a man who lived in Chartres France. They had corresponded from teenagers, but eventually lost touch – until – many years later Geoff and Innes were attending evensong at Berkswell Church and a message or note was given to them, it transpired that Jean Geroudet her French penfriend was at the church door with his wife and family. A lovely reunion which I'm pleased to say has carried on to this day, all past their three score years and ten by now (2001).

They did exchange visits and eventually we met them Jean (pronounced John) his wife Yolonde and son Patrick, they came here to dinner one evening, also our friends Freda and Lionel, we had "return matches" at Freda's and Innes'. We got to know them very well indeed, Jean spoke good English, Patrick's was, I think better, and although Yolande could only manage a few words, she could understand what was being said. The family were "well to do" in Chartres. (do not know how else to put it) they owned quite a lot of property, farmland and a big area of standing timber (woodland) somewhere in the centre of France. Both Jean and Patrick had been educated at the Sorbonne in Paris. Jean, later on, was teaching himself Japanese language from an English text book, it all really puts a lot of us English to shame, BUT, they did have the opportunity, I for one had to get out there and earn my living, something I have never regretted or been ashamed of despite my remarks above – Does that sound like an excuse? – because it is not. I have said many times about having problems with the English language.

Back to the Geroudet family, who also have a daughter, Annie, a lovely lady in every sense of the word, married to Jean Robert and they live in a flat in Paris. One day Freda, Lionel, Olive, Innes and myself received an invitation to go and stay in Chartres with our new friends, although we had known them sometime by now. We accepted with thanks and duly loaded up into Lionel's spacious car and away we went, we were treated like royalty in their lovely town house and quite private, plain but pretty garden. The weather did behave itself for our days out. This was the first of three visits all of which were most enjoyable and informative. On our visit there with Dorothy and Alan we were at the Eiffel Tower after 11 p.m. Alan had a trip up the tower. Dorothy could not understand why I did not go. Reasons: one cannot see much at that time of night – and – it was quite expensive, she thought I was "windy" Not so, although I do not like "heights".

It has been a pleasure to help entertain the family on their visits to England. One memorable occasion, when it was the 50th anniversary of the beginning of their friendship as pen pals, Innes thought it was all worthy of a party, so about sixteen people came from France and there was a "bit of a do" in the Reading Room at Berkswell, some people stayed in B and B and others with some of us. We had Annie and Jean-Robert, it did help because their English was very good, we had a grand gathering much enjoyed by all, and still talked about now.

Another major event for Olive and I was our ruby wedding anniversary on April 4th 1993. A party was planned in the Reading room. Jenifer volunteered to undertake the catering and we also had a bar. About seventy relatives and friends turned up and I like to think we all had a nice time. My best man Bill Green was with us with his wife Rita. Bill was also best man to our friend John Kirby, it was John that joined the Malayan Police in about 1950. I think after three years he came home on leave. He had always been shall we say, fond of the girls, and I do believe a lot of girls would have liked to be fond of him, if one sees what I mean. He was tall and had an honest open and good looking face with a great personality to match – that is my opinion anyhow. Without anything ever being said I always thought he was particularly fond of Pearl and vice versa. When he came home on leave it transpired he was "running around" with a special licence in his pocket – a marriage licence. But, Pearl, I understand was playing "hard to get". But just imagine getting wed and going half way round the world to live in a hot sticky climate and all that goes with it, snakes and crocodiles to name a couple.

John won the day in the end, they were married at St. Mary's Temple Balsall and soon departed for Malaya. They were there till Malaya became Malaysia and gained their independence. John's job as a police superintendent came to an end. Whilst in Malaya he was awarded the Colonial Police Medal for an act of bravery, being a modest sort of a guy he never said exactly what for. He was offered and accepted a similar position in Bechuanaland now Botswana (which is also easier to spell!). By this time they had at least one child, Janet. I understand he attained quite a high rank in the police force there, and after some years it all was too much and, unknown to anyone in this country, was sent to a hospital or home in this country suffering a mental breakdown, he had been back here in U.K. two weeks before his mother was informed. To cut a very long story shorter, he never REALLY got over his breakdown. He was retired from Bechuanaland on health grounds, the family came to live in Burton Green. I saw him only occasionally; by now they had 5 children and in a way, like us, their main time – after work – was devoted to the family. I must say – John's problem was, I am sure, not being able to cope with his job. He definitely was not mentally ill if – and I hope one knows what I mean.

It was some years later that he died, I did not even know how ill he must have been. We had all completely lost touch with Bill Green, but I just had to let him know. Jumping in the car and calling on his last known address on the other side of Coventry, there was no reply at the door and I knew Bill did not live there, the front garden was overgrown and in an awful mess. A knock at next door was answered and I was either given a phone number or an address. Success! The next evening. We met up again at John's funeral. His ashes are interred in a family grave in Berkswell churchyard with a memorial seat close by. It was good bye to a good pal from our younger days, a clever talented and popular man. Why does this often happen to the best?

It is not very often that Olive expresses a desire or wish, but she did one day in 1993 and it was to go and see some wild animals in their natural surroundings – a safari. I did not need much encouragement, always game – pardon the pun – if funds are available. In any case I had "had my fling" going to Australia, therefore it was all systems go. Two of my ex clients/friends had been and gave us a few suggestions and tips, so off to the travel agents to collect an armful of brochures. We eventually decided on a double safari, a week in Kenya and another week in Tanzania, flying out to and returning from Nairobi. To us it was a real adventure, staying the first very short night in Nairobi and joining our driver/courier and general carer at 7.30 am the next morning for our first weeks tour heading out towards our first game park – the Masai Mara, viewing any game (wild life) on the way. Our driver was jet black, very helpful and polite, there were just seven of us in the vehicle, referred to as a van. Specially built for rough terrain, and "roads" which were all – or almost all – dirt tracks and sometimes corrugated and rutted. Away we went with a camera camcorder and binoculars round my neck. In the first two days we saw a big variety of wild life, but no rhino or leopard so far. On to Amboseli Reserve and one night at "The Ark". A lodge similar to the famous "Treetops" – but, claimed to be better. It was a real experience, we stayed there with about 70 others for one night only, once in there was no leaving until next morning. It was here we saw "our" first rhino with a very young calf. At one end of "The Ark" – a huge wooden building – there is a water hole and a "salt lick", salt laden rock that the animals have a great desire to get to, all part of their natural diet. At one time a big herd of cape buffalo occupied the area for quite a long time, and a group of elephants were desperate to take a turn, but they had to wait until the buffalo moved away, they posed a real threat to anything with their massive horns for head-gear. The law of the jungle very much at work. We then went on to Lake Nakuru, where thousands of flamingo congregated at a soda lake which looked like a large salt pan. We saw a leopard near there, but only for a very short time of a minute or so, as he or she slunk off. Then down to the border between the two countries, with about 400 yards of no mans land between the check points. Again, quite an experience as we had to clear Kenya, change vans and drivers before crossing into Tanzania via another check point. A queue to fill in documents in a vile stinking office full of sweaty people of all colours, watching our pockets, etc. No mans land was "heaving" with people some honest and others trying to make the quick deals, changing money, etc. We were not allowed to take any currency into either country, obtaining local money from the hotels or lodges where we stayed. The one hotel in Nairobi was very good, air conditioning and so on, the lodges were all superb although some places were not much more than tents, they all had mosquito nets and candles to burn at night to deter any nasties – we were not bothered by any and no "tummy bug" problems. The food was superb and plenty of it, we did avoid salad and some fish, being full board there was very little to spend money on. After crossing into Tanzania our new driver took us for an overnight stay in Arusha, one of many places where ancient meets modern head on. Washing vehicles in a river in the town, the same water would be used for drinking further down stream. We had a nice rest in a Novotel and recharged our batteries for the next part of the safari in Tanzania. Kenya is a poor country but Tanzania is poorer, or was in 1993. We did not see much evidence of that, spending all our time in the game parks and lodges. Time was spent in the huge Serengeti Reserve where the landscape was quite varied, great plains and some rainforest areas, here and there were lakes where hippos and elephant could wallow and soak to their hearts content. It was here our driver discovered two leopard, they were hauling a kill into a tree and we observed them for over 20 minutes. The drivers can – seemingly – spot game up to half a mile away, or a well camouflaged animal just yards away. With my poor eyesight I sometimes had a job to focus onto things, but nearly always made it with the help of seven others. The best was "saved" till last – the Ngorongora Crater, but on route we called at the Olduvi Gorge where Richard Leakey has spent a lot of time hunting for and discovering pre historic remains. We had our only packed lunch on the edge of this fascinating gorge where it would have been nice to find out more about the gorge and surrounding area. Since our return I have read a little about Leakey and his exploits.

The Ngorangora crater was a volcano thousands of years ago, the floor area is in excess of 100 sq. miles, it contains just about all the species of native animals except giraffe. The crater caters for all their needs, grazing for the grazers – there is a word for them – and plenty of meat for the carnivores – fresh – but it has to be caught. The sides of the crater are quite steep and rise about 700 ft. – my guess – therefore animals have no need to escape this environment, there are streams and lakes for hippo, etc, flamingo round the edges. Rhino graze on the plains and the lions are huge specimens. In the Serengeti lodge where we stayed there was a shortage of water – it was the dry season. For our stay there, water was only available from 6 pm till I think 7 am next day, all cold, We had a jug kettle with us and managed to heat water for a wash and shave – for me, Olive doesn't shave. We were made aware of these facts in the brochure, the animals come FIRST it is their home.

On arrival at the new lodge on the rim of the crater after a long dusty drive, I/we were covered in a layer of dirt, my hair – what there is of it – felt like barbed wire. But what a super place we had arrived at, a huge bath, which was soon put to good use, I threw my clothes in as well and walked about on them, not a pretty sight. But no one was looking. The whole lodge was built in circles, the rooms, steps, restaurant the lot, fascinating. It was then another long drive back to Nairobi and home. There were strikes and long delays at the airport all in the heat and, more sweaty bodies including mine. It was indeed a memorable holiday – well not really a holiday – an experience if ever there was one.

We arrived home just in time for preparations for Christmas, holly wreaths, Christmas trees and the usual Christingle service on Christmas Eve. I am not sure where Christmas Day was spent, with the youngsters long gone we could please ourselves. Val and Jim preferred to stay at home, also Jenifer the same. Robert always hated Christmas and birthdays, so we never even saw him. Our feelings were that if the family were happy with their arrangements so were we, all free to do "our own thing".

Often we would spend the day with cousin Kathleen and Michael at Barford or Jenny's at Wellesbourne, we had "return matches" here from time to time, but the Barfordian family preferred to be at home, some of them could "disappear" and watch telly elsewhere, something we can do without most of the time – but – each to his own.

The next big thing I had to look forward to was retirement. 65 years of age on March 12th 1994. Having worked – and I mean worked, for fifty one years man and boy I was quite ready to call it a day. One or two of my mates said that "Webby" would not retire, but Webby had other ideas. I decided sometime previous to run down my activities. Since Alan and Dorothy's visit from Australia I had not worked a full week, I never managed a five day week in all the years, there was always a job to finish off on a Saturday or someone to see about work, either on Saturday or in the evening, I hated these visits giving quotes, do not get me wrong, I loved meeting my clients, except on the rare occasions when I was chasing a slow payer. At the time of my retirement the country was in quite a state of recession and my order book was dwindling down, very few jobs to undertake, I did often wonder how I would have fared had there been a need, in fact everything worked out fairly well. I had my state pension to look forward to, all fifty nine pounds per week, big deal, after fifty one years hard labour I thought the pension was an insult. After seven and a half years I now receive another fifteen pounds per week, this increase has just about been enough to pay the increase in rates/poll tax and now council tax over the year, and I still think the state pension is an insult to those that have not asked for anything and paid their way over a working life time – so there.

Thankfully I paid into a private pension scheme for thirty three years, but at the end if was not a big amount that is being paid out. Not being a big earner I was only allowed to invest about 17% of my income into a pension. However, it did provide an income that we could easily manage on, and using savings and sometimes dipping into capital for holidays, etc. It was, and still is an ambition NOT to end up as the richest bloke in Berkswell Churchyard, no fear of that anyhow. "Balancing books" was the way to do it. The twelfth was on a Saturday and a party with a difference was planned, John would be "At home" from 12.00 midday till 8.30 pm. It was Jenifer's idea to put on "John's Italian Extravaganza". Invitations were sent out, I particularly wanted some of my clients to come and they did, some sixty five relatives and friends were invited to partake of drinks and a three course meal all undertaken by Jenny ably assisted by helpers in the kitchen.

The invitations read thus:

The 12th March starts the rest of my life,
Time to slow down and relax a bit more,
Time for my garden time for my wife
Holidays and outings never a bore

You are invited to lunch tea or dinner,
You cannot go wrong, it will be a winner,
Same menu all through the day,
A drop of booze, Hip Hip Horray.

Italian chef Italian waiter,
Standing by ready to cater,
The chef is pretty, the waiters not bad
She is his daughter, he is her dad.

No presents please at our get together,
If you do insist, I'd accept a small heather,
Two pensioners will be pleased to see you
R.S.V.P – or a phone call will do.

It really did all go very well, thanks entirely to Jenny, who must have been all in at the end, she did not say, probably to tired. Our first two visitors arrived on the dot of twelve. Gladys Smith and Arthur James, sadly both have now departed to the greater life, a pair of characters if ever, in completely different ways. Gladys, widow of Sam, a farmer, could undertake and make a super job of anything a farmers wife could be expected to do, with a needle or pins and in the kitchen. Dressing poultry and gardening all undertaken in a "matter of fact" way with no "airs and graces", a lovely bubbly popular fun loving lady – the last of her kind, I cannot think of any other of her ability.

Arthur James was a retired draftsman, like Gladys loved food, any food, when it came to the choice of pudding, he always pointed to one and said he would like to try that first – after eyeing up the others. Always able and happy with a "few words" of thanks, a speech, or a toast at short notice at any occasion. A wonderful bass singing voice, he sang in the church choir for many years. Always happy to do "a turn" on the stage in a concert or play.

Any readers will be pleased to know that I am not writing about every one who came to my extravaganza. People came in a steady stream and thankfully there was always somewhere for everybody to sit until a place could be found at a table. I met everybody on arrival, fixed a drink and waited on table. The splendid menu was fit for a Duke.

Another very happy and memorable day. Jenny had left the catering trade and was working in a civil engineers office in Stratford, I think she used the party as a means of keeping her hand in, she did that alright.

What are senior citizens worth
(submitted by an old lady)

Did you know that old folks are worth a fortune... Silver in their hair, Gold in their teeth. Stones in their kidneys, Lead in their feet and lots of Gas in their stomachs.

I have become older and wiser since I saw you last, and a few changes have come into my life, frankly I have become a Frivolous old girl and I am seeing six Gentlemen every day. As soon as I wake up, Will Power helps me out of bed, then I have to visit John, then it is time for Mr Kellogg, followed closely by the refreshing company of Mr Tetley or my other friend, just called by his initials PG.

Then comes someone I do not like at all, Arthur Ritus, he knows he is not welcome, but he insists and what is more he stays for the rest of the day. He does not like to stay in one place so he takes me from joint to joint. After such a day I am really tired and go to bed gladly with Johnny Walker, what a hectic life.

Oh yes I am now flirting with Al Zeimer.

The priest called the other day and said that at my age I should be thinking of the Here After, I told him "Oh I do, all the time". No matter where I am, the bedroom, kitchen, sitting room, or even in the garden, I stop and ask myself.

Now what am I here After......

So another chapter in my life came to an end, but not quite. There were still a few little jobs left to do in fact one little mowing job was to go on for four more years, also the Christmas holly wreath making continued for some years, I enjoyed it, a bit of a challenge perhaps – and the few extra pounds was always useful. I also carried on with the W.I. market that again I did quite enjoy, and it was only spring and autumn that my produce was in demand. What I really wanted to abandon was regular commitments, having to be in a certain place at a certain time. In a way it would have been nice to be involved helping out somewhere like a National Trust Property or the like, the Berkswell Darby and Joan Club were looking for drivers. However, I never joined anything and if that is a selfish attitude so be it. Having said all that I stood for, and was elected Churchwarden again in April 1994, and that was the last time there was an election – proper – with more than two people standing for election, (writing now in 2001). As stated previously the position of churchwarden is quite demanding, but with the current Rector, the Rev. George Baisley it was much easier this time around. The Rector is very ably assisted by his wife Barbara, it was I think a big day for our church when she became fully ordained as a minister, one of the first ladies to be ordained in the country, the service at Coventry Cathedral. Later on she became an honorary canon of the cathedral, again, a great honour for her and for all of us. They, the Rector and Barbara are assisted by three licensed readers. Mary Goode, John Clements and Ric Edwards who became licensed round about 1995. So really we are well blessed for clergy in Berkswell.

I was a churchwarden for three years until April 1996, deciding not to stand for the next year, there were a variety of reasons all best kept to myself. And so I became fully "redundant" and for the first time completely free to do my own thing. I did have a "swan song", some time later on it was decided to walk the churchyard and see if any improvements could be made chiefly looking for ways to cut down on the maintenance work. Our verger was Una Clements very ably assisted by her husband John who was just about to retire from his job. There was an untidy corner between the main porch and the tower and I built a dry-stone wall in that place and planted alpine plants in and on the wall. My fellow "consultants" and I made further suggestions which were all adopted and I must say it has proved to be a big improvement all the way round.

Una maintained the churchyard to a very high standard entering the best kept churchyard competition every year. By her efforts she won for us the best kept churchyard of the whole diocese one year. I always thought, and said that the grass in the churchyard was frightened to grow as what there was found itself continually shaved off.

Not wishing to change old habits there were two holidays in 1994. Mayrhofen in Austria in June was first on the list, now that we are both retired we can toddle off any old time. June in Austria – as in many other places – is magnificent, in particular we see many species of wild flowers in bloom. In some village resorts farmers are not permitted to mow certain areas until flower seeds have set and been shed, also there are one or two high altitude rock gardens where all sorts of alpines grow all "under one roof". There is a garden on the Kitzbuhler Horn mountain above Kitzbuhl. The meadows around Seefeld are spectacular in June.

In October of '94 we visited New England USA in the fall, three days in Boston with plenty to see and do, in particular I enjoyed the Quincey Market. Not really a bloke for shops, etc. – not many men are, but every other outlet seemed to be food, eat on the premises, take away – what have you. One elderly couple on our trip were disappointed not to find roast beef, yorkshire pudding and two veg. But you can't win 'em all. The sun was shining a trad jazz band was playing, problem was I was not all that hungry. We visited Harvard University – too late for me. The site of the Boston tea party where an ancient sailing ship is on view. Some of the "Heritage Trail" was followed – a painted red line round the inner city connecting all the historical sites.

Then onto our coach for a most scenic tour of some of the New England States, staying three nights in Montreal from where we had a one day outing to Quebec and little did I think all those years ago that I would stand on the Heights of Abraham and look down on the mighty St. Lawrence river where General Wolfe knocked seven bells out of Montcalm. Miss Tattersall made history and geography come alive – for me anyhow, pity about my sums, and spelling, those lessons were never quite the same at "Balsall Academy", but my maths did improve somewhat).

I digress – again, our next port of call was just an hour or two in Ottawa, the capital city of Canada, parking the coach very close to a big open space very close to the parliament buildings. On then to the huge rambling city of Toronto its suburbs went on for miles or so it seemed. By prior arrangement we were met in the hotel by my "old" mate Derrick Wagstaff and his wife Betty, they emigrated to Canada some 25 years ago, and lived in London, Ontario some 3 hours drive away. They took us out for a Dutch treat to – I think Eddy Murphy's restaurant where we had a lovely meal and a long long chat as one can imagine. Derrick's father Bert was chauffeur at Berkswell Hall. Col. Wheatley died in 1943. From then on there was only one car to look after and hardly any driving, before the war (1939) there were quite a few including a Rolls Royce and Mrs Wheatley drove around in a huge Armstrong, as big as a hearse like a mini bus. She never looked left or right, but scruffy kids playing at the roadside were "ten a penny" anyhow. Derrick is a first class electrician, capable of setting all the electrics for a factory assembly line, he worked very hard indeed on a long apprenticeship at Lee Beesley in Coventry. That completed he was called up for two years, National Service in the army.

Niagara Falls was next, after a tour of Toronto and a ride up the C.N. Tower, one of the tallest structures in the world. As the tower was a magnificent building feat, the Niagara Falls was a spectacular natural spectacle. I had a boat ride on the "Maid of the Mist" right up into the spray caused by the tumbling waters of the falls, altogether a most magnificent experience.

On then to New York for three nights, the whole time filled with sightseeing, including a helicopter flight over Manhatten, following 5th Avenue on the way out and the river on our return. We were staying at the Pensylvania Hotel which was the New York "residence" of the Glenn Miller Orchestra and the phone in the room bore the famous number "Pensylvania 65,000" as in the tune of the same name. The hotel was right opposite Madison Square Garden, the huge building where many famous sporting events – including boxing – are held. Also pop concerts and so on. Then it was home time for a bit of a rest, jet lag caught up with me on this one, but that would not put me off.

For the next year or two events fell into some sort of a pattern, a nice "design" as far as I was concerned, not getting up too early in the mornings, eight fifteen will do I suppose – if I'm awake. Sometimes in the mid winter it would sometimes be nine o'clock, a bit of a waste of time perhaps, but it was MY time was it not. Time in the garden AM and PM pottering in the greenhouse and battling against the greenfly, pigeons, etc. and the elements, I could always go indoors if it rained. No book-keeping to do except keeping an eye on the finances which did not take up much of my time. Our main highlights were and still are visits for supper/dinner with our friends and their visits here, our friends are good cooks and we are fortunate to have sampled many delights in the company of super folks.

The garden was open two or three times in the year, we have also had visits from gardening clubs and the like. Many new friends and acquaintances have been made, most of them have remained long standing which makes it all very nice and well worth a bit of effort. We tend not to go out a lot, we visit gardens open to the public now and again, getting our own back if you like.

Again holidays form an important part of life for me, I will not go into great detail, but 1995 in Scotland visiting gardens in the south-west and as far north as Callender in the Trossacks. In the autumn another ambition was fulfilled with a holiday to Zimbabwe and in particular the Victoria Falls also visiting safari parks and finishing up with a week in Mauritius.

Another wish was made reality in 1996 with a visit to Switzerland staying in Wengen, a village resort, traffic free, in the mountains close to Interlaken, the Bernese Oberland had always fascinated me with its cog railways connecting the villages and mountain areas. Grindlewald and Kleina Scheideg for example, although it was late July there were lots of wild flowers to be seen, especially at high altitude.

1997 we were back in Seefeld, Austria tramping the "hills" to the best of my ability, arthritis was not too bad but long hikes were out, fortunately there are plenty of shorter ones. However, I am thankful and satisfied with what I can do. This holiday turned out to be the last Olive and I went to in a group, there were no problems, but from now on "things" seemed to happen in a different way, just as way back the other holiday "gang" as we called ourselves sort of disbanded, youngsters grew up, we were perhaps a bit better off and could "dip our toes" in other waters, fashions change, but we are still the best of pals with all our old "playmates".

I know I said how nice it was to be "free" of local organisation commitments, – and It is – I had always thought I would like to be involved with Berkswell Museum, not part of it though. So eventually I was invited and made welcome on the museum committee.

The museum is situated behind the almshouses in the gardens, originally two cottages dating back to around 1500. Part of and administered by Berkswell Charity Trustees and offered the property for use as a village museum in 1981. I am fairly sure the museum was an ambition of the late Kenneth Hope and certainly a lot of material belonging to him formed the nucleus in the beginning. Almost the entire collection has been donated by

Berkswell people. Well worth a visit on a summer Sunday afternoon or by appointment. And talking of Museums, etc.

HOW TO KNOW YOU'RE GROWING OLDER
Everything hurts and what doesn't hurt doesn't work.
The gleam in your eyes is from the sun hitting your bifocals.
You feel like the night before and you haven't been anywhere.
You get winded playing chess.
Your children begin to look middle aged.
You finally reach the top of the ladder and find it's leaning against the wrong wall.
You join a Health Club and don't go.
You know all the answers but nobody asks you the questions.
You look forward to a dull evening.
You sit in a rocking chair and can't get it going.
Your knees buckle but your belt won't.
You're 17 around the neck, 44 around the waist and 105 around the golf course.
You just can't stand people who are intolerant.
Your back goes out more often than you do.
You stop looking forward to our next birthday.
You burn the midnight oil after 9.00pm.
You sink your teeth into a steak and they stay there.
You regret all those temptations you resisted.
The little old grey haired lady you help across the street is your wife.
You get all your exercise from being pallbearer for your friends who exercised.
You remember today that yesterday was your wedding anniversary.
You start a sentence but forget what you................

WE ARE SURVIVORS!
(For those born before 1940)

We were born before television, before penicillin, polio shots, frozen foods Xerox, plastic, contact lenses, videos, Frisbees and the pill; before radar, credit cards, split atoms, laser beams and ball point pens; before dishwashers, drip-dry clothes, air conditioners, electric blankets, tumble driers and before man walked on the moon.

We got married first and *then* lived together (how quaint ! I hear you say). *We* thought 'fast food' was what one ate in Lent, a 'Big Mac' was an oversized rain coat and crumpet was toasted for tea. We existed before house husbands, computer dating, dual careers, and when a 'meaningful relationship' meant getting on well with your cousins.

We were born before day care centres, group homes, disposable nappies, and sheltered accommodation was where you waited for a 'bus. *We* had never heard of FM, tape decks, electric typewriters, jet aircraft, artificial hearts, word processors, yoghurt, or men wearing ear rings. For us, time sharing meant togetherness, a chip was a fried potato, hardware meant nuts and bolts and software wasn't even a word. Before 1940, 'Made in Japan' meant junk, the term 'Making out' referred to how well one did in exams. Stud was something that fastened a collar to a shirt and 'going all the way' meant staying on the 'bus to the terminus. In *our* day, cigarette smoking was fashionable, grass was mown, coke was kept in the coal house, a joint was a piece of meat you had on Sundays and pot was something that you cooked in. Rock music was grandmother's lullaby, Eldorado was an ice cream, a gay person was the life and soul of the party and nothing more, whilst aids just meant beauty treatments or help for someone in distress.

We, who were born before 1940, must have been a hardy bunch when you think of the ways in which the world has changed and the adjustments we have had to make. No wonder we are so confused and that there is a generation gap today ...*but*... by the grace of God, We have survived!

Berkswell was home to two millionaires before the second world war one was Colonel C.J.H. Wheatley of Berkswell Hall and Sir Charles Hyde, Baronette who resided at The Moat above the village. They both departed this life during the war, only a few months apart. Miss Maud Watson and her sister Lillian were daughters of the Rector of Berkswell and Maud defeated her sister in the first ladies singles championship at Wimbledon.

R.E.S. (Bobby) Wyatt lived at Carol Green and captained Warwickshire and England at cricket. Jeremy Huggins lived at Berkswell Grange in Truggist Lane with his three brothers and parents, he became Jeremy Brett the actor, perhaps best remembered for portrayal of Sherlock Holmes. Memorabilia of all three can be seen in the museum. A recent refit has really improved the museum, pop in sometime.

1998 was a very eventful year for Olive and I, with a "sting in the tail" for me, we must have gone away on some sort of holiday before July, but it is what happened afterwards is a little bit more noteworthy.

We had been approached at least three times by the person who owned the field at the rear end of our garden, the field is about four acres and the owner whose house was in Kelsey Lane, and part of the property had been trying to obtain planning permission to develop the land into housing and were we interested in joining in. On one occasion the idea was to demolish our house and put a roadway in off Windmill Lane, there was no way we could agree with that, upsetting our good neighbours. However, the field and part of our rear garden was "green belt land" and that was taboo as far as Solihull Council were concerned.

Then sometime later on one of our neighbours, next door but one, died and the executor tried at least twice to get planning approval on that property, probably getting on for an acre. Those applications were refused and

that was that. When in July 1998 we received a letter from a property company saying they were interested in buying our property at a greatly
enhanced price, above market value I did not even raise an eyebrow, and
put the letter "behind the clock" with all the others. I came across it again
some weeks later when sorting for something else perhaps and was a little
curious, it was a new approach after all.

I rang the phone number on the letter and requested some sort of
explanation, to which this nicely spoken man said that he would prefer to
come and see us. I am a little dubious about these arrangements sometimes, and as he said we would be under no obligation whatsoever we
agreed that he could come over. He arrived very punctual at the appointed
time, and we introduced ourselves and I said I suppose you would like to
walk over our property? "Yes please" said he, and down the garden path we
all strolled, we informed him as to what was ours as he consulted his sketch
plan and, asked a few questions, had a good look round and made an offer
for the "back land", there and then, not sure whether it showed or not but
we were both flabbergasted. As explained before, the bottom end of our
garden is double the width of the frontage, when we sold the building plot
in 1960 we retained all the back land. He wanted to acquire all the wide
area which would have left us with quite a small garden in comparison to
what we owned. Naturally the whole deal was subject to gaining planning
permission about which he was almost certain the company would get.

Then I informed him that part of all three properties he was interested
in was in the green belt. "No", he said, but I did not argue. We said that
really we did want to keep some of the land he required, but we were naturally interested in his offer and ideas.

He told us that he was sure that all our wishes – and his, could be
achieved, and with that we all had a much needed cup of tea, and he departed leaving us a bit bewildered, and me just a little apprehensive, this was
the first time anything quite like this had happened to me/us before –
although – as previously stated I have been very fortunate – or lucky over
the years. But, still had to work hard to get there.

Olive and I were soon on our way to Solihull and the planning department at the Council House, to discover – sure enough, that none of our
garden was part of the green belt. A chat at the solicitors was next on the
list, to be informed that this sort of development, known as "windfall land"
was quite common and was taking place in this area. A day or two later I
was talking to daughter Jenny on the phone and telling her all about it, she
said she had means of checking out the firm we were talking to. Back came
the answer that they were perfectly alright – as far as she could tell. They
had been in business for over thirty years and the fellow we were dealing
with struck me as being straight and honest.

During the next months we talked quite a lot, on and off to the devel-
oper, plans were being drawn up as the other two property owners had to

come to an agreement, we just had to sort out and agree where the new boundary should be. Eventually, after the company had liaised with Solihull Council as to what they would and would not permit, we ended up with ten metres, (33 feet) of the wider part of our property, this suited us fine as this width would form a buffer-zone between the building site and us, also our neighbours.

Then began the anxious time of uncertainty, would the plans be passed? Or what if? Why and when. We decided not to tell anyone about the proposed project until the plans were submitted – or just before. All our neighbours had the same letter in the first place anyhow, it was hardly discussed with the other two interested parties, we just "sweated it out". However, the developers were so confident that plans would be approved so we were very hopeful. It was a large garden and I was 69, and, when someone comes along offering money for something not needed, well there is only one thing to do. Eventually the "bubble burst" and everyone knew about the proposed development, opposition groups were formed and at the end of the day there were well over fifty objectors, which naturally is every-ones right to do.

It was one Sunday evening when a neighbour discovered plans to develop were to be submitted soon, one of the other interested people told them, they came to see us in floods of tears and so on, all of which was quite understandable. What I could not understand was their failure to investigate the letter we all received in the first place. Eventually the day came when the meeting to consider the plans arrived, I went along to Solihull with a neighbour also involved and met a cool reception from a few people in opposition, however, in the long run after lengthy discussion – for and against, it was passed – three in favour two against, with two abstaining, were they "windy" of getting the blame – we will never know. Really it was all downhill from then on, all the business via the solicitors, payments were made as arranged. The whole business was carried out in an honest straight forward manner, everything the developers said they would undertake was carried out to the letter – and more so. Just as it should be in fact, but not always happening in this day and age.

So, in the financial sense we were able to "jump over the fence" and sample life from the other side, after almost seventy years of careful spending and watching the coppers I could now go out and if I/we saw anything we wanted or fancied we could have it without a count up. Yes, I know we have had some very special holidays which cost a few quid, but without what I call our good fortune – it is not actually a fortune – those holidays would soon have become a thing of the past. My idea was to do things while we could, not wait for retirement and then "set the world on fire". Strange as it may seem everything seems the same, we still "gad about", etc, there is now a nice feeling of security which we really did not have before. More than a few people are very much opposed to this sort of development and

I have pointed out to many that this sort of thing has been going on in Balsall for over 50 years. I was talking to a friend one day and said that what is now called Balsall Common was always known as plain Balsall in the past, I also said that I was fed up with people that came to live here then want to prevent others from doing the same (opposing development, etc). My friend said "Yes John, they are the ones that put the Common bit onto Balsall". No comment from me. It must be said, however, that a lot of newcomers provided towards my income and I am grateful to them all. At the end of the day no friends have been lost here and, though we may not be flavour of the month, "most people have been honest enough to say that given the same circumstances they would have done the same thing. So once again good fortune came my way, Lady Luck however one likes to put it, but it was a hard graft to buy the place in the beginning.

Probably on the strength of the deal or, just fulfilling another of my "holiday ambitions" Olive and I went to the Canadian Rocky Mountains and Vancouver in September 1998. The "Air Canada" pilots were on strike, which interfered with the holiday schedule somewhat, but all the tour was fulfilled to the letter. A grand tour with nice people and fair weather was also good, we had an extended stay in Vancouver at the end of the tour and met up and entertained by relatives of friends living in Balsall Common – neither of which had anything to do with "the common bit". The Rocky Mountains is a place I would dearly like to return to in the future. The cost of living "seems" far lower over there, almost everything being about one third cheaper than U.K.

Early in November I was literally "stopped in my tracks", on a Friday evening I developed a severe pain just below belt level and self diagnosed a pulled muscle. The day before I had taken my mower in the trailer to do the final mow for a client and friend and I went off without the "skid board" to unload and re load with, so I lifted the mower on and off and thought no more. In the past I quite often "pulled a muscle" and the pain soon eased off and disappeared, but not this one. I phoned the surgery on Saturday and the emergency hospital number on Sunday evening because I was in some discomfort to put it mildly. I told them that I thought it was a pulled muscle and was told to rest and take Paracetamol tablets, which I did, but on Monday morning found me at the doctors surgery where I related the same story. I was put on an E.C.G. apparatus and an appointment was made for me at Solihull Hospital the following Friday – 4 days hence. After a miserable week, sleeping downstairs in a chair on some nights I turned up at the hospital. Within an hour, they had taken blood and urine samples. I had another E.C.G. session and a good "going over" by a doctor, also an X-ray, it was then decided that I was to be admitted, I was just glad something was happening, when I was put on a Hepperon drip and ended up on a trolley bed.

Once admitted it was more or less the same procedure all over again, this time by a German female doctor, who really knew her stuff. Whatever, at two p.m. I was pushed onto a ward, which was in semi-darkness, but discovered it was siesta hour. We were instructed to rest and try and sleep between one and three p.m.

Wow, what a turn up, my pulled muscle turned out to be a blood clot on the lung, after another uncomfortable night the pain disappeared. The "posse" came round the ward about 10 p.m. 3 or four doctors, including the one that had given me the going over earlier – still on duty – poor soul she was in a worse state than me, all in and tired out. I was given "something to help you sleep", and I never want another, talk about night-mares I had day and night-mares. Dreams occur with me every night, singing, dancing, conversation all logical. This night I was talking to a friend and he was a small carved wooden statue – like one would see in a church – we had a real old chin-wag, but it was all weird. That was one of many. I was confined to my bed space, trips to the bathroom was by wheelchair and as I felt O.K. I could not understand why, it was only later that I was told that if the clot moved it could have been the end of John Henry Webb, Gardener – retired.

My stay was for ten days and I had many kind visitors and received forty nine "get well" cards, it was a very nice feeling I must say. They all looked after me very well in the hospital and I found the catering was very good too, with quite a choice. It was altogether an experience probably – no certainly – one that I could have done without, however, I am still around and enjoying life, even if I have not got as much "puff" as before.

Since my spell "in dock" Deep Vein thrombosis has come to the fore and it is interesting to note that we had been to Vancouver and back just weeks before. I am now taking warfarin tablets daily to keep my blood thin. As a little sideline I now go around biting rats

I'm Fine, Thank You

There's nothing the matter with me
I am as healthy as can be.
I have arthritis in both my knees,
And when I talk, I talk with a wheeze.
My pulse is weak, and my blood is thin,
But I'm awfully well for the shape I'm in.

Arch supports I have for my feet,
Or I wouldn't be able to walk down the street,
Sleep is denied me night after night,
But every morning I find I'm alright,
My memory is failing, My head's in a spin,
But I'm awfully well for the shape I'm in.

The moral of this tale I unfold,
That for you, for me who are getting old.
It's better to say, "I'm fine," with a grin,
Than to let folks know what a shape we're in.

How do I know that my youth is all spent?
Well, my get-up-and-go has got-up-and-went.
But I really don't mind, when I think with a grin,
Of all the fine places my get-up has been.

Old age is golden, I've heard it said,
But sometimes I wonder as I climb into bed,
With my ears in a drawer, my teeth in a cup,
My eyes on the table until I get up.
E'er sleep overcomes me, I say to myself.
Is there anything else I can lay on the shelf?

When I was young my slippers were red
I could kick my heels high over my head.
When I grew older, my slippers were blue,
And still I could dance the whole night through.

Staying with our French friends in Chartres, France. Left to right standing: Innes Brett, Jean
Geroudét, son Patrick. Lionel and Freda Holtom.
Seated: Yolande Geroudét, John and Olive

Now when I'm old, my slippers are black.
I walk to the shops, and puff my way back.

I get up each morning and dust off my wits,
Pick up the paper and read the Obits,
If my name is still missing, I know I'm not dead,
So I get a good breakfast and go back to bed.

As I said before quite an eventful year 1998. I had only been out of hospital a day or two when there was an awful pain in one of my feet, so, back to the surgery, where my usual doctor was not on duty, I saw A.N.Other who said it was a foot infection and prescribed anti-biotics, there was no lumps or broken skin and I had my doubts. Having had a little experience of gout some years ago that is what I thought it was, but no more self diagnosis for me. However, the pain did not go away, and two days later I was back at the surgery to report to my doctor regarding my hospital stay, the doctor had my notes and file in front of him and mentioned my foot. "Lets have a look" " said he and promptly said "Gout". He put me on more pills and discontinue the anti-biotics. My gout is still with me, but thankfully never too bad, keep taking the tablets they say. I do as and when it is necessary.

Another happening came to an end, there was no wreath making that year, sort of forced retirement. We still were some way off discovering whether plans would be passed for development of the adjacent land. It was nice, we were free to attend carol concerts and the like, before there had been absolutely no time for any sort of leisure. Although for some years we always had a "works outing" for a Christmas lunch somewhere, it started when my neighbour Ken started helping me out. It was usually Ken and his wife, Olive and myself and sometimes another guest, probably if someone had been a help to me during the year. The outing was always a Christmas lunch at some hostelry, a glass of whatever and then return home for tea of coffee, we still go out for a pre Christmas "do", but it is now a lunch for retired persons.

1999 proved to be a much more calm year, I had regular trips to Solihull Hospital to see "The vampires" who took a sample of blood to determine the daily dose of warfarin, I now go to the surgery in Meeting House Lane and the results are posted to me two days later, much more convenient.

The garden as always took up a lot of my time, I love it all and the exercise does me good. It was a job to know what to do, and what not to do regarding the proposed development. The development company were so confident that it would all be passed and I decided to let nature take over the area of garden under offer. As I said before it was not until July 1999 that the plans were finally approved. At the beginning of '99 I was taking things a bit steady, the clot on my lung had been more serious than I imagined, I was soon "out of breath" when tackling a strenuous job, there was some permanent lung damage. However, it was to be my 70th birthday in March and daughter Jenny thought there should be a party. It is a waste of my time to object or argue and, one might have gathered I like a "bit of do" anyhow. Jenny undertook the catering, there were drinks from the off licence and the party was being held in the church hall at Wellesbourne. It was more handy there for Jenny. We had – in my opinion – a good do, Jenny pulling out all the stops with a very nice feast. Our friend Innes entertained with a talk – a retired teacher who had spent most of her teaching years at Berkswell C of E. A very humorous rambling called "An apple for the teacher". It was all the more funny for me because I knew who she was talking about.

Holidays this year were, first of all in June, our usual "fix in Austria", staying this time in Kitzbuhl, we had stayed close by but never in the resort before. As usual it was really nice although once more the weather was not all that special, but as always we made the best of it. The spring flowers were just as nice although not as many as we have seen in other places.

Later on in September we ventured to Riva Del Garda. A resort town on the shore of Lake Garda in Italy, we do like Italy, the people are nice and friendly, the food we like and it is clean, sad to say but better than here at home. Why? Why? Why? Do some people treat the place in England as a rubbish dump, I often wonder what some homes are like. Garda is nice, mountains in the north where we stayed, but very flat at Sirmione at the southern end. We had a tour by coach and ferry around Lake Garda one day, and I thought Sirmione was very interesting, including the castle built right on the lakeside, almost surrounded with water. From the sublime- as they say – there was also an ice cream shop the likes I have never seen before, what a pity we had just had lunch.

Public transport was good, but the best was visiting other towns and villages by the very efficient ferry service, which was just a minute or two from the hotel. Yet another memorable holiday.

Christmas 1999 was upon us and, another "first" for us, we spent Christmas at home on our own. We had had invitations to go elsewhere, but for various reasons decided to stay at home. It was very nice indeed and that is not taking away the happy times we have spent in other homes over the years, we have always enjoyed "going away" to relatives and friends but to be able to do EXACTLY what we wanted – and when was also very nice indeed.

Time flies, but despite what has been said before I did join the Berkswell Museum committee, meetings usually twice a year. I also got involved with the millennium plans – the committee – and although most of the planned events, etc. for the millennium were on computer, etc. it was most interesting. The main idea of the millennium project in Berkswell was to produce a record of Berkswell Parish at the turn of the century. This I feel was achieved and a tremendous lot of hard work was undertaken to bring the plans to fruition. Cartography of the parish was undertaken, the area being divided into map squares, people took on a square and recorded what happened there. Crops in fields, types of hedge rows trees and so on.

A video was produced showing a year in the parish, the school, meetings of parish organisations, the life of the church, etc. Every thing that takes place features miles of video tape which was edited down to just less than one hours viewing time. A C.D Rom was made, Berkswell ancient and modern is on this, I have a copy and have only seen little bits so far. One day I will try and see it all on some kind souls apparatus, if I can operate the thing.

A book was produced which contains over 60 individual impressions of Berkswell at the millennium, contributions from all age groups. An eye opener for me and I would imagine lots of other people as well. It will be interesting to read it again after a few years.

Hundreds, if not thousands of photographs were taken by some very gifted people and they were/are on sale. However, pride of place must go to the parish map, designed and made by local people.

The map is made in five sections the big map in the centre measuring 4 foot by 4 foot with four panels, one on each side and top and bottom. There are over 40 listed buildings or ancient artefacts in the parish including the well, stocks on the green the animal pound and windmill. They have all been worked onto tapestry and placed on the map in the correct location. All sorts of features have been added, woods, field, the lake, sand quarry. Agriculture is to the fore, tractors, animals birds, etc. Transport i.e. cars, a train, even Concorde. Around the outside in the surrounding panels local places are incorporated, the parish organisations, even local people around the parish and village at the millennium, a work of art painstakingly put together over many hours by a dedicated group of lady stitchers. The map is on display in the Reading Room and well worth a visit, perhaps on a Sunday afternoon in the summer when tea and home made cakes are served. Visit the museum on the same day.

Millennium celebrations took

Yours truly at work

place in Berkswell the first weekend in July 2000. The official opening ceremony was performed by the Mayor of Solihull, prior to the unveiling of the map by T. Wheatley-Hubbard, grandson of the late Colonel Wheatley and Mrs Christobel Wheatley. Late of Berkswell Hall, now converted into apartment flats, the stables altered to mews type dwellings, almost a small village on its own.

An exhibition in the Reading Room over two days and the church fete was held on the Saturday afternoon. A B.B.Q. and bonfire in the park took place in the evening, as we were just about to depart for the B.B.Q. the heavens opened up and we chickened out and put our supper under the grill. However, many brave souls braved the elements and had a super evening. I think they were probably a bit younger than Olive and I. Certainly more enthusiastic.

On Sunday morning a village play (mummers type) was performed in various parts of the village centre finishing up with a short service in church.

A millennium picnic followed in the Rectory garden with all sorts of entertainment as well. The weekend concluded with Choral Evensong in Church. It was most unfortunate for Olive and I, we had our garden open under the National Garden Scheme on the Sunday of the celebrations, the two events completely unconnected. I was very much involved manning the plant stall at the fete on the Saturday where we sold just about every plant, and there was a "cargo" to sell, we had a very busy and enjoyable afternoon.

On the following morning I had to start all over again getting plants ready for sale here at the open garden. We always sell plants which makes money for The Helen Ley M.S. Care Home at Blackdown near Leamington. We did get to evensong, daughter Jenny came over and closed up after the visitors had departed.

We pushed the boat out again (twice) for our year 2000 holidays, again it was an ambition to return again to Oberammergau to see the passion play, held every ten years. Staying at Thaur (pronounced Tower) about 3 miles from Innsbruck. Nice hotel and company, etc. but for us not such a nice location and the weather was not too clever. The play was superb, once again all day 9.30 – 12.15 and 3 – 5.30. A long time, but we did not notice time or any discomfort being totally absorbed with the play. The seating had been very much improved since we were there in 1980.

Later on in October we had a trip to New Zealand, both holidays this year with SAGA. We have nothing but praise for Saga from booking till our return home. I had been looking in brochures for some time looking for the holiday we wanted. Most important was the length of time spent in New Zealand. It is a long way, and it seemed much longer coming back, we may only go once therefore we wished to make the most of it regarding seeing the sights. Quality of overnight stays and not to do it all on a "whistle stop" excursion. I am pleased to say all these aspirations were fulfilled.

We had Pat, our tour manager and "mother hen" – although one never got that impression. She was there to help us all – a very nice group of people, all easy to get on with throughout the trip. Glenn Miller was our driver/courier on the North Island, a nice bloke who really knew his country, we were well informed in a humorous way throughout.

We travelled to Cape Reinga in the far north, the Bay of Islands on the east side. An interesting one night farm stay near Cambridge, also Rotorua and the hot springs, just a short look at Wellington, the capital before crossing to the south island on the ferry. Another coach and driver met us and took us a short ride for our one night stay at Pickton, on then to lovely Christchurch and then to Queenstown. Really into some beautiful scenery by now. Milford Sound next with a boat trip out as far as the open sea, a wild untamed area, the south west of the south island and long may it continue. Dunedin was our next destination, where amongst other sights we saw albatross on a headland, they had come to this spot to breed (it was spring time there) the only place on any mainland that they ever come to. Then on to Lake Ohou (Oh Oh) staying in a motel on the side of the lake, miles and miles from anywhere, so peaceful, quiet and stunning scenery. Back then to Christchurch, a flight to Auckland at the end of the best holiday ever. We were so fortunate with the weather, wall to wall fine and sunny, there were just two wet spells in the late afternoon. New Zealand has everything one could possibly wish for. One slight problem for us in England it is a long way away. We did opt for an extension of five days to Raratonga the main island of the Cook group. Was the grass skirts the attraction?, not really, I forgot my shears anyhow. We were as close as we would ever by to the South Sea Islands and I thought a few days to relax after a busy tour would be just right, it was hot and humid and altogether a nice trip. I did realise even more so that we are definitely not beach people, there was plenty of water sports and swimming, but the sand gets every where does it not, however, it was another new experience for us.

Again it was Miss Tattersall at Berkswell School who taught us about the South Sea Islands and lots and lots of other places that we have visited over the years. We have been so fortunate to be able to visit some of these distant lands and meet a few of the local inhabitants, not really surprising to discover their ambitions aspirations and ideas of what life is all about is just about the same as ours. So, who puts the spanner in the works and jiggers things up for many people on this earth.

During the year 2000 it was discovered, at a routine visit to the optician, that I had cataracts on both eyes, I am pleased to say that was just about put right just about within twelve months, quite successfully at Solihull Hospital. At the end of the year Olive and I resigned as parish secretaries of the Children's Society after over 20 years of opening collecting boxes held by individuals in the area.

This rather conveniently brings us to the end of the year 2000 and in my opinion the end of the millennium – I.e. the end of 1000 years NOT 999 years.

So far at the age of 71 it has been a wonderful life for me, Christians are not supposed to speak of "luck and fortune", but how else can I explain the many lucky or fortunate happenings during my lifetime. It has not always been easy, I have had a working life really and really enjoyed it all. A dear old pal once told me to work hard and play hard. BUT! One must work hard first, my pal could not read or write, but he was a "wise old owl" out of the top drawer.

At the present time we jog along with plenty of things to occupy our time, we take longer over meals, always have a coffee break at 11 a.m. and a pot of tea at 4 p.m. I did that when I was working, a habit I am not pre-pared to change. I read more, never made time before, biographies and nos-talgic books I like, and have just discovered fiction and what of the future? Yes, I am concerned and interested in what is happening in the world around us. Most of the events most of us have no control over, I have no wish to be young again and think life is very difficult for lots of people, teenagers find-ing their way in life. Employment, getting work and how long for? However, I do believe that if the will and ambition is there, the sky is still the limit – or is it the limit? With space craft and the like flying around.

Ambitions and thoughts on travel are never far away from me, our next objectives are a return to Switzerland. Canada and the voyage to Alaska and The Norwegian Coastal voyage, NOT all in one go. However, if I was told that there would be no more holidays for me I do not think it would bother me all that much. I might lose my memory (heaven forbid) then I would get these writings out and start from page one.

I have lived through interesting times, in my childhood very few cars on the road, no radio set in our house till I was eleven, it was about 1962 when we first had a telephone. I had a motor bike when I was 21, after ask-ing my parents permission or blessing, don't think I really had the blessing. It did 70 m.p.h. down hills with the wind behind me.

A van came on the scene – mainly for business use in 1960 and a car in 1962. Our first very small TV in about 1963.

* * *

There is much to look forward to in the future, in April 2003 Olive and I hope to celebrate 50 years or marriage. Olive, one of the two women in my life. The other one was my mother who was always there with encourage-ment and advice, and Olive always allowed me my head to follow ideas and new directions. A wonderful wife, mother and best pal.